Feminisms at a Millennium

Feminisms at a Millennium

Edited by **Judith A. Howard and Carolyn Allen**

The University of Chicago Press
Chicago and London

The essays in this volume originally appeared in various issues of SIGNS: JOURNAL OF WOMEN IN CULTURE AND SOCIETY. Acknowledgment of the original publication data can be found on the first page of each essay.

The University of Chicago Press, Chicago 60637
The University of Chicago Press, Ltd., London
© 2000 by The University of Chicago
All rights reserved. Published 2000
Printed in the United States of America
04 03 02 01 00   5 4 3 2 1

Library of Congress Cataloging-in-Publication Data

Feminisms at a millennium / edited Judith A. Howard and Carolyn Allen.
     p. cm.
     Includes bibliographical references and index.
     ISBN 0-226-01443-6 (cloth) — ISBN 0-226-01444-4 (pbk.)
     1. Feminist theory — History. 2. Feminism — History. I. Howard, Judith A. II. Allen, Carolyn.

HQ1190 .F44234 2000
305.42'01 — dc21

00-046719

The paper used in this publication meets the minimum requirements of American National Standard for Information Sciences — Permanence of Paper for Printed Library Materials, ANSI Z39.48-1984.

Contents

Judith A. Howard
Carolyn Allen

Introduction
Feminisms at a Millennium

eattle welcomed in the new millennium with a headline quote from its mayor, Paul Schell, in the *Seattle Times:* "I AM NOT A WUSS" (Broom 2000). With this unusual proclamation, Schell captured various of the (gendered) anxieties that beset the earth as we slipped quietly into a new year, century, and millennium, marked even by those whose religious, cultural, and political beliefs did not count this moment as millennial.

What was Schell responding to? One month before the millennial passage, Seattle had hosted the meetings of the World Trade Organization (WTO). It was an event the city had anticipated with pride, an event city leaders had assumed would mark Seattle's emergence on the global scene as a major urban, sociopolitical, commercial center. What transpired is now old news, but suffice it to say these expectations were naive at best. A week of intense battles between city police and a multinational coalition of protesters ended with 500 people in jail, significant property damage to key downtown stores (mostly those targeted as using abusive labor practices), and allegations about anarchist rioters on the one hand and police abuses on the other. The chief of police resigned, and the mayor was subjected to intense criticism for having failed to take seriously the depth and scope of the protests, which had been planned as carefully as the WTO meetings themselves. The meetings, it turns out, were also wracked by dissension and failed to result in any agreements, other than to meet again.

Almost a month later, a few days before the end of 1999, an alleged terrorist was detained while trying to enter the United States in Port Angeles, Washington, in possession of major amounts of nitroglycerin. The FBI and CIA announced their concerns about terrorist plans to wreak havoc in three U.S. cities for the millennial transition, including Seattle. The media fanned the public's anxieties, and Mayor Schell decided to cancel the main city-sponsored New Year's party, limiting the midnight fireworks to a skimpy five minutes. In light of the extreme quiet that prevailed when the new millennium began, the media announced Seattle a party pooper. Late-night TV talk show host Jay Leno cut from scenes of revelers in Paris, New York City, and D.C. to a view of an almost bare room with three people watching TV and said, "And now, live from Seattle." Even the weather (never Seattle's strong suit) contributed to Schell's ignominy, clouding over just in time to obscure the special light display that was to read "2000."

Why do we begin with this narrative? To be sure, *Signs* is just now completing a five-year editorial term in Seattle, and events in this city and region have been of special import to its editors and staff. More significantly, however, caught up in these events are themes of gender, nationality, global interdependence, hegemonic domination by transnational corporations, racial and ethnic identities, and complex intersections among these systems. In one or another way, almost all of the essays in this issue speak to these themes. Some give voice to anxieties, others are more hopeful; some reflect back, others look forward. All were written in the months preceding the millennial transition. When January 1, 2000, dawned over a twenty-four-hour period around the globe, it seemed anticlimactic; it was, simply, another day. Our collective responsibilities for addressing the concerns of the moment, whether individual, familial, friendship, work, national, or global, were still there.

We knew we wanted many voices in this issue. We asked the members of our international advisory board, our associate editors, and the former editors of *Signs* to write short essays on anything they wanted to emphasize at the millennial transition. To ensure a generationally diverse set of voices, we also asked them to identify more junior scholars whom we then also invited to participate. The essays you are about to read are provocative. We take some space in this introduction to highlight several themes that arise persistently.

The rubric of millennium: "Duration means invention"

Three of the essays, by Catharine Stimpson, Mary Romero, and Elizabeth Grosz, focus directly on the rubric of "the millennium," an arbitrary, ambivalent moment designating two thousand years since the birth of the founder of Christianity, only one among a variety of world religions. And, as Stimpson reminds us, the Millennium in Christian narratives is a drastic, vengeful, lunatic vision. Although elements of a millennial vision can be seductive for feminists — allowing hope that patriarchies are not inevitable, for example — utopian moments also divide people into two clear camps, the saved and the damned; feminists have learned to be wary of clean dichotomies. The notion of an external salvation also undermines the necessity of feminist work here, now, by living people. And millennial visions tend to be deeply violent, in contrast to feminist principles of nonviolence. What they have in common is that both millennia and feminisms provide visions. For Stimpson, feminist visions at this moment in time include skepticism about the possibility of a monolithic vision, recognition of the need for a way to think about differences and their consequences, and a need to find some shared beliefs and commitments.

Romero articulates why suspicion about the concept of commonalities endures, underscoring that each temporal marker that achieves sociopolitical recognition and commemoration is invariably a positive celebration of freedom, affluence, and power for some and a marker of domination, oppression, and poverty for others (e.g., the 500th anniversary of the presumed "discovery" of the "New World" by Christopher Columbus). The Christian millennium, in particular, celebrates progress toward an end, and in its teleological character differs profoundly from, say, the Buddhist emphasis on dialectical cycles of life that transcend specific bodies. Romero argues that feminist reflections provoked by the millennial moment must be intensely alert to the economic and political structures that shape both ideologies and the material circumstances of human lives, for Western millennial "progress" is often achieved at the expense of deteriorating conditions for other women.

Grosz stresses that our understandings of relations between past and present have implications for our conceptions of the future. When we assume that pasts are like presents, we end up with predictable futures. In contrast, when we seek a history of singularity, she argues, we have a future of surprises and the past endures only in its "capacity to become something other" (1019). Grosz's point is echoed in Cynthia Enloe's emphasis on the capacity for surprise. Listing some of the events at the close of the twentieth century that surprised her — for example, the NATOization of human rights, the appearance of Russian women in brothels in Thailand, the British arrest of Augusto Pinochet (temporary, as it turns out) — Enloe suggests that being open to surprise, having one's predictive assumptions thrown into confusion, may be a useful attitude for feminists to adopt in the coming century. Paola Bono and Federica Giardini propose a new metaphor for feminist thought, the *taglio,* that exemplifies this power of the unexpected: they describe a *taglio* as a cutting line, a fracture in how we look at and experience ourselves and the world, possibly inventing unexpected points of view from which to find and create meanings. Some of the changes they observe at the end of this century, such as a weakening in the power of the patriarchal symbolic system for both women and men, are contested by other contributors to this volume, but Bono and Giardini's emphasis on practices, on interactions of experience and thought, also resonate with other essays.

The practice of theory and the theory of practice

Lessons of political/theoretical strategizing: Looking back
Several of the essays assess key theoretical and political trends of the past several decades of feminist thinking, with an eye toward speculating about wise courses of action and scholarship in contemporary times. Drucilla Cornell looks to her own political past for lessons for the new millennium, focusing on the practice of consciousness raising (CR), a group creation of voice. Consciousness raising, for Cornell, was an experiment in radical democracy, challenging the moral norms of femininity and of what could and could not be spoken. She and the members of her CR group, called Las Greñudas, struggled to find representational practices that would allow women to be taken seriously, without producing racist or classist effects. She argues that this project of radical democracy, then and now, is about opening space for new moral, ethical, and political representations of feminism itself. Sandra Harding also draws on her autobiography in thinking about trajectories for the new millennium. Harding echoes Cornell's appeal for a re-energized democracy, suggesting that we could use the millennium to mark the emergence of an envisioned democratic time in which democratic negotiation — redefined primarily by those who have not had it — would become the prevailing mode of interpersonal, institutional, and global interactions.

Similarly, Karen Brodkin examines her history in the civil rights and feminist movements for clues about ways forward. She traces the numerous benefits that she, a white middle-class feminist, reaped from affirmative action and speaks powerfully to the combined effects of social movements and urban uprisings of the sort that generated Medicare, Medicaid, Head Start, the reform and expansion of AFDC, and major expansions of public schools. She observes that, even with all of the recent backsliding, the establishment of New York's and California's more widely accessible systems of higher education is a good part of why universities today are still much more diverse than they were when the sixties began. She clearly attributes the success of those earlier social justice programs to the coalitions of social movements. In the face of today's wholesale shift away from public responsibility for social services, Brodkin argues that feminists and women's studies programs must return to the political activism that was part of their central mission twenty-five years ago.

Lessons of political/theoretical strategizing: Looking forward
Laura Brace and Julia O'Connell Davidson identify several "best practices" that avoid ahistorical universalisms and homogenizations but also attest to

the realities and material bases of exploitations. They cite Kamala Kempa-doo's (1999) research on sex work in the Caribbean, which situates the particularities of migrant women's sex work in a framework that recognizes systemic inequalities at local, regional, and global levels. Brace and O'Con-nell Davidson argue eloquently for greater dialogue between general theo-rists and those whose research and theorizing is more explicitly situated and historicized. Kathy Rudy offers a similar approach in her assessment of hegemonic feminisms: she suggests that U.S feminists should examine our own beliefs, historicizing and contextualizing multiple feminisms, in order to facilitate coalitions with other women. Rudy offers her analysis as a route toward interventions in favor of social justice. Whether similar po-litical analytic strategies work for those in both colonizer and colonized positions and whether the parameters of social justice are always clear, she argues, need to be considered explicitly. Certainly Tani Barlow's trenchant critique of U.S. women's embrace of "international feminism," and the ways this move signals the triumph of a particularly American way of em-powering women, give one pause.

Globalization: "Benvenuto in Macintosh"

"The party means you never have to say you're sorry" (1059). Or so says Sue-Ellen Case in her send-up of the globalization, indeed the transcen-dence, of time, of space, of political investments — of pretty much every-thing — leaving narcissistic academic nomads to enact the fashions that cir-culate around the globe. (Not so far from the Nike-wearing man shown on CNN tearing down the Nike logo from the store's roof in Seattle dur-ing the WTO protests.)

Comments on globalization also mark several of the essays that focus on the profound recent changes in Europe. Rosi Braidotti speaks to the character of late twentieth-century war, noting that it is often not labeled war, even as thousands of civilians are murdered or flee ethnic cleansings. What appears unchanging is nationalism, often the trigger for the intense militarization of Western cultures. Yet nationalism, Braidotti reminds us, is itself an imagined idea that generates an illusory sense of unity over inco-herent, fragmented ranges of internal regional and cultural differences. Braidotti argues fiercely for dislodging the belief in natural foundations, values, meanings, or beliefs as the only way she sees to generate political resistance adequate to the "specific paradoxes of our historical condition" (1063). She does not reject the European Union as a possible site of such resistance but cautions against its vulnerability to conservative agendas. While Braidotti stresses the power of military technologies, Liana Borghi and Ilaria Sborgi speak to the more pervasive and everyday spread of (gendered) Internet technologies: an Apple computer in Italy greets its user in a sexy female voice, "Benvenuto in Macintosh." They maintain that technoscience has allowed the local to become global, so that feminists must not only decode hegemonic structures of technical discourse but also recognize how technoscience recodes feminist discourses.

Małgorzata Fuszara traces a portrait of gender politics in Poland that stands in marked contrast to Braidotti's argument for distancing from nationalisms. Fuszara sees feminism as a clear possibility in Poland, stressing that there have been women in positions of political power for some time, and notes there are dozens of women's organizations and initiatives, many of them organized around feminist issues such as abortion, wage differentials, and family violence. She speaks also of an active and rapidly growing gender studies program at Warsaw University and traces debates about this academic institutionalization that echo those common among U.S feminists. Implicit in Fuszara's essay is the importance of viewing feminisms within their particular historical and national contexts.

The contradictory tendencies toward homogenization caught within globalization, on the one hand, and the multiple particularities expressed in nationalisms, on the other, must be located within the analytic of imperialism, Mrinalini Sinha argues. Revealing that the structure and ideology of middle-class British feminism was indelibly marked by its imperial location, Sinha demonstrates that the colonial feminism of Indian women was no more articulated within specific macropolitical structures than was British feminism (or other colonial feminisms). She argues more generally that these (and other) feminisms are co-implicated in a shared history of a "system whose economic, political, and ideological reach was worldwide" (1079).

Uma Narayan employs a similar analysis in unpacking the homogenizing of cultures, emphasizing that culture-specific essentialist generalizations, rooted in colonial histories, are just as dangerous and as socially constructed as gender essentialisms. She warns of selective labeling through which those with social power designate some practices as cultural preservation and others, those that challenge the status quo, as cultural betrayal. What to do? Narayan emphasizes the importance of attending to differences in values among members of the "same" culture and to affinities among members of "different" cultures. Her analysis, like many others in this volume, speaks to the progressive possibilities of cross-cultural feminist alliances.

Therese Saliba, too, attests to the complex imbrications of gender, nation, religion, and sociopolitical history in her assessment of Arab feminisms at the millennium. Saliba touches on the contradictory implications of liberal nationalism for women, the complex (and often uninformed) debates about Islam, and the importance of localized struggles that seek a non-Eurocentric framework in which Arab women may seek indigenous identities. She concludes that some of the greatest contributions of Arab feminism have been in exploding constraining categories — Orientalist, Islamic, nationalist, multicultural, and feminist, all of which express colonizing tendencies — a point echoed by other contributors to this volume. Oyeronke Oyewumi's use of African constructions of family and gender roles to reveal the hegemony, and limitations, of a white, U.S., nuclear-family model in feminist analyses of gender and family argues a similar point.

Taken together with these commentaries on feminisms in Arab countries, in Africa, in India, in Poland, and in other European contexts, Barlow's portrayal of international U.S. feminism, in which political and media figures speak to presumed common feminisms in supranational contexts, should raise caution flags. Barlow characterizes this version of international feminism as a "series of totalizing theories that . . . will not admit the tangibility of any social forms in excess of their own drive to represent 'the interests of the world's women'" (1103). What she describes is a new form of colonialism that requires both analysis and resistance.

While these essays focus on relationships across U.S. and other national and multinational contexts of feminism, several other contributors focus instead on the complex interdependencies of border work. Patricia Fernández-Kelly attests to the signal contributions of early scholarship on gender and development, emphasizing through analysis of *maquiladoras* the exploitation both of women as preferred providers of cheap labor and of men deprived of the right to work. Fernández-Kelly echoes other contributors in stressing that gender discrimination can be understood only as part of larger orders of domination that affect men as well; gender, she maintains, is the pivot around which class divisions organize. She stresses the importance of more comparative theory. Edna Acosta-Belén and Christine Bose also offer a comparative analysis, stressing the complex situations of racial and ethnic minority women in the Americas. They note the interplay between the structural conditions of Latinas in the United States and the transnational connections that various Latinas maintain with their respective countries of origin. They also cite the scholarly and pedagogical consequences of such interplay, demonstrating how academic Latinas from both North and South have created alliances across ethnic studies, Latina studies, and women's studies programs by encouraging these programs to focus on global gender and ethnic issues.

Human rights

Bringing together concerns with political strategizing and analyses of globalization, other contributors emphasize struggles for human rights and social justice. Dorothy Q. Thomas offers an incisive critique of the U.S. government's resistance to international accountability and of U.S. activists' failure to move beyond a kind of "learned insularity" (1123). At the same time that a powerful movement for women's human rights has emerged internationally, U.S. women's and civil rights groups, according to Thomas, tend to see human rights as pertaining to the rest of the world but not to the United States. Two points are particularly salient: (1) Global movements for human rights are organized around the indivisibility of civil, political, economic, social, and cultural rights, but, in the United States, broad-based approaches to rights are uncommon. (2) Human rights is founded on a principle of intersectionality that permits simultaneous race, class, and gender analysis, in contrast to much U.S. rights-based organizing. Given the increasingly globalized political and economic environment, U.S. insularity impoverishes struggles for justice.

Hilary Rose argues that the emphasis on human rights should be broadened to include environmental protections; she speaks of a wide-ranging biomedical assault on the environment and, echoing Thomas, notes that European feminists are markedly more active in their opposition to these assaults than are U.S. feminists. Rose is both optimistic, noting that feminism is forging a synergistic relation with environmentalism, and pessimistic, tracing the immense powers of capital over a global workforce and the backsliding of countries now retreating from rights they once accorded women and children. Echoing other authors in this volume, Rose argues for alliances across differences to accomplish sustained resistance to social injustices.

Henrietta L. Moore offers a more conceptual echo of Rose's call for struggles across differences, focusing specifically on the fraught politics of difference. Arguing for a commitment "to the continuing and irresolvable contest of the existence and meaning of unifying ideals," Moore maintains that difference "has no meaning outside its self-constituting relation to a posited universal or shared horizon" (1132). She takes issue with the claim that adherence to general principles involves the erasure of distinctiveness, maintaining instead that struggles for social justice must be forged in a collaborative milieu.

The essays by Beth Richie and by Michelle Fine and Lois Weis both make concrete the struggle for social justice, emphasizing violence against women. Richie sounds a caution. She is clear about the many successes of the feminist antiviolence movement, in terms of services, individual support, and public policy initiatives and funding, but she also points out that the success of the "it can happen to anyone" logic has suggested a race and class neutrality to gender violence that excludes low-income women and women of color. She speaks especially to the dangers of relying on law enforcement as the major strategy for procuring women's safety, seeing this as one of many signs of expanding state power, while everyday safety in communities of color is threatened by more aggressive policing, increased use of force, and mass incarceration. Fine and Weis speak to very much the same issues, underscoring a "twinning of State and domestic violence against women" (1141), both direct and indirect, in the form of massive state withdrawal of welfare support, decreased support for public education, and parallel increases in dollars for prisons. Both essays argue that antiviolence activism needs to focus not only on individuals but also on state-initiated or sanctioned abuse of women.

Introspections on the academy

Academic disciplines: Words, numbers, and wisdom

Not surprisingly, the academy itself comes under scrutiny in this volume. Several of the essays concern the academy as a whole; others focus on specific disciplines and the extent to which feminisms have made inroads in them. Dorothy Smith provides a telling framework for the essays on this theme, reminding the reader of the profound power of social institutions. She focuses on schooling as an institution that produces inequities, an institutional order that extracts organization from the connectedness of people's everyday activities by linking multiple settings and thus becoming independent of particular individuals. She cautions, in contrast to some social theorists, that working in the institutional order does not inherently accord agency and argues that schools are a key part of those institutional processes that allocate agency differentially and thus profoundly impair democracy. Smith does not take up, but we may want to ask, what these processes will look like, both in schools and in other institutions, as the workings of power at the millennial transition become apparently freer of particular institutions, more fluid, more geographically mobile.

Academic writing also receives its share of critique. Ruth-Ellen Boetcher Joeres raises two issues that have plagued discussions of academic feminisms for at least the past two decades: the reliance of some feminist scholarship on specialized language that limits its readership to an academic few, and an apparent abandonment of feminist activism in favor of theorizing. Catherine Belsey sets up a different conundrum on a similar topic: how to write, as a feminist, in ways that provoke the reader to ideas, to thinking, of her own? She recommends inconsistencies, questions, unanswered problems. Both Joeres and Belsey suggest that feminist academic writing should *do,* rather than be or mean, and what it should do is provoke thought and motivate readers to action.

In some ways Elaine Marks argues an opposite tack. She reflects with deep concern on what she sees as a steady, longtime move toward separation of the political from the poetic. She is eager to see a return to the literary imagination and a reinvestment in teaching students how to read literary texts. In words that she seems surprised to be writing, she speaks even of her dismay that many students now seem not to recognize mythological or biblical references associated with the canon that has been so strongly under attack. Sydney Kaplan, too, takes up themes of literary criticism, and her reflections speak both to the power of feminist literary criticism and to her belief in its continued importance. Kaplan's own academic history mirrors the development of feminist literary criticism; she suggests that the women authors she studied in graduate school in the 1960s (Dorothy Richardson, Virginia Woolf, May Sinclair, Rosamond Lehmann) were, in the absence of feminist professors, her mentors. Kaplan argues for feminist criticism as cultural critique, with its grounding in the real-life experiences of people and its origins in intense longings for a better world, possibly against Marks's current worries.

Londa Schiebinger also takes stock of her field, science. In contrast to her 1987 *Signs* review, in which she highlighted gender distortions in science, in this essay she asks whether feminism, now a presence in science for almost two decades, has changed science. She discounts the idea that simply encouraging more women to enter science will necessarily produce change but at the same time stresses the need for governmental funding and initiatives on women and gender in science and argues for multiple arenas for change: research priorities, domestic relations, university structures, classroom practices, and relationships between home and work. Hard-core realities that impede enactment of such changes are traced by Julie Nelson in her assessment of feminism and economics. As Nelson observes, "neoclassical economics is a parody of what feminist scholars of science argue against" (1178). She argues for redefining economics from its contemporary emphasis on rationality and market forces to an emphasis on "provisioning," exploring how we provide the means to sustain and enjoy life. Nelson's redefinitions echo contemporary agendas among feminist sociologists and other social scientists.

Women's studies and feminisms

And what about women's studies, a radical experiment twenty-five years ago but now, as a number of the essays wonder, perhaps overly institutionalized? Barrie Thorne reflects on the shifts, some markedly positive, others possible cause for concern. Among the reasons for optimism are the establishment of women's studies programs in more than seven hundred U.S. colleges and universities, the existence of more than thirty feminist journals, and the establishment (and vitality) of sections on gender in virtually all major disciplinary organizations. Causes for concern are the ways the academy may have changed feminists and women's studies programs, producing a loss of critical edge and political momentum of ideas and infighting among scholars, especially between theorists in the humanities and empiricists in the social sciences.

Judith Stacey echoes Thorne's observations, focusing particularly on several paradoxical challenges to the future of academic feminisms. Drawing on Dorothy Smith's trenchant critique of her own and Thorne's earlier work (Stacey and Thorne 1985; Smith 1996), Stacey points to the growing conservatism of the surrounding political climate and the academy's increasing dependence on technological and managerial forces, as evidenced by, for example, university retrenchment, the backlash against affirmative action, and assaults on tenure and on scholarship and teaching on gender and race. Stacey marks two paradoxes. First, the very growth of transdisciplinary feminist scholarship has generated greater disciplinary specialization. Feminist scholarship within disciplines is now so considerable that few scholars can gain comprehensive knowledge of the feminist literature even within their subfields; doing significant work across the disciplines is even more difficult. Second, there are intellectual forces from many sides that challenge universalistic theories of gender, which raises some tough questions: If feminists can no longer profess the primacy of gender as a category of analysis, is there a disciplinary or discursive domain that can be claimed as distinctly feminist? At a practical level, does this then undermine requests for expanded curricula, departmental resources, and staff? How does one recruit feminist faculty whose work does not center on gender?

In contrast to the caution sounded by Stacey, Irene Dölling and Sabine Hark argue for transdisciplinarity as a way to address the threatened loss of critical potential that accompanies the increasing institutionalization of women's and gender studies. For Dölling and Hark, transdisciplinarity means constituting disciplines less around a single core than around multiple knots in a netlike structure. The task for women's studies would be to trace the paths of these intersections and interlacings, to continually reflect on artificially drawn and contingent boundaries and what they exclude, including the boundaries and exclusions created by feminisms' own premises and constructions.

Barbara Charlesworth Gelpi offers autobiographical reflections on the circumstances of feminist faculty at Stanford, her institution, over the twenty years since she began a five-year term as editor of *Signs*. Though acknowledging problems with the concept of "community," Gelpi sees in recent campus events heartening signs of community like those she recalls from the earlier years: a panel of recent alumnae from feminist studies leading a workshop for current seniors worried about the job market, for example, and a reception for new faculty well attended by a wide range of new women faculty, with unusually high numbers in fields traditionally dominated by men. At the same time, she notes the poor attendance of senior faculty at the reception, many of them negotiating the demands of the speed-up in academic institutions that the great majority of readers will recognize. Gelpi notes as well a worrisome undertone to the overall tone of celebration: thinking of recent negative personnel decisions, disproportionately concerning women faculty, she asks how many of these women will gain tenure? Jean O'Barr, another former *Signs* editor, also speaks to the mixed bag of signs for optimism and signs for concern. O'Barr adopts a format hauntingly familiar for many readers: lists. She offers both a list of tough challenges — being able to communicate with varied audiences, figuring out how to negotiate a career trajectory that honors both our intellectual passions and the values of those who sit in judgment on us, keeping political commitments central, learning to work with those who differ from us, being conscious of both our privileges and our disempowerments, keeping the long view — and a list of things to do: recognize that we know how to do several things at once, procure space, foster coalitions, change structures, persevere, and, last but not least, rest.

Almost all of these comments on academic feminism attest to the urgency of coalition. Three essays that comment on black women's studies and black feminisms suggest a profound disjuncture between academy and practice. Noliwe Rooks gives a thumbnail review of the circulation of ideas, scholarship, and theoretical paradigms in black women's studies today and concludes that scholarly space is shrinking, both among African Americanists and among feminists, in sharp contrast to the flourishing of such work in the late 1980s. Nell Irwin Painter allowed us to print an e-mail she sent us expressing intense frustration that, looking around her at the conditions of young African American historians, she was simply unable to write the "progress" part of a millennial narrative. In striking contrast, Barbara Ransby's assessment of the past decade of black feminist practice traces the development of a loose network of black feminist activists provoked, in part, by the Clarence Thomas appointment, efforts to give Mike Tyson a hero's welcome, and the Million Man March. She points to a decentralized, group-centered, grassroots democratic model as central to the continued work of this large progressive movement, as well as to the ideological tenet that race, class, gender, and sexuality are interdependent factors that cannot be separated and ranked. Such markedly different assessments of black feminisms within and outside the academy are yet another reminder of the stifling institutional constraints of contemporary higher education.

Karen Brodkin's response to the question of where women's studies should go is concrete: (1) curricula should be reorganized around analyses of the counterpoint between the gendered racism of public policy and the various challenges to it; (2) programs should become much more visibly involved in fights to preserve and expand affirmative action; (3) as the biggest organized voice of feminism, women's studies should take the lead in amplifying feminist voices and initiating the coalition-building needed to reanimate campus and community movements. France Winndance Twine shares some of these critiques of women's studies and academic feminisms more generally, but she emphasizes a relatively underrecognized theme in this issue, the absence of working-class members, and particularly working-class people of color, among such programs. Twine goes beyond the not-infrequent call to consider hiring more women of working-class backgrounds to argue for a more sustained and deeper approach, exhorting feminist scholars to "challenge the aristocratic leanings of institutional reward structures" both internal and external to their departments (1229). In light of the elimination of many of the grants and low-interest loans that have been essential to allow working-class students access to a university education, these challenges are vital.

Barbara Laslett and Johanna Brenner in some senses combine Brodkin's and Twine's key points, exhorting academic feminists to confront the class structure of the academy and of women's studies. They detail many of the changes in the academic work environment—cuts in public funding, the rapid growth of temporary workers compared to tenure-track faculty, a general speed-up, and, especially, the overproduction of Ph.D.s relative to the supply of academic jobs. This last trend pointedly exemplifies the class structure of academic feminists: Laslett and Brenner voice the uncomfortable truth that the collective networking that is part of feminist organization in academia helps only a lucky few to negotiate career hurdles. They call for senior feminists to acknowledge the historical particularity of their own current positions and to develop strategies that confront the distributions of power within and between academic institutions: to create multi-issue coalitional politics, for example, to form alliances with the least powerful groups on campus, and to help unionize graduate students and faculty. Laslett and Brenner bring us back to Smith's reminder that education is a social institution, with all the inequities and hierarchies this entails.

Embodied subjects

Tina Chanter is one of the few contributors to comment explicitly on the relationships between sex and gender. Distinguishing three possible under-standings—necessary (sex determines gender), arbitrary (sex and gender are completely independent), or contingent (gender is related to, but not determined by, bodies)—Chanter argues for contingency. When we fail to investigate bodies and materiality, she reminds us, we fail to think through the complexities of race, class, and other axes of oppression that are also part and parcel of physical bodies.

Traise Yamamoto speaks against the reduction of race to figure, to repre-sentation, cautioning that whether race is viewed as a biological essence or, according to contemporary wisdom, as a social construction has not really made much difference in the existence and scope of racist repression. Ya-mamoto argues that much feminist theory has not yet come to terms with racialized embodiment and, indeed, has violently erased the body. Devon Mihesuah takes a related tack in her reflections on possible intersections between feminist studies and American Indian women's studies. Noting that the majority of Indians today are "mixed-bloods," she describes the complexity of the ensuing identity politics. Many are dissociated from their tribes' cultures but still possess strong Native identities. Moreover, there is no single authoritative Native women's position and no one feminist theory of Native women. Thus, reiterating a point made by many others, Mihesuah maintains that these labels often are umbrella terms that do not adequately represent those they are assumed to comprise. She argues for attending to the complexities of differences through respectful ethno-graphic methods.

Many of the authors draw on their own histories for insights and reflec-tions about the contemporary academy, feminisms, and political visions. At the same time, very few specifically take up questions of age and aging. An exception is Anne Fausto-Sterling, who revisits her own intellectual and pedagogical history to think about what it means to age within the academy. As a profession that matches teachers who are steadily growing older with students who, on the whole, remain late adolescents, teaching presents certain challenges. Fausto-Sterling suggests that it might make sense for universities to allow—indeed, to encourage—scholars to shift their focus as they age. She asks whether teaching is a profession better suited to younger colleagues who share more experiences with their students. Equally to the point, she finds herself drawn to a new direction, critical science studies, that would seem to alleviate some of the specific challenges for feminists teaching science and scientists teaching women's studies students.

Judith Kegan Gardiner addresses both aging and masculinities, urging feminist scholars to engage with age and masculinity studies to promote a more gender-just future. Gardiner ruminates on variations of new masculinities that have taken the place of midcentury breadwinner roles and suggests that gender maintenance and power stability rely more now on emotional socialization than on force, admitting for men some narrowly targeted empathic moments. Such moments modernize older conceptions of gender, albeit in a controlled manner, opening up possibilities of more democratic masculinities.

Thomas Gerschick approaches masculinities through a theory of the connections between disabilities and gender. Gerschick argues that because bodies are so central to doing gender, people with disabilities are vulnerable to being denied recognition as women and men. Further, having a disability diminishes women's already devalued status, whereas for men, masculine gender privilege contradicts the stigmatized status of having a disability. (White, financially comfortable) disabled men experience a status inconsistency that women in parallel circumstances do not; thus, doing gender is a deep conundrum for disabled men—one that, while troubling, may also contribute to the democratizing of masculinities to which Gardiner refers.

Nancy Woods takes up the question of women's health policy at the beginning of the twenty-first century, assessing an agenda for women's health published by the National Institutes of Health (NIH). In Woods's view, the sections of the report on specific diseases and problems could "transform the landscape of women's health research" (1272). At the same time, though, she notes that it places little emphasis on the health consequences of poverty, on the gendered allocation of work, or on a global perspective of women's health. And, of course, it remains to be seen whether the recommendations in the report are in fact embraced by the scientists who judge the merit of research proposals and shape science policy for the NIH.

David Eng proposes the fascinating thesis that melancholia, with its generalized representation as depression, has come to describe numerous subjectivities around the globe. Following Wendy Brown, Eng argues that identity politics are structured around discourses of injury and unresolved grief. Marginalized peoples are coerced both to relinquish and to identify with socially stigmatized positions; the melancholia that results, suggests Eng, is deeply political, for the proliferation of melancholia beyond its gendered distinctions means that feminisms can no longer think about gender in isolation from sexuality, race, and postcoloniality. Eng concludes that the expansion of melancholia as nascent political protest resituates gender and feminisms at the millennium as a crucial site for progressive politics.

Cultural productions

"Attend concerts. Buy CDs. Listen up," commands Susan McClary, urging readers to support female musicians (1286). McClary and Ellie Hisama both reflect on the remarkable successes of recent music by women artists and the growth of feminist music theory. McClary sounds a more cautious note, recognizing that such successes may be short-lived, and also worries about the general disavowal of the term *feminist* by many of these women artists. She expresses concern as well about the aggressively market-driven music industry.

Hisama begins by citing an older friend who wishes she had been born fifteen years later so that her formal training could have included studying music by women and feminist scholarship about music. Hisama reflects on her own training, which incorporated some of the elements that her friend missed, a generational pattern echoed in many of the fields represented by the authors in this volume. Hisama attests to a burgeoning richness of feminist work in music, including biennial "Feminist Theory and Music" conferences, greater numbers of women faculty in music departments, and the growth of feminist music theory. At the same time, she echoes McClary's worries, noting that only 20 percent of the members of the Society for Music Theory are women. Hisama offers a powerful example of how to intertwine feminist scholarship and pedagogy in a description of her classroom analysis of John Zorn's representations of Asian women in his CD "Torture Garden." Hisama's analysis is a trenchant exploration of racist and misogynist narratives in music and also a fine example of how feminist analyses reveal and question such narratives.

Tamara Underiner takes up the realm of theater, pondering how to encourage her drama students to recognize and confront their privilege in ways that do not reify a difference between white and other—that is, that are not undone by the twin dangers of fetishization of or indifference to difference. Underiner argues for "deploying the dramatic canon with a vengeance" (1295), using it to illustrate institutionalized and invisible whiteness produced in the rhetoric of liberal humanism. Examining plays such as Suzan-Lori Parks's *The American Play,* Underiner reconfigures identity as too situational and relational to be approached through fixed categories of race, gender, and class and argues instead, as do many of the authors, for multiple positionings and transformative alliances across these categories.

Conclusion: Collaborations and alliances

As we have noted, many of these essays endorse efforts toward alliances and collaborative political agency, even while recognizing the complexities that endanger effective allied action. Within the microcosm of their friendship, Dale Bauer and Priscilla Wald explicitly model both the commitments and the challenges that collaboration entails. In a lovely irony, their collaboration for this volume began with a misunderstanding, and their approaches to their topic differed markedly. Wald wanted to focus on the challenges of working in coalition and on feminist activism, and Bauer wanted to address collaboration at a more conceptual level, focusing on Lauren Berlant's analyses of intimate female identification. As they push their ideas, they realize that they disagree fundamentally on what to do with principles of coalition: Bauer argues for invention of a new genre for public female discourse, but Wald sees coalition as inherently protean and thus does not think a new form can be truly "genre-shattering." Ultimately they do not impose a false unity in their conclusion but simply end by acknowledging both their disagreements and their mutual respect.

These fifty-plus essays by a disciplinary and generational range of feminists, mostly academic, are inspiring, troubling, provocative, despairing, celebratory. They use a variety of methods, autobiographical, theoretical, epistolary, and pedagogical; they stress the need for politically contextualized coalitions across differences and for serious, engaged analysis of and activism within academic institutions; and, at the same time, they plead for equally serious and engaged activism outside those institutions. We read these essays as deeply thoughtful about, and at the same time strikingly committed to, feminisms: all of these authors speak with passion.

We began this introduction with reflections on the WTO protests in December of 1999, as the century and the millennium were about to close. Nelson Mandela and Graça Machel visited Seattle just a few days after the WTO meetings ended and offered their observations on the organization: Mandela described the WTO as part of a welcome process of globalization that no country should avoid. "But," he said, "the WTO, under its current rules, favors the powerful. Power today is still monopolized by the West, and their moral fiber leaves a lot to be desired. They use the World Trade

Organization in order to make a maximum profit, not for humanity, but for the ruling classes in their respective countries" (quoted in Sanchez and Ostrom 1999). In his commentary on these events, Mandela referred to the African notion of *ubuntu,* the belief that humans are persons only in their relation to, support of, and responsibility for others. As feminisms move forward, change shape, reinvent themselves differently in a variety of locales, we look to the practice of conversations, collaborations, and coalitions to enact the *ubuntu* crucial to feminism's futures.

Sociology Department (Howard)
University of Washington

English Department (Allen)
University of Washington

References
Broom, Jack. 2000. "Canceled Celebration Puts Focus on What Kind of City We Are, Our Appetite for Risk." *Seattle Times,* January 2, A1.
Kempadoo, Kamala. 1999. "Continuities and Change: Five Centuries of Prostitution in the Caribbean." In *Sun, Sex, and Gold: Tourism and Sex Work in the Caribbean,* ed. Kamala Kempadoo and Cynthia Mellon. Lanham, Md.: Rowman & Littlefield.
Sanchez, Roberto, and Carol M. Ostrom. 1999. "Mandela Isn't Shy about His Views." *Seattle Times,* December 9, B2.
Schiebinger, Londa. 1987. "The History and Philosophy of Women in Science: A Review Essay." *Signs: Journal of Women in Culture and Society* 12(2):305–32.
Smith, Dorothy E. 1996. "Response to Judith Stacey's and Barrie Thorne's Essay." *Perspectives: The ASA Theory Section Newsletter* 18(3):3–4.
Stacey, Judith, and Barrie Thorne. 1985. "The Missing Feminist Revolution in Sociology." *Social Problems* 32(4):301–16.

Catharine R. Stimpson

On Being Transminded

Afit between the millennium and feminisms? The more one thinks about it, the more awkward it becomes. This is true whether one is exploring the millennium in the flickering light of historical inquiry or the strobe light of today's hyperbole about it.

Historically, the millennium is a drastic passage in a prophetic Christian narrative, at once hopeful, vengeful, and lunatic. According to Revelation 20, a chapter in the concluding book of the New Testament, for 1,000 years absolute evil will be defeated; Satan will be chained and sealed up. Absolute good will triumph, and Christ will reign on earth in person. Enthroned beside him will be the martyrs, those "beheaded for the sake of God's word and their testimony to Jesus, those who had not worshiped the beast" (Rev. 20:4). After the millennium, Satan will be released. He will organize a cosmic war, but heaven will eventually beat him and his hosts down again. The Last Judgment will follow, and then the splendors of a new heaven and a new earth.

This millennial vision has served as a template for subsequent utopian visions, including those of feminism. They imagine a dualistic world in which the forces of good, be they sacred or secular, will eventually defeat the forces of evil. Such a clean-sweep victory will usher in a perfect world, for feminists one purged of patriarchy and its sufferings. To be sure, utopian dreams have provided feminism with some necessary oxygen. They have inspired and encouraged people to work for a future that is different from and better than the present. However, utopian dreams, including those of feminism, have their dangers. Like Christian millennialists, utopianists can divide our messy, multiplicative world into two camps: the saved, to which they belong, and the damned, whom they shun and abhor. Ensconced within the party of the saved, the utopian dreamer, while alert to many evils, can be blind to others. One thinks, instantly and anxiously, of the feminists who accepted racism.

The sense of history in Revelation is also profoundly alien to feminism, for it assumes that divine forces will ultimately control events on earth. Feminists can believe in the sacred, and many of us do. However, feminist work is done here on earth by us earth dwellers. We cannot count on any

[*Signs: Journal of Women in Culture and Society* 2000, vol. 25, no. 4]

god or goddess to rescue us. We are our own and each other's saviors. Nor can we see the end of history. Instead we see the necessity of doing feminist work in history in order to change it.

Moreover, although individual women are capable of violence, feminism is a nonviolent movement. In contrast, the biblical millennial vision is militantly violent. The millennium begins and ends with great, savage wars. To be sure, feminism can be hard, exhausting work, as arduous as it is joyous. It is only realistic that feminist rhetoric often speaks of struggle. Women did not win the vote because they demurely requested it, and no woman leaves a battering husband with a song in her heart and a smile on her lips. But if the anti-Soviet movement in Czechoslovakia was the Velvet Revolution, feminism has been the velvet and silk and linen and cotton and polyester and Gore-Tex revolution. One of its most significant wagers with history is that it can alter the most profound ways in which people feel, believe, and behave without resorting to the blood and gore described in Revelation, without guns and shrapnel-loaded bombs.

Interestingly, despite all the drumbeating and hoopla, much of the discourse about the millennium in the United States has also been comparatively pacific. We are as apt to use the bloodless and neutral term *Y2K* as the term *the millennium*. In so doing, we construe a party of the saved and a party of the damned, but the party of the saved consists of the corporations, agencies, and people who have upgraded their computer programs, while the party of the damned consists of those who have not. Our Y2K discourse offers feminists two mild opportunities. The first is to quantify and measure the past, to brand the skin of time.[1] Who, TV panelists ponder, have been the Greatest Artists of the twentieth century? Of the past 1,000 years? The past 2,000? Who have been the Greatest People? Here feminism and women's studies insist that women, who have paid their historical dues, must get their historical due. This first opportunity is the sedate companion to the second — the chance to party on down. Clearly, the peacefulness of Y2K makes celebrating more seemly than it would be if Satan and his minions were on their Darth Vaderish march. This strain of Y2K party rhetoric flamboyantly invites us aboard the good ship Millennial Lollipop in order to spend money, guzzle champagne, and boogie. Here each feminist with spare change must choose what to do — whether to hide until the last bit of confetti has been swept up (probably by a woman) or to pick up her big MAC lipstick and go for it.

[1] The most notable example of this effort to capture history as it concerns women and feminism is a special issue of the *New York Times Magazine,* "Women: The Shadow Story of the Millennium" (May 16, 1999).

I am, then, a sardonic agnostic about the millennium and Y2K. However, even the most belligerent agnostic must admit that Revelation has for centuries fed the human appetite for vision by offering an implacably vivid picture of the world—not as it is but as it might and should be. One reason feminism has proved so powerful is that it too provides a vision. The most influential feminists have had imagination enough to see below the crust of custom and beyond the horizon of convention. To be sure, individual feminists have been swept along by historical forces that galvanize changes in gender roles and relations—shifting patterns of women's work; the lessening reliance on physical strength in war and work, which is altering traditional rules of masculinity; the new reproductive technologies, which are altering traditional rules of femininity; and a more universal belief in human rights and democracy. Nevertheless, we have also had our visionaries.

The stress on the differences among women that has pervaded feminism—and even more so women's studies—in the past thirty years has bred a valuable skepticism about the possibility of any monolithic vision compelling a broad, heterogeneous group of women. Simultaneously, we have realized that no single word, such as *feminism,* can name a broad, heterogeneous movement for the betterment of women's lives. I use the word *feminism* because it is an important element of my historical period, but other words can do for other people. The more international feminism becomes, the more women it reaches, serves, and touches and the more the differences among women become apparent. Experiences and interpretations of experience proliferate. So do needs and desires. One hears with near-simultaneity the voices of a lower-caste woman in India negotiating her new role as village leader, a middle-class woman in Syria whispering to a journalist about the nature of her arranged marriage, a law graduate in New York City describing her preparations for the bar exam, and an undocumented worker giving birth to a daughter in a border town in Texas. Nor do women change in lockstep with each other. On the same day, one finds accounts of U.S. women starting up Internet companies and Afghani women being broken down by the Taliban.

This multiplying multiplicity creates two needs. The first is for a way of thinking about differences and their consequences. When the intellectual histories of the last part of the twentieth century are written, they will, I believe, show how directly its citizens confronted this need. Think, to give three examples, of the concept of cosmopolitanism, the picture of a varied public world; of the concept of intersectionality, a picture of a state of being in which several strains of identity meet as if they were at a crossroads; or of the concept of hybridity, a picture of a state of being (be it genetic, psychological, or aesthetic) in which several strains of identity have together bred something that is of, but different from, them all, just as the color purple mixes red and blue and black and white yet differs from each in its purpleness.

I have been experimenting with the use of the prefix *trans* and the compound words that it initiates as the building materials for still another way of thinking about our differences and their consequences. This industrious syllable signifies doing something—going across, through, over, beyond, outside of, or from one place, person, thing, or state to another. Thus *trans* is the prefix for English words that mean actively moving through and among all sorts of differences. Examples abound: *transportation* is our word for going from one place to another, literally or metaphorically; *translation* for taking one language into another; *transaction* for dealing with each other; *transilience* for leaping from one thing to another; *transgender* for operating across gender boundaries. Significantly, each of these words implies a *transition,* passing from one stage to another. If I were to listen carefully to the English translation of a feminist text written in Thai, I would go through a transition. That is, I would change cognitively and psychologically to a less ignorant and provincial condition. Feminists must be transminded, that is, constantly aware of the many differences among women and men and then able to act among, with, and on these differences. This can be so delicate and time consuming that it undercuts a feminist belief that the transformation of culture, society, and education is just around time's corner.

Despite the ever-multiplying differences among women, the second need that feminists must meet is to find some commonalities, some shared beliefs and commitments and principles. The awareness of differences that transmindedness demands is compatible with this activity. Indeed, translations and transactions are the tools feminists should use to divine a mother lode of unity. The more numerous our differences, the more urgent the need for something, at least one thing, that we hold in common. Otherwise, all we will see in each other are our differences, and this, no matter how theoretically interesting, is no basis for coalition building and ground gaining.

One commonality is a revulsion at the harms women and children suffer and the adamant determination to stop the silencings, sweatshops, rapes, beatings, batterings. Only brutes, perverts, and gender traditionalists so rigid that they embody a form of perversion would disagree with this. Surely, even if we repudiate millennial thinking, we can also gather behind a vision of the future. I once imagined a feminist future abstractly as a place where "equity" and "rights" would be as common as sunshine in equatorial climes. I now imagine a feminist future more metaphorically. It is first a place of sufficient bread where all of us have enough to eat and where all of us are physically secure. It is next a place of roses where all of us have a sense of self, the ability to participate in democratic communities, and the capacity to love fully and freely. Finally, it is a place of keyboards where all of us have access to literacy, education, and the technologies that will shape the twenty-first century. Bread, roses, keyboards: my rubrics for a unifying vision of the future. Keyboard is, of course, a nice pun. For a keyboard is not only the plastic rectangle on which I type these words. It is also the instrument on which one transposes keys and strings into music. This music will not be the strident military chords of millennial wars but the melodies, harmonies, and solo improvisations of a future that one must imagine if one is to survive honorably amidst the tears, hopes, creativity, and tatters of the Y2K present.

Graduate School of Arts and Science
New York University

Mary Romero

Marking Time and Progress

As I ponder the significance of the millennium for feminists, I recall the number of times my generation has been called upon to mark an era. There was a centennial, a bicentennial, a quincentennial, and now the millennium. The meanings behind each of these occasions were shaped by controlling interests. Differing responses to the era revealed conflicting positions and statuses within specific economic, political, and religious power structures. Thus, while in 1976 the United States officially commemorated two hundred years as a democratic nation, some submerged and dominated nationalities condemned the era as two hundred years of oppression. When states and government organizations officially celebrated the "discovery" of the New World, the disenfranchised reminded us of five hundred years of conquest. Once again conflicting interests are revealed as we celebrate the second millennium and debate its significance. It is helpful to reflect on the meanings and implications of an era based on the Christian notion that two thousand years have elapsed since Christ was born. How does the peculiar marker called the millennium highlight ideological constructs, uniting some communities and separating others? What does it reveal about individuals, communities, and nations within the world system and the emerging global economy?

While Stephen Jay Gould (1988) has made us aware of the extent to which the date of the millennium is completely arbitrary, as a social construction and belief it is all too real in its consequences. Depending on their brand of Christianity and capitalism, people are anxiously awaiting anything from the apocalypse to the second coming, from "party like it's 1999" to the global scare of Y2K. Everyone should be aware that non-Christians — Jews, Muslims, Hindus, and Buddhists, as well as atheists — identify different historical figures and calendars as more crucial to their beliefs, sense of time, and construction of meaning in everyday life. At the same time, the worldwide recognition (and use) of the A.D./B.C. distinction is evidence of Christian hegemony and Western control over communication. The successful interlinking of religion with economics and politics, that is, of Christianity with capitalism and representative democracy, forces us to interrogate history and quality of life from the perspectives of

[*Signs: Journal of Women in Culture and Society* 2000, vol. 25, no. 4]

a male triad of god (father, son, and holy ghost) supported by faithful followers — many who have tinkered a bit with the church's official images, constructing modifications and additions to include god(s) and goddess(es) that reflect their own ethnic, racial, class, sexual, and gender image and likeness. So while we can point to Christian hegemony marking time and constructing meaning, there is clear evidence that worldwide conversions did not occur without resistance and a process of acculturation that incorporated aspects of indigenous cultures.

Marking transitions from one era to another invokes a process that measures the transformation of quantity into quality; things go along from day to day and year to year and suddenly we proclaim that we are entering a new era. These ontological breaks make it possible to evaluate and assess history in terms of difference and similarity. Many women are using the millennium to assess the material and spiritual histories of women globally and to reevaluate the ideological constructs that are considered feminist. I am struck by certain assumptions made in these reflections. On the occasion of the millennium, feminists find ourselves reflecting on past political and economic struggles. Simultaneously, we attempt to project the path that needs to be traveled before all women's lives are erased of sexism. However, selecting the millennium as *the* commemorative occasion marginalizes non-Christians and further reinforces the Christian cultural (and in some cases political and economic) domination that Jewish, Muslim, Hindu, Buddhist, and other women experience in their everyday lives.

In addition, the reflection on and assessment of feminist strategies and goals, like other millennial musings, is grounded in and predicated on Western assumptions of progress. The millennium concept carries with it an inescapable unilinear, progressive, and evolutionary worldview. Simultaneously, the very word *millennium* implies the Christian teleology of the end times. In essence, the millennial concept is a representation of humankind on a long march from the beginning to the end. Despite feminist emphases on inclusion, diversity, and difference, which broaden tolerance, frameworks, and agendas by including an *s* at the end of *feminism,* the premise lurking at the heart of Western feminism is of an evolutionary process with each stage an improvement on the previous one. Western formulations of history as progress, of life as consumption, and of spirituality as the world to come leave out such relations as growth and decay, life cycles, dialectical relationships, circularities (infernal and otherwise), universalities, repression and the return of the repressed, and the everyday progressive/regressive experiences of human relationships.

My concern with embedded and unquestioned assumptions is that reflection on feminisms at the millennium easily blinds us to the economic and political structures that condition ideology. Feminisms, like any ideology, are products of concrete struggles and not simply products of intellectual development. Each form and type of feminism identified and nurtured in research and writing is actualized through a social process involving the economic and political institutions to which it is connected. Thus the economic and political restructuring that opens professions to women in one country cannot be isolated from the economic and political restructuring that drives women in other parts of the world to immigrate and seek work as maids, nannies, and caregivers. While identifying the undeniable gains that women have made in some segments of society (nationally and globally), U.S. feminists need constantly to critique choices and strategies to assure that sexism has indeed been eliminated and not just shifted to another segment of the female population. As the song "Are My Hands Clean?" by Sweet Honey in the Rock (1985) says, women's triumphs, privileges, defeats, hardship, and oppression are closely linked. The journey of the blouses we wear to make our proclamations about feminisms at the millennium began in the cotton fields of El Salvador and was completed in the sweatshops of Haiti or downtown Los Angeles. The female labor embodied in this commodity brings us together as women, but gender is camouflaged beneath other identities: farmworker, seamstress, factory worker, sales clerk, cashier, or laundress, as well as designer, model, marketer, manager, or corporate executive.

I began to make these connections while listening to a presentation by a well-known and highly regarded feminist sociologist speaking at an international conference. In her assessment of where women had been and where they should be going, she discussed employment rates throughout the world. Comparing women's employment rates appeared to me to be based on an unexamined assumption that more women in the labor force meant a better quality of life for women and thus progress. The research presupposed that paid employment outside the home increased women's independence in the family and community. Local conditions, international inequities, quality of family and community life, economic and political restructuring, along with exploitation, low wages, and poor working conditions were not figured into the equation. Moving women into the labor market was treated as a positive step, an advancement for women, and a move up the evolutionary ladder toward a feminist utopia. Like much research, the design was based on a Western feminist ideology that sees employment outside the home as progressive and as the same for all women.

When labor-force participation is experienced as fulfilling and rewarding, women's paid labor certainly has numerous positive attributes, yet women's increased labor participation can also be related to the overall erosion of wages, forcing more than one family member into the labor market. When experienced as dangerous, demeaning, and drudgery, and when paid labor contributes little above subsistence-level wages, women's entrance into the labor force is less a sign of progress than of regress. The quantification of women's lives in terms of wages or labor-force participation, like marking the millennium, does not capture the important issues of quality of life—at work, at home, and in one's community and nation-state. If we do not incorporate an analysis of these structures, we fail to make important connections that are not linear or progressive: rich-poor, beautiful-ugly, young-old, native-alien, or how such binary categories rely upon the existence of the other. Social, economic, and political "progress" made under certain feminist political and economic regimes is structurally linked to the exploitation, regression, and devolution of other women. By failing to consider how different feminisms are connected to specific economic, political, and religious power structures and how particular forms of feminism directly benefit some and hinder others, we obscure the fact that our own progress may be connected to the deteriorating conditions of other women. At this point, being inclusive and diverse is not enough to hold feminisms together; we need a broader understanding of the complexity of how the different perspectives are linked, both in conflict and in mutual struggle.

The millennium milestone may turn out to be inclusive and to develop significance for our pursuit of feminisms by shifting attention away from concepts like tolerance, diversity, and difference and toward concrete political links and connections. Recognizing the political and economic structures hindering or promoting a feminist perspective in one part of the world and tracing what links those structures to other feminisms can move feminists toward a common agenda. I suggest an agenda that denies, in practice, that any one feminism can pass judgment on another and offers instead a process of self-critique that works toward the elimination of barriers for other feminisms.

School of Justice Studies
Arizona State University

References

Gould, Stephen Jay. 1998. *Questioning the Millennium: A Rationalist's Guide to a Precisely Arbitrary Countdown.* New York: Crown.

Sweet Honey in the Rock. 1985. "Are My Hands Clean?" Lyrics by Bernice Johnson Reagon. Washington, D.C.: Songtalk.

Elizabeth Grosz

Histories of a Feminist Future

> The more we study the nature of time, the more we shall comprehend that duration means invention, the creation of forms, the continual elaboration of the absolutely new.
> — Bergson 1944, 14

am delighted that *Signs* has given me this opportunity to raise some speculative questions about the time and future of feminism. The marking of the millennium is clearly an arbitrary, and ambivalent, designation: two thousand years since the nominal birth of Christ may not prove the most apt occasion for feminist reflections on pasts and futures; nevertheless, social rituals, those marked by a calendar date, by an anniversary, provide as good an excuse as any for engaging in reflections on the past and speculations about the future. I do not intend here to undertake any prognostication, predicting what a feminist future might look like. Unlike the futurologists, whose (impossible) role is to foresee trends, to make predictions, and to extrapolate from existing knowledges and practices into a future that still resembles the present, I am more interested in clearing a conceptual space such that an *indeterminable future* is open to women.[1] This idea of an open future, uncontained by the chains of the determinism that constrain the future directly through the past, that is, a future yet to be made, is the very lifeblood of political struggle, the goal of feminist challenge.

I

Time is marked not only by calendars and clocks, by uniform measurement and abstract calculation (of the kind represented by millennial celebrations!) but also by movement, through an incalculable force of passage that resists counting and numeration. The past, present, and future are composed not only of dates but also, in a more complex and incalculable

[1] A history of futurology could be undertaken that would reveal that the various images of the future it projects are not only invariably mistaken as predictions of the future but are also fascinating revelations of contemporary obsessions, readable pictures of the present that produced them.

[*Signs: Journal of Women in Culture and Society* 2000, vol. 25, no. 4]

way, of events. How we understand the relations between past and present has direct implications for whatever conceptions of the future, the new, creation, and production we may develop.

The past is assumed to be fundamentally like the present, and thus the past provides a preeminent source for the solution of contemporary problems. The more and the better we understand the past, the more well-armed we are to face a future that is to a large extent a copy or reformulation — the variation on a theme — of historical events. It is for this reason we need to cultivate memory, as the art, and scholarship, appropriate to memorialize the past. Such a view of history can at best understand the present in terms of a concretization of the past, the culmination or fruition of what has been. It sees the future in terms of tendencies and features of the past and present. The problem with such a model of time and history is that it inevitably produces a predictable future, a future in which the present can still recognize itself instead of one open to contingency and the new. What is needed in place of such a monumental history is the idea of a history of singularity and particularity, a history that defies repeatability or generalization and that welcomes the surprise of the future as it makes clear the specificities and particularities, the events, of history.

This is one of the paradoxes of historical research in general: histories, reconstructions of the past, are in fact illuminations of a present that would not be possible without this past. The time of the historian is strangely dislocated, somewhere between the past and the present, but not entirely occupying either. For the feminist historian, these paradoxes are particularly exacerbated: the task of the feminist historian is not simply to acknowledge that the writing of the past is more a story about the present but also that it involves the linking of the past and present to a possible future. The project of the feminist historian must be, in part at least, the forging of relations between the sexes, and among members of each sex, along lines that dramatically diverge from the present. The past, a past no longer understood as inert or given, may help engender a productive future, a future beyond patriarchy. Time, the very matter and substance of history, entails the continual elaboration of the new, the openness of things (including life, texts, or matter) to what befalls them. This is what time *is* if it is anything at all: the indeterminate, the unfolding and emergence of the new.

The future is the domain of what endures. But what endures, what exists in time and has time as part of its being, is not what remains the same over time, what retains an identity between what it was and what it will be. Time involves the divergence between what was (i.e., what exists in virtuality) and what is actualized or capable of actualization. The past endures, not in itself, but in its capacity to become something other. This becoming infects not only beings in/as duration but the world itself. This is why feminist history is so crucial: not simply because it informs our present but more so because it enables other virtual futures to be conceived, other perspectives to be developed, than those that currently prevail. In this sense, the astute feminist historian stands on the cusp of the folding of the past into the future, beyond the control or limit of the present.

II

I want to raise a series of hypotheses, some of them quite speculative, meant to highlight rather than elaborate social and political issues, which I hope will raise in relief the questions of what feminist history might be and what feminist theory must be in order to support feminist futures. When we write a history of the past from the point of view of the future, one of the most urgent tasks is to think in the *future anterior,* the tense that Luce Irigaray favors in her textual readings: what will have been, what the past and present will have been in light of a future that is possible only because of them. I postulate three working hypotheses, then, about history and its inherent binding of past to present and future.

1. In studying history, we are not simply gleaning texts, artifacts, and events as they occurred in themselves; we are not unearthing "facts" from the past, like little nuggets of gold that have their own intrinsic value. Rather, what *counts* as history, what is regarded as constituting the past, is that which is deemed to be of relevance to concerns of the present. It is the present that writes the past rather than, as positivist historiography has it, the past that gives way to the present. This is not to say that the present is all that is left of the past; quite the contrary, the past contains the resources to much *more* than the present. Rather, it is only the interests of the present that serve to vivify or reinvigorate the past. The past is always propelled, in virtual form, in a state of compression or contraction, to futures beyond the present.

2. Rather than the past being regarded as fixed, inert, given, unalterable, it must be regarded as being inherently open to future rewritings, as never "full" enough, to retain itself as a full presence that propels itself intact into the future. This is Jacques Derrida's crucial claim about identity and iteration.[2] The identity of any statement, text, or event is never given in itself. Neither texts, nor objects, nor subjects have the kind of self-presence

[2] In particular, see Derrida 1976, 1988.

that gives them a stable and abiding identity; rather, what time is, and what matter, text, and life are, are becomings, openings to time, change, rewriting, recontextualization. The past is never exhausted in its virtualities, insofar as it is always capable of giving rise to *another* reading, another context, another framework that will animate it in different ways. What Derrida makes clear is that the significance, value, or meaning of a text or an event is given only in the infinitely deferred future. So that when we are "doing" history, not only are we writing the event, we are positively reinscribing it, producing it anew, writing it as an opening up to a life that is not exhausted in its pastness.

The past is not a diminished or receded former present, a present that has faded into memory or carried in artifacts that intrude in the present. The past is the virtual that coexists with the present. The past, in other words, is always already contained in the present, not as its cause or its pattern but, rather, as its latency, its virtuality, its potential for being otherwise. This is why the question of history remains a volatile one, not simply tied to getting the facts of the past sorted out and agreed on. It is about the production of *conceivable futures,* the future here being understood not as that which is similarly contained in the present but, rather, that which diverges from the present, one uncontained by and unpredicted from within the present.

3. The past is the virtuality that makes both history and memory possible. Neither history nor memory should be equated with the past itself. As latency or virtuality, the past is larger, more complex, and more laden than any history can present—including feminist history. There can be no complete, or even partial, history, no objective reconstruction, no extraction of the truth of history. What I am getting at is that the past always and essentially gives rise to multiple histories, histories undertaken from different perspectives of the present. This multiplicity is not given through the complexity that the present adds to the past, the present layering or enriching, spotlighting, the details of the past. Such a picture is rendered more complex through the necessity of recognizing what the fissured and latent past enables, for the past is uncontainable within any one history or even all cumulative histories.

This claim is based on Irigaray's understanding of sexual difference as the perspective that has yet to take place, whose place is in the future anterior—which, when it occurs, will have transformed the ways all knowledges, all practices, and all relations have been understood, from perspectives whose positioning has never been occupied or taken place before.[3]

---

[3] See Irigaray 1985, 1994.

There is another way of undertaking history — even feminist history — or another way of undertaking any activity or discipline than that which is presently available. The past cannot be exhausted through its transcription in the present because it is also the ongoing possibility (or virtuality) that makes *future* histories, the continuous writing of histories, necessary. History is made an inexhaustible enterprise only because of the ongoing movement of time, the precession of futurity, and the multiplicity of positions from which this writing can and will occur.

Comparative Literature Department
University at Buffalo, State University of New York

References

Bergson, Henri. 1944. *Creative Evolution*. Trans. Arthur Mitchell. New York: Modern Library.

Derrida, Jacques. 1976. *Of Grammatology*. Trans. Gayatri Chakravorty Spivak. Baltimore: Johns Hopkins University Press.

———. 1988. *Limited Inc*. Trans. Samuel Weber and Jeffrey Mehlman. Evanston, Ill.: Northwestern University Press.

Irigaray, Luce. 1985. *This Sex Which Is Not One*. Trans. Catherine Porter with Carolyn Burke. Ithaca, N.Y.: Cornell University Press.

———. 1994. *An Ethics of Sexual Difference*. Trans. Gillian Gill with Carolyn Burke. Ithaca, N.Y.: Cornell University Press.

The Surprised Feminist

Predicting never has been my preferred vocation. Friends have to bribe me to go with them to sci-fi movies. Reading academic "ten-year plans" almost never puts me on the edge of my seat. So, I confess, I am quite daunted at the prospect of responding to the enticing invitation from *Signs* to spell out even my tentative hunches about where feminist scholarship — especially activist-minded scholarship — will be heading in the new century.

Surprise. I have come to think that the capacity to be surprised — and to *admit* it — is an undervalued feminist attribute. To be surprised is to have one's current explanatory notions, and thus one's predictive assumptions, thrown into confusion. In both academic life and activist public life in most cultures, one is socialized to deny surprise. It is as if admitting surprise jeopardizes one's hard-earned credibility. And credibility, something necessarily bestowed by others, is the bedrock of status. To deny surprise, to sweep confusion under the rug, thus may be especially tempting for feminists, since in societies ranging from Serbia to the United States, from Vietnam to Italy, our purchase on status is insecure at the dawn of this new millennium. Better to assume the "Oh, well, of course it would turn out like that" pose.

This, however, seems to me to be an increasingly risky, if understandable, inclination. Being open to surprise, being ready to publicly acknowledge surprise, may be among the most useful attitudes to adopt to prepare one's feminist self for what now lies ahead of us.

For all of my daily attempts to listen to and mull about the world, I did not predict, did not anticipate these late twentieth-century occurrences:

The NATO-ization of human rights
The fall of Suharto
The collapse of the Brazilian economy
The Canadian Inuits' adoption of a gender-equality principle for
    their new territorial Nunavut parliament
The recruitment of girl children into the Sierre Leone rebel army
The rise of the Kosovo Liberation Army

[*Signs: Journal of Women in Culture and Society* 2000, vol. 25, no. 4]

The British arrest of Augusto Pinochet
The decision to award male scholars scarce fellowships at Radcliffe's
    Bunting Institute

All of these events and the dynamics that brought them about are deeply gendered. That is, women and men played different roles in them. Moreover, they have had quite different effects on various ideas about femininity and masculinity. The ways particular women of distinct citizenship statuses, social classes, ethnic groups, and racialized identities respond to each of these events is certain to determine the respective depth or shallowness of its long-term consequences in the new century. My surprise at Suharto's 1998 fall suggests that I underestimated the breadth of certain Indonesians' political disaffection, even though I was trying hard to chart the organizing efforts of Nike's Indonesian women sneaker-factory workers. My surprise at Ottawa officials' 1996 agreement to establish Nunavut and at local Inuits' decision to institutionalize a fifty-fifty legislative representation reveals the inadequacy of my long-standing curiosity about the politics of Native Canadian women. Being caught off guard by the Kosovo Liberation Army's militarized emergence is a result of having paid insufficient attention to the impacts of Slobodan Milosevic's oppressive policies on Kosovar young men's ethnicized sense of their own masculinity.

The list of embarrassments goes on. My feminist eyebrows went up at:

The success of the Women's National Basketball Association
The post–bubble economy corporate layoffs of Japanese clerical
    "office ladies"
The reemergence of butch/fem role-playing among many young
    American lesbians
The rising number of Mexican men working in border *maquiladoras*
    (assembly plants)
The appearance of Russian women in brothels in Thailand and
    Israel

Admitting my surprise is the only way I am going to be able to take fresh stock of my feminist analyses of developments both far afield and close to home. If I worked hard enough, I probably could manage to fit the current unemployment of Japanese clerical workers into my existing concepts of the sexual division of labor. I could explain Japanese corporate executives' decisions to lay off some of their most feminized labor not in terms of the classic workings of cheapening labor but in terms of those executives' acceptance of equally classic notions that privilege men's employment in times of economic depression. Likewise, I might be able to explain the success of the American women's professional basketball league in terms of patriarchy's famed adaptiveness. After all, at the same time gifted women athletes are gaining a thin slice of ESPN's prime-time television coverage, Reebok and Nike are commodifying those same women's bodies, and more and more men are vying to coach those women's (and their younger schoolgirl sisters') sports teams. That is, whenever one is surprised, one most likely can manage to squeeze the new development into a comfortable, worn conceptual shoe. And this effort is worth the try. Maybe an existing idea does satisfactorily explain the surprising phenomenon. Certainly, sexual divisions of labor and adaptive patriarchy are not concepts that any feminist should rush to dump. But one needs to make that explanatory effort in a spirit of willingness to let go, willingness to think afresh.

It is often in the classroom that a feminist academic is most routinely tested in her commitment to acknowledging surprise. Say I have just made a point — about Canadians' political culture, or about the role of misogyny in fueling the Rwandan genocide — when a student raises her hand and describes something she has observed that doesn't jibe at all with my analytical argument. What do I do? I am tempted to commend the student for her interesting contribution but then to move right into reworking it so that it somehow confirms my point. What I need to do, though, is to pause and say, "Gee, that's surprising. Let's all think about what this new information does to my earlier analysis." It is amazing how much guts, or at least stamina, it takes to do this. It may take even a larger dose of these resources to do it on a prestigious conference panel or in an intense strategy session.

Just since starting to draft this short essay, I've had to practice the art of admitting surprise at a number of developments:

The Columbine High School massacre in Colorado
The nightly televised images of Kosovo refugee "women-andchildren"
Tony Blair's out-militarizing all of his NATO colleagues
Learning about a strand of Tibetan culture that celebrates male warriors
The Pentagon's decision to extend its Junior ROTC military training program down into middle schools

When the latest news is so dismayingly patriarchal, it is natural for anyone with a hint of feminist consciousness to think, "Here we go again." The much-heralded new century seems likely to bring only more of the same. Yet there is a very fine line, sometimes, between a sharp vision that can see clearly the perpetuating dynamics of patriarchal structures and a cynicism that dulls curiosity—curiosity about exactly why two Colorado boys use guns and explosives to express their masculinized adolescent alienation or about precisely what gender rearrangements are occurring in an Albanian tent city. Seeing patriarchy, even misogyny, is not enough. In each instance, we need to know exactly how it works and whether, even if continuing, it has been contested. At a gross level of analysis the patriarchal outcomes may seem to be more of the same, but discovering what is producing them may come as a surprise.

Thus, as we enter the twenty-first century, feminists inside and outside academia need to be on our guard against a cynical form of knowing. We need to send the roots of our curiosity down ever deeper. We need to stand ready to be surprised—to admit surprise and build on it. It is bound to enliven our teaching, broaden our conversations, and make more savvy our strategies.

Government Department
Clark University

Paola Bono
Federica Giardini

Crisis and Adventure

Times of crisis are, or may become, favourable occasions for adventurers.
And we are adventurers.
—Muraro 1995, 1

R ather than marking a true turning point, the end of a millennium
can become a pretext to repropose a founding gesture for feminist
thought: what we call in Italy a *taglio,* that is, a cutting line, a fracture
in our way of looking at, experiencing, signifying ourselves and the world;
also the practice of choosing—perhaps inventing—unexpected points of
view from which to find and create meaning. To *cut away from* established
categories; to *cut into* the discursive, social, and symbolic organization of
"reality," gambling on its interpretation; to practice disbelief, questioning
given understandings and orderings of "reality." These are gestures that
still can problematize the so-called naturalness, necessity, and inevitability
of previously available narratives.

This crisis point is not simply a break in the linearity of events; it is the
very movement of a thought that is also a practice and therefore becomes
a political action as well. Primacy of practice is a fruitful interaction of
experience and thought, of one's lived situations and their theoretical elaboration. Interpreting is not simply an intellectual activity when it entails
changing one's perception of oneself and of one's position in the world,
changing one's way of relating to that position and ultimately to the world
itself. Practice, never solitary, always interactional, denies the Marxian di-
chotomy between interpretation and change: interpretation, in fact, *can*
change the world.

Looking at the Italian sociopolitical situation in its European and global
context on the cusp of the new millennium, we feel that a *taglio* has indeed
occurred: "Patriarchy is over, it has lost women's trust and it is over . . .
and now? What will happen to the world and to ourselves, now that the
patriarchal symbolic order no more regulates, and will ever less regulate,
women's lives and their relationship with men?" (Libreria delle Donne
di Milano 1996, 1–2). The crisis takes the form of a weakening in the

[*Signs: Journal of Women in Culture and Society* 2000, vol. 25, no. 4]

signifying power of the patriarchal symbolic system for the lives of both women and men; becoming an interpretative lens, the *taglio* calls to mind and into question several issues that we think are theoretically, politically, and experientially relevant today. We can do little more than sketch some of them rather briefly in our contribution to this millennium issue; ours is, of course, a subjective contribution but also one rooted in our relations to other Italian feminists and in our deep allegiance to the Italian feminism of sexual difference.[1]

1. Some Italian women have ventured an interpretation of our historical times, characterized by rapid and often dramatic change, as bringing about the "end of patriarchy." For a crisis is also a moment when everything seems to precipitate — as in chemical preparations — so that a new compound comes into being. However, because we are thinking of human lives, in this case there is no formula to foresee the results of the various combinations. Nonetheless, some trends are clearly visible: the demateralization of markets, norms, subjectivities, bodies and vital processes such as death and life, forms of communication, and national borders (and, conversely, the violent, authoritarian, reactionary reclaiming of these same borders), all of which we strive to reread in the light of the practical, materialistic discourse of sexual difference.

The strength of this discourse lies in never accepting already codified dualisms and oppositions, always questioning — and acting upon — the underlying symbolic order that produces and assigns codes and meanings. In Italian thought on sexual difference, the emphasis has been on *practices*, on the material dimensions of the naming of experience, and on the necessity and capacity of turning experience into a source of theoretical reflection in and through the relation with (some) other women. Experience is a dimension that is often still concealed both in dominant theories that privilege only the linguistic-textual dimension and in political interpretations that focus on formal or global phenomena. This lack of attention to experience downplays the disturbing friction of each person's unique

---

[1] Who one is and where one speaks from are always relevant features, more so in a cross-cultural situation such as this: two Italian feminists (and Italian feminism is still a newcomer on the English-speaking scene, although it has a rich and varied history) writing for a U.S. journal and an international audience. So we feel a few words about ourselves are appropriate: we belong to different generations and disciplines — Paola is around 50 years old, a literary critic and scholar teaching English drama at the University Roma Tre; Federica is around 30, a philosopher working on her Ph.D. in the same university — but we are both on the editorial board of the journal *DonnaWomanFemme,* perhaps the oldest and certainly one of the most respected Italian feminist journals. What we think about the coming millennium is steeped, on the one hand, in our personal life stories, marked as they have been by Italian feminist thought and action, and, on the other, in the current Italian sociopolitical situation.

experiences, seen as contingent, subjective elements of secondary relevance. It behooves us, then, to reassume a thought-in-practice mode at the beginning of the new millennium.

2. Taking as a starting point political passion and its interconnection with the thought of sexual difference, two recent issues of *DonnaWoman-Femme* (*DWF*) (1997a, 1997b), titled "Politics: A Difficult Love Story" and "On the Edge of Time," have underlined and questioned the implications of the changing relationship between women's politics and institutional politics. Rooted in the awareness of a gap between the two, reflections on political action now need to go further if we want to understand and reinterpret some fundamental features of the present.

While the public sphere has expanded, particularly where women's lives are concerned, the sphere of traditional politics has not grown proportionally. On the contrary, the so-called decision-making places have been reduced to increasingly limited citadels of power. The norms and laws produced by these sites are increasingly less adequate in attributing meaning to existence(s). This provokes a sense of emptiness and suspension, even in what was once the feminist community. No longer able to portray itself in terms of either pure opposition or total estrangement, and having to take into account a widespread female presence in the most disparate public places and institutions, feminism must understand the forms that political action marked by sexual difference might take. Political reflection can no longer count on a shared "us," on a clearly defined community or a movement. The overwhelming need to give voice to differences among women without falling into a fruitless individualism emerges. *Donna-WomanFemme* answers this need with a concept of "related singularities" (1998, 6), in which each woman in her difference and differences identifies the conflicts and openings emerging out of her own situation and then makes them a point of comparison with other women.

Among the challenges we have to face are the growing meaninglessness for many people of the institutions of the state and, consequently, a gamble on the ability for societal self-regulation; the need to reconsider the figure of the mother given the changes arising from the diffusion of new reproductive technologies; the transformation of means of production linked to the ever-increasing presence of women in the workforce; and the call to personalize the impersonal and thus reenact in a new form the "personal is political" axiom.

That more and more Western women can now lead emancipated lives risks reproducing a split between the public and the private, as emerges, for example, in the caregiver role. Taking on the responsibilities and gratifications of public life may result in delegating caring activities (looking after children and elderly parents, making the house a pleasant place, etc.) to others, to immigrant women, for example, whose presence continues to increase in Italy. This in turn leads us to reflect on the underlying conflict between public time and private time.

3. The possibilities presented by this crisis call for a reconsideration of the historical dimension of feminist thought. It is a matter of addressing differences among women, including the different positions that come into play in the establishment of a symbolic order. The so-called "end of the feminist community" (*DWF* 1997a, 6–7) also raises the question of "a present not contemporary onto itself" (Boella 1993, 9–14) and the possibility of maintaining a certain tension between various positions with respect to the historical origin of feminism in the 1970s. For indeed there are important differences among the positions of the women who contributed to that rebirth, at times interrupting their relationship with tradition in order to make room for new symbolic forms, and also between their positions and those of younger women who can count on that history, having as their starting point situations decidedly different from those of their feminist forebears. In fact, the generational shift that presents itself at the end of this century is marked by its own distinct characteristics. In place of the "matricide" accomplished in the transition from the feminist horizon opened up by Simone de Beauvoir to the new horizon of sexual difference feminism, recent generations can do more than just break away from their antecedents. For instance, the line of feminist thought that has highlighted the issue of the mother-daughter relationship permits one to consider relations with women "coming from afar" in ways that intermingle continuity and difference. Now this difference can be considered in a historical dimension, given both the changed conditions of today's women and the existence of a historical trend of development that is already feminist. Certain feminist "figurations" need to be reconsidered as well, from symptoms of the effects of symbolic exclusion, such as the hysteric, to the primacy of everyday grassroots political action with respect to institutional politics—an idea that in Italy marked a clear distinction between feminism as a movement and institutional feminism, a distinction that should be reconsidered in order to examine what political action might mean in the hands of the young women of today and of the future.

4. Last but not least, masculine identity (at least in the West) seems to repeat its own worn-out patriarchal forms. Masculinity today is often characterized by a disorientation that does not always result in the assumption of one's own partiality but, on the contrary, can produce gestures of violent restoration of the patriarchal symbolic order; however, this disorientation also opens a potential space for the male sex to become estranged

from itself. The gamble of the philosophical idea of sexual difference, which always questions preconstituted identities, consists in the construction of a common space for subjects who are marked by a constitutive gender alterity and can no longer aspire to a self-contained unity that is totally binary and representable. Thus sexual difference points to a move beyond the reattribution of fixed identities for the two sexes and outlines a possible future of relationships based on experienced differences that do not result simply in an indistinct plurality.

Department of Communication in Literature and Performing Arts (Bono)
Department of Philosophy (Giardini)
University of Rome Tre

References

Boella, Laura. 1993. *Le parole chiave della politica.* Mantova: Scuola di cultura contemporanea.

DWF. 1997a. "Politics: A Difficult Love Story." *DonnaWomanFemme* 34–35(2–3).

DWF. 1997b. "On the Edge of Time." *DonnaWomanFemme* 36(4).

DWF. 1998. "Tempi moderni: Editoriale." *DonnaWomanFemme* 39–40(3–4).

Libreria delle donne di Milano (Milan women's bookstore). 1996. *E' accaduto non per caso.* Milan.

Muraro, Luisa. 1995. "Introduction." In *Oltre l'uguaglianza: Le radici femminili dell'autorità,* ed. Diotima, 1–3. Naples: Liguori.

Drucilla Cornell

Las Greñudas: Recollections on Consciousness-Raising

The second wave of feminism, as it has come to be known, started out as an experiment in radical democracy. We called that experiment "consciousness-raising," which was the method of group formation characterizing the movement. All those who came into feminist consciousness-raising groups were to be given a voice and heard with seriousness. It may sound strange to put it that way, as if such a group could give to women what they did not have — a voice. But that was exactly the point. Together, we could find a way to learn both to speak among ourselves and to address a broader public by providing ourselves with the support we could not find alone. Voices were not just something we had, a natural attribute of our human being, but also something we helped each other develop as we struggled to articulate who we were and who we sought to become in the movement we were creating. Since everyone's voice was to count as equally important in the group and in the formation of the group's political agenda, these "spaces" were as often about contest and profound disagreement as they were about agreement.[1] By letting women speak and represent themselves — initially, these tended to be women-only spaces — the process of change was already taking place no matter how deeply women initially disagreed on questions such as what it meant to be oppressed as a woman, how race and class played out in that oppression, and what kind of change we ultimately had to make in order to truly challenge patriarchy. By patriarchy, I mean the state-enforced and culturally supported norm of heterosexual monogamy as the only appropriate organization of family life. This imposed family structure, as I have argued elsewhere,[2] inevitably reinforces rigid gender identities through the psychic laws that are purportedly necessary for the perpetration of these families and the achievement of so-called normal mature sexual differentiation.[3] In the course of

---

[1] I put *spaces* in quotation marks because these spaces were not just literal but also moral and psychic.

[2] See Cornell 1998, chap. 2.

[3] For a more elaborate discussion of what I mean by psychic laws and their relationship to actual legal law, see Cornell 1999. Psychoanalytic theory, in all of its diversity, shares one thing in common: the elaboration of psychic laws that are ethically justified in the name of

[*Signs: Journal of Women in Culture and Society* 2000, vol. 25, no. 4]

democratic struggle among ourselves, we were already achieving an ethical and political purpose, which, following Marilyn Friedman (1995), I will call "demoralizing the genders," even if some consciousness-raising groups never engaged in more traditional activism. The phrase is clearly ironic, and I will return to the misunderstanding of that irony shortly. By "demoralizing" the genders, Friedman means that we seek to denaturalize the narrow moral symbolism and mythologies through which masculinity and femininity are defined and which in turn create moral divisions of labor, codes of how men and women are supposed to behave, and what kinds of moral characters are appropriate for them to develop (1995, 70). Consciousness-raising groups ethically challenged the moral norms of femininity just by insisting that public contest over the meaning of our "sex" should take place. This leads to another aspect of radical democracy that was to be practiced.

Our "sex," under the patriarchal moral code, was what was to be kept in secret as part of the sexual shame associated with femininity. The frank discussion in these groups about everything from getting breasts to having periods, to living with pregnancy, to exploring our bodies, was clearly an effort to release ourselves from shame. Our groups were radical in the content of what was made appropriate for public discussion and group engagement. We had a slogan for this: "The personal is political." Moralism about what was appropriate to say about our "sex" would have gotten in the way of this symbolic and representational practice.

My own consciousness-raising group, made up of Latinas and African-American women with the exception of myself, spent hours discussing the specificity of how we were femmed differently because race and class were integral to the mapping of femininity onto femaleness. Our group was formed in 1974, largely due to the efforts of Muriel Hirschfield, an African-American woman, after she and I were fired for union organizing at our jobs as phone operators at Columbia University.[4] At a group discussion, one Latina used the example of her mother's insistent warnings of the dangers in Anglo society of appearing *greñuda* — uncombed. *Greñuda,* in Spanish, implies that a properly femmed Latina must whiten herself

---

achieving adequate separation and individuation. I am aware that many psychoanalytic theorists would not put it this way because these laws, such as the incest prohibition, e.g., are explained as an inevitable part of enculturation or part of what it means to be a sexually differentiated individual. It is beyond the scope of this essay to defend my argument that psychoanalysis should defend these laws ethically rather than try to show their inevitability through "scientific explanation."

[4] It is legitimate to write that we were fired for union organizing because the National Labor Relations Board found union organizing to be the reason for the firing.

through ladylike hairstyling, a particular mode of braiding that would show that her hair was not "nappy." But *greñuda* is not literally about hairstyling. It is a metaphor about how a Latina is not supposed to appear or behave. For our group member, her femming was inseparable from how she was to distinguish herself morally from all that was "black." After that evening, we called ourselves *las greñudas* to represent what we were struggling against, even though we knew that we did not all share her experience and that the metaphor would mean different things to each one of us in the group. Yet as a group, the name represented our solidarity in a struggle for what we proudly called freedom. Later in my life I would understand this kind of representational practice as inversion or mimesis, which through its conscious appropriation inverts the moral meaning it was originally meant to carry (see Irigaray 1985; Cornell 1991, 147–52). We saw ourselves as creating new representations of ourselves as a group without minimizing the differences of race, class, ethnicity, and national backgrounds among us.

We took our commitment to new forms of representation and democratic practice into the political battles that arose out of our coming together as a group. One of our members was a prostitute who had organized a prostitutes' collective. We joined with her and the other collective members to do what was necessary to allow the women to escape from their pimps. Another project was getting men who were parents of group members' children to keep up with their support payments. We would go to the man's workplace and call on his "brothers" and "sisters" to help us address the problem. We had great success, as "brothers" were reminded by their own coworkers of their responsibilities by having food pelted at them in the cafeteria, smoke bombs put in their lockers, and other creative and collective measures used to ensure that the necessary support was delivered. We never considered hiring a lawyer, not because none of the women in the group could afford a lawyer but because bringing in the state was never an alternative for this group of Latinas and African-American women, for whom the state, and particularly the police, generally were not considered sources of protection. The whole idea here was to find a representational practice that would allow women to be taken seriously, to get their needs met, not to bring in the state against men who, although behaving badly, were never identified as the enemy.

Our representation of ourselves as feminists was inseparable from our antiracism and our attempt to dignify the Spanish language. We were not claiming that the name we gave ourselves was an adequate description of some truth about Woman or that, in a like manner, it captured our essence as women. Indeed, we did not share the same experiences of oppression.

As a result, it was crucially important for us to bear witness not only to our differences but also to the privileges, including the privilege of a potential "passing," that could separate us from one another. As a white woman, I was called to witness in front of my sisters that I could never share their experiences of oppression as women of color. I was always already represented by the larger society, as a white woman, and could not simply step out of the privileges that were inherent in that representation.

This leads me to a crucial point: representation is inevitable. Representation is what gives us our reality. But we are not passive before these representations, as if the world is simply imposed on us so that we are effectively limited by how we are shaped by the symbolic codes that give us meaning, including the meaning of the moral symbols of conventional stereotypical gender hierarchy. We are always both consciously and unconsciously engaged in representing who we are in the very process of becoming a "presence" to ourselves and to others (see Cornell 1998, 34–37). The feminism we practiced in our consciousness-raising group, which clearly understood the centrality of rerepresenting ourselves in accordance with our attempt to explode the limits of how we had to be in the world, did not essentialize the meaning of these representations. They were understood to be just that — representations, an aesthetic mode of knowledge[5] that also allowed us to develop a politics in accordance with political and ethical aspirations to challenge the hegemonic meanings of sexual difference.

Nor, then, was the use of *las greñudas* simply strategic, deployed as a means to an end. The end was integral in the name, which we understood to be both political and ethical: political in that it challenged the behavior appropriate to women in public, and ethical in that it challenged how we had been hemmed in from divergent race, class, and ethnic positions. As the only white woman in the group, I came to see myself as not only oppressed because I had been femmed so as not to have access to certain kinds of pursuits — in my own case, being a mathematician — but also privileged, even if I saw some of the privileges of white femininity as themselves a prison.

Of course, I am not describing what actually went on in all consciousness-raising groups, but I am arguing that the insistence on radical democracy was crucial to the practice we both conceived and lived. It is this insistence that realizes profound respect for the potential richness of the symbolic field of sexual difference. Without this respect, the power of our experiences is diminished by a feminist moralism that tries to tell us, in the name of feminism, how we are to behave as women, as feminists, or both.

---

[5] See Cornell 1999 for more on this notion of aesthetic knowledge.

Let me be clear about what I mean by feminist moralism. I mean the remoralization of gender in the exact opposite sense of what Friedman means by demoralization.[6] In other words, if in different guises we moralize gender and reinscribe a moral division of labor by attributing a specific set of moral behaviors to men or women as a class, we are engaged in remoralizing gender. We see this kind of remoralization, for instance, among younger antifeminists who argue for a new chastity (see Decter 1972). But antifeminists are not the only ones who engage in this process. Feminists do it, for example, when we argue that it is only men who are enticed by sexually explicit literature because it is part of their rapacious nature. Such statements often pose as descriptions, but I argue that they are moral generalizations — not so much about who men actually are but about how masculinity is symbolically encoded.

I am aware, of course, that my story of my own consciousness-raising group proceeds through recollective imagination, by which I mean that the story that I tell proceeds through a narration of its moral as I imagine its significance for a future ethical orientation for feminism.[7] It may even risk the nostalgia of an "old girl" reminiscing about her youth on the picket line, but I take that risk because this radical herstory is often obscured in accounts of the second wave of feminism. The second wave was not, for many of us, a school in which we "girls" learned to enter and were allowed to gain access to straight, white, male-dominated professions. If, in my imaginative recollection, there is a moral to the story of my consciousness-raising group, it is not that we are left with a political demoralizing antiessentialism.[8] Nothing in the struggle to demoralize gender, in the sense that I mean it, involves us in denying the need for the ethical, political, and aesthetic representations of who we are — and even the need for a legal

---

[6] Friedman's argument that gender is moralized is as follows: "Morality, I suggest, is fragmented into a 'division of moral labor' along the lines of gender, the rationale for which is rooted in historic developments pertaining to family, state, and economy. The tasks of governing, regulating social order, and managing other 'public' institutions have been monopolized by men as their privileged domain, and the tasks of sustaining privatized personal relationships have been imposed on, or left to, women. The genders have thus been conceived in terms of special and distinctive moral projects. Justice and rights have structured male moral norms, values, and virtues, while care and responsiveness have defined female moral norms, values, and virtues. The division of moral labor has had the dual function both of preparing us each for our respective socially defined domains and of rendering us incompetent to manage the affairs of the realm from which we have been excluded" (Friedman 1995, 64).

[7] For a longer discussion of how I have defined and used the phrase *recollective imagination*, see Cornell 1993, 23–24, 31–32.

[8] I have defended such a moral and legal right to personality and named it the "right to the imaginary domain" (see Cornell 1995).

translation of these into a conception of the right of personality—as long as it is conceived to be consistent with the overall project of our struggle for freedom. Freedom here is understood as our freedom to be otherwise than in the limited, restricted personae of masculinity and femininity. There is a confusion, for example, that laws and movements against sexual harassment need to involve themselves in this remoralization.[9] This project of radical democracy is about opening up a space for new moral, ethical, and political representations of feminism itself, as much as it is against the specific kind of moral symbolization of sexual difference integral to gender hierarchy.

Defined as such, this project encompasses feminists who come from a wide variety of philosophical and political traditions (see Butler 1990; Brown 1995). What has come to be called "postmodern feminism" is better understood as this project to demoralize gender.[10] We are reminded of a radical project of democratic representation that always remembers the metaphor of silencing as that which led us to create spaces in which new voices could articulate themselves and be taken seriously in the first place. There is terrible irony, given our herstory, in the moral imposition of silence on some women because they do not engage in behavior that some feminists decree necessary for a "proper" feminist.

Women's Studies, Political Science, and Law
Rutgers University

References

Brown, Wendy. 1995. *States of Injury: Power and Freedom in Late Modernity*. Princeton, N.J.: Princeton University Press.

Butler, Judith. 1990. *Gender Trouble: Feminism and the Subversion of Identity*. New York: Routledge.

———. 1995. "Contingent Foundations." In *Feminist Contentions: A Philosophical Exchange*, by Seyla Benhabib, Judith Butler, Drucilla Cornell, and Nancy Fraser, 17–34. New York: Routledge.

Cornell, Drucilla. 1991. *Beyond Accommodation: Ethical Feminism, Deconstruction, and the Law*. New York: Routledge.

[9] Katie Roiphe (1993), e.g., makes this mistake by arguing that laws against sexual harassment and date rape require the remoralization of gender.

[10] For example, both Judith Butler and I are not entirely comfortable calling ourselves postmodernist, although we are often taken as such. Both of us have questioned whether there is a unique historical period that could be meaningfully designated as postmodern, let alone one that we are in and that further describes a certain kind of feminist politics (see Cornell 1992; Butler 1995).

———. 1992. "The Ethical Message of Negative Dialectics." In her *The Philosophy of the Limit,* 13–38. New York: Routledge.

———. 1993. *Transformations: Recollective Imagination and Sexual Difference.* New York: Routledge.

———. 1995. *The Imaginary Domain: Abortion, Pornography, and Sexual Harassment.* New York: Routledge.

———. 1998. *At the Heart of Freedom: Feminism, Sex, and Equality.* Princeton, N.J.: Princeton University Press.

———. 1999. "Introduction to the New Edition: Feminist Hope." In her *Beyond Accommodation: Ethical Feminism, Deconstruction, and the Law,* 2d ed., xv–xxxviii. Lanham, Md.: Rowman & Littlefield.

Decter, Midge. 1972. *The New Chastity and Other Arguments against Women's Liberation.* New York: Coward, McCann & Geoghegan.

Friedman, Marilyn. 1995. "Beyond Caring: The De-Moralization of Gender." In *Justice and Care: Essential Readings in Feminist Ethics,* ed. Virginia Held, 61–77. Boulder, Colo.: Westview.

Irigaray, Luce. 1985. *This Sex Which Is Not One.* Trans. Catherine Porter. Ithaca, N.Y.: Cornell University Press.

Roiphe, Katie. 1993. *The Morning After: Sex, Fear and Feminism on Campus.* Boston: Little, Brown.

After the Common Era

an women have a millennium? It is tempting to answer this question with "yes, but not at the millennium," to borrow a well-known argument from Joan Kelly-Gadol (1977). For one thing, what could it mean for women to celebrate the millennium? Were my Christian identity robust, the millennium could mark an important milestone for me. Perhaps it could do so if I felt loyalty to a Western civilization that often claims ancient Greek and early Christian origins. Here it would not be an exact date that was commemorated but something like the idea of ancient origins and shared pride in our achievements. Lacking such allegiances, however, the millennium feels to me like a call to celebrate someone else's story of history toward which I have considerable ambivalence, at best.

Moreover, there is little positive connection between millennial history, as I shall refer to it, and either women's history or the history of feminism. After all, such periodization schemes pick out milestones for a group "for itself"—for a group self-consciously identifying itself as such. It was only the emerging feminism of the early 1970s that enabled me to claim allegiance to women as a self-conscious social group with a public agenda. I can't remember ever even wondering prior to the reemergence of feminism what it could mean for women to be such a group. Patriots, Christians, Jews, and the working class were such groups, but in my mind, women were not. The suffragettes, as they were demeaningly called, who achieved perhaps a paragraph in the total collection of elementary, secondary, college, and graduate school texts that I had been assigned, appeared to me as a piece of isolated historical exotica, in the same category as Joan of Arc and Marie Curie. No sense of impending historical change reached me through the descriptions of these extraordinary women—although to those more knowledgeable and hopeful about women's futures, both the suffragists and Marie Curie no doubt held great promise.

So if women and feminists cannot now commemorate a millennium of history in which we can see the reflection of our own activities (let alone two such millennia), perhaps we can nevertheless look forward to one that our distant relatives will celebrate. Women, and the feminisms that have helped bring them to consciousness as a self-defined group, can have their own calendars, their own time.

The thrill of women's time

Feminism has not lacked its theorists of "women's time," such as Kelly-Gadol and Juliet Mitchell. Mitchell described as a "world historic event" for women the availability of cheap and reliable birth control, which, for the first time, she argued, allowed women to become self-conscious historical actors planning our futures unburdened by relatively uncontrollable pregnancies (1973). With this event, women's history began, and, upon reading Mitchell, I personally thrilled at the thought of joining what passed for history in those days. Although these little devices that were to give me access to history purportedly had been "available" for several decades before I read Mitchell, they were controlled by the state and by families. When I was twenty-three, in the week before my marriage, I had to be accompanied by my mother to get the family doctor's contraceptive prescription. The strategies we young women used to join history before the unfettered legalization of contraceptives I leave to your imaginations or recollections.

At the same time that I thrilled to Mitchell's recasting of my lot in history, Betty Friedan's analysis of women's gathering resistance during the post–World War II years to being shut out of challenging jobs in the name of "the feminine mystique" helped me to understand my mother's and my own different but equally ambivalent dreams about who we could become — about, one could say, premature recruitment by history for my mother and the confused feelings toward it that I, like she, experienced.

She was seven when she and her siblings were abandoned to an orphanage by their well-to-do father, who ran off with his secretary, and by their newly indigent mother, who had no relatives or social services to support her and her five children. But my mother went on to graduate from college (Phi Beta Kappa even) and then to work in advertising in New York City in the late 1920s. In the 1930s she supported the family when my adored father, who had had his own series of struggles and achievements, was out of work for several years during the Depression. She had many pregnancies, five of which produced me and my siblings. After my father died, she joined Vista at the age of sixty-three, and worked to provide adequate nutrition for migrant workers' children. Both the barely suppressed pain of her childhood and her continuing determination to flourish in whatever circumstances life might bring have haunted me all my life.

So, too, was I haunted prior to the emergence of feminism by an ambivalence much like hers toward claiming this new role in history—although I certainly cannot lay responsibility for it primarily on her. For her, "woman" was never a chosen, proclaimed category of identity. Wife and mother first, then neighbor, and often still sister to the younger siblings she had helped to raise—these were her loyalties, and they remained her frequently announced allegiances even in the later decades when she taught elementary school and then worked as a school librarian. "I'm just a house-wife," she would say to the census interviewer, as he also recorded her full days of paid work. She had a deep ambivalence, verging occasionally on hostility, toward the idea of women claiming not just equality with men and their roles in the public sphere but also the right, the need, and the desire to shape public life from within it as we collectively thought desir-able. She thoroughly supported my career dreams and plans and was proud of my achievements at school and work, but she thought me selfish to wait almost a decade after marriage to have children.

Had I spent that decade developing my own career and place in history? No. I had worked to support my husband through graduate school and then graded papers and in other ways advanced his career. Women's time may have started, but I didn't know it. Then feminism came along and, as they say, the rest is history.

Whose time is women's time?

So, the question I ask myself is this: What do or could feminists count as significant historical markers? Mitchell imagined a bright new beginning to women's history, and in important senses she was right. But that was then, and this is now. My mother had her reasons not to claim "woman" as a political identity. But is "woman" even a—let alone *the*—significant category for me to claim in this moment of intersectional, multicultural, postcolonial, transgender flourishing, not to mention a moment of pon-dering how to turn gender into a category within history rather than some-thing always already there, prior to history, as historians have called for? I'm quite sure "feminist" is such a significant category; numerous caveats notwithstanding, there are many contexts in which I am happy and proud to claim it. Of course, I only very cautiously claim it in international con-texts, including interactions with students from other cultures, where it is thought to be too conservative, too radical, or too Western. We are enter-ing a period of collective negotiations and resignifications of the term in university settings among generations and among feminists, as well as be-tween women's studies programs and the disciplines. In community and international settings too, the term is under negotiation. Yet *feminist time* remains far less problematic for me at this point than *women's time;* the intersectional and multicultural issues alone are enough to make me doubt the usefulness of the latter term's falsely unifying energy.

Perhaps, if we are lucky, the era we have been entering in the past few decades will be referred to as democratic time (problematic as the term *democracy* may be). The self-identified group with which I feel most affinity with respect to public time is a fictive solidarity of groups that could tell similar stories of struggling through the debris of the end of the imperial fiction of a Common Era. We do so even as our lives are more and more closely linked by global political, economic, and social commonalities. From the rapid expansion of global capitalism, Western media representations, and Western governmental forms to the escalation of large-scale environmental changes, we can no longer retain the fiction of cultures that are materially isolated from each other. Yet gone too is the plausibility and legitimacy of the integrationist, melting-pot, single cultural ideal of the sort that the millennium and its Common Era are supposed to mark. The Common Era becomes simply a bookkeeping convenience, a bureaucratic device, which is not exactly something deserving a great deal of celebration.

So perhaps we could use the millennium to mark the beginning of the emergence of an envisioned "democratic time." Cultures have their own significant milestones to commemorate whenever these might occur, but Y2K could mark the end of a prehistory and the beginning of a — hopefully long — era when democratic negotiation — as redefined by those who have suffered from too little of it — becomes the prevailing mode of interpersonal, institutional, community, and global interactions. Now, there is a good excuse for a fine party, for a celebratory event with dear friends and loved ones, and for jokes expressing only a slight anxiety about the dire bureaucratic scenarios of the old Common Era.

Graduate School of Education and Information Studies
University of California, Los Angeles

References

Kelly-Gadol, Joan. 1977. "Did Women Have a Renaissance?" In *Becoming Visible: Women in European History,* ed. R. Bridenthal and C. Koonz, 137–64. Boston: Houghton Mifflin.

Mitchell, Juliet. 1973. *Women's Estate.* New York: Random House.

Laura Brace

Julia O'Connell Davidson

Minding the Gap: General and Substantive Theorizing on Power and Exploitation

O ver the past decade, general theorists within feminism have developed increasingly sophisticated responses to questions about how best to theorize power and subjectivity. This has involved bringing the "unsettling power" of theory to bear on the model of power that informs one longstanding theoretical tradition within feminism (Butler and Scott 1992, xvii). Nancy Fraser points out that feminist thinkers from Mary Wollstonecraft to Catharine MacKinnon and Carole Pateman have understood "women's subordination . . . first and foremost as the condition of being subject to the direct command of an individual man. Male dominance, accordingly, is a dyadic power relation in which a male superordinate commands a female subordinate. It is a master/subject relation" (1997, 225).

This dyadic master/subject model understands male power as domination and in the process fixes the meanings of sex and gender, masculinity and femininity. It is an approach that strives for security of identity, for a settled feminist territory. Critics have argued that this is bound to be homogenizing, reductive, and ahistoricizing, that it assumes and oversimplifies precisely that which feminism needs to explain. Rather than imagining women as "a definable empirical group with a common essence and identity," feminists need to uncover and transform "all the discourses, practices and social relations where the category 'woman' is constructed in a way that implies subordination" (Mouffe 1992, 382). To this end, theorists such as Joan Scott (1988), Elizabeth Spelman (1990), Iris Young (1990), Chantal Mouffe (1992), Anne McClintock (1995), Leonore Davidoff (1995), Nira Yuval-Davis (1997), and Ruth Lister (1998) have begun to formulate various ways of addressing the multiplicity of subject positions that women, as bearers of classed, racialized, national, ethnic, sexual, and aged as well as gendered identities, occupy in relation both to men and to each other.

These theorists may disagree as to how, precisely, the articulation of

Signs: Journal of Women in Culture and Society 2000, vol. 25, no. 4]

these multiple subject positions should be addressed and how, if at all, they relate to broader social structures, but at the level of general theory a consensus is emerging around the need for a more complex, nuanced, and relational vision of gendered power. Such attention to complexity is very often missing from contemporary feminist analyses of *substantive* questions about human rights issues such as prostitution, pornography, trafficking, and migrant domestic work. Though there are feminist writers who draw on recent developments in general theory to celebrate the "sex work" of a small elite of white Western women (see, e.g., Bell 1994), the work of those who are concerned with the sex industry and global traffic in women *as sites of exploitation* is typically informed by theories advanced in the 1970s and 1980s (e.g., Brownmiller 1975; Dworkin 1981; and MacKinnon 1987).

In the 1990s, feminist analyses of the ways women are subordinated through specific practices have thus tended either implicitly or explicitly to reaffirm the assumption that universal claims about women and men (subjects and masters) as internally undifferentiated groups can and should be advanced. Sheila Jeffreys, for example, insists that "prostitution is a form of brutal cruelty on the part of men that constitutes a violation of women's human rights, wherever and however it takes place" (1997, 348), while Kathleen Barry tells us that "prostitution makes all women vulnerable, exposed to danger, open to attack" (1995, 317), that pornography "is a collective, social-class representation of women's vulnerability" (318), and that women who migrate to work in prostitution may not be trafficked in the traditional sense but are "vulnerable to the only means of economic existence available to them because they are women, and because they are women they are homeless, and poor" (196; see also Russell 1993, 1998; Jeffreys 1994; Kitzinger 1994).

These authors present trafficking, prostitution, and pornography as phenomena that both epitomize and replicate the master/subject model of power, creating and reflecting women's identity as subordinate. In this sense, there is a very real gap between substantive and general feminist theorizing on power and oppression. Those who identify women as an oppressed group look warily across the divide, suspecting those on the other side of disloyalty, of "thoughtless theory" that is bound to undermine feminism as politics (Riley 1992, 121).[1] This lack of dialogue is un-

---

[1] The gap reappears in scholarly journals and other forums for feminist debate because of an institutionalized "division of labor" between academics and the mechanics of the refereeing process. Papers that draw on empirical studies of sexual exploitation are sent for peer review to acknowledged experts on the substantive field, which very often means they are sent to individuals who are firmly wedded to a nonrelational view of power. Meanwhile,

helpful to our understandings of both substantive and general theoretical issues. Take, for instance, questions about the articulation of gender, race, and class. "Radical" feminists usually do acknowledge racism and economic marginalization as factors that render some women especially vulnerable to sexual and other forms of exploitation. However, they do not even begin to engage with the insights of 1990s post- or neocolonial feminist theory, which teaches that "race, gender and class are not distinct realms of experience, existing in splendid isolation from each other; nor can they be simply yoked together retrospectively like armatures of Lego. Rather, they come into existence *in and through* relation to each other—if in contradictory and conflictual ways" (McClintock 1995, 5).

This reluctance to take on board recent theoretical developments stems, perhaps, from a fear that poststructuralist thinking will dissolve all basis for political action by fragmenting the female subject into a series of incommensurable subjectivities (see Jeffreys 1997). However, we want to argue that some of the most interesting and politically significant empirical work being undertaken today is precisely that which recognizes diversity and invites examination of the contradictory and conflictual ways gender, race, and class come into existence in and through relation to each other. Kamala Kempadoo's research on sex work in the Caribbean (1994, 1998, 1999), for example, highlights the need for historically specific accounts of the construction of relations of subordination in given geopolitical spaces. Her detailed portraits of migrant sex workers in Curaçao undermine the universalism implicit in Barry's (1995) analysis of migrant women prostituting because, as women, "they are homeless, and poor," and they also firmly situate the particularities of migrant women's actions and experiences in a framework that recognizes systemic inequalities and injustices at regional and local, as well as global, levels. "Migrant sex workers in the Caribbean," Kempadoo observes, "like many of their counterparts elsewhere in the world, stand at the nexus of oppressions and exploitation around gender, sex, class, nationality, and race" (1998, 130). Kempadoo does not pretend to provide a comprehensive theoretical account of prostitution as an institution, and readers may, of course, take issue with her more general position on sex work. The value of her work is that it illuminates the complex and often contradictory interplay between racialized, economic, and gendered processes that have historically shaped, and that

---

papers that discuss oppression in a more abstract, theoretical fashion are rarely reviewed by scholars who are actively engaged in research in substantive areas.

continue to shape, women's sexual exploitation in the Caribbean. In so doing, it contributes to a body of research evidence that can be used to inform more sophisticated feminist political and theoretical responses to prostitution.

Our vision of feminism's terrain is further complicated by research exploring the fact that women can sometimes be more than complicit in sexually exploitative practices. Jacqueline Sánchez Taylor's (1997, 2000) work on female sex tourism, for example, draws attention to *relationships* among subjective gender, race, and class identities, and it poses challenging questions for feminists who give primacy to patriarchal power relations in their analyses of sex tourism. The relationship between (some) Western women's class and racialized privilege and the construction of Otherness and subordination is also a feature of Bridget Anderson's (1993, 1998, 2000) research on migrant domestic workers in the European Union. Anderson's analysis of the ways female employers raise their own status through the degradation of "their" domestic workers is revealing about linkages between hierarchies of gender, race, class, and nation in European societies. Her work also shows very clearly the political and theoretical dangers of refusing to recognize that there can be real and material conflicts of interest between different groups of women.

These are just a few examples of researchers who refuse the comforting ahistoricism of universalism without losing sight of the realities of exploitation and its material bases, and they can hardly be accused of lacking political commitment. Rather, their willingness to explore the uneven and contradictory ways in which social categories and identities (such as race, class, heterosexual, prostitute, and woman, e.g.) develop in relation to each other and to explore social relations that are gendered, racialized, and classed represents a commitment to the development of realistic strategies for transformation. Theory need not be "thoughtless," and its "unsettling power" need not imply a hopeless fracturing and relativism. Indeed, as Anderson argues, "We must first acknowledge differences between women in order to make connections" (1998, 6). Research that seeks to locate the diversity of women's experience in the contemporary world within theoretical frameworks that allow for the identification of underlying structural mechanisms that shape difference, as well as commonalty, actually has the potential to protect us from moral relativism and political complicity. Such potential will be realized only if and when there is greater dialogue and critical exchange between general theorists and those whose research and theorizing is focused on substantive issues. It is our hope that in the next decade, this kind of critical dialogue will flourish and the gap between general and substantive feminist theory will begin to close, bringing us together on solid ground.

Department of Politics (Brace)

Department of Sociology (O'Connell Davidson)
University of Leicester

References

Anderson, Bridget. 1993. *Britain's Secret Slaves: An Investigation into the Plight of Overseas Domestic Workers in the United Kingdom.* London: Anti-Slavery International.

———. 1998. " 'Just Like One of the Family'? Migrant Domestic Workers in the European Union." Ph.D. dissertation, University of Leicester.

———. 2000. *Doing the Dirty Work? The Global Politics of Domestic Labour.* London: Zed.

Barry, Kathleen. 1995. *The Prostitution of Sexuality.* New York: New York University Press.

Bell, Shannon. 1994. *Reading, Writing, and Rewriting the Prostitute Body.* Bloomington: Indiana University Press.

Brownmiller, Susan. 1975. *Against Our Will: Men, Women, and Rape.* Harmondsworth: Penguin.

Butler, Judith, and Joan Scott, eds. 1992. *Feminists Theorize the Political.* London: Routledge.

Davidoff, Leonore. 1995. *Worlds Between: Historical Perspectives on Gender and Class.* Cambridge: Polity.

Dworkin, Andrea. 1981. *Pornography: Men Possessing Women.* New York: Perigee.

Fraser, Nancy. 1997. *Justice Interruptus: Critical Reflections on the "Postsocialist" Condition.* London: Routledge.

Jeffreys, Sheila. 1994. "Representing the Prostitute." *Feminism and Psychology* 5(4):539–42.

———. 1997. *The Idea of Prostitution.* Melbourne: Spinifex.

Kempadoo, Kamala. 1994. "Prostitution, Marginality and Empowerment: Caribbean Women in the Sex Trade." *Beyond Law* 5(14):69–84.

———. 1998. "The Migrant Tightrope: Experiences from the Caribbean." In *Global Sex Workers: Rights, Resistance and Redefinition,* ed. Kamala Kempadoo and Jo Doezema, 124–38. New York: Routledge.

———. 1999. "Continuities and Change: Five Centuries of Prostitution in the Caribbean." In *Sun, Sex and Gold: Tourism and Sex Work in the Caribbean,* ed. Kamala Kempadoo, 3–33. Oxford: Rowman & Littlefield.

Kitzinger, Celia. 1994. "Problematizing Pleasure: Radical Feminist Deconstructions of Sexuality and Power." In *Power/Gender: Social Relations in Theory and*

Practice, ed. H. Lorraine Radtke and Henderikus Stam, 194–209. London: Sage.

Lister, Ruth. 1998. *Citizenship: Feminist Perspectives.* Basingstoke: Macmillan.

MacKinnon, Catharine. 1987. *Feminism Unmodified: Discourses on Life and Law.* Cambridge, Mass.: Harvard University Press.

McClintock, Anne. 1995. *Imperial Leather: Race, Gender and Sexuality in the Colonial Contest.* New York: Routledge.

Mouffe, Chantal. 1992. "Feminism, Citizenship and Radical Democratic Politics." In *Feminists Theorize the Political,* ed. Judith Butler and Joan Scott, 369–84. London: Routledge.

Riley, Denise. 1992. "A Short History of Some Preoccupations." In *Feminists Theorize the Political,* ed. Judith Butler and Joan Scott, 121–30. London: Routledge.

Russell, Diana, ed. 1993. *Making Violence Sexy: Feminist Views on Pornography.* Buckingham: Open University Press.

———. 1998. *Dangerous Relationships: Pornography, Misogyny, and Rape.* London: Sage.

Sánchez Taylor, Jacqueline. 1997. "Marking the Margins: Research in the Informal Economy in Cuba and the Dominican Republic." Discussion Paper in Sociology no. S97/1. University of Leicester, Department of Sociology, Leicester.

———. 2000. "Tourism and 'Embodied' Commodities: Sex Tourism in the Caribbean." In *Tourism and Sex: Culture, Commerce, and Coercion,* ed. Stephen Clift and Simon Carter. New York: Pinter.

Scott, Joan. 1988. *Gender and the Politics of History.* New York: Columbia University Press.

Spelman, Elizabeth. 1990. *Inessential Woman: Problems of Exclusion in Feminist Thought.* London: Women's Press.

Young, Iris Marion. 1990. *Justice and the Politics of Difference.* Princeton, N.J.: Princeton University Press.

Yuval-Davis, Nira. 1997. *Gender and Nation.* London: Sage.

Difference and Indifference: A U.S. Feminist
Response to Global Politics

eminism in the United States is at a crisis point with respect to transnational politics. The reshaping of capitalism and our increasing awareness of the limits of Western thought bring to U.S. feminist scholarship a new consciousness of the need to understand cultural difference. As an ethicist who has worked primarily on Western-oriented moral issues, I find this academic interest in globalization both exciting and daunting. In the short space allotted here, I begin to think through various dilemmas emerging for U.S. feminists as we turn to global issues. What are the diverse moral and religious convictions underpinning the lives of women across the globe and how can we begin to understand them? How can we inquire about practices that are foreign to us in ways that capture some of the complexities involved in different constructions of reality? How can we step outside our own assumptions and view our own lives through the lens of another? If women across cultural and national borders have little in common, how can we organize together against oppression? How can we be sensitive to difference and politically progressive at the same time?

One way of thinking about these questions begins with the idea that because human meaning is socially constructed, different cultures have different understandings of reality, embodiment, gender, materiality, and so on. Thus, any metanarrative that seeks to describe otherness in Western terms (such as the human rights discourse associated with liberalism, the essentialism of radical feminism, or the materiality embedded in orthodox Marxism) simply exports Western theories into other locations and hence functions as another form of colonization. Any politics that believes that everyone relates to reality in the same way is unacceptable. Liberation should always be seen in local terms, not described universally. There is no general map of what human liberation looks like, no way to determine political progress except from within the parameters of a given culture. There is, then, no place to stand that would allow someone objectively to view women's position cross-culturally. The only acceptable kind of political interventions that can be made, according to such an approach, are those that align themselves with local resistance, working with women

[*Signs: Journal of Women in Culture and Society* 2000, vol. 25, no. 4]

with progressive viewpoints across the globe to make arguments—based on their own internal histories, beliefs, habits, customs, and sacred texts—that counter oppressive forces. Because all political involvement should recognize that human life is organized differently in different times and locations, those Westerners who see themselves as concerned activists should work first to avoid universalizing assumptions and practices in their transnational interventions.

Another approach, more deeply invested in certain configurations of liberation, embraces certain metanarratives to assist political progress. From this point of view, cultural sensitivity often leads to political indifference. We are not afraid to intervene in blatant cruelties and injustices here at home; why, then, should we back off unjust situations abroad? In other words, why should the meaning of liberation change from context to context? Why should we shy away from universal claims about justice and liberation? A woman starving in El Salvador is similar to a woman starving in New York, the argument goes, and both hungers should be satiated; a woman who is beaten by her fundamentalist Christian husband in the United States is similar to the Saudi woman who suffers domestic abuse authorized by the Koran, and both acts should be resisted. From this perspective, attending too closely to racial, ethnic, national, or religious difference can lead to a kind of relativism that obscures the importance of human dignity and material needs.

It seems to me that a third alternative is available. In order to avoid the problems associated with each of these positions, we could begin our political reasoning with the recognition that U.S. feminism is constituted not by one unanimous theory but rather by a loosely organized set of theories, convictions, and practices. While there is no one benchmark or litmus test for feminism, it is nonetheless characterized by certain sets of codes, signals, beliefs, habits, familiarities, actions, intuitions, and so forth. If we start by examining these practices, we can readily identify several central themes shared by many within the tradition. For example, while most U.S. feminists would fully endorse a political agenda that works toward more just worldwide resource allocation, many are also skeptical that orthodox Marxism alone would bring about full liberation for women. While some feminists see important connections among women of all backgrounds, others focus primarily on their differences. What I propose, then, is an understanding of feminism as constituted by these conflicts, as well as an understanding that we, as feminists, are enmeshed in and related to an entire grid of (sometimes conflicting) convictions.

If we understand feminism as a phenomenon rooted in historical practices, we can appeal to this history as we engage in political struggles in different contexts. Rather than beginning our theorizing with a debate about the value or evil of metanarratives in general, U.S. feminists can begin with an examination of our own platforms, beliefs, and configurations. Rather than trying to develop generalizations that are true for all people at all times, we can understand ourselves as being formed by a discourse (feminism) that has a history of valorizing various forms of liberation. If we start our politics with ourselves, with our own history, we are more likely to avoid the dangers of hegemonic metanarratives and open up a space for increased sensitivity to difference, for, if we begin by understanding who we are, what has been important in our Western feminist context and why, we can then move to build coalitions with women in other locations by working to the nature and significance of their own lives.

Such a posture contains risks for U.S. feminists. Implicit in the project of expressing our politics as contingent realities rather than universal truths is the obligation to try to understand the ways others describe their own worlds and realities. We must take seriously the fact that U.S. feminist agendas are filled with flaws and shortcomings that can be seen only from outside, from systems with different histories and values. Other structures of meaning may capture us, various aspects of other worlds may draw our interest and attention. Once we realize the values configured by non-Western formulations, we may become increasingly dissatisfied with what we have at home.

Beginning not with metanarratives but with the convictions we find within our local feminist communities allows us to be specific without being hegemonic. On issues from abortion to sexual harassment, from women-only space to affirmative action, we must start by examining and explaining what has been critical to us. Doing so can help us avoid universal pronouncements associated with various metanarratives of liberation, as well as the hesitancy to get involved that can accompany discourses of cultural diversity. Rather than approaching a non-Western community either with the presumption that a given configuration of liberation (such as Marxism or liberalism) is appropriate for all or with the idea that local constructions of reality are always better and should remain uninfected by Western theories, I believe we must be willing to share our ideas of what liberation looks like for us while at the same time being open to the possibility that other formulations, in different ways on different maps, may be more liberatory. Such a posture allows us, in short, to pay attention to difference, without leading us down the path to indifference.

Women's Studies Department
Duke University

The Party

You are invited to The Party: New Year's Eve, 1999. The celebration of the new millennium. There are so many things a girl will have to know in order to successfully arrive; it might be useful to review them here.

First, how can we determine, across time zones, the proper time for The Party to begin? No need to be concerned; the notion of an Internet time has now been established. There will soon be a global cybertime that will tick through the corporate software of Microsoft into the transnational zone of the Internet. The well-dressed woman need only glance at her newly designed Swatch (the ads are already running), which will show both the local time and the Internet time to know just when to jack in to the celebration. We are now giddily swerving toward a global time—a cybertime—that is disconnected from place, or even from space, as we have traditionally experienced it. Why be nostalgic for those old time zones, anyway? They were designed around a century ago only to make sure that the trains could travel on schedule or that those traveling sales-men could meet their company's representatives in "other" places. So we won't miss the sentimental rendition of "Auld Lang Syne" ringing through the computer speakers, for this new time is not the time of memory. It is a time suspended in our newly designed cyberspace, which can register only a digital present. Since there will be no memory attached to this time, we will need a new design for subjectivity, if one at all. Remember what those postmodernist boys were proposing? That popular male couple, De-leuze and Guattari, for instance? A surface without the retainer of depth? Swatch it on, girl. And give those old psychoanalytic rags to the Salvation Army. Over here in Singapore, they say the smartest thing those Chinese dynasties did was to employ a new historian for every dynasty.[1] The Party will do more than that—it will ring in a new time, at its own, original midnight.

All dressed up and nowhere to go? You needn't be content with cyber-space alone for your partying. The Party for some of the best people

---

[1] My thanks to Professor Ban Kah Choon for this idea.

[*Signs: Journal of Women in Culture and Society* 2000, vol. 25, no. 4]

will start at the international date line; then they will jet here and there, following the sun as it rises.[2] Oh, we used to have such high hopes for nomadism. Remember (oops, what an outdated notion in the new time) Rosi Braidotti imagining it as a "rooted, corporeal, material subjectivity" (1994, 3–4)? Those were the good old days. Of course, Braidotti did invoke a "transatlantic feminist core," which, over here in Singapore, makes us feel as if our roots are not showing (18). Nevertheless, nomadism now seems to suggest a change of mood. It just doesn't feel subversive, what with all that wailing and all those tears from various diasporas: people fleeing Kosovo or the Kurds on the dry mountain roads. And then there is the nomadism of transnational capital: the whir of sewing machines in those wandering economic zones, in which, for example, Nikes replace army boots in the "new" (as they like to say on CNN) Vietnam. Oh well, *better to be the victim of fashion than of invasion,* as women have long repeated to one another. Oh, and then there are those nomadic places, rather than people. Just where did the German Democratic Republic go? Who owns Hong Kong? So, The Party must be a traveling one. Just to celebrate its new global invitation list, it has got to happen on jetliners, crossing borders, while taking advantage of duty-free shopping.

Now, just who should you take to The Party? Here's where gender comes in. We can now count on the global process of regularizing gender to advise us in this matter. In spite of niggling ethnic uprisings here and there or from within certain religious communities, which insist upon their own specific gender practices, the new "youth culture," as it is termed, has heard the call of transnational gender identification. Now MTV and hot Web sites are (uni)forming gender codes. Mobbed cyber cafés in places such as Slovenia, Sweden, Thailand, England, Brussels, Singapore, Canada, Indonesia, and the United States serve up the same Web sites and chat rooms, where cyber foreplay repeats global gender codes of seduction.[3] Ah, America Online, as they say. Accordingly, MTV stages the big picture of a global gestural system of heterosexual seduction. Dance sequences and

---

[2] New Zealand will first see the dawn of 2000. The recently created New Zealand Millennium Office has sold out several tour packages, using the Maori words *Akuanei, Apopo, A-Kautere,* meaning "Today, Tomorrow, Together." The first inhabited area to see the sunrise is Pitt Island, where tourists will rush up Mt. Hakepa for the view and, of course, photo opportunities.

[3] For example, the *Jakarta Post* exclaims that, in spite of the economic crisis, Internet cafés are proliferating. The Internet came to Indonesia at the end of 1994, with ten thousand people using the cafés in Jakarta and new ones opening in Yogyakarta, Surakarta, Surabaya, etc. (*Jakarta Post* 1999).

facial expressions are fixed to gendered bodies, then broadcast out to accompany the world market in music. When you regularize global capital, you just seem to regularize everything.[4]

So one appropriate escort, if you want to look internationally heteronormative, might be a boyish-looking white man with streaked blond hair or, rather, someone who resembles Leonardo Di Caprio. At least he is the talk of the town in Beijing and Shanghai. *Titanic* grossed around thirty-four million U.S. dollars in China. Its success in India is threatening a once-vital national cinema there, marking the international triumph of Hollywood cinema. In Thailand, where Di Caprio's film company is tearing up a local island to make his latest movie, he was so mobbed by people seeking his autograph that he engaged special escorts of his own.[5] I suppose the image of a young man on a sinking ship does have some allure for those who have hit the iceberg of the International Monetary Fund, sinking into the Asian Crisis. But what would he wear? Well, he could certainly find something at the Gap, which should really be called the Seam(less). It's just everywhere. Or he might wiggle into any one of those ubiquitous T-shirts sold in the transnational franchises of Planet Hollywood. The name Planet Hollywood seems to say it all. So no more anxiety about exactly how men and women should appear. Sometime in the 1980s, when those multinationals decided to conserve their energies by deploying the same ads throughout their global markets, gender codes had to be globally fixed. How else could seduction and allure travel with the fashions? No more localizing the look.

However, if this new globalization of gender regularization bothers you, you may subscribe to the global regularization of the gender critique. In academia, it is one of the hottest Anglo-American exports. It has the added attraction of appearing in English, the new transnational language, or appearing as a component of "American Studies," which includes its "subversive" perspectives under the rubric of "American." Feminism, as we have known it, then, is helping to set the terms of the discussion of gender around the globe. Just how to translate those difficult terms? No problem. Learn English through feminism.

---

[4] President Clinton has said that Americans "must embrace the inexorable logic of globalization" and that this includes "everything from the strength of our economy, to the safety of our cities, to the health of our people" (*International Herald Tribune* 1999, 1).

[5] Twentieth-Century Fox stands accused of breaching Thailand's National Park Act for its filming of *The Beach*. Allegedly, bribes of more than $100,000 were offered to access the parks of Khao Yai and Phi Phi. The studio has already paid $234,364 in a bond against damages. It insists it will "restore" the beaches and parks to their original condition after filming. The trial begins in March 1999 (*Straits Times* 1999).

But to return to our preparations for The Party. Some of us may prefer to take an escort of our own sex, or gender, or maybe some simulation of the "other" one, or the real copy of the simulation, or the juridical iteration of one of the gender codes, or the performative excrescence of the phallic mother's lack! I mean, we could not show up with one of those retro "lesbians." After all, this "queer" escort marks another transnational success. Taiwan and Hong Kong have now enjoyed "gay pride parades," as they are called, as have Sweden and many countries in the European Union. I'm proud to see how our movement is aiding in global regularization processes regarding the way we articulate our sexuality. Why, even the terms *butch* and *femme* have helped so many needy people who otherwise could not have articulated their sexual alliances (Thongthiraj 1994). And what a discourse queer theory has given us! So redolent with the airs of seduction and emotion. Take "juridical subject," for instance, to be whispered in your date's ear at the chiming of midnight, or maybe "performative" to describe what you would like to do when alone. If you want to get maudlin, at midnight, just think back to that early feminist project in which we were going to abandon all that patriarchal language of Eurocentric male philosophy. But really, we have discovered that it just does best capture our subcultural goings on! I wouldn't dream of going out without my European accessories from, for example, the House of Lacan, or my Eau de Foucault, or without that D&G on my bag. But, being a feminist, I want to make sure that I Benetton them up, by referring to colors I have borrowed from Jennie Livingston's endlessly wearable film, or better yet, by adding something in which you just can't tell *what* someone really might be, though they do entice with the possibility of that je ne sais quoi. Adopt any color, that is, but red. It has faded out almost everywhere but China. Anyway, who needs Planet Hollywood when we've got our own Queer Planet!

There have been times in history when the word *Party* has been capitalized — when it even signified an international call to organize. Remember Warren Beatty and Diane Keaton in *Reds*? How, finally, American Leftists were trapped inside the USSR, forced to propagandize, even to die on some Communist train in an Arab country? No more horror shows, please. When we say The Party, we don't mean ideology. We don't even mean government. Oh puhleease. The Party is all about having a good time. Dressing up. Good cybersex. And, of course, traveling. For those of us in academia, jetting from country to country to give that same old talk documents our "international reputation," read *fame*. I just love to watch the trail of my travels spread out behind me in the ozone. Academic star quality, at last, after all those tweeds. And the sooner the better. Preferably, one should begin traveling the circuit when still a graduate student. By the time one is an assistant professor, one should be well known and oft invited to deliver enough subversive strategies to earn tenure from the Institution.

And just remember, we are now beyond those unfortunate feminist social codes of the past: no more hot debates, no more tears, no more embarrassing personal statements. Always be polite to the institutions that house your critique. Not only that, but now that even the state universities are required to entice corporate funds, how do you expect to help the future of higher education if you cannot be properly introduced to the CEO? The Party wants the best for you, but not necessarily for everybody else. So, when you make your reputation by suppressing those old feminist traditions of the collective, or when you abandon the politics of citation, as it was called, as you seek to deliver your own hand-stamped version of "strategies," or when you write feminist theory that politely overlooks its social application, just remember: The Party means you never have to say you're sorry. Happy New Year!

Theatre and Dance Department
University of California, Davis

References
Braidotti, Rosi. 1994. *Nomadic Subjects.* New York: Columbia University Press.
International Herald Tribune. 1999. "Clinton Calls on U.S. to Accept Global Role." *International Herald Tribune*, Jakarta ed., February 27–28, 1.
Jakarta Post. 1999. "Internet Cafes Grow despite Economic Crisis." *Jakarta Post*, February 5, 5.
Straits Times. 1999. "You Ruined Our Park." *Straits Times,* February 15, Life! sec., 2.
Thongthiraj, Took Took. 1994. "Toward a Struggle against Invisibility: Love between Women in Thailand." *Amerasia Journal* 20(1):45–58.

Once Upon a Time in Europe

I. Speed and simultaneity

The end of the millennium is hardly inspiring in the specific periphery of the globe I happen to inhabit: former Western Europe, which has just become the European Union. The century ends here as it began: not with a whimper but with a bang. I am writing this in the midst of the NATO air strikes against the Serbs in the Balkans. Contemporary cultural critics have argued that the war machine—the most advanced brand of today's technology—resembles a huge logistical complex aimed at the swift and efficient delivery of weapons onto targets. The proliferation of micro wars on a global scale makes a mockery of the concept of peace, which is by now replaced in the media with expressions such as "a state of pre-hostility." It is with great speed, dictated by altogether new kinds of simultaneous events, that thousands of ethnic Albanians are pouring across the borders of Kosovo to flee Slobodan Milosevic's ethnic cleansing and NATO's bombings. As it did over fifty years ago, with the exodus of Jewish Europeans, Roma, and antifascist and homosexual refugees, Europe witnesses once again its own population fleeing from murderous political violence. Nationalism, the century-old virus of the European mind-set, is still claiming victims in that zone of turbulence that is the Balkans, engendering multiple forced and deeply painful brands of nomadism. These high-tech wars without armies but with plenty of civilian casualties (also known as "collateral damage") rest on techniques and strategies strangely reminiscent of terrorist attacks: hit-and-run target-servicing operations, systematic environmental damage, and embargoes on oil and other prime-necessity materials. A diffuse and all-pervasive fear about the possibility of a bomb going off, an "accident" happening any minute, anywhere, is the political logic of late postmodernity in the "advanced" world.

If I could start my work on feminist philosophy all over again, I would think a lot more systematically about the increasing militarization of Western culture. I would keep high on the agenda the interconnections of war, European nationalism, and technology. Now and in years to come, these same questions, crossed over with issues of ethnicity, nationality, and sexual difference, reach a peak of intensity and relevance. Let us hope that they will not necessarily bring along more murderous violence. I do believe that Europe will evolve into a multiethnic and multicultural space, but in order to do so, masculinism, nationalism, and demented ethnocentrism have to be removed from the European mind-set, so as to stop constructing difference in terms of negative otherness.

II. Complexity and instability

The only constant in today's world is change. Under the impact of fast technological transformations and equally speedy reorganizations of socioeconomic structures, stability has left our lives. Complexity and instability have come to the fore as dominant principles in European human and social sciences. Over the past two decades, several movements of critical thought (psychoanalysis, poststructuralism, feminism, deconstruction, postcolonial critiques, social sustainability movements, and so on) have undermined the unitary vision of the subject, the authority of experience, and the belief in fixed identities.

All communities, even and especially national ones, are "imagined"; that is, they are held together by complex flows of affects, identifications, and power relations between the self and society. The complexity of this interaction is such as to blur any categorical distinction between the self and whatever lies outside it. It is not uncommon to think about networks of power relations, and even to represent the self, as an interactive web that stretches across different layers of the social, the discursive, the symbolic — a split, fluid, complex, and multilayered vision of a nomadic self. For instance, the idea of national identity itself has been challenged by a postmodernist critical perspective, inspired by Gayatri Spivak and other feminist postcolonial and black thinkers, that shows that common ideas of nation are to a large extent imaginary tales, which project a reassuring but nonetheless illusory sense of unity over the actually disjointed, fragmented, and often incoherent range of internal regional and cultural differences that make up a nation-state. Feminists, moreover, know that the legitimating tales of nationhood in the West have been constructed over the body of women, as well as within the crucible of imperial and colonial masculinity.

The fact that these allegedly universal or all-encompassing ideas of nation or national identity are in fact flawed and internally incoherent does not make them any less effective, nor does it prevent them from exercising hegemonic power. But an awareness of the lack of coherence, consistency, and inner rationality of what Lyotard named the "master narratives" of the

Western world does open new spaces for critical opposition. It is not because masculinism, nationalism, and racism have superior inner rationality or logic that they have become hegemonic. Quite the contrary: it is because of their dominance that they have appropriated exclusive claims to rationality and logic.

Thus, awareness of the profoundly unstable structure of fundamental categories of political and philosophical analysis, far from giving way to a suspension of belief in the permanence of power, results in the quest for new forms of resistance. I would value very highly a project of elaborating forms of political resistance that are suited to the specific paradoxes of our historical condition. More specifically, I would emphasize as a political priority the project of dislodging the belief in the natural foundations and consequently the fixed nature of *any* system of value, meaning, or belief. In this respect, the deconstruction of essentialized identities of any kind, but especially those that are historically linked to the concept of Europe, will remain at the heart of my intellectual and political project.

III. Recasting European identity

The project of European unification, with the recent introduction of the common currency, the Euro, has already put questions of European identity and citizenship and questions of access, entitlement, and participation at the center of feminist social and political agendas. The changes brought about by the new technologies in terms of globalization have accelerated the decline of nation-states and the rise of new geopolitical configurations such as the European Union.

The concept of European identity is particularly contested at present. As a conservative project, the European Union was aimed at streamlining the reconstruction of Europe in opposition to the Soviet-dominated countries of the east, and thus it was a major pawn in Cold War politics. As a progressive project, however, the European Union is also an attempt to come to terms with the historical decline of European nation-states and, more specifically, of European nationalism. The project of European federation dates back to the end of World War II to the Marshall Plan and the reconstruction of the war-torn European economy. The Allied forces, led by the U.S. government, were determined to prevent further intra-European infighting and thus aimed to link some of these countries in a federal system in order to squash the nationalistic spirits that had ravaged the continent of Europe. The European Union of the present is nothing more or less than the dismantling of the European nation-states in favor of a federated system. It was and still is a postnationalist project.

In the absence of a concerted involvement of feminists in the progressive potential of the European project, more conservative forces are setting the agenda. There is a real danger of re-creating a sovereign center in the new European federation. This is also known as the "Fortress Europe" syndrome, which has been extensively criticized by feminists and anti-racists who warn against the danger of replacing Eurocentrism with a new "Europ-ism," or a belief in an ethnically "pure" and self-reliant Europe.

My agenda for the new millennium gives high priority to the reconstruction of a postnationalist, feminist, and antiracist European identity. "Europe" as a progressive project today means a site of possible political resistance against the nationalism, xenophobia, and racism that could accompany the process of European federation.

IV. Lightness and becoming

In a historical context that has been haunted and daunted by the notion of "crisis"—of European values and identities, of the economy, of the family, and of nearly everything—feminist practice has been a horizon of hope and regeneration. Feminism has shaped my intellectual, political, and personal life to such an extent that I cannot imagine any other possible agenda for the spatiotemporal grid that constitutes my existence. The political passion that is feminism has led me to drift in directions whose purpose and worth became evident only a posteriori. Thus, I moved from Melbourne to Paris to follow Foucault's seminar but, once I got there, I discovered Deleuze and Irigaray instead, and they changed my life. I had the honor of meeting Simone de Beauvoir only to realize that an abyss separated us, in terms not only of age, but also of culture, values, and, ultimately, politics. I still loved her and attended her funeral with a broken heart. That, for me, was the real end of the millennium. Things happened along the way, as I followed not so much a line but a zig-zag path of becoming that connects the life of the mind to the desire to act upon the world, with and for other women, so as to make a difference. However critical and alternative, feminism is for me also an affirmative culture of positivity, hope, and tremendous creativity and intelligence. It has put wings on my feet and on my mind, made me laugh and made me cry, and I would not have it any other way. I just hope that those who come after us will have as much fun.

Women's Studies Department
Utrecht University

Liana Borghi

Ilaria Sborgi

Tender Buttons: Misprisions of the Feminine and Millennial Appropriation

This is the country where Vita ran away with Violet. From this computer, Gertrude Stein's country place, Bilignin, is not too distant. What was Alice's *omelette aux fines herbes* really like before the age of hormones and intensive pest control? Out of the window, a plump mimosa nods in the spring breeze above the hazy blue coastline. Around the corner a lava of cement covers one of the most beautiful regions of the world. We have made nature redundant. Pine trees, cypresses, brush, and blooming fruit trees survive in spots, promising more natural enclosures further inland. But the future is right here, already spent before its coming, the tame black squirrel with its mangy tail hobbling on the minute, electronically enclosed front garden.

Many miles down the same coast, on a nature reserve in the Italian Riviera, where the Goddess once ruled her shrines and the Madonna is now worshipped in the sanctuaries, the local authorities of the Cinque Terre have permitted construction of a huge fish farm. It was the only unpolluted stretch of coastline left in the area. The denaturing of context has become commonplace, from artificial insemination to fish farms, even though we may both dread and welcome its signs. Is it the nostalgia for a point of origin in clean waters that makes us mourn the constant, inconsiderate erosion of our earth's resources?

In the culture of this stretch of land, women and men alike have been taught to care about things, animals, and people. The fabric of the world, like any worn piece of cloth, needs constant mending. But somehow women themselves were never mended and were always on the mend. Last year, a man on trial for rape was acquitted on the grounds that he could not have taken off the woman's jeans without her help. Seeing a pair of jeans now makes us wonder when violence will cease to be a woman's problem and become the responsibility of all beings. Some Italian feminists, upholders of difference, believe that there exists a primary women's politics concerned with the sphere of personal relations that does not communicate at all with the official politics of men. One may not endorse their analysis, possibly on the grounds that we are all implicated in a ceaseless un/raveling construction of global—not just male-to-female—networks of power, requiring constant translation. But these women have detected a "glocal" problem that expresses the need for a collective becoming-other, a need to enact some feminine measure of enabling desire, which may or may not be the policy of turning the now gendered apparatus of care into a global structure beyond gender.

Walking the unspoiled wood paths of the Cinque Terre, it seemed far-fetched to read the change from the Goddess to the Madonna, the substitution of an all-powerful matriarch with a figure of patriarchal mediation, as a form of early denaturalization of the feminine, a form of encroachment on the female body writ large on the natural world. Yet so it is read by our women's histories and fictions. Umpteen science fiction stories tell tales of expropriated women's bodies and functions or the recoding of gender through reproductive practices, genetic mutation, transplants, and prosthetic surgery. But this same denaturalization, no longer a fiction, is also being read as an enabling escape from the curse of anatomy. In vitro fertilization, cloning, and even male extrauterine pregnancies offer possibilities beyond the strictures of a given sex or gender. It can be difficult, at times, not to see this process as an ongoing basic power struggle between women and men. More than a quarter century ago, in a visionary passage, Shulamith Firestone (1970) proposed her famous neomarxist equation recommending that, just as the workers must appropriate the means of production, women must appropriate the means of reproduction. But this heroic resolution appears obsolete in the present complex material world of technoscience, made up by so many visible and invisible actors and agencies—human, not human, cyborg. "Reproductive politics are at the heart of questions about citizenship, liberty, family, and nation," says Donna Haraway; hence, they are at the heart of "a conscientious feminist search for what accountability to freedom projects for women might mean" (1997, 189, 191).

Haraway's words urge us to decode and challenge what she calls the informatics of domination, to be alert and conscious of the paradoxes of technoscientific culture, to look at reproductive politics both as the reproduction of hegemonic discourses and as a process of denaturalization that can enable a plurality of recodifications of gender—for in the paradox (re)lies the challenge.

"Feminisms at the Millennium" itself is a title informed by paradox. On the one hand, it refers to the plurality of feminist challenges to hegemonic cultures; on the other, it places this plurality within the chronotopic confines of Western culture or, more precisely, of Christianity. What year will it be in the Jewish calendar or the Islamic one? How many other numbers will be attributed to this year? In light of these questions, the phrase "feminisms at the millennium" indicates a glocal paradox or, rather, suggests that we question the paradox of glocality. If the term *feminisms* suggests a plurality of voices, the term *millennium* suggests a hegemonic process of "inglobation," not so much a hybrid between private and public, local and global, but a process of assimilation where the local becomes global. Like the Y2K computer bug: a glocal paradox that, on the one hand, threatened a worldwide collapse of computer systems, the informatics of domination, and the hegemonic structures of technoscientific discourse located in the access and use of informatic technology and, on the other, exposed the global implications of the local, Western-Christian matrix of such discourse, even for the majority of the world population who do not participate in such technologies and power.

"Think different," says the now famous slogan of Apple computers, echoing many feminist slogans. Think through, across, with, and within differences, contemporary feminisms might add. Yet if the challenge of feminisms is to decode and recode hegemonic structures of discourse, it should also go the other way and address the ways hegemonic discourse — for example, technoscience — decodes and recodes feminist discourses, slogans, and terminologies. Apple's ad for its new, "colored" iMac provides an interesting glocal paradox for feminist reflections.

By implementing a user-friendly interface, Apple literally brought the computer into our homes. On the Internet, we can connect a "personal" computer with a global network of computers. We can make glocal connections. And, now, Apple's latest "interfacial" revolution comes "in colors." According to Steve Jobs — the man behind Apple's commercial "resurrection" — the option of choosing the color of one's computer interests its user-buyer more than its megahertz. And what user-buyer does Apple have in mind, we might ask? A puzzling question if we consider the iMac ad and how it stresses this color feature. In the ad shown on Italian television, the iMac monitor is presented in its various color options (tangerine, grape, strawberry, and lime) on a white background. The monitors appear on screen in sync with the rhythm of a Rolling Stones song, "She's a Rainbow," which says, "She comes in colors everywhere / She combs her hair / She's like a rainbow / Coming colors in the air / Oh, everywhere / She comes in colors." There is no other comment to the monitor images except the Apple slogan at the end of the ad, "Think different." And what user-buyer does Apple have in mind, we might ask again? What is the difference between the discursive structure of address in this ad and that of a car ad in which the car's beauty and appeal are equated to that of a sexy woman? If we are beginning to suspect that Apple might be thinking of a male user-buyer, the Italian case scenario not only reinforces this suspicion but eliminates other possible answers. If in fact we turn on an Apple computer in Italy, "she" will tell us, with a smiling face, "Benvenuto in Macintosh," using the masculine to address her user, as if she were welcoming a man. Once again, the machine is feminized, the user-buyer-controller is conceived as male. Is it a question of denaturalization or renaturalization? Whose context is it? And in any case, whose culture? Whose (cultural) reproduction? "Think different." Where does this leave us feminists at the millennium?

Dipartimento di Filologia Moderna
Università di Firenze

References

Firestone, Shulamith. 1970. *The Dialectic of Sex: The Case for Feminist Revolution.* New York: Morrow.

Haraway, Donna J. 1997. *Modest_Witness@Second_Millennium.FemaleMan© _Meets_OncoMouse™:Feminism and Technoscience.* New York and London: Routledge.

Feminism, the New Millennium, and Ourselves: A Polish View

I **n 1993,** *Peace and Democracy News* published an article by Ann Snitow on the future of feminism in postcommunist countries that provided an outsider's diagnosis of the situation, which naturally differed from the one Polish feminists might make as insiders. However, the text was a convenient starting point for discussion among Polish women scholars. Along with several works on women in Central and Eastern Europe also published in the United States in the 1990s, it provoked us to take an interest in feminism, its prospects in our country, and our own participation in it.[1] These texts elicited a number of responses and further questions from Central and East European women involved in the feminist movement: Do we agree with diagnoses given in these works, or do we see the situation differently? Why is it that Polish feminists and our Western counterparts often seem to be missing each other's point? While apparently discussing the same subject, are we actually thinking of very different things? Do we really understand each other, or do we often fall prey to a number of intercultural misunderstandings, stereotypes, and mistaken expectations?

Rereading these relatively recent texts now testifies to the speed with which time flows and change takes place in our part of the world. Some factors that earlier articles such as Snitow's cited as obstacles to the development of feminism in Poland are outdated; some were not perceived by Polish women themselves as such then, nor are they today. The subjects and problems I find most frequently in discussions of feminism in Poland today tend to focus on three specific issues, each a somewhat different formulation of the same question about the nature of feminism in and around us. The first concerns women and power and the relationship between that issue and feminism. The second is the issue of women's rights, and the third is the question of feminism itself—whether it exists and has future

---

[1] The results of one such discussion were published in Poland, together with a translation of Snitow's text, as Fuszara 1995.

[*Signs: Journal of Women in Culture and Society* 2000, vol. 25, no. 4]

prospects in Poland and whether there is a thing that might be called the shared experience of women in our part of Europe. I begin with the first.

Women and power

In Poland, discussions of women and power tend to develop into discussions of women's participation in public life and, especially, in government. There are several reasons for this narrowing of the subject. One is the feeling — regained after many years, or, rather, for most women and men, gained for the first time — that these institutions, which for decades had just a window-dressing role instead of genuine authority, have now taken their due place in the process of government. For the first time, women feel that we have — or at least should have — an impact on the composition of those institutions. Hence our recurrent questions: Is it important for women to hold offices directly related to the process of government (and if so, for what reasons)? Should feminists support all women striving for power or only those who share our particular aims? Is it right and possible that we support such women?

Many Polish feminists have regarded the rapid decrease in women's participation in the parliaments of all Central European countries since 1989 as another indication of women's absence from areas where actual power is exercised: once these bodies begin to achieve real power, women are excluded. However, I find this interpretation inconsistent with what is usually said in debates on women's participation in power in Central Europe, where the decrease is often blamed on women's passive attitude, their "escape into privacy," or their rejection of politics as a dirty, evil, and corrupt area of life. While similar arguments — especially the last one — can be heard from feminists too, they tend to implicate entire societies, not specifically women. There are many stereotyped opinions, repeated by the media and debaters outside feminist circles, about women's low participation in politics, many of which operate on the notorious principle of "blaming the victim," where women themselves are supposedly at fault for their small representation among politicians. Proponents of this view claim that women consider men to be better at politics and that they refuse to participate in the process, offer no support to women politicians, and see the issue as unimportant. However, the findings of opinion surveys belie such theses. Polish women tend to see it as an advantage when a candidate is a woman, and they generally vote for women whenever possible (see Fuszara 1994; Siemieńska 1994). They also believe that the proportion of women in high offices is too small: over half (55 percent) state that there should be more women in government, an opinion voiced much less frequently by men (31 percent). Men and women also differ greatly on another point: 33 percent of men and as many as 54 percent of women call for steps to increase women's participation in public life, while 54 percent of men and 35 percent of women oppose such steps.[2]

Often mentioned by way of explanation of the weak response to feminism in postcommunist countries as well is the fact that rights were "given" to women there, without struggle. As a consequence, for a long time there was no need for, and today there is no rich tradition of, women's movements with a broad social base to shape conceptions of important women's issues. According to this position, not having been forced to fight for their rights and become organized, Polish women are now passive and feel that they can make gains without their own contribution and effort. Because the guarantees of women's rights during the nineteenth century were greater in Poland than elsewhere in Europe (e.g., in France), it is sometimes argued, Poland developed a tacit agreement—an armistice that prohibits the use of strong oppositional measures. Yet, the struggle for women's participation in public life often requires defining the situation in the language of conflict.[3] Only when the situation is thus defined can women genuinely participate in public life and enter into negotiations capable of bringing about social change and conflict mitigation or resolution.

Questions about women's rights

Many Polish feminists, however, oppose the thesis that rights were simply "given" to women. Uncovering the history of women, we also uncover their endeavors—though perhaps not in the form of fierce struggle—for specific rights. More and more often, we also find that what were given were merely symbolic rights that lacked actual import. An example is the provision on gender equality in the communist constitution (adopted in Poland in 1952). Admittedly, women did not have to struggle for its inclusion in the basic law; on the other hand, though, the constitution and its provisions pertaining to women were of declaratory nature only and provided no grounds for protecting one's rights in a concrete case. While women gained numerous posts in areas, such as the judiciary, that were dominated by men in other countries, they were still unable to defend women against gender bias in those areas. Polish women, then, are well

[2] "Udział kobiet w życiu publicznym: Prawne gwarancje rownosci plci" (Women's participation in public life: Legal regulations on gender equality). Research conducted by Social Opinion Research Centre, January 17–21, 1997, on a sample of 1,101 adult Poles.

[3] However, as Grażyna Borkowska (1996) argues, women's issues have almost never been articulated this way in Poland.

aware that constitutional gender equality may be accompanied by actual inequality of rights in social life, and they often manifest a skeptical attitude toward legal regulations as means of counteracting inequality.

Opinions on the best approach tend to be inconsistent among both women and men. As few as 30 percent of women and 20 percent of men favor a gender-equality law that would parallel the constitutional regulation, and only 17 percent of men and 25 percent of women support a quota system that would legislate the minimum participation of women in public institutions. Yet, comparing answers to the question whether the quota should be introduced to those about possible effects of such regulation reveals a characteristic inconsistency: over half the women (51 percent) say that it would be a just method of reducing discrimination.[4] While many men and women agree that the introduction of such a system might lead to at least mitigation if not abolition of the existing discrimination on account of gender, many are repelled by the very terms *handicap, discrimination,* or *quota,* rather than by the mechanism per se.

Questions about feminism

What is feminism to us? Can it be found in Poland? What actions, areas, and activities can be called feminist? What do we gain and lose because of the delayed onset of feminism here as compared to the West? What do our contacts with Western feminists look like and why? Such questions are posed frequently in Polish debates on feminism, and, of course, there are even more answers than questions. Some definitions of feminism focus on the exercise of power at all levels, and others stress an awareness on the part of women that can lead to social change. Others emphasize women's organization around shared values or solidarity with other women for the sole reason that they are women. For others, the basic feature of feminism is a specific philosophy of existence and expression, or a more personal identification with practical activities for women's rights.

There are a large number of women's organizations in Poland, and, indeed, the *Directory of Women's Organizations and Initiatives* of 1999 lists more than 200 groups, including feminist, vocational, and church movements; groups formed within political parties or universities; and Polish branches of international women's organizations. They are highly diversified, ranging across a variety of areas in which a problem pertaining to women has been noticed and defined, from initiatives and organizations aimed at increasing women's political participation to those that advocate

[4] "Udział kobiet w życiu publicznym: Prawne gwarancje rownosci plci."

for working women, to groups offering counseling in the area of family planning, abortion, and birth control, to counseling and consultation centers and hostels for women and children who are victims of domestic violence. Voices can also be heard, however, that deny the strength of these women's groups because they often have nothing in common with an explicit feminism. In contrast, though, some argue that organizations originally formed to represent the interests or defend the rights of their women members often tend to develop into groups extending women's awareness and many times become feminist groups themselves.

Another obstacle to the development of feminism in our part of Europe is the influence gained after 1989 by the rightist ideology, which is strengthened, especially in Poland, by connection with the Catholic Church. In Poland this is manifested by an attempt to appropriate feminism for different ends: some Catholic periodicals even use the term *new feminism*. Admittedly, they invoke some of the concepts articulated in feminism — for example, recovering the now forgotten history of women — but they also promote a model of traditional femininity that is focused on the family and the roles of wife and mother. It is difficult to say whether the actual impact of such attempts will consist mainly in the appropriation of the term or whether it will have more far-reaching consequences. Paradoxically, it might also inadvertently benefit feminism by, for example, decreasing mainstream opposition to the term and to people who identify themselves with it.

This brings me to the supposed unpopularity of feminism in Polish society. I have asked myself whether feminism is indeed unpopular and, particularly, what Polish society really knows about it anyway. In a 1996 survey, I asked the following question: "If your friend or relative asked you what the term 'feminism' means, what would you say? How do you define the term?"[5] The answers confirmed my hypotheses: 56 percent were unable to respond to the question at all and thus had neither correct nor mistaken associations. Among the rest, the biggest proportion explained the term "feminism" through a reference to equal rights (12.4 percent) and women's struggle (e.g., for their rights; 11.2 percent). A similar answer was given by a further 6 percent of respondents, who saw feminism as an action, trend, or defense (e.g., of women's rights or interests). Other respondents (8.2 percent) understood feminism as women's movements or organizations or referred to women's rights (e.g., "women's right to work"; 6.4 percent). The concepts of freedom, liberation, and indepen-

[5] Research conducted by Social Opinion Research Centre, March 1996, on a sample of 1,158 adult Poles.

dence of women were used to explain feminism by 5.4 percent of respondents. A similar number of respondents (5 percent) saw feminism as women's domination and expansion, women's rule, and female quest for conquest and domination, and 0.5 percent regarded it as opposition against men, "boycott of men," or "refusal to recognize men." Still another group (3.8 percent) knew only that the term had something to do with women. The degree of a person's knowledge of feminism depended mainly on his/her education, place of residence, and age. A decided majority (over 70 percent) of elderly persons (age 65 and over) with a low educational level, living in rural areas, and earning small wages could provide no answer whatsoever. Most striking is the education factor: among the university educated, the answer "don't know" was given by 1 percent; among those with only elementary education, it was 81 percent.

The best sources of feminist understanding and knowledge are gender studies programs offered by universities, such as the postdiploma gender studies program at Warsaw University (established in 1996). Before this program was founded, gender issues went unaddressed in the official process of education at Polish universities, although there were some scholars who took an interest in and held isolated lectures or classes on the subject at their respective faculties. There was an explicit need for an institutional framework and space for introduction of broad interdisciplinary gender studies. In the case of Poland, postgraduate studies proved the best institutional form in this respect. They follow a rather flexible formula, for despite the requirement that the curriculum be accepted by various levels of university authorities, it can actually be shaped quite freely.

The organizers of the program aimed at grouping the largest possible community of scholars to address gender concerns in Poland. Such programs both make it possible for persons involved in teaching and research on gender problems to come together and form a community of scholars into the subject and also initiate the process of introducing gender problems into the general curricula of individual universities. The hope is that someday the gender dimension will become a regular part of university curricula and that its inclusion will be considered necessary and self-evident.

To conclude, I would like to add my personal reflection on the advantages of participation in feminism. To scholars, it opens important and interesting intellectual perspectives as an interdisciplinary inquiry that examines the world from a joint viewpoint. The best examples are discussions between scholars from different disciplines. Feminism is a great intellectual adventure that offers the possibility of going beyond the limited discipline in which each of us is normally involved and of taking a look at many other disciplines from a common viewpoint that permeates culture, law, literature, and theology and makes it possible to find a shared approach to the world. For this reason, I believe that, despite the immense obstacles, both feminism in general and feminism in postcommunist Europe have great prospects for development. During the first year in Warsaw, the gender studies program had forty students; three years later, there were more than 140. In fact, gender studies may even prove the fastest developing university branch of study in our part of the world at the beginning of the new millennium.

Institute of Applied Social Sciences and Gender Studies Program
University of Warsaw

References

Borkowska, Grażyna. 1996. *Cudzoziemki: Studia o polskiej prozie kobiecej* (Foreigners: Studies on Polish women's prose). Warsaw: Instytut Badan Literackich Polskiej Akademii Nauk.

Fuszara, Małgorzata. 1994. "Rola kobiet w polityce w ich własnych opiniach i programach partii politycznych przed wyborami 1993" (The role of women in politics in their opinions and parties' programs before elections in 1993). In *Kobiety: Dawne i nowe role* (Women: Former and new roles), 45–58. Warsaw: European Council Information and Documentation Center.

———. 1995. "Feminizm i my" (Feminism and we). In *Spotkania feministyczne* (Feminist meetings), 14–21. Warsaw: Polygraphic.

Siemieńska, Renata. 1994. "Wybierane i głosujące: Kobiety w wyborach parlamentarnych III Rzeczpospolitej" (Electing and voting: Women in the parliamentary elections of the Third Republic of Poland). In *Kobiety: Dawne i nowe role* (Women: Former and new roles), 27–44. Warsaw: European Council Information and Documentation Center.

Snitow, Ann. 1993. "Feminist Futures in the Former East Bloc." *Peace and Democracy News* 7(1): 40–44.

Mapping the Imperial Social Formation:
A Modest Proposal for Feminist History

My remarks are drawn from the ways I attempt in my own current work to address some of the broader questions that have been opened up by contemporary feminist historiography. I am at work on a feminist history of the interwar period that focuses on the contributions of the women's movement in India and of Indian feminist agency to the outcome of the struggle between British imperialism and Indian nationalism at a crucial historical conjuncture. Here I confine my remarks to the contemporary implications of a particular heuristic model that I adopt for this study. This model, which I call an "imperial social formation," will serve as my point of entry into some of the debates that have surfaced in conflicts about the direction of feminist scholarship in the late twentieth century.[1] Some of the recent developments — especially those associated with the denaturalization of the category "women," the focus on discourse as a subject of historical analysis, and the attention to issues of "difference" — have provoked in some quarters a sense of crisis about the future of feminist scholarship and of feminist politics more generally.[2] While not subscribing to these diagnoses of crisis, I would like to offer, by way of the model of the imperial social formation, a provisional attempt at engaging the potential of the current situation in feminist scholarship.

The model of an imperial social formation draws on what Rosemary Hennessy (1993) has called a "global social analytic." Such an analytic is global in two senses: first, it engages with "national" and "local" histories as they are imbricated in a world system fashioned by imperialism and colonialism; second, it understands the "social" as the intersection of the political, economic, and cultural/ideological, none of which can be reduced to any of the others. The further point about the heuristic model of an imperial social formation, however, is that it draws attention to the concreteness of particular historical conjunctures whose dynamics are shaped

---

[1] For an elaboration of this model see Sinha 1995.

[2] For an insightful critique of the discourse of "crisis" invoked in some contemporary feminist scholarship, see Dingwaney and Needham 1996.

[*Signs: Journal of Women in Culture and Society* 2000, vol. 25, no. 4]

not by predetermined foundations—whether structural, ontological, or discursive—but by the outcome of specific struggles in history. It is thus that the agon of history provides the site for the invention of subject positions and for the theorization of autonomy and agency.[3]

On one level, perhaps, this framework of an imperial social formation is useful in engaging the real challenge beyond merely a pluralizing shift in terminology from "feminism" to "feminisms" posed to feminist scholarship by the discrepant histories of different women's movements as they have emerged in insistently varied political contexts. The project of historicizing early Indian feminism in late colonial India, for example, provides some interesting lessons for feminist scholarship regarding the conceptual implications of engaging fully with the discrepant histories of feminism.[4] The pioneering work of Kumari Jayawardena, as well as that of a host of other scholars of women and feminism in late colonial India, has helped establish that "feminism was not imposed on the Third World by the West" (1986, 2) but arose out of important material and ideological changes that affected women in the third world. Yet the view that early Indian feminism lacked a proper "revolutionary feminist consciousness" (Jayawardena 1986, 107–8), partly because of its imbrication in the broader nationalist struggle against colonial rule, has been much harder to shake.[5] Indeed, the desire for a "pure" feminist consciousness, against which early Indian feminism was found wanting, ultimately undermines the effort to historicize Indian feminism because it removes feminism itself from the specific history of its own production. What the conceptual map of an imperial social formation adds to the study of early Indian feminism, then, is precisely to make visible the fact that neither feminisms nor women are ever articulated *outside* macropolitical structures that condition and delimit their political effects.

The juxtaposition of Indian and British feminisms within the framework of an imperial social formation, indeed, exposes the "provincial" or parochial history of certain dominant versions of feminism in Western Europe and North America that have been falsely universalized as the normative or paradigmatic form of feminism (Chakrabarty 1992). When nationalist feminism in India and imperial feminism in Britain are brought within the same field of analysis, the consequent reconstitution of the object of study permits an analysis that demonstrates that middle-class feminisms in

---

[3] I am indebted for this formulation to Wess 1996.

[4] On the "woman question" and the emergence of middle-class Indian feminism in colonial India, see Forbes 1996.

[5] For a discussion of this point, see John 1989 and Mohanty 1991.

late colonial India and in imperial Britain were both produced within the prevailing, and symbiotically connected, discourses of empire and nation. The point is not simply that many British feminists were imperialist in their attitudes toward Indian women but rather, as Antoinette Burton (1994) has so persuasively demonstrated, that the very structure and ideology of middle-class feminism in Britain was indelibly marked by its imperial location. For, as Burton suggests, efforts to challenge the Victorian construction of woman as Other and to identify women with the nation were mediated via the role accorded to the Empire in middle-class British feminist discourse. The analytical framework of an imperial social formation thus gives the lie to any attempt to salvage a univocal history for feminism, however shorn of its imperial or racial baggage, as a default frame of reference.

The further point of bringing British and Indian feminisms into the same field of analysis, however, is to demonstrate their co-implication in the history of the combined but uneven evolution of a system whose economic, political, and ideological reach was worldwide. From such a perspective the Indian traditions that supposedly mark the cultural authenticity and autonomy of Indian feminism are themselves revealed to be far less pristine and far more shaped by the broader processes of colonial modernity than a strict nativist rhetoric would concede (Mani 1998). Indigenous traditions, on which the claims to a distinctive "Indianness" often rested, were themselves formed and transformed in the colonial encounter in ways that belie the comfort of a "pure" genealogy. The tendency to stop merely with the assertion of cultural difference, then, dodges the embarrassment of histories that, while discrepant, cannot be understood as absolutely separate. Indeed, the mutual constitution of British and Indian feminism within a common global system reveals the limits of any effort that simply substitutes various discrete national or cultural feminisms for a putatively universal feminism. For the model of an imperial social formation favors analyses of "invented traditions" over a multiculturalism that too often rests on an exaggeration of cultural autonomy and purity.

On another level, moreover, the analytical framework of an imperial social formation can also be useful, in the wake of the denaturalization of various categories of identity and of humanistic notions of individual agency in contemporary feminist scholarship, for reconceiving the role of the subject in the process of historical change. Here the social dimension of the model serves to critique the excesses of both discourse analysis and structural determinism, which too often conceive historical processes either as a play between discourses or as the unproblematic reflection of fixed structural positions. They thus also theorize resistance and agency either from mere deviancy or from a human essence outside of history. By contrast, however, the model of the imperial social formation theorizes resistance and agency from within the rivalry of contending norms that emanate from historical struggles.

The project of foregrounding the subject formation of the modern Indian woman in late colonial India thus offers some insights for thinking about issues of change and agency in feminist scholarship more broadly. The work of Partha Chatterjee (1986, 1993), for example, has had an important impact on the recognition of the particular discursive construction of the modern Indian woman in the gendered discourse of "official" Indian nationalism, which offered new subject positions for elite and middle-class Indian women as the guardians of that supposedly most authentic realm of the Indian nation: its inner or spiritual realm. The invented traditions for which the modern Indian woman became the unique signifier did not necessarily preclude the emancipation or self-emancipation of Indian women in the late nineteenth and early twentieth centuries. Yet Chatterjee's conclusion that, "unlike the women's movement in nineteenth- and twentieth-century Europe or America, the battle for the new idea of womanhood in the era of nationalism was waged in the home" (1993, 133) ultimately elides the agency of both organized women and the discourse of early Indian feminism in the nationalist project (Sarkar 1997). The search for women's autonomy in the home, away from the public and political organizations of women in the outer/material world, concedes too much determinative force to the discursive construction of a "derivative" Indian nationalism that invested the subject position of the modern Indian woman as the bearer of its own supposed authenticity. Against the excesses of discursive determinism, the model of an imperial social formation posits instead a conception of agency emerging out of specific conjunctures and struggles.

Indeed, the social dimension of the imperial social formation model makes visible the specific historical conditions for organized women's rhetorical invention of new subject positions within the discourse of early Indian feminism. The modernizing discourse of a liberal middle-class Indian feminism, along with the creation of new subject positions for the modern Indian woman as not merely the bearer of Indian tradition but as herself the agent of nationalist modernity, became "rhetorically sayable" in the outcome of the historical struggles of the interwar period.[6] In Robert Wess's useful gloss on Kenneth Burke's analysis of rhetoric, language as action inscribes "rhetorical sayability" rather than either Enlightenment certainty or Romantic authenticity (Wess 1996). It is precisely the charting

---

[6] Here I am drawing on Wess's (1996) distinction between "rhetorical realism" and "rhetorical idealism." For an elaboration of this idea in the specific context of early Indian feminism, see Sinha 1999.

of this inscription that is enabled through attention to the concreteness of specific historical conjunctures.

The interwar period was marked both by changes in the struggle between colonialism and nationalism and by various challenges to Indian nationalism from radical gender and caste critiques by subaltern (plebeian) movements, as well as by the very different challenge represented by communal (religious sectarian) movements. The anticaste Self Respect Movement in Madras Presidency, for example, represented an alternative and more radical restructuring of gendered and caste hierarchies than Gandhian nationalism. It was against such challenges that the gender, caste, class, and communal assumptions that had hitherto marked the ideal subject of nationalist discourse were reconstituted in the figure of the liberal bourgeois citizen-subject constructed as politically neutral. The further point, however, is that the discourse of early Indian feminism assumed an essential unity of womanhood as a prototype for this putative "national" citizen-subject. Its most crucial ideological service to the nationalist project, indeed, lay in normalizing the liberal-bourgeois citizen-subject—allegedly above considerations of gender, caste, class, and community—as the normative subject of political discourse in late colonial India. The contribution of early Indian feminism in the interwar period, then, was to invent new subject positions for the modern Indian woman as the generic Indian citizen. In so doing, it also provided ideological cover to a hegemonic nationalism compromised by gender, caste, class, and communal contradictions.

If the invention of a new subject position by organized Indian women in the context of the contested origins of the citizen-subject defies reduction to the discourse of "official" Indian nationalism, it also resists an easy, direct correlation with the socioeconomic background of the women themselves. It cannot be read simply as a reflection of the predominantly Hindu, upper-caste, and elite background of the members of the nascent all-India women's movement. For the inventions of new subject positions, as Wess points out, are not merely "afterthoughts" but are themselves the "forces that galvanize bodies for the role they play in making history" (1996, 27). It is in this sense, then, that the particular rhetorical choices and agency of organized women in the invention of new subject positions acquires its crucial historical significance.

The model of the imperial social formation acknowledges the structural force of the macropolitical economic system as well as the social divisions inside various imagined communities. At the same time, it allows for change—and thus political agency—because it exposes the concept of discourse to the effects of historical struggles, on the one hand, and to the force of rhetorical invention, on the other. Historical conjunctures determine what is rhetorically sayable, but the rhetorical acts of subjects — acts that invent new subject positions in history — produce change. My proposal, therefore, is for a mode of analysis that is simultaneously global in its reach and conjunctural in its focus.

History Department
Southern Illinois University at Carbondale

References

Burton, Antoinette. 1994. *Burdens of History: British Feminists, Indian Women, and Imperial Culture, 1865–1914.* Chapel Hill: University of North Carolina Press.

Chakrabarty, Dipesh. 1992. "Provincializing Europe: Postcoloniality and the Critique of History." *Cultural Studies* 6(3):337–57.

Chatterjee, Partha. 1986. *Nationalist Thought and the Colonial World: A Derivative Discourse.* London: Zed.

———. 1993. *The Nation and Its Fragment.* Princeton, N.J.: Princeton University Press.

Dingwaney, Anuradha, and Lawrence Needham. 1996. "The Difference That Difference Makes." *Socialist Review* 26(3–4):5–47.

Forbes, Geraldine. 1996. *The New Cambridge History of India: Women in Modern India.* Cambridge: Cambridge University Press.

Hennessy, Rosemary. 1993. *Materialist Feminism and the Politics of Discourse.* London: Routledge.

Jayawardena, Kumari. 1986. *Feminism and Nationalism in the Third World.* London: Zed.

John, Mary. 1989. "Postcolonial Feminists in the Western Intellectual Field: Anthropologists and Native Informants?" *Inscriptions* 5:49–73.

Mani, Lata. 1998. *Contentious Traditions: The Debate on Sati in Colonial India.* Berkeley: University of California Press.

Mohanty, Chandra. 1991. "Introduction: Cartographies of Struggle: Third World Women and the Politics of Feminism." In *Third World Women and the Politics of Feminism,* ed. Chandra Mohanty, Ann Russo, and Lourdes Torres, 1–47. Bloomington: Indiana University Press.

Sarkar, Sumit. 1997. *Writing Social History.* New Delhi: Oxford University Press.

Sinha, Mrinalini. 1995. *Colonial Masculinity: The "Manly Englishman" and the "Effeminate Bengali" in the Late Nineteeenth Century.* Manchester: Manchester University Press.

———. 1999. "The Lineage of the 'Indian' Modern: Rhetoric, Agency and the Sarda Act in Late Colonial India." In *Gender, Sexuality and Colonial Modernities,* ed. Antoinette Burton, 207–21. London: Routledge.

Wess, Robert. 1996. *Kenneth Burke: Rhetoricity, Subjectivity, Postmodernism.* Cambridge: Cambridge University Press.

Undoing the "Package Picture" of Cultures

Many feminists of color have demonstrated the need to take into account differences among women to avoid hegemonic gender-essentialist analyses that represent the problems and interests of privileged women as paradigmatic. As feminist agendas become global, there is growing feminist concern to consider national and cultural differences among women. However, in attempting to take seriously these cultural differences, many feminists risk replacing gender-essentialist analyses with culturally essentialist analyses that replicate problematic colonialist notions about the cultural differences between "Western culture" and "non-Western cultures" and the women who inhabit them (Narayan 1998). Seemingly universal essentialist generalizations about "all women" are replaced by culture-specific essentialist generalizations that depend on totalizing categories such as "Western culture," "non-Western cultures," "Indian women," and "Muslim women." The picture of the "cultures" attributed to these groups of women remains fundamentally essentialist, depicting as homogeneous groups of heterogeneous peoples whose values, ways of life, and political commitments are internally divergent.

I believe that many contemporary feminists are attuned to the problem of imposing Sameness on Other women but fail to register that certain scripts of Difference can be no less problematic. Cultural imperialism in colonial times denied rather than affirmed that one's Others were "just like oneself," insisting on the colonized Others' difference from and inferiority to the Western subject. Insistence on sharp contrasts between "Western culture" and "Other cultures" and on the superiority of Western culture functioned as justifications for colonialism. However, this self-portrait of Western culture had only a faint resemblance to the political and cultural values that actually pervaded life in Western societies. Thus, liberty and equality could be represented as paradigmatic Western values at the very moment when Western nations were engaged in slavery, colonization, and the denial of liberty and equality to large segments of Western subjects, including women.

Anticolonial nationalist movements added to the perpetuation of essentialist notions of national culture by embracing, and trying to revalue, the imputed facets of their own culture embedded in the colonialists' stereotypes. Thus, while the British imputed "spiritualism" to Indian culture to suggest lack of readiness for the worldly project of self-rule, many Indian nationalists embraced this definition to make the anticolonialist and nationalist argument that their culture was distinctive from and superior to that of the West. Thus, sharply contrasting pictures of Western culture and of various colonized national cultures came to be reiterated by both colonizers and colonized.

Prevalent essentialist modes of thinking about cultures depend on a problematic picture of what various cultures are like, or on what I call the "Package Picture of Cultures." This view understands cultures on the model of neatly wrapped packages, sealed off from each other, possessing sharply defined edges or contours, and having distinctive contents that differ from those of other "cultural packages." I believe that these packages are more badly wrapped and their contents more jumbled than is often assumed and that there is a variety of political agendas that determine who and what are assigned places inside and outside a particular cultural package.

The essentialist Package Picture of Cultures represents cultures as if they were entities that exist neatly distinct and separate in the world, independent of our projects of distinguishing among them, obscuring the reality that boundaries between them are human constructs, underdetermined by existing variations in worldviews and ways of life. It eclipses the reality that the labels currently used to demarcate particular cultures themselves have a historical provenance and that what they individuate as one culture often changes over time. For example, while a prevailing picture of Western culture has it beginning in ancient Greece and perhaps culminating in the contemporary United States, a historical perspective would register that the ancient Greeks did not define themselves as part of "Western culture" and that "American culture" was initially distinguished from "European culture" rather than assimilated to it under the rubric "Western culture." The *Shorter Oxford English Dictionary* indicates that the use of the term *Western* to refer to Europe in distinction to "Eastern" or "Oriental" began around 1600, testimony to its colonial origins. Similarly, "Indian culture" is a label connected to the historical unification of an assortment of political territories into "British India," a term that enabled the nationalist challenge to colonialism to emerge as "Indian." Labels that pick out particular cultures are not simple descriptions that single out already distinct entities; rather, they are arbitrary and shifting designations connected to political projects that, for different reasons, insist on the distinctness of one culture from another.

The Package Picture of Cultures also assumes that the assignment of individuals to specific cultures is an obvious and uncontroversial matter. Under the influence of this picture, many of us assume that we know as a simple matter of fact to what "culture" we and others belong. I invite readers who think that they are members of Western culture or American culture to ask themselves what they have in common with the millions of people who would be assigned to the same cultural package. Do I share a common culture with every other Indian woman, and, if so, what are the constituent elements that make us members of the same culture? What is *my* relationship to Western culture? Critical reflection on such questions suggests that the assignment of individuals to particular cultures is more complicated than assumed and that it is affected by numerous, often incompatible, political projects of cultural classification.

The Package Picture of Cultures mistakenly sees the centrality of particular values, traditions, or practices to any particular culture as a given and thus eclipses the historical and political processes by which particular values or practices have come to be deemed central components of a particular culture. It also obscures how projects of cultural preservation themselves change over time. Dominant members of a culture often willingly discard what were previously regarded as important cultural practices but resist and protest other cultural changes, often those pertaining to the welfare of women. For instance, Olayinka Koso-Thomas's work reveals that in Sierra Leone virtually all the elaborate initiation rites and training that were traditional preliminaries to female circumcision have been given up because people no longer have the time, money, or social infrastructure for them. However, the rite of excision, abstracted from the whole context of practices in which it used to be embedded, is still seen as a crucial component of "preserving tradition" (Koso-Thomas 1987, 23). Feminists need to be alert to such synecdochic moves, whereby parts of a practice come to stand in for the whole, because such substitutions conceal important dimensions of social change.

Feminist engagement with cultural practices should be attentive to a process that I call "selective labeling," whereby those with social power conveniently designate certain changes in values and practices as consonant with cultural preservation and others as cultural loss or betrayal. Selective labeling allows changes approved by socially dominant groups to appear consonant with the preservation of essential values or core practices of a culture, while depicting changes that challenge the status quo as threats to that culture. The package picture of cultures poses serious problems for feminist agendas in third-world contexts, since it often depicts culturally dominant norms of femininity, along with practices that adversely affect women, as central components of cultural identity and casts feminist challenges to norms and practices affecting women as cultural betrayals (Narayan 1997).

Giving up the Package Picture's view of cultural contexts as homogeneous helps us see that sharp differences in values often exist among those described as members of the same culture while among those described as "members of different cultures" there are often strong affinities in values, opening up liberating possibilities with respect to cross-cultural feminist judgments. For instance, the values and judgments of a Western feminist may diverge greatly from those of politically conservative members of her "package," while they might converge quite strongly with those of an Indian feminist counterpart. A Western feminist accused of imposing Western values in her negative judgment of an Indian cultural practice could, for instance, point out that her judgments correspond closely to those of some Indian feminists. Making this assertion does require her to be informed about Indian feminists' analyses of the practice and to use her critical judgment when such analyses disagree, as sometimes happens. Feminists can avoid the Package Picture of Cultures by attending to the historical variations and ongoing changes in cultural practices, to the wide range of attitudes toward those practices manifested by different members of a culture, and to the political negotiations that help to change the meanings and significances of these practices. Such attention would facilitate informed and astute feminist engagement with women's issues in national contexts different from their own.

Philosophy Department
Vassar College

References
Koso-Thomas, Olayinka. 1987. *The Circumcision of Women*. New York: Zed.
Narayan, Uma. 1997. *Dislocating Cultures: Identities, Traditions, and Third World Feminism*. New York: Routledge.
———. 1998. "Essence of Culture and a Sense of History." *Hypatia* 13(2):86–106.

Therese Saliba

Arab Feminism at the Millennium

By the Islamic calendar the current year is 1421. For the often forgotten Christian minorities of Arab lands, particularly those in Bethlehem (West Bank), the millennium marks the 2,000th anniversary of Christ's birth, an occasion to remind the world that the subject of the Christian era was not only Jewish but also Palestinian, in this land torn by a century of nationalist struggle. For those with apocalyptic visions—from American right-wing Christians who foresee Israel's conquest of Jerusalem as the fulfillment of biblical prophecies, to the U.S. government with its continued bombings against an Iraq devastated by a decade of economic sanctions—the role of U.S. policy in the region is to speed along this cataclysm. In North America, demographers predict that Muslims will constitute the second largest religious group shortly after the millennium. From colonialism to globalization, the West has imposed on the region known as the "Middle East" not only its own conceptions of time, history, and geography but also transnational economic structures, globalized/U.S. culture, and even its own brand of liberal feminism. In challenging these interpretive frameworks and the power structures they support, Arab feminists and Middle East scholars and activists continue to negotiate the contested terrains of women's relationship to nationalist and Islamic movements and of the hybrid identities of Arab and Muslim women in the diaspora.

Initially, the post-Orientalist scholarship on Arab women that has flourished in the past two decades sought to critique exoticized, reductive representations of Oriental and Muslim women oppressed by their culture.[1] Feminist debates of the 1980s centered on the heterogeneity of Arab women's experience, the critique of Islam as an all-encompassing category, and the primacy of various categories of analysis—sexuality, socioeconomics, and the legacy of colonialism and the nationalist response—in shaping Arab women's lives. This scholarship extended feminist analysis beyond the bounds of liberal Western feminist discourse. As Elizabeth Fernea writes,

---

[1] The post-Orientalism trend has followed the publication of Edward Said's *Orientalism* (1978) and the rise of feminist poststructuralism.

[*Signs: Journal of Women in Culture and Society* 2000, vol. 25, no. 4]

"Feminism [is] synonymous with America and fast food" for many Arab women (1998, 414).

Recent critiques of modernity situate both "feminist" and "nationalist" formulations within the modernizing assumptions of European liberal political philosophy; thus much recent scholarship has focused on the contradictory implications of liberal nationalism for women (Ahmed 1992; Booth 1997, 836). Marilyn Booth, for example, argues that although the "Famous Women" biographies in early twentieth-century Egypt constructed "a bourgeois class identity" with "the nation as the primary community" (1997, 837), Egyptian women's emergence into public life allowed them to "transgress the neat boundaries nationalist [male] thinkers . . . set for them" (839). In a similar vein, Julie Peteet's study of Palestinian refugee women in Lebanon asserts that the nationalist discourse of "maternal sacrifice," while limiting, also offered women a "validating position from which to launch a critique of the movement and its leadership" (1997, 104). Although nationalist struggle at times has offered Arab women a platform from which to challenge local institutions and cultural practices, the historical connection between feminism and nationalism in the Middle East and the legacy of cultural imperialism have more often discouraged the examination of "local institutions and cultural processes" (Kandiyoti 1996, 19). The emergence of "transnational feminism" in the 1990s has brought a turn in scholarship that reflects women's activities in these processes and has provoked debate about culturally specific practices versus "universal women's rights." Intersecting with transnational cultural and economic forces, and sometimes in reaction to them, these localized struggles seek a non-Eurocentric framework from which Arab women may search for indigenous identities and gain economic and legal rights within their societies.

The Palestinian struggle for self-determination and national sovereignty remains at the center of regional conflict and the nationalism/feminism debate. In 1990, Palestinian women activists began to critique the "poverty of nationalism" (Said 1998), focusing on its traditional gender roles, in order to set forth a specific women's agenda within emerging institutions to promote democracy and equality. While much post-Oslo analysis refers to women's contributions to the "state-building" process, some critics argue that the very terms of the Oslo agreement preclude Palestinian aspirations for an independent state.[2] Within this ambiguous transitional phase

[2] The Oslo Peace Agreement was signed by Israel and the Palestine Liberation Organization in September 1993.

from grassroots *intifada* activism to bureaucratic state and society building, women activists characterize their roles as intervening in public-policy formation to bring about "positive change in women's lives" (Johnson 1997, 3, 9). Yet, as in the nationalist struggle, the women's movement in this transitional period has played a marginal role in policy making (7).

In measuring the gains and losses made by the Palestinian women's movement, feminist scholars document contradictory social trends: "Rising educational levels and political participation exist alongside negative indicators of their low labor force participation and persistent high fertility" (Johnson 1997, 3). Given the Palestinians' formidable economic crisis, marked by economic dependence on Israel and lack of sovereignty over land and resources, feminist scholars predict limited possibilities of major social transformations (Taraki 1997, 21). Another major obstacle to women's empowerment has been the social conservatism within Palestinian society, which some feminists attribute to the "resurgence of traditional thought," associated particularly with the rise of the Islamic Resistance movement (*Hamas*) (Ashrawi 1998, 189; Kawar 1998). Others, however, emphasize the conservative tendency within Palestinian nationalist ideology, which has "wittingly or unwittingly idealized the traditional division of labor and gender hierarchies" and reinforced "primordial loyalties and identities" (Taraki 1997, 15). Lisa Taraki asserts that, despite popular representations of Palestinian society as "revolutionary," it is indeed "traditional." Thus, targeting Islamist forces as the main source of a gender backlash may be too reductionist and further alienates Islamist women from a women's movement that tries to appeal to women across differences of religion, class, and education. Moreover, the limited gains for women during both the nationalist struggle and this transitional phase reflect, in many ways, the impoverished nationalism of the Palestinian Authority with its imaginary state, as well as the failures of the "nation-state" as "a European construct that has largely failed to meet the needs of majorities of peoples in the Arab world" (Joseph 1998, 368; Majid 1998a). These emerging critiques of the nation-state and its exclusionary ideology, alongside the pressures of globalization, have rendered "nationalist struggle" increasingly ambiguous at the millennium.[3]

[3] Although many Western feminists have argued that nationalism is incompatible with feminism, nationalist struggle has been a necessity for Palestinians fighting for self-determination and their survival as a people. Recently, however, the implications of nationalism have been complicated by globalization and by what some theorists describe as the erosion of the power of the nation-state. Yet in the Middle East and Africa, where the nation-state is a creation of colonialism, national formations have often served to strengthen the power of autocratic rulers in the service of the West. Furthermore, given the exclusions of

The rise of Islamic women's movements throughout the Arab world has further challenged the secular, liberalizing assumptions of feminism by focusing primarily on progressive readings of Islamic texts to argue for a more egalitarian Islamic tradition that enhances women's rights.[4] This "Islamic awakening" has been attributed to two major factors: the indigenous response to Western cultural imperialism (Ahmed 1992) and accommodation to declining economic conditions, wherein established Islamic institutions replace the eroding welfare state and veiling becomes a functional response to increasing economic competition between men and women (Macleod 1991; Hatem 1993). In her recent study of the women's mosque movement in Cairo, however, Saba Mahmood asserts that these analyses often "neglect the religious arguments of the women themselves" (1998, 153), whose search for piety and submission is often interpreted as "false subjectivity" (135) within feminism. Marnia Lazreg has argued for "a phenomenology of women's lived experience to explode the constraining power of categories" (1988, 95); yet Mahmood's analysis suggests that devout Muslim women are rendered silent "non-subjects of feminist history" because they are understood to uphold patriarchal domination (1998, 148). In this sense, some variants of the Islamic women's movements cannot be interpreted within feminist frames of liberal or progressive notions of equality. In other words, as Anouar Majid has argued, Muslim identity "does not lie in accepting a bourgeois definition of the human" (1998a, 346). In dismantling the assumptions of the liberal-humanist tradition and its feminist variants, these movements pose a further challenge to feminism in particular and a more problematic confrontation to international human rights conventions in general.[5]

These debates about Islam as an alternative to Eurocentric liberal humanism are occurring at a time when the "Islamic threat" has become the new enemy of the post–cold war era, and Arab and Muslim populations are on the rise in Western metropolitan centers.[6] Recent feminist scholar-

---

nationalist ideology, Zionism being a prime example, intellectuals such as Azmi Bishara and Edward Said argue increasingly for a binational state in Israel/Palestine, rather than an apartheid separation that creates fragmented, politically ineffectual Palestinian bantustans (see Bishara 1995; Said 1998).

[4] See Ahmed 1992 and any of Fatima Mernissi's works.

[5] For an example of this often heated debate, see the exchange among Anouar Majid, Suad Joseph, and Ann Elizabeth Mayer in the Winter 1998 issue of *Signs* (23 [2]: 322–89).

[6] While the Muslim population in the United States is estimated at approximately seven million, the majority of American Muslims are African American (42 percent) or South Asian (24.4 percent), with Arabs constituting only 12.4 percent (Nu'man 1992, 13). In addition, Arab Americans (some non-Muslims) constitute approximately three million in the United States alone.

ship on Arab and Muslim women in the Americas has sought to dismantle assumptions about Muslim women in the "first world" by focusing on their hybridized identity negotiations within Orientalist, Islamic, and multiculturalist discourses (Khan 1998). Evelyn Shakir's *Bint Arab* (1997), for example, includes oral histories of Arab women immigrants who confront both political and religious racism engendered by U.S. policy in the Middle East and anti-Arab media representations and whose identity negotiations defy essentialized notions of "Arab" and/or "Muslim" identity. This emerging cultural politics emphasizes "the mixing that occurs in urban spaces in contemporary diasporic communities" (Khan 1998, 489) and further highlights how existing racial and ethnic constructions have effectively rendered Arab and Muslim women invisible within multicultural and political discourses.

Within the past two decades, innovative scholarship and activism, as well as the increasing availability of Arab women's literature in English translation, have brought Arab women out of their seclusion within Middle East departments into wider feminist circles. This scholarship has sometimes reinforced, sometimes questioned, the liberalizing discourses of modernity, liberal nationalism, and feminism that have been applied or misapplied to Arab women's experiences. Perhaps the greatest contributions of Arab feminism at the millennium have been expanding methods of feminist analysis and exploding the constraining categories—whether Orientalist, Islamic, nationalist, multicultural, or even feminist—whose often colonizing tendencies have bound Arab women.

Third World Feminist Studies
Evergreen State College

References

Ahmed, Leila. 1992. *Women and Gender in Islam: Historical Roots of a Modern Debate.* New Haven, Conn.: Yale University Press.

Ashrawi, Hanan. 1998. "An Interview with Hanan Mikhail Ashrawi: The History of the Women's Movement," by Dima Zalatimo. In *Palestinian Women of Gaza and the West Bank,* ed. Suha Sabbagh, 184–91. Bloomington: Indiana University Press.

Bishara, Azmi. 1995. "Bantustanisation or Bi-nationalism?" Interview by Graham Usher. *Race and Class* 37(2):43–49.

Booth, Marilyn. 1997. " 'May Her Likes Be Multiplied': 'Famous Women' Biography and Gendered Prescription in Egypt, 1892–1935." *Signs: Journal of Women in Culture and Society* 22(4):827–90.

Fernea, Elizabeth Warnock. 1998. *In Search of Islamic Feminism: One Woman's Global Journey.* New York: Doubleday.

Hatem, Mervat. 1993. "Toward the Development of Post-Islamist and Post-nationalist Feminist Discourse in the Middle East." In *Arab Women: Old Boundaries, New Frontiers,* ed. Judith E. Tucker, 29–48. Bloomington: Indiana University Press.

Johnson, Penny. 1997. *Social Support: Gender and Social Policy in Palestine. Palestinian Women: A Status Report.* Vol. 5. Women's Studies Program, Birzeit University.

Joseph, Suad. 1998. "Comment on Majid's 'The Politics of Feminism in Islam': Critique of Politics and the Politics of Critique." *Signs* 23(2):363–69.

Kandiyoti, Deniz. 1996. "Contemporary Feminist Scholarship and Middle East Studies." In her *Gendering the Middle East,* 1–27. Syracuse, N.Y.: Syracuse University Press.

Kawar, Amal. 1998. "Palestinian Women's Activism after Oslo." In *Palestinian Women of Gaza and the West Bank,* ed. Suha Sabbagh, 233–44. Bloomington: Indiana University Press.

Khan, Shahnaz. 1998. "Muslim Women: Negotiations in the Third Space." *Signs* 23(2):463–94.

Lazreg, Marnia. 1988. "Feminism and Difference: The Perils of Writing as a Woman on Women in Algeria." *Feminist Studies* 14 (Spring): 81–107.

Macleod, Arlene Elowe. 1991. *Accommodating Protest: Working Women, the New Veiling, and Change in Cairo.* New York: Columbia University Press.

Mahmood, Saba. 1998. "Women's Piety and Embodied Discipline: The Islamic Resurgence in Contemporary Egypt." Ph.D. dissertation, Stanford University.

Majid, Anouar. 1998a. "The Politics of Feminism in Islam." *Signs* 23(2):321–61.

———. 1998b. "Reply to Joseph and Mayer: Critique as a Dehegemonizing Practice." *Signs* 23(2):377–89.

Mayer, Ann Elizabeth. 1998. "Comment on Majid's 'The Politics of Feminism in Islam.'" *Signs* 23(2):369–77.

Nu'man, Fareed H. 1992. *The Muslim Population in the United States: A Brief Statement.* Washington, D.C.: American Muslim Council.

Peteet, Julie. 1997. "Icons and Militants: Mothering in the Danger Zone." *Signs* 23(1):103–29.

Said, Edward. 1978. *Orientalism.* New York: Pantheon.

———. 1998. "The Poverty of Nationalism." *Progressive,* March 8, 27–29.

Shakir, Evelyn. 1997. *Bint Arab: Arab and Arab American Women in the United States.* Westport, Conn.: Praeger.

Taraki, Lisa. 1997. *Palestinian Society: Contemporary Realities and Trends. Palestinian Women: A Status Report.* Vol. 1. Women's Studies Program, Birzeit University.

Family Bonds/Conceptual Binds:
African Notes on Feminist Epistemologies

Family talk, if not family values, is everywhere. The rhetoric of family values has been useful in legitimizing oppression as well as in mounting oppositional movements against it. Lately, a number of scholars have focused renewed attention on the uses of family as trope and as ideology in the constitution of political projects, in academic discourses, and in policy formulation, even in arenas that appear to be only distantly related to this social institution. British sociologist Paul Gilroy (1992) draws attention to the ubiquity of family rhetoric and the misogynist and exclusivist ways it is deployed in "Americocentric" black nationalist discourses. In a recent paper titled "It's All in the Family," Patricia Hill Collins (1998) documents the widespread use of the metaphor of the family and the endless readings this metaphor unleashes when employed to analyze discourses of race, gender, and nation and their interconnections in the United States. In her perceptive critical review of Anthony Appiah's *In My Father's House* (1992) African philosopher Nkiru Nzegwu (1996) invites us to read Appiah's grand philosophy of culture as a manifesto on the family and to focus on the way he privileges the European nuclear family even as he purports to be writing about Africa.

Undoubtedly, family discourse is everywhere. But the question that is often left unasked and that is implicit in Nzegwu's critique of Appiah is, which family, whose family, are we talking about? Clearly, it is the Euro-American nuclear family that is privileged, at the expense of other family forms. In this article my objective is twofold: to focus on feminism — specifically white feminism — as a particular discursive site from which to investigate the scope and depth of family rhetoric and to articulate African family arrangements in order to show the limit of universals. I suggest that feminist discourse is rooted in the nuclear family and that this social organization constitutes the very grounds of feminist theory and a vehicle for the articulation of values such as the necessity of coupling and the primacy of conjugality in family life. This is in spite of the widespread belief among feminists that one important goal is to subvert this male dominant

[*Signs: Journal of Women in Culture and Society* 2000, vol. 25, no. 4]

institution of the family and the belief among feminism's detractors that feminism is antifamily. Despite the fact that feminism has gone global, it is through the Euro-American nuclear family that many feminists think. Thus, I argue that the controlling concept of feminist scholarship—woman—is actually a familial one because it functions as a synonym for wife. The woman at the heart of feminism is a wife. Once this subject's antecedents are known and her "residence" is exposed, the limitations of concepts such as gender and other terms in feminist scholarship become more intelligible.

Home gals

In her thoughtful analysis of the "problem of exclusion" in feminism, Elizabeth Spelman (1988) tries to account for the discrepancy between Simone de Beauvoir's (1952) rich theoretical insights on the multiple forms of oppression and her practice of focusing on only white middle-class women and considering their experience universal. Spelman is quick to note that it is not enough to say that Beauvoir was merely exhibiting her own race and class privilege by using her experience to represent that of others. Rather, Spelman asks what might be in the language or methodology or theory employed by Beauvoir that allows her to disguise from herself the assertion of privilege she so keenly saw in other women of her own position (1988, 58). I agree. Spelman explains the tension as a consequence of feminism's political nature: Beauvoir may have ignored the differences among women because it was clear to her that a strong case for political change must be a universal one. This may well be true, but as an explanation for a theoretical lapse that continues to plague many feminist accounts even today, Spelman's interpretation is inadequate.

It seems to me that the problem with Beauvoir's account, a problem that continues to plague feminist theory, is fully explained by recognizing that the woman in feminist theory is a wife—the subordinated half of a couple in a nuclear family—who is housed in a single-family home. Beauvoir and others theorize as if the world is a white middle-class nuclear family. It is not surprising that the woman who emerges from Euro-American feminism is defined as a wife. According to Miriam Johnson, "in the West the marriage relationship tends to be the core adult solidary relationship and as such makes the very definition of woman become that of wife" (1988, 40). Because race and class are not usually variable within a family, white feminism that is trapped in the nuclear family does not acknowledge race or class difference. Methodologically, the unit of analysis is the nuclear family, which construes women as (white middle-class) wives because this is the only way they appear within the institution. The extent of the feminist universe that takes her as its subject, then, is the home.

The concept of "white solipsism"—the tendency to "think, imagine, and speak as if whiteness describes the world" (Spelman 1988, 116)—has been offered as one explanation for the inattention to race in much feminist research. However, the problem is also a perceptual one structured by the inability to see even the home as a bounded and limited place, one among many points from which to appreciate the world. The tendency of white feminists such as Beauvoir and Nancy Chodorow (1978), who universalize from their own experience, is not so much tunnel vision as it is truncated vision—a result of the fact that the world is not available for perusal from within one's home, CNN notwithstanding. The woman at the heart of feminist theory, the wife, never gets out of the conceptual household. Unconsciously, like a snail, she carries the house, along with the notion of one privileged white couple and their children, with her. The problem is not that feminism starts with the family but, rather, that it never leaves it and never leaves home.

From the logic of the nuclear family follows a binary opposition that maps as private the world of the wife in contrast to the very public world of the man (not "husband," for the man is not defined by the family). Her presence defines the private; his absence is key to its definition as private. This observation explains another vexing problem in feminist scholarship, namely, the problem of male absence as typified by the convention in scholarship of using the term *gender* as a synonym for *women*. The absence of men from the spatial structure of the nuclear family is reproduced when men's presence is not registered in feminist discourse. The woman in feminism is specifically a wife, for if she were a generic woman, she would have to be constructed in relation to some other thing every time she is mentioned. As wife, however, her position and location are always already configured and understood; thus the would-be other gender can be dispensed with.

The spatial arrangement of the nuclear family as private space in which only the wife is in her element does not allow for gender as a duality. No wonder *women* and *gender* are virtually synonymous terms in many studies that purport to be about *gender* relations (which should in fact include both men and women). The nuclear-family origin of much feminist scholarship yields a flawed account even of gender, the category it claims as its ground zero. Rather than construing the white nuclear family as a culturally specific form whose racial and class characteristics are essential to understanding the gender configuration it houses, much feminist scholarship continues to reproduce its distortions across space and time.

Going global

The idea that the woman in feminism is a wife is not a new one. A number of researchers on gender in African societies have shown that feminist anthropologists of Africa tend to focus on social categories that they perceive to be defined by men, equivalent to the category of wife in the West. What is new is the identification of its point of origin within the West. In my book *The Invention of Women: Making an African Sense of Western Gender Discourses* (Oyewumi 1997), I argue that in much feminist anthropological research, *woman* is used as a synonym for *wife* both conceptually and linguistically, and *husband* as a synonym for *man*, as demonstrated in the following comment on Yoruba women: "In certain African societies like the Yoruba, women may control a good part of the food supply, accumulate cash, and trade in distant and important markets; yet when approaching their husbands, wives must feign ignorance and obedience kneeling to serve the men as they sit" (Rosaldo 1974, 19–20). The problem is that *oko*, the Yoruba category rendered as *husband* in English, is not gender specific; it encompasses both males and females. Females too assume the role of husband; thus some of the "husbands" alluded to in the quote are women. There is little understanding that African social arrangements, familial and otherwise, derive from a different conceptual base.

In much of Africa, "wife" is a four-letter word. While not a vulgar term in itself, *iyawo* (as one example) is quintessentially a subordinate category. Consequently, many women traditionally have not privileged it in identifying themselves. (Although with the colonial imposition of the practice of married women being labeled with the name of their conjugal partners, European-style, this African value is under serious assault.) Wifehood tends to function more as a role than as a deeply felt identity, and it is usually deployed strategically. Across Africa, the category generally translated as *wife* is not gender specific but symbolizes relations of subordination between any two people. Consequently, in the African conceptual scheme it is difficult to conflate woman and wife and articulate it as one category. Although wifehood in many African societies has traditionally been regarded as functional and necessary it is at the same time seen as a transitional phase on the road to motherhood. *Mother* is the preferred and cherished self-identity of many African women.

Furthermore, the predominant principle organizing African families has been consanguinal and not conjugal: blood relationships constitute the core of family. Many brothers and sisters live together, along with the wives of brothers and the children of all. In this kind of family system, kinship is forged primarily on the basis of birth relations, not marriage ties. Normatively, then, wives are not considered members of the social arrangement called "the family." The African family does not exist as a spatially bounded entity coterminous with the household, since wives as a group belong to their birth families, even though they do not necessarily reside with their kin groups. There are other African family arrangements that complicate the issue further. For example, in the Akan family system in Ghana, families are traditionally matrilineal and matrilocal.

In all African family arrangements, the most important ties within the family flow from the mother, whatever the norms of marriage residence. These ties link the mother to the child and connect all children of the same mother in bonds that are conceived as natural and unbreakable. It is not surprising, then, that the most important and enduring identity and name that African women claim for themselves is "mother." However, motherhood is not constructed in tandem with fatherhood. The idea that mothers are powerful is very much a defining characteristic of the institution and its place in society.

African constructions of motherhood are different in significant ways from the "nuclear motherhood" that has been articulated by feminist theorists such as Chodorow (1978). In her account, there is no independent meaning of motherhood outside the mother's primary and sexualized identity as the patriarch's wife. The mother's sexual ties to her husband are privileged over her relationship to her child; she is not so much a woman as she is a wife. It is only within the context of an isolated nuclear family that Chodorow's arguments about the infant's gendered identification with the mother make sense. This is the effect of an assumption that the mother appears as a wife (gendered relational being), even to the child. In a situation such as the African household arrangement, where there are many mothers, many fathers, many "husbands" of both sexes, it is impossible to present the relationship between mother and child in those terms.

The five-centuries-long process of globalization has blurred all sorts of boundaries across the globe. At the turn of the millennium, therefore, one of the most important issues facing feminism is the fragmentation of the category woman — the subject of feminism. This is usually understood as a challenge posed by postmodernist accounts of social (un)reality. But, I am quick to point out that the historic challenges to a monolithic racial and cultural understanding of feminism's subject predate postmodernism. Black American feminists are notable pioneers in this regard. The feminist anxiety over the disappearance of woman is unnecessary; she never existed as a unified subject in the first place. Moreover, if, as I have argued here, the taken-for-granted identity of the woman invoked in much feminist scholarship is that of "nuclear wife," her disappearance may not be regrettable. On the contrary, her demise may clear the way for "women" to be all they want to be.

Black Studies Department
University of California, Santa Barbara

References

Appiah, Kwame Anthony. 1992. *In My Father's House: Africa in the Philosophy of Culture.* New York: Oxford University Press.

Beauvoir, Simone de. 1952. *The Second Sex.* New York: Vintage.

Chodorow, Nancy. 1978. *The Reproduction of Mothering: Psychoanalysis and the Sociology of Gender.* Berkeley: University of California Press.

Collins, Patricia Hill. 1998. "It's All in the Family: Intersections of Gender, Race, and Nation." *Hypatia* 13(3):62–82.

Gilroy, Paul. 1992. "It's a Family Affair." In *Black Popular Culture,* a project by Michele Wallace, ed. Gina Dent, 303–16. Seattle: Bay.

Johnson, Miriam. 1988. *Strong Mothers, Weak Wives: The Search for Gender Equality.* Berkeley: University of California Press.

Nzegwu, Nkiru. 1996. "Questions of Identity and Inheritance: A Critical Review of Kwame Anthony Appiah's *In My Father's House.*" *Hypatia* 11(1):175–201.

Oyewumi, Oyeronke. 1997. *The Invention of Women: Making an African Sense of Western Gender Discourses.* Minneapolis: University of Minnesota Press.

Rosaldo, Michelle Zimbalist, and Louise Lamphere, eds. 1974. *Woman, Culture, and Society.* Stanford, Calif.: Stanford University Press.

Spelman, Elizabeth. 1988. *Inessential Woman: Problems of Exclusion in Feminist Thought.* Boston: Beacon.

International Feminism of the Future

I n July 1999, the U.S. women's soccer team won the Women's World Cup (WWC). I did not watch the game. I had professional reasons for scanning the press coverage, however, as I am a historian of modern China, teaching in a U.S. women's studies department. After years of engineered tensions—the so-called campaign finance scandal, political loyalty witch hunts in the Asian American community, "spies" in the Department of Defense, the Belgrade Chinese embassy bombing, Hillary Clinton's speeches in China in 1995—geopolitics would surely give the final match between the People's Republic of China (P.R.C.) and the United States a fillip unthinkable were the opposing team from almost any other nation.

Embedded in the U.S. press coverage of the women's soccer victory are two characteristic operations I have learned to worry about in the four years that I have taught and considered the definition of "international feminism," which is what my faculty line is called.[1] First, in the terms of this feminism, recognition of the achievements of U.S. women requires that the achievements of the other country's women disappear. Richard Sandomir's essay "Just Who Was the United States Playing for the Championship?" (1999) raised this troubling matter in the nonacademic

---

[1] As it is currently constituted, international feminism contests non-U.S. feminist claims to the Enlightenment heritage (national, communist, and socialist feminisms) while also expanding the neoliberal geopolitical notions that seek a Great Power relation between the United States and the rest of the world. This thing called "international feminism" is an ideological package—a well-financed, resurgent, neoliberal, United States–focused effort to establish common ground for feminism. Commonality may be a United Nations– or Ford Foundation–sponsored projection of women's human rights and global democratization processes. Or it may be a geopolitical maneuver that panics public opinion, like the recent allegations of state-backed female infanticide in China made by rightist factions in the U.S. government as cause to deny that country most-favored-nation trade status. In any case, though international feminism is a kind of cultural liberalism that points to the universal similarity of women on the grounds that we all seek the same sort of justice, the United States is simply the place where more women—as in the example of the WWC soccer team—have achieved it.

[*Signs: Journal of Women in Culture and Society* 2000, vol. 25, no. 4]

press. "Maybe," he wrote, noting the strange erasure of the enemy team, "this is what happens when your scientists are accused of filching American nuclear secrets and President Clinton is at the Rose Bowl." Actually, he went on, sport internationalism seems to be boiling down to simple national chauvinism, or, as he put it, the attitude that "China's players mattered far less than America's." The presence of a U.S. female sportscaster, Wendy Gebauer, herself a former "international" player for the American team at the 1991 WWC, did not affect the scenario.

Second, although it tends to be erased, the other country is actually the necessary medium through which "international U.S. feminism" takes shape. Sandy Bailey of *Sports Illustrated for Women* reflected this logic on July 12, 1999, in a PBS *News Hour* interview when she said, "It [soccer] is the sport of the world," while football is "the sport of our [i.e., American] men." Her point in drawing this distinction was to argue that, to succeed commercially, women's sports must draw male viewers. Since American male consumers prefer American football and seem reluctant to have American women playing American football, the American female athlete must win internationally to get male consumers to buy women's sports. Listening to "a caller from Seattle" on National Public Radio's *Talk of the Nation* explain, the morning after the game, that when "we" beat the Chinese team *she* felt empowered, the familiar pieces fell into place. The caller was voicing the common belief that the victory of the U.S. soccer team on the global stage signaled the triumph of a particularly American way of empowering women.

But there is a third element that is routinely present in the popular press and that could be called the ideological content of international feminism: the argument that, although the other country's women are just like us, they also are different, primarily because they are devalued. In Hillary Rodham Clinton's well-publicized speeches, women around the world are seen to heed the U.S. women's achievements even despite their own oppressive states. They can do so without disloyalty to local cultures because international feminism connects undervalued local women with the universalizing value of (U.S.) dollars. So, while including the three tropes of environmental feminism, human rights feminism, and feminist sensitivity to local differences that I argue are likely to be at the core of the doctrine of international feminism in the new millennium, Clinton's "Remarks to the United Nations Fourth World Conference on Women" in Beijing on September 5, 1995, made explicit this question of value. "However different we may appear," she argued, "there is far more that unites us than divides us." "We" (meaning the U.N. and non-governmental organization representatives in her audience) have come to the P.R.C. "to find common ground" where women can meet women. "As an American," Clinton stated,

> I want to speak up for women in my own country . . . who are raising children on the minimum wage, women who can't afford health care or child care, women whose lives are threatened by violence, including violence in their own homes, . . . who are fighting for good schools, safe neighborhoods, clean air and clean airwaves. . . . I speak for them, just as each of us speaks for women around the world who are denied the chance to go to school, or see a doctor, or own property, or have a say about the direction of their lives, simply because they are women.

"If there is one message that echoes forth from this conference," she concluded, "let it be that human rights are women's rights. . . . And women's rights are human rights, once and for all."[2]

This was not only a bit of a non sequitur (the road out of poverty is through human rights), it also pronounces an exculpatory internationalism, arguing that the commonality of women is an effect of the capital invested in them. "Whether one talks about my country or any country," she claimed in her "Remarks to the NGO Forum" the following day, the principles of economic self-help on the Grameen Bank model can be applied precisely because the needs of the world's women can all be addressed in similar ways. Since one of the primary differences among women is that some women have American dollars and others do not, it gave the First Lady pleasure to announce that "the United States would make an effort to enhance educational opportunities for girls so that they could attend school in Africa, Asia, and Latin America" and that that effort, "funded with United States' dollars, is being organized in countries throughout those continents by NGOs."[3]

My point in all this is that the new international feminism is already operating in a domain of the more-than-national, where it alleges to overcome U.S. parochialism. This is true of both its academic articulation and its media profile, as well as of official White House policy on international women's human rights. Specially marked educational materials — conference volumes, internationalist reports, movies, listservs, and so forth — frequently claim the mantle of international feminism and propose that,

[2] Hillary Rodham Clinton, "Remarks to the United Nations Fourth World Conference on Women," Beijing, China, September 5, 1995. See the First Lady's Web page at http://www2.whitehouse.gov/WH/EOP/First_Lady/html/China/.

[3] Hillary Rodham Clinton, "Remarks to the NGO Forum," Huairou, China, September 6, 1995. See her Web site (n. 2 above).

because it specializes in the representational practices needed to bring women into history, U.S. women's studies, more than any other academic project, should develop internationally in the future.[4] So the drive to represent women in history, in women's studies, in the human sciences, and consequently in the Real itself, is congruent with the drive to represent women's civil rights internationally in individual, transformed national civic orders. This is assumed to be a first step in universalizing women's rights as human rights beyond all parochial, local, and national boundaries. First, different communities of women must learn to fix their presence in the representational orders; then, on the basis of that equality, the world's women will advance "our" human rights. Or that is the theory.

United States–financed international feminism is likely to form a future neoliberal orthodoxy. Indeed, because the elements of international feminism are already so pervasive, my undergraduate students tend, rather uncritically, to embrace arguments that reconsolidate the liberal relation of universal and particular in international law, which not only universalizes law but also regards crime as a common ground for all women. As Charlotte Bunch (1995) puts it, the common ground of feminism is the body of the woman and the violence committed against it, including violations of women's right to reproductive health, the universality of rape, and the allegation that women are universally locked out of public and into private spheres. Human rights feminism, then, rests on the discourse of the state and civil society.

Of course, this discourse generally leaves unexamined the old saw that women's interests run counter to their national interest. What is particularly compelling about the reworked cliché regarding other women's collective alterity in relation to their national states is the way that visibility/invisibility does not rest on either similarity or difference but rather invokes both similarity and difference at the same time (as is clear in Hillary Clinton's 1995 speeches). This is also obvious in the drama of female genital mutilation (FGM) that plays a regrettably unreflective role in popular media versions of international feminism. In discussions of "violence against women" (the one event that supposedly links every female), women are both similar to (as victims, if not of FGM, then of one of its analogues such as breast implants, liposuction, genital reconstruction, etc.) and also different from (since breast implants are analogically similar to FGM but different from it in specificity and degree of violence) each other.

These internationalized and flexible market-sensitive or donor-agency

---

[4] Many of these, however, tactfully recognize that some communities of women disavow feminism altogether.

feminisms evade some simple questions. They rest on the kind of internationalism (an ideological complement of the international state system) that makes it difficult to talk seriously about social relations of production, simple political economy, and ideologies of citizenship, and, most troubling for a teacher, they unduly obscure the conditions of their own production. That in itself makes them uncomfortably ideological. Time after time in my class for women's studies majors, "Teaching International Feminism in a Global Frame," I have to ask, "Where does this idea come from?" "What assumptions are conditioning this idea, or making it possible?" "Why does the 'global' that these international feminisms talk about seem so familiar?"

It is fair to conclude that the international feminism initiative is congruent with ongoing drives to restructure global capital. But no matter what international feminism turns out to be in the end, it is now a series of totalizing theories that cannot admit to an outside of feminism and will not admit the tangibility of any social forms in excess of their own drive to represent "the interests of the world's women." This latter claim rests on the pretension that international feminist work lies beyond all specific nations and thus is beyond even U.S. parochial concerns. Students find this claim incredibly liberating. On the basis of international feminist theory and U.S. capital, they, like Clinton, can participate in what they tend to view as a cosmopolitan, generous, antiracist feminism. That is how international feminism presents itself as *supra*national and in an opportune position to represent all women equally by disregarding (somehow) the superficial differences of skin tone, social standing, and customary practice while, always respectfully, taking into account local specificities.

Students do come to recognize that knit into these tropes of environment, law, and culture is a newly retooled ideology promising unmediated access to women from other countries. At least one student each year voices concern after watching a videotape that alleges to unmask a conscious Chinese state policy of mistreating babies in state-run orphanages. One student told the class that while she realized that she could not make the report of another woman's degradation the proof of her own enlightened feminism, what she really wanted to do after seeing "Return to the Dying Room" was to get a tape recorder and go to China and make those Chinese women confess to her who had forced them to kill their baby girls! She wanted to compel them to explain what she interpreted as their lack of personal volition. The student thought she was doing international feminism when, actually, she was reproducing the same imaginary relation of the U.S. and the P.R.C. that characterized U.S. press coverage of the WWC soccer game. The achievements of women in the other nation disappear while at the same time forming a mirror in which a U.S. student sees her own enlightened self-interest.

There are alternatives to the ideology of international feminism. For example, what happens to the European Enlightenment tradition of feminist internationalism when Chinese Marxist feminist Professor Li Xiaojiang lays claim to it in a theoretical project that argues for women's rights from an explicitly nationalist position?[5] More than a decade ago, Li Xiaojiang pointed out the masculinity of the modernist subject in the work of her own contemporaries. However, she allied herself with her colleagues on many points including the need to promote Enlightenment ideologies. She also has set up schools for women, encouraged feminist scholarship and media outreach campaigns, and contributed her own initiatives inside and outside the purview of the state. What make Li "Chinese" are precisely her nationalism and the specificities of the feminist tradition (a revolutionary movement to liberate women that is already a century old) that she invokes. What make her an Enlightened thinker are her claims on the Marxist, feminist, and liberal political philosophies that are the lingua franca of the modern world. What make Li a part of the sort of international feminism that I am spotlighting in this essay are her status as a global signifier of Chinese women and the amount of Ford Foundation contributions that her projects have absorbed in the past decade. Finally, what make her one of a whole cohort of theorists who work in the domain of women's liberation theory and feminism but are not international feminists are her connections with the likes of Dai Jinhua, Meng Yue, Li Yinhe, Josephine Ho, Kin Chi Lau, Karl Ning, and many others from the Chinese world of letters.

Historians persistently question attempts to universalize or reduce the category of woman to one thing or another, an imperative that requires me to read Li Xiaojiang because she is a theoretical predicator of subjects for women. People are thinking in other parts of the world, sometimes in the frame of international feminism and sometimes outside it. But why are international feminists not reading the feminist archives or the intellectual work of men and women who are not co-religionists, co-ethnics, or co-citizens? Perhaps the heritage of the state socialist experiments should be seen as part of feminisms that call themselves international rather than as the degraded other of international feminism. What about critical traditions or intellectual heritages that exceed the grasp of international femi-

---

[5] The resurgence of Chinese feminism in the late 1980s occurred during a neo-Kantian trend in Chinese cultural criticism that was the ideological wing of a larger political movement. See Wang 1996; Barlow 1997.

nism per se? Can a feminism that precludes the histories of thought in other places ever really be international? Reading international feminism in the context of critical claims from elsewhere may be a historian's practice, since we do tend to be more concerned with the truth claims than with truthfulness when it comes to ideologies such as international feminism. A chauvinistic, international feminist sportscaster's claim to epistemological authority when explaining the superiority of the U.S. women's soccer team, however, begs for analysis. (Certainly the same holds true with Clinton's proposition that women's bodies increase in value relative to the number of U.S. dollars invested in them.) More even than its core assumptions about environment, rights, and locality, this hunger for epistemological authority is what seems most elemental to international feminism and consequently most in need of our thoughtful attention.

Women Studies Department
University of Washington

References

Barlow, Tani. 1997. "Woman at the Close of the Maoist Era in the Polemics of Li Xiaojiang and Her Associates." In *The Politics of Culture in the Shadow of Capital,* ed. Lisa Lowe and David Lloyd, 506–43. Durham, N.C.: Duke University Press.

Bunch, Charlotte. 1995. "Transforming Human Rights from a Feminist Perspective." In *Women's Rights/Human Rights: International Feminist Perspectives,* ed. Julie Peters and Andrea Wolper, 11–17. New York and London: Routledge.

Sandomir, Richard. 1999. "Just Who Was the United States Playing for the Championship?" *New York Times,* July 11, sec. 1, p. 24.

Wang, Jing. 1996. *High Culture Fever: Politics, Aesthetics, and Ideology in Deng's China.* Berkeley and Los Angeles: University of California Press.

Reading the Signs: The Economics of Gender
Twenty-Five Years Later

I **distinctly remember** opening with anticipation the first issue of *Signs* as a recent migrant from Mexico and a graduate student of social anthropology at Rutgers University. The appearance of the pioneering publication roughly coincided with the first International Women's Conference held in the city where I have spent most of my life. I saw the two corresponding events as harbingers of discovery. The leading article in the first issue of *Signs* was a small masterpiece of durable power that I still assign to students with satisfying results.[1] Throughout the years, the journal has published lasting contributions to our understanding of women's experience. It is therefore fitting at the end of the century that we reflect in *Signs* on the accomplishments of more than two decades and the intellectual riddles that still await resolution.

The mid-seventies ushered in a period of momentous revelations in the study of gender. For the first time, in a systematic way women were made visible as subjects and agents. To be sure, there had been precursors, male as well as female, who had noted the particularities of women's experience and attempted to explain them. But it was only in the seventies that scholars deliberately set out to fill the gaps in understanding created by patriarchal and Eurocentric biases. Infused by feminist verve, they produced a wealth of new insights based on investigation rather than speculation.

This was especially true in understandings of political economy. Publications such as Ester Boserup's *Women's Role in Economic Development* (1970) and Rayna Reiter's *Toward an Anthropology of Women* (1975) set the standard for a new kind of scholarship. Still essential, these books contain a creative research agenda and a potent intellectual mission. Their objective was scientific in the sense that they sought to articulate precise explanations on the basis of empirical evidence. A main question concerned the puzzling inferiority of women's socioeconomic status. Skeptics saw this as a limited purpose more suitable of militants than scholars. Yet a better grasp of gender inequality has proven essential to advance all the great themes in the

---

[1] The essay is Smith-Rosenberg 1975.

[*Signs: Journal of Women in Culture and Society* 2000, vol. 25, no. 4]

social sciences. What began as a specialized concern has become, despite external resistance, an indispensable aspect of contemporary knowledge. That was a conspicuous and irreversible achievement.

Unraveling the causes and consequences of female subordination was not an easy task. Plausible explanations remained elusive even after ideological beliefs that saw women's servility as a function of physical weakness, biological limitation, or godly design were refuted. In need of redress were the paucity of information about women in multiple settings and the lack of coherent explanatory frameworks. Exemplary projects by Annette Weiner (1976), Eleanor B. Leacock (1972) and Diane Bell (1983) revealed extensive variations in gender inequality; authors such as Karen Sacks (1975), Kate Young (1978), Heidi Hartmann (1976), and Maxine Molyneux (1979) and produced an incipient theoretical body that centered on the mechanics of patriarchy, the distinctions between productive and reproductive labor, and the critical demarcation between public and private domains; and research by the likes of Helen Safa (1974), June Nash (1977), Lourdes Benería (1982), and Carmen Diana Deere (e.g., Deere 1986; Fagen, Deere, and Coraggio 1986) made clear the effects of capitalist expansion on the status of women. It is difficult to think of richer or more original contributions to scholarship than those made by early students of women and development.

Inspired by those efforts, I set out in the late seventies to conduct my own dissertation research on the circumstances surrounding female employment in Mexico's *maquiladora* (assembly-plant) program. By now the story is well-known, but it was new two decades ago when I looked for a job at a garment shop in Ciudad Juarez—minutes away from El Paso, Texas—to perform what anthropologists call "participant observation." My purpose was to apply the findings of the new literature on women to the understanding of an emerging phenomenon: the internationalization of production. The Mexico–United States border, joining a poor country and the richest nation in the world, provided an ideal setting. In addition to work as a seamstress, my project included a survey of more than five hundred workers and over fifty in-depth interviews. Earnest and inchoate, it became a point of reference mostly because it shed light on critical aspects of industrial restructuring and its relationship to gender.

Maquiladoras were one of the first manifestations of a major trend whose effects are only now becoming apparent. The North American Free Trade Agreement between Mexico and the United States is a direct descendant of that experiment. The relocation of factory work to less-developed areas like the Mexican border, and the ensuing epidemic of plant closings in advanced industrial nations, signaled a shift in the balance of power between workers and employers. In old industrial cities such as Detroit, Pittsburgh, Baltimore, and Philadelphia, the diminution of manufacturing employment adversely affected a preponderantly male labor force, weakened the unions to which many of its members had belonged, and brought about the enduring stagnation of average family wages. In Korea, Mexico, and the Caribbean, the appearance of plants operating as subsidiaries or subcontractors of transnational corporations announced a movement away from earlier attempts at autonomous industrialization and toward greater dependence on world markets. In both rich and poor countries, economic internationalization paralleled the massive incorporation of women into the formal workforce.

The narrative that emerged from my research and from other studies of women and development centered on the notion of exploitation, understood as the appropriation of human labor without commensurate compensation. Women had become the preferred providers of cheap labor in the age of globalization for reasons akin to those for their subordination in earlier times. Dependent on men, devoid of resources or true political standing, and charged with domestic responsibilities that often clashed with work outside the home, women had few alternatives but to accept jobs that were repetitive, poorly paid, and dangerous.

Few would dispute the accuracy of that general account, but, from a theoretical standpoint, it led to a cul-de-sac. Compelling accounts of the abuses caused by masculine greed soon became the single, resounding message and a priori conclusion of the literature on women and development. This gave the field a flattened, uninspired tone, and, more important, it had the unintended consequence of representing women as passive victims, and men, by inference, as the true agents of economic change. Without a strong focus beyond the notion of patriarchy, authors had few paths to traverse in their search for fine distinctions. A field that had been vibrant with promise in the seventies risked stagnation at the end of the eighties.

Fortunately, the past decade has witnessed a burst of renewed creativity, mostly thanks to a new generation of scholars willing to examine women's subordination in the context of other kinds of inequality.[2] Yet more effort is needed by way of theorizing gender as a relational process that comprises variations in the experience of women *and* men. Auspicious possibilities for achieving that goal emerge from studies of the intersections between gender and class. It grows increasingly difficult to see these two domains as separate effects of the exercise of power. Gender is better understood as

---

[2] See, e.g., Scheper-Hughes 1992; Hondagneu-Sotelo 1994; Yelvington 1995; Gutmann 1996; Freeman 1999.

the pivot around which class divisions organize. Female subordination can be properly explained only as part of larger orders of domination that critically affect men. Especially when backed by law and custom, women's dependent status acts as a two-edged sword. It enables the preservation of an exploitable labor pool within the domestic realm, but it also serves to control men, especially those in the working classes. Until recently, equating masculinity with the ability to support women and children functioned as a potent mechanism to secure male compliance not only in the world of work but also, even more tellingly, in hazardous male-only endeavors such as warfare.

My own research reveals other turns and twists in the geometry of gender and class. The economic shifts that started in the seventies dealt a severe blow to preexisting gender arrangements. As more women entered the formal labor force, it was reasonable to expect that they would gain greater autonomy and a more equitable footing with men. To a substantial extent that forecast has been realized. In the United States, wage differentials based on gender have decreased in the past twenty years. In places like Ciudad Juarez too, even the low pay earned by women in the *maquiladoras* has offered them a modicum of independence.

But there has also been a conspiracy of reality against sanguine hope. In both rich and poor countries the new premises surrounding gender have paralleled devastating assaults on workers of both sexes. The reduction of gender-based wage disparities in the United States is partly a result of the diminishing capacity of men to command adequate compensation. Even more alarming are the effects of industrial decline on racial minorities, especially black men. Almost gone is the family wage that granted ordinary Americans unprecedented prosperity earlier in the twentieth century. The tendency is toward the atomization of the labor force in terms of gender. Women's greater autonomy is now linked to an expectation that all individuals, regardless of their sex or domestic responsibilities, will support themselves. All this raises pressing issues that await analysis. The improvements in women's status may be real, but they have come at a cost that is apparent only when taking the widest outlook.

There is more to the story of gender than women's exploitation and dependence. Having pinpointed the specificity of female experience, let us now place it in the larger, more bountiful landscape of comparative theory.

Sociology Department
Princeton University

References

Bell, Diane. 1983. *Daughters of the Dreaming.* Melbourne: McPhee & Gribble; Sydney: Allen & Unwin.

Benería, Lourdes. 1982. *Women and Development: The Sexual Division of Labor in Rural Societies.* New York: Praeger.

Boserup, Ester. 1970. *Women's Role in Economic Development.* London: Allen & Unwin.

Deere, Carmen Diana. 1986. "Agrarian Reform, Peasant and Rural Production, and the Organization of Production in the Transition to Socialism." In Fagen, Deere, and Coraggio 1986, 97–142.

Fagen, Richard R., Carmen D. Deere, and José Luis Coraggio, eds. 1986. *Transition and Development: Problems of Third World Socialism.* New York: Monthly Review Press.

Freeman, Carla. 1999. *High Tech and High Heels in the Global Economy: Women, Work, and Pink Collar Identities in Barbados.* Durham, N.C.: Duke University Press.

Gutmann, Mathew C. 1996. *The Meanings of Macho: Being a Man in Mexico City.* Berkeley: University of California Press.

Hartmann, Heidi. 1976. "Capitalism, Patriarchy, and Job Segregation by Sex." In *Women and the Workplace: The Implications of Occupational Segregation,* ed. Martha Blaxall and Barbara Benton Reagan, 366–94. Chicago: University of Chicago Press.

Hondagneu-Sotelo, Pierrette. 1994. *Gendered Transitions: Mexican Experiences of Immigration.* Berkeley: University of California Press.

Leacock, Eleanor B. 1972. Introduction to *The Origin of the Family, Private Property, and the State,* by Frederick Engels, 7–67. New York: International.

Molyneux, Maxine. 1979. "Beyond the Domestic Labour Debate." *New Left Review* 116 (July/August): 3–27.

Nash, June, ed. 1977. *Ideology and Social Change in Latin America.* New York: Gordon & Breach.

Reiter, Rayna R., ed. 1975. *Toward an Anthropology of Women.* New York: Monthly Review Press.

Sacks, Karen. 1975. "Engels Revisited: Women, the Organization of Production, and Private Property." In Reiter 1975, 327–34.

Safa, Helen I. 1974. *The Urban Poor of Puerto Rico: A Study in Development and Inequality.* New York: Holt, Rinehart, & Winston.

Scheper-Hughes, Nancy. 1992. *Death without Weeping: The Violence of Everyday Life in Brazil.* Berkeley: University of California Press.

Smith-Rosenberg, Carroll. 1975. "The Female World of Love and Ritual: Relations between Women in Nineteenth-Century America." *Signs: Journal of Women in Culture and Society* 1(1):1–29.

Weiner, Annette. 1976. *Women of Value, Men of Renown: New Perspectives in Trobriand Exchange.* Austin: University of Texas Press.

116 **I** Fernández-Kelly

Yelvington, Kevin A. 1995. *Producing Power: Ethnicity, Gender, and Class in a Caribbean Workplace.* Philadelphia: Temple University Press.

Young, Kate. 1978. "Modes of Appropriation and the Sexual Division of Labor: A Case Study from Oaxaca, Mexico." In *Feminism and Materialism: Women and Modes of Production,* ed. Annette Kuhn and AnnMarie Wolpe, 123–46. London: Routledge & Kegan Paul.

Edna Acosta-Belén

Christine E. Bose

U.S. Latina and Latin American Feminisms: Hemispheric Encounters

The growing globalization of the world capitalist economy, which will continue its expansionist trend into the new millennium, represents a decisive turning point in any reappraisal of the evolution of women's movements and conditions in the developed and developing countries of the Americas. This essay tries to capture some of the major theoretical developments and realities shaping the experiences of U.S. Latinas and Latin American women in the era of globalization.

Any analysis of this nature must begin with the recognition of the fundamental differences in the historical, cultural, and socioeconomic factors that have shaped U.S. Latinas' and Latin American women's experiences. Moreover, it also requires consideration of the interplay between the structural conditions that Latinas face in U.S. society and the transnational interconnections that different Latino/a groups maintain with their respective Latin American and Caribbean countries of origin. Contemporary transnational interconnections and bidirectional contacts between the United States and the countries of the Americas are increasingly creating overlap among U.S. Latino-focused ethnic studies, women's/feminist studies, and Latin American and Caribbean area studies. While area studies programs in the United States primarily emerged from cold war foreign policy concerns, programs that focus either on the collective U.S. Latino/a experience or on individual nationalities, such as Chicano, Puerto Rican, Cuban, or Dominican studies, are rooted in a long history of socioeconomic and civil rights struggles. Indeed, the liberation movements of the 1960s and 1970s influenced the advent of both ethnic and women's studies academic programs. The original impetus of Latino/a and women's studies was to critique prevailing paradigms and produce new knowledge about traditionally marginalized groups. Although the field of women's studies challenged patriarchal structures and the androcentric constructs, behaviors, and exclusionary canonical practices of the Western tradition, it was initially dominated by the experiences of white middle-class women.

Signs: Journal of Women in Culture and Society 2000, vol. 25, no. 4]

At the same time, ethnic studies was focusing on issues of racial and ethnic oppression and cultural nationalism, without paying enough attention to the sexism, heterosexism, and racism found within these groups. Out of the subordination of Latinas and their initial exclusion from both a male-dominated ethnic studies movement and a white-dominated women's movement, Chicanas, puertorriqueñas, and women from other disenfranchised U.S. ethnoracial minorities began to forge and articulate a feminist consciousness and a collective sense of struggle based on their experiences as members of diverse individual nationalities, as well as on their collective panethnic and cross-border identities as Latinas and women of color. These perspectives were fostered in the pioneering anthologies *All the Women Are White, All the Blacks Are Men, but Some of Us Are Brave* (Hull, Scott, and Smith 1982) and *This Bridge Called My Back: Writings by Radical Women of Color* (Moraga and Anzaldúa 1981), which made it clear that the process of constructing new, more inclusive emancipatory knowledge required full consideration of other sources of marginality and oppression. They also underscored the power differentials between women and men, and within and among groups, and denounced the culture of intolerance and the exclusionary or marginalizing practices of mainstream U.S. society and Western intellectual traditions. Furthermore, these writings established the need for women of color to engage in the processes of defining themselves, asserting their agency, and building their own intellectual traditions.

The process of problematizing and rectifying the initial shortcomings of the U.S. ethnic and women's movements was both conflictive and divisive, but it was also a necessary process that forced the emerging fields of women's and ethnic studies to pay more attention to the social, racial, and cultural factors that produce differences within and among groups at national and international levels in order to find common ground; to influence research and teaching endeavors; and to explore the potential for building intergroup solidarities and meaningful coalitions. It was quite evident that this potential could not be achieved unless it acknowledged the differences among women and the conditions that create those differences. Thus, it was U.S. Latinas and other women of color who introduced gender into ethnic studies and racial issues into women's studies. The term *women of color,* though problematic because of the same homogenizing tendencies found in the term *white women,* became widespread as a way of fostering the idea of common struggles, but, more accurately, it signaled a direct oppositional stance against the deficient and exclusionary tenets of white middle-class Western feminisms. Latinas and other women of color recognized early on that their particular civil rights struggles transcended U.S. borders and resonated in the human rights, socioeconomic, and political survival struggles of the rest of the hemisphere and other parts of the third world. This view, in turn, fostered a national and international dialogue on the intersections of gender, race, and ethnicity, on the power differentials between developed and developing countries, and on the transnational interconnections between U.S. Latinas and women from Latin American and Caribbean nations around issues such as human rights, peace, health, (im)migration, the environment, and economic restructuring.

Lesbian and gay issues also came out of the intellectual closet, and perhaps one of the most noticeable new areas of scholarship on Latinos/as in recent years has been the deconstruction of female and male sexuality and a concomitant denunciation of heterosexism. Since the publication of *This Bridge Called My Back* (Moraga and Anzaldúa 1981) and Juanita Ramos's anthology, *Compañeras: Latina Lesbians* (1987), several new studies and edited volumes on gay and lesbian issues have been published. Considering that lesbianism and homosexuality are among the most taboo subjects in the Latin American/U.S. Latino/a experience, these works contribute to breaking that silence. Most are aimed at shattering prevalent myths and stereotypes, but they also analyze the contingent nature of sexual identities, how these identities are negotiated, and how constructions of masculinity and femininity vary with sociocultural context and historical moment.

The past decade has seen increased scholarship on the pluralistic nature of feminism, the differences among women, and the many forms feminism assumes within specific communities, social sectors, nations, races, and regions (Bose and Acosta-Belén 1995). As we consider the effects of globalization, academics are still struggling to define broad-based multicultural and gender-inclusive approaches to the differences and commonalities among feminists and women's movements in various parts of the globe. Do we have an adequate conception of the variety of Western feminisms as well as of non-Western feminist discourses and women's movements? What, for instance, are some of the major differences in the development of North American and Western European women's movements, or between those in Western and Eastern Europe, Latin America and Africa, the United States and Japan, Cuba and Puerto Rico? Which issues and conditions transcend national borders and which are specific to a country or local community? Why do some women's movements not regard the state as the major instrument for improving their status, while others do? What are the factors that make women's movements more grassroots oriented in some countries than in others? What makes women's/gender studies flourish in academic settings in the United States but primarily in independent centers or institutes in most third-world countries? If feminism is considered a historically continuous and fluid movement, what are the factors that produce periods of stagnation or expansion in particular countries? If there is an international women's movement, what holds it together? And, if some of the present social and economic conditions are global and general, how can we bring about articulated forms of global action around specific issues? Which are the issues that make transnational coalitions possible? The answers to these questions are far from obvious. Nonetheless, the questions themselves underscore the pitfalls that feminism must avoid to keep from becoming another homogenizing Western master discourse that can be exported, like any commodity or development program, to "modernize" the developing world. We need to listen to the voices and experiences of women in less privileged settings. The goal of cross-border solidarities and coalitions around specific issues such as health, the environment, human rights, violence against women, prostitution, major socioeconomic inequalities, or survival in the informal economy can be advanced only if major differences among the women of the Americas are recognized and if we engage in dialogue based on mutual respect for our differences and seek a convergence of goals.

Different theoretical frameworks are needed as well. Early discussions of women and development in Latin America and the Caribbean generally took a dichotomous approach: women were viewed as either helped or exploited by development, either drawn into paid employment or excluded from it. In the latter case, theorists relegated women to the role of homemaker and ignored their contributions to the informal economy. The shortcomings of these approaches led feminists to reconceptualize work itself as an activity to be measured on a continuum from formal paid work to informal paid work to household work (Ward and Pyle 1995). This approach clearly established that development, usually thought of as an activity in the productive sphere, is not separate from the domestic sphere and that the macro and micro levels of economic analysis can and must be considered simultaneously and interactively.

International macro-level relationships need to be analyzed as well, since growth and changes in Latin American and Caribbean women's employment have been integrally tied to trends in North America and especially to the role of Latinas and other women of color in the U.S. political economy (Fernández-Kelly and Sassen 1995). For example, money sent by U.S. Latinos/as to families in their homelands constitutes a significant portion of some Latin American economies. Moreover, during the 1980s, U.S. corporate strategies began to shift, generating major employment changes, population displacements, and labor migration flows throughout the hemisphere. Increasingly, corporate emphasis has been on internationalizing the service sector, rather than manufacturing, as well as creating global markets in finance. The former "global assembly line" is transforming into what has been described as "regional clustering" brought on by corporate attempts to lower production costs through the use of computer technology rather than by moving production work from country to country (Nanda 1994). The parallel structure in the gendered division of labor within the United States and the developing countries of the hemisphere is shaping and changing women's roles. As a result, U.S. Latinas often work in the garment industry, in computer assembly, or as domestic workers — work similar to that done by women in their countries of origin — and families in both places need multiple earners.

Much of Latin American and Caribbean women's organized resistance to their subordination has been based on survival needs, often at the individual or family level as well as in the neighborhood or workplace, rather than at the level of large-scale social movements, political parties, feminist groups, or labor unions. For instance, families use multiples income strategies, with members engaging in a variety of survival efforts, such as earning wages in the formal sector, growing subsistence produce, trading in the informal sector, or performing unpaid household labor. Yet, in reaction to development models that focus on growth and increased profits for transnational corporations, often to the detriment of the environment and the well-being of native populations, women have played an active role in calling for new models of sustainable development. Since globalization implies the creation of new regional centers of capital accumulation and the formation of new alliances among social sectors at local, national, or transnational levels using new technologies (Jonas and McCaughan 1994), it also calls for similar alliances among women to combat the persistent inequalities and abuses introduced by transnational capital. Members of such women's organizations are not necessarily feminists, but their consciousness is frequently raised through praxis and through networking with other women of color at international meetings.

In sum, Latinas from the North and South have played an important role in internationalizing women's studies and in denouncing both the persistent basic inequalities and prejudices endured by third-world populations as well as their disadvantaged or subordinate position in relation to Latino men. Latina feminists in the United States increasingly are engaging in comparative work, trying to envision or imagine new models that advance knowledge of their individual ethnic group experiences and, at the same time, undertaking the difficult task of building bridges of understanding and solidarity among ethnoracial groups at national and international levels. Many Latino studies programs have already made alliances with women's studies programs, which themselves have begun to focus on global gender issues, thanks, in part, to initiatives such as the Ford Foundation's Women's Studies, Area and International Studies (WSAIS) grant program. Links among women's, ethnic, and area studies, in spite of their disparate academic and political origins, are fostered by the transnational dynamics created by the common impact of globalization on developing countries and on women of color living in capitalist metropolitan centers. However, the convergence of minds and goals among women of different races, nationalities, and classes is more an unfinished project than an accomplished fact. The second edition of *This Bridge Called My Back* has a sobering new foreword by Cherríe Moraga that touches on the state of an imagined unity among feminists of color and still poses a major challenge: "Third World feminism does not provide the kind of easy political framework that women of color are running to in droves. We are not so much a 'natural' affinity group, as women who have come together out of political necessity. The *idea* of Third World feminism has proved to be much easier between the covers of a book than between real live women" (Moraga and Anzaldúa 1983, iii).

The concerns of third-world feminists vary considerably and are not always obvious to those of us in core countries. For peasant, poor, and working-class women, the primary concern is survival: escaping war and violence or having ready access to shelter, food, and potable water for their families. Professional women strive for increased political participation and socioeconomic equality. For other women, the topics are sexuality, reproductive rights, and health issues, running the gamut from sex tourism and prostitution, female circumcision, and selective abortion to protection from AIDS and the availability of safe birth control. Still, in large parts of the world, with high rates of illiteracy, the basis of economic rights is sought in much-needed education. While these concerns may seem far away in a sense, women in many core countries share similar issues. Moreover, many third-world problems are often generated by the economic control exerted by first-world transnational corporations and international economic agencies in these countries. In this new millennium, increasing transnational migration and continuing transnational links make these issues part of a common cause.

Latin American and Caribbean Studies and Women's Studies Departments
(Acosta-Belén)
Sociology, Women's Studies, and Latin American and Caribbean Studies Departments (Bose)
University at Albany, State University of New York

References

Bose, Christine E., and Edna Acosta-Belén, eds. 1995. *Women in the Latin American Development Process*. Philadelphia: Temple University Press.

Fernández-Kelly, M. Patricia, and Saskia Sassen. 1995. "Recasting Women in the Global Economy: Internationalization and Changing Definitions of Gender." In Bose and Acosta-Belén 1995, 99–124.

Hull, Gloria, Patricia Bell Scott, and Barbara Smith, eds. 1982. *All the Women Are White, All the Blacks Are Men, but Some of Us Are Brave: Black Women's Studies*. Old Westbury, N.Y.: Feminist Press.

Jonas, Suzanne, and Edward J. McCaughan, eds. 1994. *Latin America Faces the Twenty-First Century: Reconstructing a Social Justice Agenda*. Boulder, Colo: Westview.

Moraga, Cherríe, and Gloria Anzaldúa, eds. 1981. *This Bridge Called My Back: Writings by Radical Women of Color*. 1st ed. Watertown, Mass: Persephone.

———. 1983. *This Bridge Called My Back: Writings by Radical Women of Color*. 2d ed. New York: Kitchen Table Women of Color Press.

Nanda, Meera. 1994. "New Technologies/New Challenges." Paper presented at the conference "Women in the Global Economy: Making Connections" at the Institute for Research on Women, SUNY, Albany, N.Y., April 22–24.

Ramos, Juanita, ed. 1987. *Compañeras: Latina Lesbians*. New York: Latina Lesbian History Project.

Ward, Kathryn B., and Jean Larson Pyle. 1995. "Gender, Industrialization, Transnational Corporations, and Development: An Overview of Trends and Patterns." In Bose and Acosta-Belén 1995, 37–64.

Dorothy Q. Thomas

We Are Not the World: U.S. Activism and Human Rights in the Twenty-First Century

O ver the past decade a powerful movement for women's human rights has emerged internationally. As an activist in this movement, I have often wondered why, when women from all over the world are increasingly incorporating international human rights into their work, U.S. activists are not. An effective global human rights movement provides U.S. activists with an unprecedented opportunity to strengthen their advocacy locally and increase its effect. Yet I find that U.S. women's and civil rights activists are still wondering, "What does international human rights have to do with us?" This question says a lot about the political and practical realities of work on rights in the United States during the past century, and it will have to be answered if we are to meet the challenges of the next.

That U.S. groups rarely resort to human rights is no accident. Successive U.S. administrations have done everything in their power, in the fifty-plus years since the adoption of the Universal Declaration of Human Rights in 1948, to insulate the country from international scrutiny and to prevent its residents from meaningfully invoking their international human rights. In 1951 President Eisenhower preempted the effort of several southern senators to limit his treaty-making power on the grounds that international human rights law could be used to challenge racial segregation: he simply refused to sign any such treaties. When key human rights conventions were finally taken up more than thirty years later, they were ratified in a way that made them virtually impossible to enforce legally. To this day, the United States remains one of the only industrialized nations that has yet to ratify the Convention on the Elimination of All Forms of Discrimination against Women, the chief international instrument that protects the human rights of women.

The U.S. government's determination to shield itself from international accountability arose in part out of the early efforts of U.S. civil and women's rights groups to invoke human rights in their work. In 1947, for example, the National Association for the Advancement of Colored People called on the United Nations to study racial discrimination in the United

[*Signs: Journal of Women in Culture and Society* 2000, vol. 25, no. 4]

States and to ensure U.S. compliance with international standards. And in 1966, the National Organization for Women's founding charter explicitly identified it with "the worldwide revolution of human rights taking place within and beyond our borders." Such actions fueled the U.S. government's fear that powerful local constituencies would use international standards and scrutiny to expose and challenge domestic abuse. Its systematic effort over the past fifty years to forestall such action, in particular by never or only nominally ratifying key human rights treaties, has effectively shut down the human rights dimension of U.S. rights advocacy. As one activist put it to me, in a country where much civil and women's rights work is advanced through litigation, an international law that cannot be enforced in U.S. courts has no meaning.

But why should United States–based activists allow themselves to be caught in a trap that is not fully of their own making? The "meaning" of human rights is by no means exclusively legal, nor does effective human rights advocacy—in the United States or anywhere else—depend primarily on the courts. In fact, in many countries, local women's rights activists invoke human rights for its moral authority and value as an educational, mobilizing, and advocacy tool. In Botswana, activists have argued that the country's sex discriminatory citizenship laws run contrary to fundamental notions of human dignity and freedom. They used the Convention on the Elimination of All Forms of Discrimination against Women to educate women about their human rights and to mobilize popular support to change the law. Ultimately, this effort led to successful litigation and legal reform. One of Botswana's most vocal women's human rights activists is now a judge on the country's high court. Given that our own courts are less and less friendly to civil and women's rights litigation, one wonders why this alternative human rights strategy that combines documentation, education, mobilization, advocacy, *and* litigation doesn't have a more contagious effect.

That U.S. groups don't use human rights may result not only from U.S. government policy but also from persistent tensions in domestic women's and civil rights advocacy. According to the principle of indivisibility, one of the defining characteristics of human rights is that civil, political, economic, social, and cultural rights are inextricably linked to and dependent on one another. In this sense, international norms could provide a framework for advancing *all* rights in the United States that is simply not available domestically. A human rights approach to domestic violence, for example, would focus not only on the right to be free from violence and to see it prosecuted and punished but also on rights to adequate health care, housing, education, and employment. Such a broad-based rights approach is rare in U.S. rights work, and the government strenuously opposes it.

Human rights is also founded on the principle of intersectionality meaning that it applies to all people equally without distinction based or race, color, sex, language, religion, political or other opinion, national or social origin, property, birth, or other status. As such, a human rights approach lends itself to simultaneous race, class, and gender analysis, for example, in a way that a civil rights approach usually does not. Human rights work on rape as genocide in Rwanda, for example, invoked an intersectional analysis of both ethnicity and gender that did not require survivors to split their experience into categories to pursue their legal claims. Such an intersectional approach, while it recognizes difference, eschews rigid conceptions of identity and provides the basis for more multi-issue organizing and advocacy than commonly occurs in the United States today.

Any U.S. group that wants to adopt a human rights approach to their domestic work is also faced with the paucity of financial support for doing so. U.S. foundations that fund human rights work do so largely out of their international programs and generally do not include human rights in their domestic portfolios. Even if financial resources were available, human resources would remain a problem, for few U.S. women's or civil rights organizations have human rights experience and, although many activists who work in human rights are *from* the United States, not many have experience working *on* the United States. This is all beginning to change, but U.S. groups are still caught in a vicious cycle: not knowing exactly how human rights might be relevant to their work, they don't seek funding to incorporate it; unless they seek such funding, though, they lack the resources to determine its relevance.

These obstacles are largely institutional. The more entrenched problem is a kind of learned insularity that may prove more difficult to overcome. Decades of isolationist U.S. policy have produced a bifurcated rights reality in the United States. Even seasoned activists think that civil rights applies to "us" and human rights to "them." Activists in the United States repeatedly express the sentiment that "we don't have time to work on human rights; we have too many rights problems here at home." In a deep sense, U.S. activism has cut itself off from the predicament and promise that it shares with the rest of the world community. We have lost sight of our common humanity and, with it, our common purpose.

Given the increasingly globalized environment in which we struggle, persistent U.S. insularity can only make for poor government policy and impoverished domestic advocacy. With this is mind, several United States–based groups are stepping up their domestically focused human rights activities. Amnesty International USA, Human Rights Watch, and the International Human Rights Law Group, three of the largest United

States–based human rights organizations, all have programs that focus on human rights in the United States. WILD for Human Rights, a newly created San Francisco–based organization, focuses on the United States's meaningful ratification and implementation of human rights treaties and on training United States–based activists to use human rights fact-finding, mobilization, and advocacy strategies. The Atlanta-based Center for Human Rights Education reaches out to grassroots activists with human rights education and training tailored to local concerns. Boston's Women's Rights Network helps local domestic violence groups to incorporate human rights strategies into their work. And the Kensington Welfare Rights Union in Philadelphia is spearheading an economic human rights campaign that involves poor peoples' organizations across the United States.

Eleanor Roosevelt once said that human rights begins at home. Feminists the world over live by this maxim and work to free women from domestic drudgery, violence, and isolation. But how lasting will our liberation be if we simply exchange the confines of the home for those of the nation? How free can we be if our government can still assert "domestic jurisdiction" to escape accountability for rights violations? What is the cost to freedom of colluding in such isolationism? How free might we be if we challenged this closed-door U.S. policy and joined with activists all over the world to ensure that human rights apply everywhere, including here?

Human Rights Program
Shaler Adams Foundation

Building a New Dream with Gaia?

So how am I to read this word *millennium:* as signifying a date in a taken-for-granted calendar whose cultural and religious roots we know but dismiss or as part of a persistent evangelism still recruiting the world around a Christian project? With Islam the new demon for the West, I want to go on complaining about such compulsory Christianizing, even while feeling more than a little sympathy for those believers whose sacred calendar is once more appropriated for a commercial opportunity. Multiculturalism has to be built every day, for history is too powerful to casually ignore.

But even treating the "M" word as a modest dateline, the problem remains that I find thinking about feminisms today basically impossible. How can even an Emily Dickinson brain hold simultaneously a recognition of the exhilarating cultural achievements of feminisms together with the agony and poverty of so many women and their children in so much of the world? My pleasure in the intellectual and cultural achievement of the diversity of feminisms is not just aesthetic, or even just about "us," that group with whom I identify in loving quarrel, or even about the feminist books, paintings, music, and plays and the sciences that we create and debate. Most of all, even though there is rather little agreement among "us," I read the poly-epistemic sieges laid by feminists and our allies against the monolithic hegemony of the old knowledges as critical for our survival.

My sense of who and what is included in that *our* has also undergone a profound transformation over the past three decades. Today I include both human and nonhuman entities. It is shorthand, but culturally and politically not only women but also nature have become historical subjects. In this new feminist political ecology, either both survive or neither does. Seventies feminism—with the exception of some of our finest science-fiction writers—was primarily focused on women and our relations with men. The nature that we fought to defend against a hugely capitalized biomedical assault, which claimed, of course, to be in our best interests, was that of our own bodies.

The environment was merely a backdrop for most of the struggles of 1970s feminists; we were indeed our bodies ourselves. Feminism fought biology's misogynist representations of women's nature and also simul-

[*Signs: Journal of Women in Culture and Society* 2000, vol. 25, no. 4]

taneously struggled to expose biology's linguistic conjuring trick of claiming complete correspondence between the study of life and life itself. The struggles within industrialized countries where white feminists fought for the right to choose while black feminists battled an ongoing eugenic history have their global counterparts. The issue of survival of the "race" both for black feminisms and for the feminisms of the South meant that they were first to recognize that the defense of the environment was identical — at least for the great mass of women if not for the elites — with the struggle for life itself. While strict Lovelockeans may flinch at the thought of Gaia demanding suffrage, it serves well as a metaphor for the necessary political space required by and for the socioecosystem. The Gaia hypothesis, initially proposed by Nobel laureate James Lovelock, sees the entire earth as one living system, but the idea has since been picked up and used much more evocatively by the environmental movement. Whereas first-wave feminism fought for the vote for women at the opening of the century, at its close, Gaia too demands a vote.

While it is widely recognized that the feminisms of North and South are necessarily different, it is increasingly common to speak of Euro-American feminisms. Here I want to insist that the specificity of the geo-historical experiences of Europe and North America maintains important differences among the two continents and cultures. Although individuals move about with extraordinary fluidity, taking our histories with us, the structures of space and time still shape and frame us. We homogenize them at our intellectual and political peril, for false homogeneity makes it impossible to see situated danger. Europe is, for many reasons, much more politically exercised than the United States about Monsanto, the Clinton administration's love affair with the biotechnology industry, and the World Trade Organization. Gaia may have been called into existence by the South, but now Europe welcomes her too.

Although I see this as a huge struggle being played out globally with biosocial survival as the stakes, the immense political and intellectual engagement of feminist activists and scholars in biopolitics has changed the constructions of the macropolitical agenda. In this still emerging agenda, feminism is increasingly coming into a synergistic relation with environmentalism. Of course this optimistic reading sets to one side those harsh private struggles with the embodied self (e.g., the cult of thinness or, for that matter, healthism as a consumerist response to the public problem of a sickness-producing biosocial environment). But it is a mistake to cast private and public struggles in permanent opposition; the boundaries between personal consumerism and the pursuit of public objectives are the subject, rather, of permanent negotiation. Thus the consumer demand that food be adequately labeled celebrates the ideology of the market by increasing choice to the individual consumer and also offers the possibility of mass consumer resistance to products deemed unsafe or unethical.

Increasingly a number of these struggles that start in the private end up on the state's doorstep. In Europe, consumer resistance to genetically modified foods forms the paradigmatic case. Typically, the state faces both ways: it both fosters the biotechnological industry as a major wealth producer and has the responsibility to regulate the industry to protect public health and the environment. Nowhere is this private-public connection more evident than in the challenges the new genetics brings to our most intimate lives. Even leaving aside the serious issue of the emergence of an unemployable, uninsurable genetic underclass, the proliferation of genetic tests for would-be parents and pregnant women shapes how we think not only about ourselves but also about the kind of children we should permit to come into existence. To date there is not one genetic therapy that works and the only therapy available is the abortion of an affected fetus. The old state eugenics is for the most part dead, replaced by a pervasive consumer eugenics. That confusing, confused, intimate moment when someone says to herself, "I want to have a baby," is the site of tremendous pressure to receive genetic information and choose responsibly. The new medical ideology of informed choice rests with special weight on the shoulders of pregnant women, and its very intimacy makes it extraordinarily hard to resist. Indeed, coping with the new genetics requires a more or less heretical move against the legacy of the Enlightenment that even the most postmodern among us may find hard to take. It is to question the idea that knowledge, in this case genetic knowledge, is necessarily desirable. Choosing when not to know is part of a new cultural struggle to defend our personal freedom not to be policed inside our own heads by biomedical constructions of normality.

Nonetheless, global shifts in the structuring of production have given a footloose capital immense powers over a global workforce in which women and children hold weak positions. The loss of collectivity and the growth of individualism have contradictorily witnessed the assertion of new rights against male violence and abuse, yet ironically many of these gains are being made in countries where a large minority of women and their children are increasingly relegated to lifelong poverty. Even the Scandinavian welfare states, which took women's equality and the state's contribution to child care most seriously, are rolling back, leaving women and their dependents exposed to market forces. Britain, whether governed by Thatcherism or New Labor, energetically rows itself across the Atlantic away from the European welfare capitalism of its common past, eager to embrace the hard U.S. model. It is sad to watch young newly elected Labor women in parliament who grew up within the women's movement and mouthed feminist values offer little or no defense against their own government's assault on lone mothers.

It is not only the rise of poststructuralist feminisms but also the collapse of the Soviet system that have been part of a loss of a sense of solidarity, a weakening of that imagined community of women worldwide. That fostering of solidarity between intellectual and activist feminists and working-class and poor women common to the projects of radical and socialist feminism is now seriously eroded. Today, feminist bourgeois careerism, replete with networking and mutual support within the group (an unholy echo of the old boy's network) celebrates its success, pretty much indifferent to the social pain and exclusion of less advantaged women.

But what do I do with the bitter knowledge that, despite the material and cultural advantages of some, most women live increasingly meager lives in the advanced capitalist countries or are dying prematurely of hunger and war in the developing world? I am part of that generation who grew up believing that the death camps marked the nadir of civilization and that we (meaning all decent people) would never again tolerate this, only to find, from Rwanda to Bosnia to Kosovo, that liberal democratic governments can and do tolerate genocide and mass rape. Sure, there were picket lines, and it was some comfort to stand with the Women in Black, but never for a moment was there the same mass moral outrage in the United States and Europe as against the Vietnam War. These places and people were all far away, their deaths were those of the Other in an Other place. Not really our problem. Our governments seem to be more concerned not to break a single infantry soldier's fingernail than to stop the killing. But where were we? Was all that stuff about multiculturalism, diversity, and antiracism basically a cultural shift and a politic trapped within the iron cage of the nation-state, within fortress Europe, or even within our academic feminist communities? And can the recognition that the entire biosocial system is at increasing risk help us build not the old dream of a global sisterhood but a new dream with a new Gaian sense of "us"? Best of all, since I wrote the first draft of this essay, the last year of the old millennium provided an inspiring augury that the answer could be yes! At Seattle in 1999, the nongovernmental organizations improbably and gloriously defeated the corporate power of the World Trade Organization. What a great start for whatever we call the dateline.

Sociology Department
City University

Difference and Recognition: Postmillennial Identities and Social Justice

Will the millennium mark a genuine watershed or not? It is tempting at the moment to fall prey either to catastrophic predictions of unprecedented change and transformation or to cynical denials of the significance of the millennial moment. A moment is indeed all it is, and one that takes place at very different times around the globe. But, fleeting or not, change is inevitable. At the end of the last millennium most deliveries in London were made by horse and cart; in the year 2000 transport and communication are light-years ahead. In 1899, Freud published *The Interpretation of Dreams,* but almost no one had heard of the Viennese physician; in 2000, Freudian insights are common currency in popular culture, and large numbers of us are bowdlerized Freudians. Our interior and exterior worlds have been transformed, in ways that few people could have foreseen in 1899.

Marking time by calendars is an arbitrary process. Political and religious regimes have often sought to impose their own ways of controlling time. It was not until October 1, 1949, that Mao Zedong declared that China would follow the Gregorian calendar. When the monk Roger Bacon informed the pope in 1267 that the Julian calendar gained time over the true solar year with the result that a surplus of nine days had accumulated, it raised the terrifying possibility that Christians might be celebrating Easter and other holy days on the wrong date. The year 2000 will be 5760 according to the Jewish calendar, 1420 according to the Muslim, and 1378 according to the Persian (Duncan 1998). Time marks out our differences, political and religious.

The millennium, then, is perhaps a good moment to reflect on differences and the problem of recognition. Difference is the philosophical, personal, and political concern of the moment. Looking back from the perspective of 2099, the last years of the second millennium might well appear beset by the uncontrollable forces of difference and their accompanying and inextricably entwined questions of identity. From a number of perspectives, it would appear that what Freud called the fetishism of minor

[*Signs: Journal of Women in Culture and Society* 2000, vol. 25, no. 4]

differences has taken hold: in the explosion of ethnic and national identities, in the differentiation of interest groups, in the demonization of immigrants, in the upsurge of multicultural protest, and in the forms of political and personal confrontation around the globe in which multiplicity has suddenly been transformed into particularism. On a personal and philosophical scale, particularism is the response to the problem of universality and to the erosion of specificities — identities, histories, needs, rights. In a very general sense, it could be argued that the problem of the new millennium, or at least of its opening centuries, will be the problem of citizenship and the associated issue of social justice.

Reflecting on this point as a feminist produces a strange sense of dislocation, since one of feminism's political imperatives and guiding principles has been the extension of social justice through the assertion of difference and the accompanying demand for recognition. This demand had no sooner been formulated than it was challenged on the grounds that it was itself exclusionary because it did not recognize differences among women. In other words, the recognition of difference along one dimension was insufficient. This must necessarily be so because differences are never singular; they are always contextual and relational. The affirmation that women have different contexts and histories, that they have suffered multiple and various forms of subordination and discrimination, and that their situation in the world is the product of differential relations between groups of people — classes, nations, races, ethnic and religious groups, and so on — should have been relatively easy for a reflective and self-critical set of feminist theories to absorb and act on. In one sense, of course, it has been fairly easy, as much feminist writing evinces. However, in another sense, it was impossible because of the continuing oscillation of the particular and the universal or, to put it another way, because of the relation between any difference and the context or ground in which it is asserted. It is therefore not surprising that some feminist scholars are still accusing others of failing to recognize significant differences or, perhaps more tellingly, of privileging some forms of difference over others — as in the sexual difference debate. The idea that identities are always a matter of multiple affiliation is easier to accept philosophically than it is to act on politically. Accepting multiple affiliations means giving up — albeit sometimes only temporarily — the privileging of one form of difference. However, once that privilege goes, then what distinguishes individuals or groups from the larger context in which they are situated?

Quite a number of scholars have characterized this as the dilemma of democracy: the oscillation between the demand for specific recognition and incorporation into a collaborative milieu within which the demand for recognition can be made and acted upon. Multiculturalism is frequently cited as an example of a demand for the recognition of specificity that presumes the national community it affects to reject. No claim based on particularity will ever erase the universal, since differences are only differences in certain contexts. The problem, of course, is that living with differences means having to live with the effects of the differential power of certain groups to identify, name, and recognize difference. Feminism's internal critique of the assumptions underlying the category woman is a good example of this point. The recognition of difference is only a starting point because the purpose of recognition is to transform the context in which differences are lived. In certain ways, it could be argued that feminism has been successful in this regard in a variety of ways, in different parts of the world, and to differing degrees: more women work, more women participate in political processes, the sexual division of labor has shifted, cultural and societal attitudes have changed. There are, of course, cynics who point out that such changes have been entirely minimal or that those changes that have taken place have had little to do with feminism per se and more to do with structural economic changes. One way to measure the success of feminism is to assess the degree to which it has provoked a backlash: a response from others that some important aspect of their identity is being ignored.

It seems clear to me, as a feminist anthropologist, that principles of social justice and moral citizenship should be defended, but this also means living with the constant threat of their potential failure. This situation is complicated by the frequent assertion that it is impossible to adhere to overarching political ideals, both because there are no generally agreed-upon meanings attached to these ideals and because liberalism is a Eurocentric particularity masquerading as a universal. The problem here is that one of the consequences of the demand for the recognition of difference is the growth of a philosophical and political orthodoxy in which adherence to general principles involves the erasure of distinctiveness. Anthropology has been complicit in this insofar as it has defended cultural distinctiveness through relativist forms of argument without a very clear understanding that cultural recognition presupposes a context that is not defined by those cultures. Critics of anthropology, however, have often used this very point to claim that anthropology is by its nature Eurocentric.

Self-recognition and cultural identity are perhaps becoming more important as the millennium closes than they were when it began because, in a more differentiated world, where cultural, racial, ethnic, sexual, and religious differences are contiguous and constantly reinforced aspects of daily living, the demand for the recognition of differences grows almost exponentially. There is no apparent limit to the demand for the recognition of difference because to concede to a limit means to admit to a defeat or, more precisely, to allow the self potentially to be overwhelmed by another. It is sometimes argued that ethical communities could grow up and social justice be maintained through the acknowledgment that identities are never one and indivisible, but always composite and hybrid, and that identities have to be sustained in a collaborative milieu and should not be conceived of as exclusive. This would certainly be a start, but it underestimates the degree to which individuals and communities already understand — directly or indirectly — that the other is part of the self, that individuals and communities are hybrid, that "mainstream" society is constituted through its minorities. The very violence of identity politics — in all of its forms — in the contemporary world attests to this fact. The challenge for the next millennium, then, is not to be overwhelmed by difference and to commit to the continuing and irresolvable contest of the existence and meaning of unifying ideals. Difference can only reproduce itself in the context of such a debate because it has no meaning outside its self-constituting relation to a posited universal or shared horizon (Norval 1994; Laclau 1996; Salecl 1998).

Anthropology Department
London School of Economics

References

Duncan, David Ewing. 1998. *The Calendar: The 5,000-Year Struggle to Align the Clock and the Heavens — and What Happened to the Missing Ten Days*. London: Fourth Estate.

Laclau, Ernesto. 1996. "Universalism, Particularism, and the Question of Identity." In *The Identity in Question*, ed. John Rajchman, 176–89. New York: Routledge.

Norval, Aletta. 1994. "Social Ambiguity and the Logics of Apartheid Discourse." In *The Making of Political Identities*, ed. Ernesto Laclau, 51–62. London: Verso.

Salecl, Renata. 1998. *(Per)versions of Love and Hate*. London: Verso.

Beth E. Richie

A Black Feminist Reflection on the Antiviolence Movement

For the feminist-based antiviolence movement in the United States, the new millennium marks the beginning of an interesting third decade that poses particular challenges and concerns for Black feminist activists and our work to end violence against women. The mainstream social movement, organized over twenty years ago in response to an emerging consciousness that regarded gender violence as the most extreme point along the continuum of women's oppression, can claim numerous victories, such as legal reforms that protect the rights of battered women and sexual assault survivors, the criminalization of sexual harassment, and legislative moves to call attention to the needs of children who witness domestic violence. In addition, an elaborate apparatus of social services has been developed to provide emergency shelter, crisis intervention counseling, medical and legal advocacy, and ongoing assistance with housing, employment, and custody issues that women who experience violence need. African-American and other women of color have been at the forefront of the most radical dimensions of this work.

Services and support at the individual level have been matched with an array of academic and public policy initiatives designed to address violence against women. There are several journals dedicated to presenting new research and intervention discussions related to gender violence, and at least four university-based research centers focus on violence against women. Each year witnesses a growing number of national conferences on issues related to gender violence, which attract a range of audiences, some with more activist goals and others with more professional and bureaucratic interests. The National Institute for Justice, the Centers for Disease Control, the Departments of Housing and Urban Development and Health and Human Services, and — paradoxically — even the Department of Defense have established federal initiatives that attempt to reduce or respond to violence against women in this country. The feminist campaign at the grassroots level has influenced government and public policy to a considerable extent, which has resulted in a significant influx of public funding for victim services, law enforcement training, and prevention services. This growth, due in no small part to the grassroots activism of survivors and

[*Signs: Journal of Women in Culture and Society* 2000, vol. 25, no. 4]

other women, has deeply influenced the mainstream consciousness. Evidence of this influence appears in several recent public awareness campaigns and opinion polls that suggest that tolerance for gender-based violence has decreased significantly in the past ten years. Feminist activism has paid off; we have witnessed a considerable shift in public consciousness with regard to the problem of violence against women.

Arguably, a critical dimension of the public awareness campaign that has led to this expansion in resources for, and the credibility of, the antiviolence movement in this country is the assertion that violence against women is a common experience, that any woman or child can be the victim of gender violence. In fact, many of us who do training, public speaking, teaching, and writing on violence against women traditionally begin our presentations by saying, "It can happen to anyone." This notion has become a powerful emblem of our rhetoric and, some would argue, the basis of our mainstream success. Indeed, many people in this country finally understand that they and their children, mothers, sisters, coworkers, and neighbors can be victimized by gender violence — that it really *can* happen to anyone.

The ideas that any woman can be a battered woman and that rape is every woman's problem were part of a strategic attempt by early activists to avoid individualizing the problem of domestic and sexual violence, to focus on the social dimensions of the problem of gender violence, and to resist the stigmatization of race and class commonly associated with mainstream responses to social problems. This approach was based not only on the empirical data available at the time but also on the lived experiences of most women who — at many points in our lives — change our behavior to minimize our risk of assault. This generalized construction helped to foster an analysis of women's vulnerability as both profound and persistent, rather than as particular to any racial/ethnic community, socioeconomic position, religious group, or station in life. As a result, from college campuses to private corporations, from public housing complexes to elite suburban communities, and in all manner of religious institutions progress has been made in increasing awareness that violence against women is an important social problem that requires a broad-based social response.

And yet, as a Black feminist activist committed to ending violence against women, something seems terribly wrong with this construction at this point in time, something that leaves many African-American women and other women of color still unsafe and renders our communities for the most part disconnected from the mainstream antiviolence movement. I would even argue that the notion that every woman is at risk — one of the hallmarks of our movement's rhetorical paradigm — is in fact a dangerous one in that it has structured a national advocacy response based on a false sense of unity around the experience of gender oppression. For, as the epistemological foundation of the antiviolence movement was institutionalized, the assumption of "everywoman" fell into the vacuum created by a white feminist analysis that did not very successfully incorporate an analysis of race and class.

In the end, the assumed race and class neutrality of gender violence led to the erasure of low-income women and women of color from the dominant view. I contend that this erasure, in turn, seriously compromised the transgressive and transformative potential of the antiviolence movement's potentially radical critique of various forms of social domination. It divorced racism from sexism, for example, and invited a discourse regarding gender violence without attention to the class dimensions of patriarchy and white domination in this country.

Put another way, when the national dialogue on violence against women became legitimized and institutionalized, the notion that "It could happen to anyone" meant that "It could happen to those in power." Subsequently, the ones who mattered most in society got the most visibility and the most public sympathy; those with power are the ones whose needs are taken most seriously. When mainstream attention to the needs of victims and survivors was gradually integrated into the public realm of social service and legal protection and became visible in research studies, "everywoman" became a white middle-class woman who could turn to a private therapist, a doctor, a police officer, or a law to protect her from abuse. She consumed the greater proportion of attention in the literature, intervention strategies were based on her needs, she was featured in public awareness campaigns, and she was represented by national leaders on the issue of violence against women.

So what began as an attempt to avoid stereotyping and stigma has resulted in exactly that which was seen early in the antiviolence movement as a threat to the essential values of inclusion, equality, and antioppression work. The consequence of this paradigmatic problem is that victimization of women of color in low-income communities is invisible to the mainstream public, at best. Worse yet, when poor African-American, Latina, Native American women and other women of color are victimized, the problem is cast as something other than a case of gender violence.

Similarly, scholarship and activism around racial/ethnic and class oppression often ignores gender as an essential variable. This argument is supported by the growing body of research on women who use drugs, women in prison, women who live in dangerous low-income neighborhoods, lesbians of color, or young women who are involved with street gangs. Where women and girls are included in these studies or activist campaigns, they are seen as "special cases" within those populations rather than as women per se. Gender is not considered a central, defining part of their identity, and their experiences are subsumed by other master categories, typically race and class. They are essentially de-gendered, which renders them without access to claims of gender oppression and outside the category of individuals at risk of gender violence.

It is here, at a critical crossroads, that I ponder my work in the antiviolence movement as a Black feminist activist and academic. From here I offer critical observations and make recommendations for the future. First, it seems that to continue to ignore the race and class dimensions of gender oppression will seriously jeopardize the viability and legitimacy of the antiviolence movement in this country, a dangerous development for women of color in low-income communities, who are most likely to be in both dangerous intimate relationships and dangerous social positions. The overreliance on simplistic analyses (as in the case of "everywoman") has significant consequences for the potential for radical social change. I suggest that we revisit our analytic frame and develop a much more complex and contextualized analysis of gender violence, one rooted in an understanding of the historical and contemporary social processes that have differentially affected women of color.

I argue for a reassessment of the responses that have been central to antiviolence work—in particular, the reliance on law enforcement as the principal provider of women's safety. For over a decade, women of color in the antiviolence movement have warned against investing too heavily in arrest, detention, and prosecution as responses to violence against women. Our warnings have been ignored, and the consequences have been serious: serious for the credibility of the antiviolence movement, serious for feminist organizing by women of color, and, most important, serious for women experiencing gender violence who fall outside of the mainstream.

The concern with overreliance on law enforcement parallels a broader apprehension about the expansion of state power in the lives of poor women of color in this country. Just as the antiviolence movement is relying on legal and legislative strategies to criminalize gender violence, women in communities of color are experiencing the negative effects of conservative legislation regarding public assistance, affirmative action, and immigration. And, while the antiviolence movement is working to improve arrest policies, everyday safety in communities of color is being threatened by more aggressive policing, which has resulted in increased use of force, mass incarceration, and brutality. The conflict between the antiviolence movement's strategy and the experiences of low-income communities of color has seriously undermined our work as feminists of color fighting violence against women.

Obviously, leadership emerges as central to this dilemma. While there is a renewed call for unity and diversity from some corners of our movement, others (women of color who have dedicated years to this work) are appalled at the persistent whiteness of the nationally recognized leadership. As the bureaucratic and institutional apparatus of the antiviolence movement grows—bringing more funding, more recognition, and also more collaborations with partners who do not share our radical goals—there is little evidence of increasing racial/ethnic and class diversity. Despite some notable exceptions, the lack of women of color in leadership roles in antiviolence programs is startling and contrasts sharply with the rhetoric of inclusion, diversity, and commitment to antioppression work. While there may be structural excuses for this, the fact that so few national organizations (even feminist ones) have successfully promoted the leadership of women of color is almost a mockery of the values on which the movement was built. Given the similar invisibility of women of color as leaders in struggles for racial justice (again, with some exceptions), the situation can seem dire as we face the new millennium.

Yet, for better or worse, the solutions are not enigmatic; they exist within our core values and the principles on which the antiviolence movement was organized. Feminist women of color need to step forward as never before, reclaiming our place as leaders both in the antiviolence movement and in struggles for gender equality in our communities. The antiviolence movement needs only to acknowledge the contradictions between its rhetoric and practice and to deal honestly with the hypocrisy in its work. As members of a social justice movement committed to ending oppression, we must reconsider the complexity of rendering justice by paying attention to specific vulnerabilities of race and class. As we claim victories on some very important fronts, our understanding of gender oppression must be broadened to include state-sanctioned abuse and mistreatment of women. If we are prepared to go there, we can begin the millennium ready to face the really hard, radical work of ending violence against women—for each and any woman.

Criminal Justice Department
University of Illinois at Chicago

Michelle Fine
Lois Weis

Disappearing Acts: The State and Violence against Women in the Twentieth Century

As children we held our breath, our senses filled with the musty smells of elephants, the staccato flashes of twirling plastic flashlights, the terrors of trapeze. With mystery, moustache, and elegance, the magician waved a wand, invited a woman, usually White, seemingly working class, into a box. She disappeared or was cut in half. Applause. Our early introduction to the notion of the sponsored disappearing act.

So, too, at the end of the twentieth century, we witness poor and working-class women shoved into spaces too small for human form, no elegance, no wand. And they too disappear. Disappearing from welfare rolls, from universities, being swept off the streets. Dumped out of mental institutions and poured into prisons. We write to map the State-sponsored disappearing acts of the late twentieth century, the loss of welfare rights, higher education, and public spaces for women, as a conscience point for us to re-imagine what could be, what must be, for girls and women — poor and working class — in the twenty-first century.

A tale of research

In 1992, as we embarked on interviews for *The Unknown City* (Fine and Weis 1998), we thought we were collecting 150 oral histories of the economic, educational, and activist lives of poor and working-class men and women growing up in urban America during the 1980s and 1990s. From literacy programs, Headstart centers, church basements, and GED classes, we heard stories of physical and sexual abuse from these poor and working-class girls and women — White, African-American, and Latina, ages 23 to 35. Women reported painfully high levels of violence across groups, and yet they also narrated culturally distinct patterns of going public (or not) and seeking assistance from kin, neighbors, or the State (or not).

A full 92 percent of the White women we interviewed described experience with childhood and/or adult abuse. Almost without exception, these

[*Signs: Journal of Women in Culture and Society* 2000, vol. 25, no. 4]

women reported that they had never told anyone, never sought refuge in a shelter, never sought an order of protection, never called the police. Sixty-eight percent of the African-American women we spoke with reported experiences of domestic violence, but these women were far more likely to have told others about the abuse, fled their homes for shelter, or thrown out their abusers. They were also more likely, despite their mistrust of the police, to secure orders of protection and called the police as needed (see Richie 1996 for important analysis of these issues). While 85 percent of the Latinas reported experiences of domestic abuse, many, if not most, chose to leave their men quietly late in the evening, trying to find a safe space for themselves and their children (see Hurtado 1996; Gordon 1997; Espin 1999).

No class or cultural group of women is exempt from domestic violence. Sixty percent of women killed in the United States were killed by a husband or boyfriend; 25 percent of female psychiatric patients who attempt suicide are victims of domestic violence, and between 40 percent (Del Tufo 1995) and 63 percent (Browne 1987) of New York's homeless families include women fleeing abuse at home. Over 70 percent of women entering the New York State prison system have had a history of physical and/or sexual abuse (New York State Department of Correctional Services 1996).

The "why doesn't she just leave?" question has finally been answered: Because she is as likely, if not more likely, to endure violence or homicide should she leave. Evidence from the U.S. Department of Justice suggests that a woman may be in even greater life-threatening jeopardy once she leaves or separates from an abusive man. Cecilia Castelano reports that "almost 25 percent of the women killed by male partners were separated and divorced from the men who killed them; another 29 percent were attempting to end the relationship when they were killed" (1996, 11), and Lenore Walker reports that "in one U.S. study, 70 percent of the reported injuries from domestic violence occurred after the separation of the couple" (1999, 24).

We exit this century and enter another with violence against women smarting, bound to another form of violence. That is, State-sponsored violence by which the public sphere, the State-sponsored safety net (always frayed and inadequate), has rapidly been dismantled, first by right-wing Republicans and soon thereafter by "moderate" Democrats, as poor and working-class women and their children fall through the huge holes in the webbing. And yet today, with no public accountability, working-class and poor women (and men) have been tossed from our collective moral community, in particular by severe curtailments in their access to welfare, shelter, and higher education. These very well traveled exit ramps from domestic abuse are under intensive and deliberate destruction. These are among the most devastating State-sponsored disappearing acts of the twentieth century.

Disappearing act I: Access to welfare and higher education

With the draconian disappearance of a social safety net for women—not that a very good one ever existed—we witness a twinning of State and domestic violence against women (see Gordon's [1997] analysis of women's complex relations to the State). Women's access to sustained welfare and public higher education have narrowed to a choke. These two social projects, as we (and many others) have learned, have been, quietly and profoundly, the primary strategies by which poor and working-class women have been able to interrupt what has been perversely called the "cycle of violence."

Synchronous with the dismantling of the welfare system has been the assault on public higher education, rendering it increasingly out of reach for many poor and working-class youth and adults. This has happened at precisely the time when poor and working-class women began to enroll in public higher education at unprecedented rates, in the 1980s and 1990s. The U.S. Department of Education has documented well a substantial gender discrepancy (many higher ed policy makers are worried—where are the men?), especially within public institutions among part-time students, older students, and African-American students (*New York Times* 1998a). (When there are too many men, how many policy makers worry about where the women are?) While the percentage of White male high school graduates enrolled in college dropped from 61 percent in 1970 to 55 percent in 1986, rates for females in the same period rose from 47 to 55 percent for White women and 39 to 50 percent for African-American women. Women across racial and ethnic groups are today pursuing formal education to a far greater extent than are men (see Fine and Weis 1998).[1] And today, public university tuition has risen, financial aid has dropped, and affirmative action has been struck down in the University of California and Texas systems (with Michigan in the wings), as remediation is threatened in the City University of New York system. Workfare demands that

[1] And yet, as the *New York Times* reports, "The welfare law is too tilted toward short term work activity. . . . The current law . . . sets a cap on the percentage of the welfare population that can be enrolled in educational or vocational training at any one time. By 2000, all teen age parents pursuing high school diplomas would be counted under the educational cap, thus reducing the number of adults who can enroll in training and still receive benefits" (1998b, A18).

women work, not go to school.[2] Thus, cuts to public higher education, retreats from affirmative action, restrictions on using welfare benefits to pursue higher education, and the withdrawal of remediation services has disproportionately hit young and older women returning to college.

We are arguing that these cuts to welfare and public higher education produce, in effect, women's increased reliance on the family, compelling them to remain in violent homes, to exit or delay entry into college, and to move off welfare after only a short period of time. With a retreat in the public sphere comes not only the privatization of the economy, health care, and education but also an increasing privatization of the family.

What poor and working-class women get instead

Upon reflection, it is inaccurate to claim that the public sphere has been dismantled. It may be more appropriate to point to the fact that public commitments and expenditures have been realigned to support elite and White interests and, consequently, contain poor and working-class, and often racially oppressed, children and families in underfunded schools and neighborhoods, thereby locking most out of the academy and the "booming" economy. The swell in the public sector is in prison construction. And here, the poor and working class, men and women of color, are the primary "recipients."

If we use New York State as a case, we find troubling patterns of shifting state expenditures. From 1988 to 1998, New York State cut support for public higher education in the same proportion as it increased funding for prisons (Gangi, Schiraldi, and Ziedenberg 1999). Nationally, from 1977 to 1995, the average state increased correctional funding by two times more than funding for public colleges,[3] supporting "the prison-industrial complex" (Schlosser 1998). Since 1991, the nation's violent crime rate has decreased by 20 percent, but the number of people in prison or jail has

---

[2] A recent survey by the U.S. General Accounting Office finds a sharp drop in the percentage of welfare recipients assigned to education and training programs. In Connecticut, for instance, while 85 percent of welfare-work participants were enrolled in education/training in 1994, this figure dropped to 31.7 percent in 1997; in Maryland the figures moved from 65.1 percent to 10.5 percent; and in Wisconsin from 60.4 percent to 12.5 percent. The "welfare reform" act "allows education or vocational training to count as a work activity for only 12 months, after which the student must work 20 hours a week to continue getting benefits. For many recipients," concludes the *New York Times,* "that requirement means dropping out of school" (1998b, A18).

[3] In Texas the ratio is six to one.

risen by 50 percent. In New York State, from 1971 to 1995, the inmate population has increased almost fivefold.

In 1988 New York's public university funding was double that of the prison system. Over the past decade, New York reduced public higher education spending by 29 percent, while state corrections enjoyed a 76 percent increase. During this time period, the governor raised State University of New York (SUNY) and City University of New York (CUNY) tuition. The SUNY schools saw a drop of 10,000 in the number of enrolled students. Current SUNY annual tuition costs an average of 25 percent of White families' income and 42 percent for Black or Latino families (Gangi, Schiraldi, and Ziedenberg 1999).

As for the related growth in prison expenditures, while women constitute only a small fraction of the entire prison population, they are the fastest growing subpopulation. From 1982 to 1995, the number of women in prison in New York State increased more than 300 percent. In 1997, 65 percent of New York State's women inmates had been sentenced for possession or sale of drugs, compared to 40 percent in 1994 and 12.5 percent in 1968 ("The Mentality between Prisons and Schools" 1999; *College Bound Programs* 1997). When we recognize that most of these women are undereducated, have been exposed to domestic violence, and are mothers whose children are often assigned to foster care, this public sector realignment seems profoundly mean-spirited, shortsighted, fiscally expensive, and morally bankrupt.

Disappearing act II: Spaces to support poor and working-class girls and women

We hear from women, mostly mothers, about yet another disappearing act in poor and working-class communities that is deeply related to the retreat of the State from community life. Evaporating are the spaces—in communities and schools—for poor and working-class girls and women to come together, share stories, educate, and organize. Local library branches are shutting down; streets and parks seem increasingly unsafe or are locked; public gardens are being sold off; young women report fear about neighbors "getting into my business"; calling the cops is too risky. Even social services, child-care agencies, and local programs—once upon a time, places and people to whom a girl/woman could sometimes turn for help, assistance, guidance, advice—are now viewed by most as "untrustworthy." The women with whom we spoke explain that these agencies have been transformed from (sometimes) activist/contradictory sites into explicit (often contracted) arms of the State obliged to report abuse and neglect, requiring women to give the social security numbers of the fathers of their babies, provide documentation of citizenship, and cover up any evidence of child-rearing difficulties lest they be read as neglect (Fine and Weis 1998). With the realignment of the commitments of the State with the elite, in the name of accountability public sites of help have been appropriated into sites of surveillance.

As the State retreats in public policy and practice, we worry that social responsibilities and violence are being thrust on the bodies and souls of girls and women. As German social theorist Frigga Haug (1992) has argued, when the State withdraws from social projects of economy, community, education, and family, women are assumed to have, and often take on, responsibility for social and "personal" relations. And women live, consequently, with guilt and judgment. We witness, and have been taught by the women we interviewed, that in poor and working-class communities women have no choice but to accept responsibilities that are, at base, impossible to satisfy. They are often raising two or three generations, with little material support and much surveillance. To add to the burden, African-American and Latina women confront the daily razors of racism. All of these women live with the threat of loss of their children ever dangling, and more often than we were ready to hear, under the fist of violence at home. Stuffed into spaces of danger and threat, the women see few exits, except for spirituality.

We imagine, with great respect for and in the shadows of those women who have paid the greatest price, a restored feminist public sphere that recognizes the ravaged and intimate connections among the economy, public support for education, violence against women, and a restored welfare state. In addition to the obvious need for organizing around reproductive freedoms, health care, housing, and child care, those women remind us that a restructured economy, with strong engagement of labor, must be linked with struggles for adequate funding for urban education, re-engagement of affirmative action, and remediation in public and higher education struggles. We see that economics and education cannot be separated from struggles against violence. While crime and violence are central concerns for poor and working-class women, building more and more prisons accelerates the undermining of poor and working-class communities, imprisons women, and disrupts the lives of children who are then exported through the foster care system. Finally, welfare rights must be central to a feminist project, so that resources are available for women to provide financial respite, time out, and a violence-free zone.

Domestic violence will accompany us in the twenty-first century, as will the violence done to and within communities and the violence perpetrated on working-class and poor girls and women by the State. Here and globally. Organizing for a restored public sphere—with accessible public education, available welfare and jobs, quality child care, and Affirmative Action—must be at the heart of our next generation of feminist work. Little girls are watching and waiting.

Graduate Center
City University of New York (Fine)

Graduate School of Education
State University of New York, Buffalo (Weis)

References

Browne, Angela. 1987. *When Battered Women Kill.* New York: Free Press.

Castelano, Cecilia. 1996. "Staying Put: Why, How and to What Effect Do Some Battered Women (Re)claim Their Homes." Ph.D. diss. proposal, Environmental Psychology Program, City University of New York Graduate Center.

College Bound Programs. 1997. Bedford Hills, Wyo: Center for Redirection through Education.

Del Tufo, Alisa. 1995. *Domestic Violence for Beginners.* New York: Writers and Readers.

Espin, Oliva M. 1999. *Women Crossing Boundaries: A Psychology of Immigration and Transformations of Sexuality.* New York: Routledge.

Fine, Michelle, and Lois Weis. 1998. *The Unknown City: Lives of Poor and Working Class Young Adults.* Boston: Beacon.

Gangi, Robert, Vincent Schiraldi, and Jason Ziedenberg. 1999. *New York State of Mind? Higher Education vs. Prison Funding in the Empire State, 1988–1998.* Washington, D.C.: Justice Policy Institute; New York: Correctional Association of New York.

Gordon, Linda. 1997. "Family Violence, Feminism and Social Control." In *Gender Violence,* ed. Laura L. O'Toole and Jessica R. Schiffman, 314–30. New York: New York University Press.

Haug, Frigga. 1992. *Beyond Female Masochism: Memory, Work, and Politics.* London: Verso.

Hurtado, Aida. 1996. "Strategic Suspensions: Feminists of Color Theorize the Production of Knowledge." In *Women's Ways of Knowing Revisited,* ed. N. Goldberg, M. Belenky, B. Clinchy, and J. Tarule. New York: Basic.

"The Mentality between Prisons and Schools." 1999. *Black Issues in Higher Education,* January 7, 12–14.

New York State Department of Correctional Services. 1996. "Women under Custody." April 1. Albany, N.Y.: Department of Corrections.

New York Times. 1998a. "American Colleges Begin to Ask: Where Have All the Men Gone?" *New York Times,* December 6, A1, A38.

———. 1998b. "Reforming Welfare with Education." *New York Times,* July 31, A18.

Richie, Beth. 1996. *Compelled to Crime: The Gender Entrapment of Battered Black Women.* New York: Routledge.

Schlosser, Eric. 1998. "The Prison-Industrial Complex." *Atlantic Monthly,* December, 51–77.

Walker, Leonore. 1999. "Psychology and Domestic Violence around the World." *American Psychologist* 54(1):21–29.

Dorothy E. Smith

Schooling for Inequality

The topic of schooling as an institution productive of inequities — of gender, as well as race and class — has never been, as I believe it should be, a major issue for feminism.

For more than twenty years now I've worked in a sociology department in an institute for studies in education. In the early years of my work here, I was active with women teachers in their associations, helping to build women's organization. Yet, talking with activists in other areas, I found a profound disinterest in, a turning away from, issues concerning girls and women in the school system. Although feminism has grown and developed among educators, the inequalities produced by the school system have never become a central topic for feminist thought and debate.[1] Unlike at the university level — where members of a feminist intelligentsia are intimately involved, where much work has been done on the situation of women in academic life, where feminist pedagogy is debated, and where we have access to the rich resources of women's studies — the school system is strikingly well insulated from initiatives originating in the public discourse of the intelligentsia and strikingly effective at preventing localized grassroots initiatives from generalizing throughout. I'd like to see that change.

For me, starting from women's standpoint means that inquiry must begin in the everyday/everynight actualities of people's experience; it means problematizing the objectified institutional order of large-scale corporations, of schooling and health care, of the professions, and of the academic, cultural, and scientific discourses, including the mass media. The institutional order puts people to work in particular local settings, coordinating their work translocally, largely through the medium of texts (print or electronic). The texts integral to the social organization of the institutional order are complemented by technologies or disciplined practices that produce standardized local states of affairs or events corresponding to the standardized texts. The institutional order has in a sense extracted organization

---

[1] However, useful work has been done by organizations such as the American Association of University Women (1997).

[*Signs: Journal of Women in Culture and Society* 2000, vol. 25, no. 4]

from the direct connectedness of people's everyday/everynight activities and built specialized and differentiated relations that connect the multiple settings of people's work. It has become independent of particular individuals; individuals participate in it through the forms of agency and subjectivity that it establishes.

Postmodern theory has contributed the notion that a subject, or subject position, is constituted in discourse rather than being a property of persons. Similarly, I think of agency as constituted socially; being at work in the institutional order doesn't automatically accord agency (Smith 1998). Some years back, Marilee Reimer (1988) described the way the executive work of senior secretaries in a government office in Ontario was recognized only as *delegated* from their boss. They acted but were not agents. A worker on an assembly line in an automotive plant is governed by the operation of the line; her or his movements may be strictly prescribed. She or he has no agency in that corporation. A Hispanic man on his way to pick up his father after work is stopped and hassled by police, who find nothing incriminating but search and impound his car anyway. He is advised by a friend who is a cop to pay the fine and let it go, even though it means that he will have a record. He has no sense of himself/is not recognized as an agent within the judicial process. When I give a lecture in a large university on feminist issues, although the majority of the audience are women, my interlocutors are almost exclusively male. Patricia Hill Collins (1998, 3–4) tells of teaching a second-grade class of African-American children whose experiences were silenced by the standard curriculum. Lew Dunn, a grass roots environmental activist, describes his own lack of agency: "I was intimidated by government officials. I wouldn't challenge them. I was fearful of them, to be honest with you. I feared making a mistake, saying the wrong thing. I didn't think I knew enough to challenge them" (quoted in Szasz 1994, 95). Not everyone can take for granted the capacity of agent within the institutional order.

Teaching courses in gender equity in the classroom, I have come to think that schools are an integral part of the institutional processes for the differential allocation of agency. At the outset of this phase of the women's movement, a major emphasis was on voice, silencing, exclusion. It is still a major issue among nonwhite feminists. Way back, Mary Ellman (1968) described a distinction, which she saw as both obvious and unnoticed, between women and men in intellectual matters. A man's body (today, we would say, "a white man's body") gives credibility to his utterance, whereas a woman's takes it away. If we are puzzled by the persistence of gender and race inequality in the higher reaches of corporations, the state, and intellectual activity, we should look, I think, toward relationships and groupings formed in the school system.

Schools reproduce the social organization of inequality at multiple levels. At the level of the school system as a whole, differences of class as income level appear in the segregated private schools and colleges and in the public school system by the economic and racial character of school districts. Within the school, class, race, and gender emerge as dynamic and exclusionary groupings formative in students' identities and associations (Olsen 1997). To state it very simply, some students learn that their own voices have authority, that they count and should be heard; others learn their lack. Some learn that they belong to groups that have agency in society and that they can count on being recognized as such. This forming of groups is more than the "socialization" of individuals; these are ways of relating that are projected and perpetuated beyond school.

Research on gender and schooling shows a persistent replication of gender relations that develop over time as exclusive gender groupings marked by the privileging of male voices and male activity in the classroom, playground, sportsfield, and hallway.

One of the earliest observers of this dynamic, if not *the* earliest, is Raphaela Best, who described the formation of exclusive groups among boys who defined their masculinity and its attendant privileges as antithetical to what was attributed to girls (1983). Barrie Thorne's (1994) observations in elementary schools show similar patterns on playgrounds and in classrooms, partially overlaid by, yet powerfully present in, the order of the classroom. Myra Sadker and David Sadker (1994) explore how teachers' interactions with students in the classroom contribute actively to male dominance of classroom activity (this isn't news for feminist educators who've been talking and writing about this phenomenon for twenty years or so). Alison Lee writes of an Australian high school geography class: "The most lasting impression I have of this classroom is of boys' voices . . . of male voices physically swamping girls' . . . [the boys'] voices were often loud, the physiological difference combining with the classroom spatial arrangements and their apparent sense of freedom to produce their voices in ways which asserted their presence fairly effectively. . . . There was a marked absence of girls' voices, despite their physical presence in the room" (1996, 72–73). Psychological terminology gives us the concept of low self-esteem, said to be endemic among high school girls. Peggy Orenstein records the explanation of a girl whose story, voted the best in class, featured a boy as the central character: "It was an adventure; it wouldn't be right if you used a girl" (1994, 15). In a study that asked girls and young women to evaluate their schooling from a feminist standpoint, one young woman said, "I would have trouble asking a male classmate for . . . help [with an assignment] because I would feel, even if he wasn't judging, I would feel he was judging. I would feel judged" (the same informant described a math class in which boys held up for ridicule the test results of girls who had not done well) (Smith, McCoy, and Bourne 1995, 17).

I collect such examples as indicators of social processes that reproduce circles of exclusion from agency within the institutional order. What takes shape in school is a child's membership in a collectivity that projects her relationships with others into her adult future. Paul Willis's study (1977) of young men "learning to labour" in an English secondary school describes a dynamic interplay within the school that impels the "lads" into a future of unskilled labor. We are only just beginning to explore dynamics built into the school system that organize such exclusions. The insulation of the school system that I identified at the outset of this essay allows the institutional order to deny agency to people who do not share the interests and experiences it embeds. These school dynamics are not, of course, part of the curriculum or intended in the professional training of teachers (and, in any case, individual teachers are not as powerful within the school system as students, parents, and the media imagine). Nonetheless, such dynamics are a profound impairment of the democratic process in our societies and merit feminist attention and debate as we enter this new millennium.

Sociology Department
Ontario Institute for Studies in Education

References

American Association of University Women. 1997. *How Schools Shortchange Girls: The AAUW Report, a Study of Major Findings on Girls and Education.* New York: Marlowe.

Best, Raphaela. 1983. *We've All Got Scars: What Boys and Girls Learn in Elementary School.* Bloomington: Indiana University Press.

Collins, Patricia Hill. 1998. *Fighting Words: Black Women and the Search for Justice.* Minneapolis: University of Minnesota Press.

Ellman, Mary. 1968. *Thinking about Women.* New York: Harcourt Brace Jovanovich.

Lee, Alison. 1996. *Gender, Literacy, Curriculum: Re-writing School Geography.* London: Taylor & Francis.

Olsen, Laurie. 1997. *Made in America: Immigrant Children in Our Public Schools.* New York: New Press.

Orenstein, Peggy. 1994. *School Girls: Young Women, Self-Esteem, and the Confidence Gap.* New York: Doubleday, with the American Association of University Women.

Reimer, Marilee. 1988. "The Social Organization of the Labour Process: A Case Study of the Documentary Management of Clerical Labour in the Public Service." Ph.D. dissertation, University of Toronto.

Sadker, Myra, and David Sadker. 1994. *Failing at Fairness: How America's Schools Cheat Girls.* New York: Macmillan.

Smith, Dorothy E. 1998. *Writing the Social: Critique, Theory and Investigations.* Toronto: University of Toronto Press.

Smith, Dorothy E., Liza McCoy, and Paula Bourne. 1995. "Girls and Schooling: Their Own Critique." Gender and Schooling Papers, no. 2. Toronto: Centre for Women's Studies in Education, University of Toronto.

Szasz, Andrew. 1994. *Ecopopulism: Toxic Waste and the Movement for Environmental Justice.* Minneapolis: University of Minnesota Press.

Thorne, Barry. 1994. *Gender Play: Girls and Boys in School.* New Brunswick, N.J.: Rutgers University Press.

Willis, Paul E. 1977. *Learning to Labour: How Working Class Kids Get Working Class Jobs.* London: Saxon House.

Ruth-Ellen Boetcher Joeres

Feminism and the Word Wars

It is hard for me, when I think ahead into the new millennium, not to think back as well, to remind myself of the ideas that we as feminists have advanced concerning our ongoing determination to change and improve the circumstances of women's lives. In particular, given my location in the academy, I am concerned with the pressing need for us to transmit feminist thought by means of a language that will not impede change, that will not solidify us into the complacency and rigidity of the academic institution. By extension, of course, this is tied to what I want feminism itself to be, a movement that both emphasizes the simultaneity, complementarity, and complexity of thought and action, theory and practice, and also recognizes that if one element in each of these pairs impedes the other, it will surely block the vital and continuously urgent message that we want to get across.

What brings forth such an outburst is my increasing anger in these waning days of the twentieth century at the specter of U.S. academic feminists less and less concerned with the importance of communicating not only with each other but with nonacademic feminists outside the academy and outside the United States. I spend much of my time either reading and writing or talking about words. And from that perspective, I am baffled at what I view as one of the disadvantages of having the feminist movement institutionalized in the academy—namely, its apparent need to adopt one of the worst characteristics of that institution, its separating, alienating, exclusive, and, to my mind, often ugly and off-putting language.

Perhaps I am just mourning what I sense is the end of feminist activism, at least among that large group of feminists who now reside behind the walls of the university. Perhaps I am just distressed at feminist academic prose that, to my mind, opposes action rather than inspiring or initiating it, that turns off prospective readers who might even agree with what is being said if they could just understand it. Perhaps my distress has to do

I want to thank Pamela Mittlefehldt and Susanna Ferlito for helpful comments on an earlier draft of this piece.

with the frustration I feel not only at no longer comprehending so much of the obfuscatory feminist academic prose I read but also at what feels like the willful misunderstanding and misreading of objections to such prose. It is quite common now to be labeled anti-intellectual and politically conservative by other feminist academics when one expresses disapproval of irritatingly obscure academic prose or of the implied idea that progress must somehow be marked by incomprehensibility. It is also alarming to find oneself in the situation of having feminist colleagues who otherwise share a love of words see terms such as *displeasure* or *ugliness* as "subjective" — and therefore invalid? — responses to such prose. And it is perhaps most distressing of all to see feminist graduate students feeling a need to imitate such dense language to assert their authority, belonging, and worth.

This is not a new worry of mine — I had it long before I wrote a *Signs* editorial on the subject in 1992. I have long been occupied with the phenomenon of the institutionalization of feminism in the academy, seeing the great benefits of the changes it has brought to the academic world, repeatedly pointing out to the cultural studies people, the New Historians, and even the postmodernists how much they all owe to feminist thought. I am a feminist thinker myself; I enjoy that large portion of my life that I spend reading and then writing about what I am thinking. I am also a great believer in the need for precision in language — the generalities of theory must, in fact, be circumscribed by the exactness of its discourse. I am also clear about the differences between academic and nonacademic writing; I know there is such an entity as an educated public that might be interested in what I am writing — as opposed to some other entity that will not. I believe in the wonderful ability of language to change and to transform itself, in the possibilities for new words, new concepts, new forms of verbal expression.

But what has happened to the goal of broad-based communication with one another that feminists both inside and outside the academy have always claimed to share? Why, in contrast to the current touting of such ideas as the public intellectual and the need for communication with broader audiences, does academic feminist language seem in some ways to be becoming even more obscure, more removed from the rest of the world? My local feminist bookstore, for example, long a place that has stocked every sort of feminist book ranging from the most activist to the most obscure, has decided no longer to carry feminist literary criticism because the store owners claim that there is little if any general interest in books written in a language that seems so determinedly arcane and inaccessible. Why is the gap between the closed-off world of the academy and the rest of the world so pronounced — and for me so painful — when the language of academic feminism is the issue?

I regret this ever more prevalent feminist academic language and its defenders. I am distressed because, as we move into the next century, I see feminism as increasingly relegated to the academy by dint of its inability — and perhaps its lack of desire — to connect meaningfully and usefully with the very world of women of which it is a part and with which it has always claimed such solidarity. What drew me to feminist inquiry in the first place was my sense of its difference, of its acknowledged political biases, of its desire to change the way the academy works by challenging all those concepts, such as objectivity, behind which academics have traditionally hidden themselves. Within an amazingly short time, I witnessed the marvelous effects on curricula, pedagogy, and indeed on other theories and methodologies of those galvanizing, energizing forces that feminism brought into the university. I began to see — and still do see — the great possibilities of new alignments: how the feminist insistence on breaking down disciplinary borders could create new, more open, more radical structures within that staid institution. In fact, interdisciplinarity has taken great leaps forward thanks to feminist work and the existence of women's studies departments and research centers that, by their very nature, create intellectual and practical alliances hitherto untried.

But how can interdisciplinary pursuits be undertaken without the facilitating use of a language that can be understood across borders? If my take on the growing incomprehensibility of feminist academic language is correct, soon we will all return to our own disciplinary cubbyholes — even if one of those cubbyholes is a newer discipline called women's studies — and form our in-groups and not communicate with each other anymore. I won't even bother to mention the world outside the academy, for in this dystopian scenario, feminism will be a divided thing, echoing that traditional understanding of two distinct spheres, the town and the gown. And that makes me disheartened and dismayed.

If we do not enter into the new century with a sense of alarm about these developments, then my gloomy prediction is that we academic feminists will soon be indistinguishable from the rest of the academy, just a newer tool of an entrenched and unchanging power structure. We will gain, of course, on one level: we will continue to receive tenure and promotion and approval from those in the institution who still hold the power and who tend, on any other level, to view us and our feminist beliefs with alarm. But at the same time, we will lose our uniqueness both within and outside the university, for from the perspective of the nonacademic world we will just increasingly be grouped with that amorphous structure called the academy: a place where privileged people gather to talk to one another in languages that are neither accessible nor indeed interesting to anyone else. The vital links between the academy and the activist world that feminism has, in fact, been marvelously effective at bringing about will break, and that loss seems to me to be massive, alarming, enormously regrettable, and entirely unnecessary. Clarity of thought and language should by all rights lead to clarity of action, and vice versa. Theory and practice should by all rights be dependent on and inextricably bound to one another. Beauty, passion, and effectiveness should not be restricted to one or the other realm. This chasm should not even exist.

The way we write and communicate with each other can go a long way toward bridging that chasm. We cannot all be activists in any standard sense of that word, but we can be actively and consciously alert and open to each other in how we transmit our ideas, whether we are academics or not. That is perhaps the best way for me to express the vision and the hope I have for the future development of feminist scholarship.

German, Scandinavian, and Dutch Department
University of Minnesota

References

Joeres, Ruth-Ellen Boetcher. 1992. "Editorial: On Writing Feminist Academic Prose." *Signs: Journal of Women in Culture and Society* 17(4):701–4.

Catherine Belsey

Writing as a Feminist

I was never entirely comfortable with *écriture féminine,* that impressionistic, sometimes breathless, commonly lyrical, often rhapsodic *expression* of women's difference. In an essay first published more than twenty years ago now, Mary Jacobus brilliantly indicated the limitations of an outright refusal of the prevailing conventions of rational prose: to repudiate in writing the values of coherence, logic, and argument risks confirming precisely the patriarchal assumptions it is designed to challenge, reasserting the feminine as irrational, intuitive, and intense (Jacobus 1979, 10–21). My unease marks a fear of relegating women all over again to a margin whose last resort is madness, in a prose style that may be feminine but is not thereby automatically feminist.

But "ease," you might well reply, is exactly what *écriture féminine* is designed not to offer. Its project is to surprise, arrest, shock us into awareness both of our difference and of the coerciveness of masculinist rhetorical codes in constructing a position of imperturbable mastery for the writer and, for the reader, a place of inevitable submission to the case presented. The conventions of rational prose are designed to reveal and explain what is made by those conventions themselves to appear irresistibly and, in the end, self-evidently true. But every unveiling of the truth is what Roland Barthes calls "a staging of the (absent, hidden, or hypostatized) father" (1976, 10), where the father is precisely the representative of authority but is hardly sympathetic to feminism. Transparency, lucidity, obviousness: the well-formed argument may elicit recognition and agreement, but these states of mind are relaxed, pacified. "The case has been made well," a reader might feel; "I cannot but go along with it, and what, after all, can I contribute that has not already been said?" Feminism, meanwhile, is a politics, and its advance requires from its adherents not passive agreement but active intervention. As thirty years of work in the current wave of feminism have so clearly demonstrated, the price of progress is eternal agitation. Until the last trace of oppression is removed, we cannot afford relaxation and passivity.

What Jacobus urges in that now classic essay (which is primarily about feminist reading practices) is not that feminists conform to existing

[*Signs: Journal of Women in Culture and Society* 2000, vol. 25, no. 4]

conventions not of our making but that we recognize the possibility of inhabiting them *otherwise* — in a way that demonstrates a difference of view. The issue that concerns me now is not whether women do as a matter of course write differently but whether feminists as a matter of strategy ought to do so. Feminists need, in my view, to write in a way that will coax the reader to sit up and think because, as readers, only what we have thought through for ourselves prompts us to active intervention in the world beyond the study. Agreement is not enough. In the twentieth century, women novelists from Virginia Woolf to Toni Morrison restlessly and brilliantly experimented with form, genre, modes of address, styles, but only in rare instances does academic writing, however fluent, however elegant, challenge the structural regularities of first-year composition. Could we, I wonder, devise for the new millennium some proposals, however tentative, about how feminist academic writing might challenge, stimulate, and promote the reader's production of ideas she makes her own?

The question treats academic prose as a sustained performance, asking of a specific essay not what it says or means but what it *does* — or sets out to do, since no text can compel its own reading. And the project, it seems to me, is to enlist the reader in dialogue. While universities pay lip service to academic "exchange," the main counter in their economy is still the monologue in its various manifestations: the lecture, the conference paper, the "talk." Virginia Woolf herself, who deplored lectures on the grounds that the printing press had made them obsolete (1978, 5), also pointed out acerbically that it was men who tended to write soliloquies: "The garrulous sex, against common repute, is not the female but the male; in all the libraries of the world the man is to be heard talking to himself and for the most part about himself" (1979, 65). Feminists have not been guilty of that, but while progressive teachers recognize the element of self-education that genuine exchange promotes in the classroom, might we not give some thought to the possibility of a form of writing that resembles or incites dialogue?

But how? It would clearly be contrary to my project to produce a checklist of appropriate devices. Bertolt Brecht, as a left-wing dramatist, raised a similar question and answered it by putting on display contradictions of form as well as content. Brecht's theatrical alienation devices, his on-stage placards and banners, and his direct challenges to the audience to reflect on the problems set up by the play are all designed to discourage that absorption in plot that celebrates the unresolved as "tragic." There is something to be learned here, as there is from Julia Kristeva's account of the revolutionary effect of "semiotic" invasions of rhythmic non-sense into the narrative and moral propositions of "thetic" poetry (1984). But there are differences of genre, too: an academic essay is not a play or a poem, and it deserves its own repertoire of radicalizing gestures.

Dialogue makes space for an interlocutor, where monologue is unremitting. How can writing reproduce this inclusive gesture? Not, I think, by the false coziness of a scattering of first-person plurals, the surreptitiously coercive "we shall see," "we shall discuss." Such formulations offer no real options; the "discussion" is in practice one-sided; "either join me," it seems to say, "or read something else." By contrast, feminists want readers to look up occasionally from the text, not to read another necessarily, but to reflect, compare, differ—in a word, to consider. Discontinuity helps here. Where the rules prescribe seamless transitions, might we not make the stitching visible, and thereby problematic? Moves from the personal to impersonality change the frame and alter perspective. Variations of register—from theory to anecdote, from polemic to playfulness, even in academic prose— can position the reader as active interpreter, offering at best a plurality of readings, a range of possible connections. Such shifts punctuate the text, make breaks for intervention.

Meanwhile, we should not, in my view, be afraid of difficulty. Representation (or presentation, since propositions cannot be said to exist independent of their formulation) is a problem, since there is so commonly an excess—of the signifier over intention, of meaning over vocabulary. No proposition is quintessentially more difficult than any other: ideas are hard to the degree that they are unfamiliar. An easy read probably does not say anything new. We might, in our presentation, want to exploit now and then the resources of language, its wordplay and undecidability, to indicate both the complexity of what we propose and the tug of signifying practice itself on the will to clarity.

And questions. Do they all need answers? The conventions require us to resolve the enigmas we expose, and so, perhaps, in most cases we should. But does not a residual riddle offer to puzzle the reader into renewed thought?

If questions are important, the ultimate enemy of dialogue is surely closure. To have the last word is a pressing object of desire, for academics as much as for others, and perhaps more. But it pulls against the feminist project I am putting forward here of enlisting the reader in continuing debate, since by definition it ends, at least for the moment, all discussion.

These signifying moves are all, I ought to stress, occasional, contextual, incidental—deviations from a conventional norm, not its replacement. And their common ground is surely absence—of consistency, grand simplicities, answers, and closure—appropriately enough, perhaps, from a psychoanalytic point of view, since psychoanalysis has conventionally coupled woman with absence. In Freud's account this absence was also a deficiency—of the penis and, correspondingly, of the superego, ethical sense, rationality, judgment.[1] But Freud was himself committed to mastery, the unveiling of a truth, even though his footnotes so commonly undermine this project, taking back with one hand what is given so copiously in the text with the other. In its later incarnation, however, psychoanalysis is a good deal less absolute. For Jacques Lacan, absence is the only possible condition, since no one possesses the Lacanian phallus, and this shared lack is the cause of desire.[2]

Would not these occasional absences in the text, mastery proffered and then withheld, truth glimpsed and yet elusive, make of feminist writing an object of desire, both as text and as politics?

Centre for Critical and Cultural Theory
Cardiff University

References

Barthes, Roland. 1976. *The Pleasure of the Text.* Trans. Richard Miller. London: Cape.

Freud, Sigmund. 1977. "Some Psychical Consequences of the Anatomical Distinction between the Sexes." In his *On Sexuality,* ed. Angela Richards, 323–43. London: Penguin.

Jacobus, Mary. 1979. "The Difference of View." In *Women Writing and Writing about Women,* ed. Mary Jacobus, 10–21. London: Croom Helm; New York: Harper & Row.

Kristeva, Julia. 1984. *Revolution in Poetic Language.* Trans. Margaret Waller. New York: Columbia University Press.

Lacan, Jacques. 1985. "The Meaning of the Phallus." In *Feminine Sexuality: Jacques Lacan and the Ecole Freudienne,* ed. Juliet Mitchell and Jacqueline Rose, 74–85. London: Penguin; New York: Norton.

Woolf, Virginia. 1978. *The Pargiters: The Novel-Essay Portion of The Years.* Ed. Mitchell A. Leaska. London: Hogarth.

———. 1979. *Virginia Woolf: Women and Writing.* Ed. Michèle Barrett. London: Women's Press.

[1] For what must be his most extravagant account of this view, see Freud 1977.

[2] The theme is pervasive in Lacan's work, but for a commonly invoked (and reviled) instance, see Lacan 1985.

Feminism's Perverse Effects

The title both registers my anxiety about the directions in which the fields of literary, cultural, ethnic, and women's studies have moved in the past ten years and suggests what I think we may have lost by following certain discursive directions proposed by "feminism" and rejecting others. I am myself a member of the executive committee in one department, French and Italian, and in two multidisciplinary programs, women's studies and Jewish studies, at the University of Wisconsin–Madison, and I have had a variety of experiences both in shaping the curriculum and in teaching undergraduate and graduate students during a period of sometimes intense debate about what it is we should be doing when we teach literature, culture, and language. I do not pretend to be objective in my evaluations, and, as in all writing, there will undoubtedly be "blind spots" in my arguments and even in my examples.

During the past four years I have begun each of my courses, whether graduate seminars in French, undergraduate and graduate classes in women's studies, or courses in literature in translation, with introductory comments to the students about my own unresolved questions. I warn them of my growing dissatisfaction with identity politics and studies, with the exaggerated emphasis on difference and inattention to commonalities, and with the separation into two opposing camps of cultural studies and literary studies, which mirrors a more troubling separation of the political and the poetic. If I were teaching language courses, I would add to this list the equally troubling separation of language and literature in our curriculum and in the pedagogical training of our students.

I was beginning to feel isolated in women's studies and fearful of being perceived in both women's studies and French and Italian as a closet conservative and a traitor to my own pronouncements of the 1980s. And then, within the past year and a half, I discovered that I am not alone. Among those colleagues whose progressive positions I had always felt to be close to my own (e.g., Biddy Martin, Richard Rorty), as well as among those whom I had regarded at a distance as politically incorrect (Robert Alter

[*Signs: Journal of Women in Culture and Society* 2000, vol. 25, no. 4]

and Harold Bloom), similar unresolved questions were being raised. Each one, in his or her own way, has deplored the reading of literature uniquely for signs of racism, sexism, anti-Semitism, uniquely as a document that reveals underlying discursive and cultural assumptions and presuppositions. As a student and teacher primarily of French language, literature, and culture, I have become increasingly hostile to readings of French literary texts whose unique goal seems to be to portray the French nation and French culture as villains whose main products for domestic and global consumption are sexism, racism, and anti-Semitism.

The January 1997 issue of *PMLA,* the journal of the Modern Language Association (MLA), is devoted to the teaching of literature. In her introductory essay, "Teaching Literature, Changing Cultures," Biddy Martin, the issue's editor, writes,

> Why devote a special issue to the teaching of literature? Why literature? Why now? The topic may strike readers as timely or outmoded, neutral or polemical, depending on their positions in the contentious debates over the status of literature and its relation to culture. I take a broad view of what literature entails, but the current shifting of literature departments in North American institutions to cultural studies makes me worry about the fate of reading practices that the term *literature* invites, permits or requires, the fate of reading that suspends the demand for immediate intelligibility, works at the boundary of meaning and yields to the effects of language and imagination. (8)

Similarly, in a "Point of View" column in the February 9, 1996, issue of the *Chronicle of Higher Education,* Richard Rorty writes,

> Academic disciplines are subject to being overtaken by attacks of "knowingness" — a state of mind and soul that prevents shudders of awe and makes one immune to enthusiasm. This may have happened to the teachers of literature in American colleges and universities who make up what the literary critic Harold Bloom has called "the School of Resentment." These teachers are proceeding along the same path that led philosophers, a few decades ago, to abandon inspiration for professionalism.

Harold Bloom, in his 1994 *The Western Canon,* sees his colleagues who pursue "cultural studies" converting the study of literature into "one more dismal social science" — thereby turning departments of literature into dried-up academic backwaters. As he sees it, these teachers substitute resentment over societal failures for utopian vision. (A48)

It is no simple matter, in this millennial fin de siècle, to criticize certain tendencies in cultural studies or women's studies or ethnic studies without being accused of participating in a conservative political agenda.

In 1994, when Bloom's controversial book appeared, I was shocked to discover how closely I had moved to positions from which I could have been expected (because of my long-standing affiliation with women's studies and the feminist inquiry) to be very far removed. Although Bloom's lists of canonical books were not the same as mine, in his opening chapter, "An Elegy for the Canon," he makes a case for the role of imaginative literature's place within the humanities curriculum that I can only applaud:

> Whatever the Western canon is, it is not a program for social salvation. . . . The West's greatest writers are subversive of all values, both ours and their own. Scholars who urge us to find the source of our morality and our politics in Plato, or in Isaiah, are out of touch with the social reality in which we live. If we read the Western Canon in order to form our social, political, or personal moral values, I firmly believe we will become monsters of selfishness and exploitation. To read in the service of any ideology is not, in my judgment, to read at all. The reception of aesthetic power enables us to learn how to talk to ourselves and how to endure ourselves. The true use of Shakespeare or of Cervantes, of Homer or of Dante, of Chaucer, or of Rabelais, is to augment one's own growing inner self. Reading deeply in the Canon will not make one a better or a worse person, a more useful or more harmful citizen. The mind's dialogue with itself is not primarily a social reality. All that the Western Canon can bring one is the proper use of one's own solitude, that solitude whose final form is one's confrontation with one's own mortality. (28)

The Association of Literary Scholars and Critics was formed four years ago in response to what many of its adherents felt was the politicization of literary studies in North America and particularly in the major organization for scholars and critics in North America, the MLA. Like many other active members of the MLA, I initially considered the Association of Literary Scholars and Critics to be composed mainly of reactionary scholars and teachers opposed to the opening of the canon and to many of the new approaches to literary texts that came to the United States from the European continent and Great Britain. The Association of Literary Scholars and Critics, as I understood its mission four years ago, wanted to take literary studies back to a precritical, pretheoretical moment in which the masterpieces of the Western literary tradition were transparent, and men and women, particularly men of good breeding and common sense, could discuss them among themselves in mutually satisfying ways without the noise provided by theory and noncanonical texts.

Imagine my surprise, then, upon reading the presidential address delivered by Robert Alter in November of 1997 to the Association of Literary Scholars and Critics and published in its entirety in the *Times Literary Supplement* on January 23, 1998. The title of the address, "The Recovery of Open-Mindedness and the Revival of the Literary Imagination," does suggest a nostalgic return to some golden age, a typical gesture of the ideological right. However, the essay's focus on "the literary imagination" also echoes the emphases of Biddy Martin, Richard Rorty, and Harold Bloom and has the distinction of providing excellent examples from three very different texts: the David story in Samuel 1 and 2 of the Jewish Bible; *The Red and the Black* by Stendhal; and *Ulysses* by James Joyce.

The examples are preceded by Alter's attempt to define the literary imagination, which,

> to borrow a formulation from the Frankfurt School critic, Leo Lowenthal, is essentially "dialectic", dedicated to articulating critical challenges to, or subtle subversions of, regnant ideologies, received ideas and antecedent literary conventions and values. Great literary works thus will repeatedly surprise us — that is precisely the source of pleasure and instruction in reading them — as long as we do not insist on contorting them to fit the Procrustean bed of our own preconceptions. When we as an association proclaim that we honour the power of the literary imagination, that does not involve any mystification but, on the contrary, an empirical openness to the unanticipated ways in which an original writer, warts and all, can offer an odd and illuminating perspective on familiar topics, overturn bland assumptions, or startlingly recast the very instruments of literary expression. (15)

In each of the three examples, Alter points out how "the unpredictability of the literary imagination" surprises and subverts readers' expectations.

I would like now to give an example of my own. It comes from a classroom experience in which both my choice of certain texts and the manner of reading them were vigorously contested by a group of students. The text was *Dust Tracks on a Road* ([1942] 1991) by Zora Neale Hurston, assigned in a women's studies course called "Writing Women's Li(v)es." What seemed to disturb the hostile students was that Hurston's narrative did not focus sufficiently on what the students expected to read: the unrelieved story of Hurston's oppression as a black woman growing up in the South in the late nineteenth and early twentieth centuries. The class was composed entirely of women, and all of those who were angry with Hurston (and me) were white.

These angry students did not react with "surprise" at the discrepancy between their expectations and the words of the text but rather with hostility, in part because, through no fault of their own, they have had little or no training in the reading of a literary text. Like most readers, they tend to read uniquely for information, for historical or psychological "realism." Although the first text we had read together in that course was Nelly Furman's superb 1980 essay "Textual Feminism," which insists on the importance of words, language, and the signifier and attempts to show that literature has functions other than the referential, their habits of reading were not easily challenged. Indeed, these habits are often supported by ideological positions that students, in some of their classes, are taught to look for in all the texts they read. If the students do not find evidence of racism, sexism, or anti-Semitism, they tend to assume that either the writer or the teacher is guilty of a cover-up.

The other major reason many students have difficulty reading literary texts is that, because they are not omnivorous readers, they do not hear echoes of earlier texts in the texts they read; they do not know the pleasures of intertextuality. Those of us who teach literature have for some time noted the decline in our students' ability to recognize mythological or biblical references. This now extends to references, explicit or implicit, to much of the canon of Western literature. For several years, when this topic was raised by colleagues, I responded that although our students did not have a literary culture, they had other kinds of culture, ones that we did not necessarily have. I no longer feel comfortable with this response.

In the case of *Dust Tracks on a Road,* it was impossible for some of the students to imagine that an African-American woman writer might equate telling folktales and lying, might play frequently with signifiers, as in the story "Git back/Git black" (50), told by a female character called Gold, about how the races were given color, or might use pejorative words ironically, in a particular context, when naming African Americans. In a sense, the students were denying Hurston the right to write in a certain style, the right to write against the doxa and the discourse of her time and place. They could read *Dust Tracks on a Road* only in terms of racism and sexism. And because they could not find in it what they were looking for, they denied themselves the pleasures of discovering a new and different text, another mode of writing and reading.

These are some of what I consider to be the perverse effects of and caveats for feminism at the millennium.

French and Italian Department and Women's Studies Program
University of Wisconsin — Madison

References

Alter, Robert. 1998. "The Recovery of Open-Mindedness and the Revival of the Literary Imagination." *Times Literary Supplement,* January 23, 15–16.

Bloom, Harold. 1994. *The Western Canon.* New York: Riverhead.

Furman, Nelly. 1980. "Textual Feminism." In *Women and Language in Literature and Society,* ed. Sally McConnell-Ginet, Ruth Borker, and Nelly Furman, 45–54. New York: Praeger.

Hurston, Zora Neale. (1942) 1991. *Dust Tracks on a Road.* New York: Harper Perennial.

Martin, Biddy. 1997. "Teaching Literature, Teaching Culture." *PMLA* 112(1):7–25.

Rorty, Richard. 1996. "Point of View." *Chronicle of Higher Education,* February 9, A48.

Sydney Janet Kaplan

On Reaching the Year 2000

We live in a culture obsessed with the activity of "taking stock." Every year the newspapers produce their usual collection of articles attempting to assess the meaning of the events we have just gone through. Every decade, more self-important articles appear affixing labels to the past ten years and complacently declaring how we have overcome the delusions of the "sixties" or the "eighties." I fear that whole libraries will need to be built to contain the thousands of such written accounts accompanying our entry into the twenty-first century, and I am a bit embarrassed to find myself contributing to that effort. Especially since this is the third time that I have approached a similar retrospective look at the state of feminist literary criticism, the first time for *Signs* in 1979 and the second for the anthology *Making a Difference* in 1985.

Twenty years ago when I was asked to review the work on women's studies in literature that had appeared since Cheri Register's review in 1977 (Elaine Showalter wrote the first one in 1975), I spent the summer reading nearly everything in the field. It is amazing to me now to remember that it was possible *ever* to read "nearly everything" on any subject in feminist criticism. If I tried to do that now, it might take me a lifetime. But it had also once been possible for me to read nearly everything that had been written in English (including book reviews) on Virginia Woolf, when I wrote my dissertation chapter on her back in 1969–70. The last time I checked, there were more than two thousand items listed in the Modern Language Association bibliography on Woolf (not counting the rapidly burgeoning collection of material on the Internet). In 1938, Dorothy Richardson described her struggle to invent a feminist approach to writing as a "lonely track" that "had turned out to be a populous highway" ([1938] 1967, 10), and the description aptly fits what has happened with feminist literary criticism and theory. I even wonder if the increasing preference for theory among graduate students — frequently attributed to the higher status theory seems to hold in the academy — has also to do with their recognition of the impossibility of controlling the masses of information now available on any literary subject. Theory provides ways of both selecting

[*Signs: Journal of Women in Culture and Society* 2000, vol. 25, no. 4]

and, perhaps more significantly, excluding what we now call "information overload."

When I began graduate school in 1964, there was no "feminist criticism" in literary studies; or, let us say, the field had not yet been so defined. Only a few months earlier I had read Betty Friedan's *The Feminine Mystique,* which had both excited and unnerved me. It led me to decide to attempt graduate work instead of devolving into the type of underachieving educated woman she described in her book. My impetus to study literature, then, was from the beginning motivated by a feminist impulse, but there was little to nourish it in the academic world I had just entered. I desperately needed a method of study that might help me to shape my life and extricate it from the control of the patriarchal forces I confronted both at home and in the university. I quickly discovered that I could explore the issues that many of my contemporaries were approaching through consciousness-raising by transferring the formalist methods I was learning in class to texts that had personal meaning for me — texts by women writers. Yet I should emphasize that this early work, contrary to some of the myths about the evolution of feminist criticism, neither focused on a critique of male writing nor was part of the "images of women" genre. It was *already* concerned with the intersections of literary form and the structure of gender relations — with how literary conventions embodied societal values and unconscious levels of ideology; in other words, it was, from the outset, a cultural critique.

That I was becoming a feminist critic was something I did not realize in 1964. Since there was no established body of feminist literary theory available — aside from Woolf's *A Room of One's Own,* of course, and perhaps the literary sections of Simone de Beauvoir's *The Second Sex* — I needed to build it as I wrote. My theoretical positions grew out of the novels I read for my dissertation (which formed the basis for my first book, *Feminine Consciousness in the Modern British Novel* [1975]). The authors of these novels — Dorothy Richardson, May Sinclair, Virginia Woolf, Rosamond Lehmann, and Doris Lessing — took the place for me of feminist professors (with whom I had no acquaintance): especially Richardson, with her insistence on gender differences in perception and modes of creativity, and Woolf, with her analysis of the "feminine" sentence and her subtle linking of questions of structure with questions of gender. By focusing on modernist writing, in which women's struggles for autonomy were inextricably connected to the creation of new formal structures, I found an immediate entry into the gender politics of literary study.

My sense of discovery during this process was exciting and invigorating, and it merged with the mood of optimism and change that feminism was producing throughout society at large during the second half of the 1960s. In looking back, I realize that I have spent my entire academic career as a feminist. Unlike many of my colleagues who "discovered" feminism after they had made their careers writing books that satisfied patriarchal standards for "serious" scholarship, my work from the very beginning was focused on women, although it was not always easy to be at home in the university. (I nearly was denied tenure, for one thing.) But my involvement in women studies prevented me from experiencing the kind of personal alienation that afflicts scholars who separate completely the one who writes from the one who feels.

In my second attempt at a retrospective analysis of feminist criticism in 1985, I identified the initiating impulses of feminist criticism as the passions of love and anger. Anger there still is in plenty, especially in reaction to the retrogressive politics of the past two decades and our recognition that women are in danger of losing many of the gains we have made, and such anger continues to fuel brilliant forays into cultural politics. But the passion I identified with "love" — love for the writing of women — may have become somewhat disreputable in the academy. It is assaulted by friends and foes alike: for not being theoretical enough, for falling into "essentialism," for participating in "identity politics," and for not recognizing the "death of the author." Nevertheless, for those of us who have not been bowled over by "theory" and have continued to let our own personal issues point the way, it is still the motivating force in our study of literature.

Following that personal trajectory, many of the most rewarding works of feminist scholarship have been those exploring relationships between women, and, obviously, many of these have grown out of "love" for the writing of women and for women themselves. This is true also of the many engaging and provocative studies of mothers and daughters and attempts to theorize the maternal. What I see as a possible next area of feminist inquiry is similarly linked with the personal. It has to do with the relations between mothers and sons. I am definitely *not* referring to those prefeminist paeans to mothers as inspirations for men's achievements. Instead, now that we have reached a point where so many women have achieved success on their own, it might be time to consider as subjects of inquiry our "sons" — literally and also by proxy in the form of our male students. The possibilities among the various disciplines are manifold. In my own field of literary criticism, I can imagine a few questions to begin the process: How do women writers influence men? How do the male children of women writers respond to the challenge of their mother's success? (How many students of literature remember that T. S. Eliot's mother was herself a recognized poet?) What are the new "anxieties of influence" that afflict male writers who have great women for their forebears? (Take, e.g., Michael Cunningham's novel, *The Hours,* which takes Virginia Woolf's *Mrs. Dalloway* as its point of departure.) How does the scholarship of our male students further the goals of feminism?

It should be clear by now that the questions I pose reflect my bias for a kind of feminist criticism that has become unfashionable in the academy. But I believe that if feminist criticism is to continue to matter in the new century, it must be grounded in the real life experiences of human beings. It should not break its connections with those intense and powerful longings for a better world that brought it into existence.

English and Women Studies Departments
University of Washington

References

Kaplan, Sydney Janet. 1975. *Feminine Consciousness in the Modern British Novel.* Urbana: University of Illinois Press.

———. 1979. "Literary Criticism." *Signs: Journal of Women in Culture and Society* 4(3):514–27.

———. 1985. "Varieties of Feminist Criticism." In *Making a Difference: Feminist Literary Criticism,* ed. Gayle Greene and Coppelia Kahn, 37–58. London: Methuen.

Richardson, Dorothy M. (1938) 1967. *Pilgrimage.* Vol. 1. London: J. M. Dent.

Has Feminism Changed Science?

Feminism has brought some remarkable changes to science. Who could have predicted just a decade ago that the chief scientist at NASA would be a woman or that the president of the foremost association of Japanese physicists would be a woman? Who would have expected to see *Science*, the premier science journal in the United States, debating whether a "female style" exists in science or the famous French physicist Marie Curie, once shunned by the prestigious Parisian Académie des Sciences, exhumed and reburied in the Pantheon, the resting place of such national heroes as Voltaire, Rousseau, and Hugo?

The current "science wars," as the unfortunate tussles between scientists and their critics are called, offer a certain measure of the successes of feminism in science. I was shocked to read in Paul Gross and Norman Levitt's *Higher Superstition* that "the only widespread, *obvious* discrimination today is against white males" (1994, 110), but I was more surprised by the depth of our agreement. Feminists and some of our most vocal opponents now agree that women should have a fair chance at careers, inside and outside academia. We agree that the "record of science, until recently, is — in its social aspect — tarnished by gender-based exclusions." We agree further that "baseless paradigms" in medicine and the behavioral sciences have been pretexts for subordinating women. "All this," Gross and Levitt claim, "is beyond dispute and generally recognized" (110). From a historical point of view, this depth of agreement marks an extraordinary change for women, who were admitted to American and European universities only about a century ago, to graduate programs even more recently, and who were told as late as 1950 that women simply need not apply for professorships in biochemistry. By this measure, we have all become feminists.

One area of disagreement remains, however, and here Gross and Levitt speak for many in proclaiming that "there are as yet no examples" of feminists uncovering sexism in the substance of science — as opposed to women

This essay draws from material in my book of the same title (Schiebinger 1999). I wish to thank the National Science Foundation and Pennsylvania State University for research support.

merely being excluded from this or that area of inquiry. More than a decade ago when I wrote a review essay on gender and science for *Signs,* one of my purposes was to highlight feminist critiques that revealed "gender distortions" in science (Schiebinger 1987). Providing concrete examples of the multifarious ways that regimes of inequality produced and reproduced gender in the substance of science was an important project in 1987. Today, I want to highlight a different question: Has feminism changed science? After being in business for nearly two decades, what new insights, directions, and priorities have feminists—men or women—brought to the sciences?

Let me offer the examples of two sciences in which gender studies have made deep and lasting impressions: medicine and primatology. The late 1980s saw mainstream biomedicine's great awakening to women's health concerns. Feminists began to shower infamy upon several influential medical studies that omitted women completely—notably the 1982 "Physicians Health Study of Aspirin and Cardiovascular Disease" performed on 22,071 male physicians and 0 women and the "Multiple Risk Factor Intervention Trial" studying coronary heart disease in 15,000 men and 0 women. Even in studies where women were included, the male body typically represented the normal human; the female body has traditionally been studied as a deviation from that norm (Rosser 1994).

Beginning in the late 1980s, feminist reform in publicly funded biomedical research in the United States was pushed forward through strong measures taken by the federal government. In 1986 the National Institutes of Health (NIH) initiated a requirement that medical research include female subjects where appropriate, and in 1991 distinctively female health concerns began to be addressed by the fourteen-year $625 million Women's Health Initiative. The 1990 founding of the NIH Office of Research on Women's Health represented a triumph for feminism. Between 1990 and 1994, the U.S. Congress enacted no fewer than twenty-five pieces of legislation to improve the health of American women. While many feminists argue that these reforms in clinical and biomedical medicine have retained too narrow a focus on disease management, few deny the importance of the reforms undertaken within NIH (see Fee and Krieger 1994; Ruzek, Olesen, and Clarke 1997).

Similarly, primatology has undergone a sea change with respect to gender. The composition of the profession has changed dramatically from the 1960s, when American women received no Ph.D.s, to today, when they receive 78 percent of Ph.D.s in primatology granted each year.[1] But more

---

[1] I thank Trudy Turner and Linda Fedigan for these numbers. See also Fedigan 1994.

important have been the changes in the content of the science. In primatology, as in medicine, the majority of feminist changes to date have come from reevaluations of stereotypical attitudes toward both males and females. Only in the 1960s did primatologists begin questioning stereotypes of male aggression and dominance and begin looking seriously at female behavior. They began studying the significance of female bonding through matrilineal networks and analyzing female sexual assertiveness, female social strategies, female cognitive skills, and female competition. Today, in a turnabout from the 1960s, conventional wisdom on baboons recognizes that females provide social stability, while males move from group to group. Changes in primatology have been so foundational that at least one mainstream primatologist, Linda Fedigan (1997), has pronounced it a feminist science.

Of course, feminist interventions have not occurred uniformly across all of the sciences. A lack of gender neutrality can be documented in the social, medical, and life sciences, where research objects are sexed or easily imagined to have sex and gender. The physical sciences, however, have by and large resisted feminist analysis (for a number of historically specific reasons that I have discussed elsewhere [Schiebinger 1999]). Here I turn to a different question: In the instances where positive change in science has resulted from a critical awareness of gender, what has brought success?

There is a pressing need to dispel the myth that currently has a stranglehold on many feminists and nonfeminists alike—that is, the myth that women qua women are changing science, that women have been the primary architects of foundational disciplinary changes. The question of who or what might create beneficial change in science has been confused by Americans' distrust of feminism. For many, *feminism* is still a dirty word, even among those who support the advancement of professional careers for women. Especially within the sciences, people seem to prefer to discuss *women* rather than *feminism*. This refusal to acknowledge politics—to call a feminist a feminist—has led to a simple equating of women entering the profession with change in science. Many women scientists, however, have no desire to rock the boat, and women who consider themselves "old boys" often become the darlings of conservatives.

People often conflate the terms *women, gender, female, feminine,* and *feminist*. These terms, of course, have distinct meanings. A woman is a specific individual; *gender* denotes power relations between the sexes and includes men as much as it does women; *female* designates biological sex; *feminine* refers to idealized mannerisms and behaviors of women in a particular time and place; and *feminist* defines a political outlook or agenda. Emphasizing women as the crucial element in the process of change within the sciences overlooks the hard-won successes of twenty years of academic women's studies, the role of feminist men, and much else. Introducing new questions and directions into the natural sciences requires long years of training in a discipline, sustained attention to gender studies and feminist theory, the support of universities and agencies that provide funding for such work, the existence of departments that recognize that work as tenurable, and so forth.

There is no firm starting point — no Archimedean point — that, once established, will ensure progressive reform, unless it is a critical understanding of the problem, which is in large part already available. Feminists have tended to make a distinction between getting women into science and changing knowledge. Getting women in is generally considered the easier of the two tasks. However, both require tools of gender analysis. Both are institutional *and* intellectual problems. Bringing feminism successfully into science will require difficult battles and a complex process of political and social change. Science departments cannot solve the problems themselves because the problems are deeply cultural. That does not, however, let them off the hook. Change must occur in many areas: conceptions of knowledge and research priorities, domestic relations, attitudes in schools, university structures, classroom practices, the relationship between home life and the professions, and the relationships between different nations and cultures.

Government programs are also important supports in this ongoing process. Bernadine Healy, a former head of NIH, put it simply: "Let's face it, the way to get scientists to move into a certain area is to fund that area" (*Science* 1995, 773). In the United States, advances in women's health research have been reinforced by laws requiring that grant applications include female participants in medical research. Similar efforts could be made to foster feminism in science nationwide. In Congress, the Morella Commission has called for a full review of women in science, and a federal bill proposed in 1993 would set up a seventeen-member commission to study the problems women face entering and succeeding in technical professions. No action has yet been taken (the two bills are still in committee); nonetheless, the groundwork for action has been laid. In Europe, the European Union set up a new commission in the spring of 1998 to oversee efforts to improve the status of women in European science.

These projects marry research on women and gender to government initiatives, a kind of mission-oriented science that is well precedented. The U.S. Manhattan Project was government-directed science aimed at securing national defense, and the Apollo Program to land men on the moon, the attempt to build, launch, and operate a space station, and the costly Human Genome Project are all examples of mission-oriented government science. Governments might launch a "Feminist Science and Engineering Initiative" aimed at analyzing gender in the content of the sciences and securing equality for women in science and technical fields. Such initiatives should be collaborative efforts joining the expertise of scientists and humanists.

History Department and Women's Studies Program
Pennsylvania State University

References

Fedigan, Linda. 1994. "Science and the Successful Female: Why There Are So Many Women Primatologists." *American Anthropologist* 96:10–20.

———. 1997. "Is Primatology a Feminist Science?" In *Women in Human Evolution*, ed. Lori D. Hager, 56–75. London: Routledge.

Fee, Elizabeth, and Nancy Krieger, eds. 1994. *Women's Health, Politics, and Power: Essays on Sex/Gender, Medicine, and Public Health.* Amityville, N.Y.: Baywood.

Gross, Paul, and Norman Levitt. 1994. *Higher Superstition: The Academic Left and Its Quarrels with Science.* Baltimore: Johns Hopkins University Press.

Rosser, Sue V. 1994. *Women's Health — Missing from U.S. Medicine.* Bloomington: Indiana University Press.

Ruzek, Sheryl Burt, Virginia L. Olesen, and Adele Clarke, eds. 1997. *Women's Health: Complexities and Differences.* Columbus: Ohio State University Press.

Science. 1995. *Science* 269 (August 11): 773.

Schiebinger, Londa. 1987. "The History and Philosophy of Women in Science: A Review Essay." *Signs: Journal of Women in Culture and Society* 12(2):305–32.

———. 1999. *Has Feminism Changed Science?* Cambridge, Mass.: Harvard University Press.

Julie A. Nelson

Feminist Economics at the Millennium: A Personal Perspective

As an undergraduate economics major in the early 1970s, I was shocked by the simple facts of women's lower wages and occupational segregation by sex and the facts of global economic injustice, even though the theoretical structure presented to explain these facts seemed mostly designed to explain them *away*. I felt empowered by stories of women's accomplishments and the righteousness of Title VII antidiscrimination victories. I felt so empowered, in fact, that with courageous naïveté I entered graduate school in economics with the idea of contributing to a feminist transformation of the core theories — as I could observe happening in the other social sciences — from the inside, along with studying the causes of poverty on a global scale.

The sort of cold shower of entering graduate training and academic research in mainstream economics is a bit hard to explain to those who have not felt its onslaught — who perhaps think of economics as characterized by authors (like Nancy Hartsock) who bring feminist scholarship to bear on discussions about capitalism, global inequality, or commodification, or others (like sociologist Barbara Reskin) who seriously study the gendered structure of labor markets. Economists in the neoclassical tradition, which is hegemonic in much of the industrialized world, however, would not recognize such as "real" economics. The word *capitalism,* for example, is almost never uttered within the mainstream. To acknowledge that we live in a capitalist economy would be to grant (presumably unmerited) legitimacy to the notion that there could be alternatives. The notion of comparable worth (equal pay for work of equal value) is considered wrongheaded politics, not economics, since it implicitly challenges the primacy of market forces. Markets, individual choice, efficiency — these are the central themes of contemporary mainstream economics; nonideal outcomes are said to be caused by "market imperfections." The core of graduate training consists primarily of not-very-applied mathematics based on models of autonomous, rational, self-interested agents and yielding "knowledge" in the form of either mathematical theorem-proof or statistical testing. Economic his-

[*Signs: Journal of Women in Culture and Society* 2000, vol. 25, no. 4]

tory, the nonformal side of quantitative methods such as data gathering, qualitative methods, and the study of contemporary economic institutions are considered relatively unimportant and therefore not much taught; global issues are seen more in terms of high finance than low standards of living; a self-reflective view of assumptions and methodology is assiduously avoided; and serious, progressive policy work, when it is done, is accomplished as much in spite of, as facilitated by, the core education. If it seems that neoclassical economics is a parody of what feminist scholars of science argue against in terms of core assumptions and epistemology, you are getting the picture.

Yet, somehow, a number of us persevered in becoming both economists and feminists. Some of us plowed through neoclassicism. (I followed a dual-career strategy, getting tenure at my first university on the strength of my mainstream line of work alone.) Others came up the alternative paths available in Marxist or Institutionalist study in the handful of universities where these are tolerated, and others (notably Barbara Bergmann) forged ahead with whatever worked in arguing for corrective policies. After a smattering of earlier feminist forays, in the early 1990s "feminist economics" was suddenly transformed from an oxymoron to an organization. The International Association for Feminist Economics was formed in 1991, the collection *Beyond Economic Man: Feminist Theory and Economics* (Ferber and Nelson) was published in 1993, and the journal *Feminist Economics* began publishing in 1995, marking the beginnings of a remarkable pace of international conferences and publications, not to mention a dynamic and diverse community.[1]

So who are these feminist economists, what are "we" doing, and where are we going? I will give my own, surely idiosyncratic, overview and personal wish list.

My own agenda has three parts. First, I have wanted to redefine the field of economics. Should economics remain defined as rational choice theory—a notion based in a radically Cartesian, anti-body view of the world—feminists will have relatively little to say. I want to change the central question to one of "provisioning"—how we provide for ourselves the means to sustain and enjoy life. Second, based on an analysis of the value system underlying this discipline (and other cultural constructs as well), I set out to suggest more balanced and adequate theoretical and methodological approaches, using a simple tool for stimulating creative thinking outside of the usual "masculine-associated (mind/detachment/hard) is

---

[1] On the history of feminisms in economics, see the introduction to Ferber and Nelson 1993; Albelda 1997.

good, feminine-associated (body/connection/soft) is bad" (or, in short-hand, M+/F-) dualism (Nelson 1996). Consider value (positive/negative) and gender (masculine/feminine) as separate dimensions:

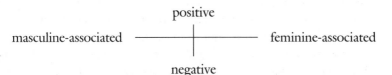

The interesting part of the thought experiment is to try to fill in the M− and F+ quadrants. I use the cells hard-rigid (M−), hard-strong (M+), soft-flexible (F+), and soft-weak (F-) to talk about how economists' obsession with being "masculine" in method (e.g., eschewing all qualitative research) cuts us off from the advantages of a more balanced approach. One can look at other issues as well: for example, the separation/connection dualism unpacks into cell entries of isolated (M−), individual (M+), related (F+), and engulfed (F−). My favorite example is that the words *virility* (M+) and *emasculation* (F−, perceived as lack of M) are quite common, but few people know the word *muliebrity* (F+, the feminine correlative of virility), and there is no word for a lack of womanly vigor. My third aim is to bring feminist insights to bear on specific real-world economic issues. My current work concerns ways to rethink and restructure "caring labor," as old dualisms of home versus market and altruism versus self-interest become increasingly anachronistic in the face of social change.

The range of feminist work in economics is wide, however.[2] Closest to the mainstream are researchers who use fairly standard methodologies to investigate models of labor-market discrimination or household behavior. The application of game-theory models to intrahousehold decision making, for example, has recently boomed. Applications of feminist insights to macroeconomics, the economics of "development" policies, and the interstices with race and class have primarily come from those scholars with Marxist, Institutionalist, or other alternative backgrounds, while policy-related work comes from all approaches. Perhaps reflecting the processes of self-selection into a profession, economics also has a small but vocal libertarian wing as well as far fewer deconstructionist or poststructural feminists than in the humanities.

Perhaps I will offend if I note that I don't necessarily consider the relative dearth of deconstructionist work a drawback. I believe that

---

[2] Diverse approaches and views can be found in the pages of the journal *Feminist Economics*, as well as in volumes such as Ferber and Nelson 1993; Kuiper and Sap 1995; Peterson and Lewis 2000.

poststructural thought, emphasizing discourse and play, and neoclassical thought, emphasizing mathematics and foundations, are not so far away from each other. Both, to my mind, in their extremes create barriers to entry for scholars not educated in specific obscurant literatures/techniques, concentrate on esoterica, promulgate a bloodless and lifeless view of the world, and fail to take into account lived experience. Caught between the wave of poststructuralist discursive play in feminist circles and my (seventeenth-century) physics-envy-afflicted neoclassical colleagues, I am reminded of the conversation between two princely brothers recounted by the Which in *The Phantom Tollbooth*: " 'Words are more important than wisdom,' said one privately. 'Numbers are more important than wisdom,' thought the other to himself. And they grew to dislike each other more and more" (Juster 1961, 74). My hope lies in a pragmatic approach, in both the informal and philosophical senses of that term. Recently I have been inspired by noting conceptual and historical parallels among some aspects of feminist epistemology; the much-neglected Institutionalist school of economics; Alfred North Whitehead's "process" thought; the pragmatist philosophy of John Dewey, Jane Addams, and William James; the notion of "mindfulness" in certain spiritual traditions; and recent developments concerning indeterminism in physics and the natural sciences, especially the work of Isabelle Stengers and Ilya Prigogine. What these have in common is the centrality of lived experience, notions of organism, flux, possibilities, and novelty. I believe they may open ways of thinking about the world — and the economy — that neither sell out the store to pure play and chance nor devolve into ideal types and determinism.

With all this fun intellectual activity on the rise, I admit that I have tended to view the topics that originally inspired me, such as labor-market discrimination, as a little dated and pedestrian and have tended sometimes to let issues of actual economic power and its abuse slide out of focus. In the past couple of years, however, I have had cause to take a refreshed interest in such on-the-ground issues. I was denied tenure at my second university and am currently waging a good old-fashioned liberal feminist legal fight. A friend of mine, recently free of an abusive partner, tells me that the most meaningful idea she picked up during recovery is the notion of a "spiral" in emotions and experiences. In employment and intellectual life, as in personal connections, we come upon the same issues again and again, but, just perhaps, with a little more wisdom each time.

Economics Department
University of Massachusetts, Boston

References

Albelda, Randy. 1997. *Economics and Feminism: Disturbances in the Field.* New York: Twayne.

Ferber, Marianne A., and Julie A. Nelson, eds. 1993. *Beyond Economic Man: Feminist Theory and Economics.* Chicago: University of Chicago Press.

Juster, Norton. 1961. *The Phantom Tollbooth.* New York: Random House.

Kuiper, Edith, and Jolande Sap, eds. 1995. *Out of the Margin: Feminist Perspectives on Economics.* London: Routledge.

Nelson, Julie A. 1996. *Feminism, Objectivity, and Economics.* London: Routledge.

Peterson, Janice, and Margaret Lewis, eds. 2000. *The Elgar Companion to Feminist Economics.* Brookfield, Vt.: Edward Elgar.

A Telling Time for Women's Studies

This is a telling time for the U.S. women's studies movement. Three decades have passed since feminist ideas began to move into the academy, and a series of recent commemorative events have marked twenty-five years since the establishment of the first women's studies programs. As the founding academic generation moves toward retirement, some of us have turned to writing memoirs and to other forms of concerted musing about the linked trajectories of contemporary feminism and of our own personal and professional lives. I've become one of the musers (see Thorne 1998), looking back on almost thirty years of teaching in sociology departments and in interdisciplinary programs variously called women's studies, feminist studies, and the study of women and men in society. My reflections swing from the past into speculations about the future, and they are laced with ambivalent feelings of satisfaction and unease.

In 1971 I left the sociology graduate program at Brandeis University with a Ph.D. and with political and intellectual passions stirred by consciousness-raising in Bread and Roses, a women's liberation group in Boston. After joining the sociology faculty at Michigan State University, I met feminists from other parts of the campus, and we became a sort of cadre, pressing the university for an affirmative-action program and for a place in the curriculum. Some of our initial struggles now seem like small matters, but at the time they loomed large as steps toward legitimacy and resources. We finally got permission to use *WS* as an "alpha code" for core and cross-listed classes and to constitute women's studies as an undergraduate thematic concentration (something short of a minor). These local efforts were fortified by contacts with feminists on other campuses and by events such as the founding of the National Women's Studies Association in the late 1970s.

From the beginning the women's studies movement had a two-pronged vision: to create interdisciplinary knowledge and spaces and to change the content of existing disciplines. As the millennium, the century, and the generations turn, we can list many signs of success. In the United States, more than seven hundred colleges and universities now have women's

[*Signs: Journal of Women in Culture and Society* 2000, vol. 25, no. 4]

studies programs, some of them granting graduate degrees, and there are more than thirty feminist academic journals. Founded in the early 1970s, the sex and gender section of the American Sociological Association now has more members than any other research division, and similar patterns can be found in the professional associations of other disciplines.

These institutional achievements are enormously gratifying, but they have come at a price, since the quest for mainstream legitimacy almost inevitably blunts the critical edge and political momentum of ideas. Much of the innovative cross-disciplinary momentum of feminism has been absorbed into the business-as-usual operations of academic disciplines, and interdisciplinary women's studies programs tend to be devalued both locally and in national academic circles. Feminist scholars, perhaps not surprisingly, have been absorbed into the vanity-envy culture of higher education—the pursuit of careers, competitive individualism, star systems, and hierarchies of privilege. On balance, some of us have come to wonder, How much have feminists changed the academy, and how much has it changed us?

The history of women's studies provides abundant material not only for contemplating the force of hierarchical institutions and traditional academic culture and careers but also for analyzing continuity and changes in the contours of knowledge. Over the last thirty years feminist ideas moved fairly rapidly and transformatively (albeit with considerable conflict and resistance) into some disciplines, such as literature, anthropology, sociology, and history. But other fields, such as economics, linguistics, and philosophy, have been relatively impermeable to feminist insights (the thriving intellectual lives of feminist economists and philosophers generally take place on the margins of those fields).

What accounts for the uneven movement of feminist ideas across the disciplines? Judy Stacey and I pondered this comparative question fifteen years ago, observing that the fields more open to feminist critique tend to be those with a relatively high proportion of women scholars, with interpretive and self-reflective rather than positivist epistemological foundations, with multiple and eclectic frameworks rather than hegemonic paradigms, and with less access to political power (Stacey and Thorne 1985). When we recently revisited this question, Judy and I queried our earlier assumption that academic disciplines would continue to march along as basically separate battalions (Stacey and Thorne 1996). Traditional divisions of knowledge reflect nineteenth-century dichotomies (public vs. private, nature vs. culture, individual vs. society) that have been thoroughly critiqued by feminists and many others; real transformation of knowledge would surely upturn these divisions. Yet the divisions persist, congealed in the organization and power structures of universities, disciplinary associations, and scholarly practices.

National and local hierarchies reveal the continuing power of the disciplines and the devaluing of interdisciplinary work and also of women and ethnic minorities. It is far more prestigious, at least in research universities, to have a faculty appointment in a "regular department" than to have a joint — or especially a full — appointment in women's or ethnic studies. On many campuses there is tension between feminist faculty based in women's studies, some of whom describe themselves as poor sisters or housekeepers, and feminists with more resources and higher status who are based in conventional disciplines. At Berkeley, one of the leaders of the academic senate publicly distinguishes "real departments" from (in his view) problematic "newcomer social programs" such as women's studies and ethnic studies. Although both of these programs have been "regularized" as departments, faculty appointments and resources have dwindled, and suspicions about their legitimacy continue to circulate.

When feminists discuss the promise and difficulties of women's studies programs, someone almost inevitably says, "We don't even know what interdisciplinarity is!" I tend to agree, but there are moments when the crossing of knowledge boundaries takes tangible and exhilarating form. The contexts of teaching have provided my most exciting moments of riding interdisciplinary waves with others. In 1973 I cotaught the first offering of the introductory women's studies course at Michigan State University with Joyce Ladenson, a colleague in literature. It was thrilling to teach poetry and fiction alongside essays by philosophers and studies by historians and sociologists. *Ideas* were front and center, and I felt liberated from the disciplining voice that tells me what I ought to teach when the subject is sociology.

In the late 1980s, when I taught a feminist theory graduate ovular (as I dared to call it in the syllabus) at the University of Southern California, students from the film school and from art history introduced me to theories of representation and the male gaze. These approaches became staple fare in my teaching and helped me recognize and write about the "adult gaze" that permeates research on children. During one semester Judith Resnick and I merged my feminist theory ovular with her law school class in feminist jurisprudence. We assigned readings from a range of theoretical perspectives, juxtaposed with court cases, empirical research from the social sciences, and a bit of literature. The unusual juxtapositions helped us see that different types of theory are like plants that flourish in one part of a garden rather than another; the theories that take hold in law may be different from those that blossom in sociology. For example, the socialist-feminist conception of gender as a social relation, a centerpiece of feminist sociology, seems to be ill-suited for the classificatory demands of legal knowledge.

I love teaching in women's studies not only because ideas spark when one is free to lay out kindling from many sources, but also because feminism provides immediately useful tools for sorting out one's life and for thinking critically about the world. When I teach women's studies to undergraduates, I experience a sense of purpose that is often lacking when I teach sociology courses. This may be, in part, because the students who take, and especially who major or minor in, women's studies tend to care about ideas and about living self-reflective and purposeful lives. Faculty in other departments sometimes volunteer to teach in women's studies because the students are so interesting and interested.

Being located in a women's studies program brings many pleasures, but there are also tensions, which, in my experience, have worsened with the process of institutionalization and the absorption of feminist ideas into separate and sometimes competing disciplines. Since the mid-1980s, women's studies programs have been sites of friction between faculty from the humanities, especially those invested in postmodernist critiques, and more empirically oriented feminists from the social sciences (although as postmodern ideas move into the social sciences, the problem seems to be easing). Tension over intellectual turf lurks in comments about who is or is not "cutting edge," about who will get to teach feminist theory courses, and about what types of theory should be taught. Feminist theory, the most valued academic currency of women's studies, has come to signify our shared intellectual life, our claims to legitimacy as a distinctive academic field, and our hierarchies of knowledge. The troubling split between reified theory and other types of feminist knowledge should be more closely scrutinized.

Women's studies programs are a site of both uneasy and engaging relationships not only across disciplines but also across generations. As one of the older generation (I'll turn 58 in the millennium year), I'm gratified that feminist ideas and women's studies courses continue to appeal to students, although I experience startling moments of generation gap. I'm a little shocked when I meet younger feminists who have nose or tongue piercings and tattoos. In those moments I feel like an older suffragist in the 1920s, wearing a long skirt and corset and encountering younger women, with bobbed hair and looser, shorter dresses, who, I hope, will carry on the struggle — with their own ideas about what to wear, what to think, how to do politics, and, indeed, whether to position themselves in some sort of feminist lineage at all. While many of my students are entranced by cyborgs and cyberfeminism, I still resonate with the metaphor of the goddess. Feminist ideas and passions continue to metamorphose, which, all in all, is a hopeful dimension of this telling time.

Women's Studies and Sociology Departments
University of California, Berkeley

References

Stacey, Judith, and Barrie Thorne. 1985. "The Missing Feminist Revolution in Sociology." *Social Problems* 32 (4):301–16.

———. 1996. "Is Sociology Still Missing Its Feminist Revolution?" *Perspectives: The ASA Theory Section Newsletter* 18(3):1–4.

Thorne, Barrie. 1998. "Brandeis as a Generative Institution: Critical Perspectives, Marginality, and Feminism." In *Feminist Sociology: Life Histories of a Movement*, ed. Barbara Laslett and Barrie Thorne, 103–25. New Brunswick, N.J.: Rutgers University Press.

Is Academic Feminism an Oxymoron?

academic: . . . scholarly to the point of being unaware of the outside world. . . . Formalistic or conventional. . . . Theoretical or speculative without a practical purpose or intention. Having no practical purpose or use.

feminism: Belief in the social, political and economic equality of the sexes. The movement organized around this belief.[1]

R**eaders,** please put away your books and take out a pen and paper. This is a pop quiz. Select from the following three statements about contemporary academic feminism the only one that was not written by a feminist: 1. "The institutionalization of women's studies at some visible colleges and universities has made scholars forget the founding tenets of women's studies as they slavishly attempt to recreate it in the image of the traditional disciplines." 2. "We should be yoking together Women's Studies, Ethnic Studies, Jewish Studies and Queer Studies under the rubric of Liberation Studies." 3. "Feminism is more threatening than Marxism, and therefore more resolutely repressed but ultimately all the more irrepressible than Marxism."[2]

The correct answer, paradoxically enough, is the laudatory view of feminist thought in the last statement. Michael Burawoy, a prominent Marxist sociologist, offered this affirmation of the enduringly radical promise of feminist sociology in his response to a retrospective assessment (Stacey and Thorne 1996) that Barrie Thorne and I provided of "The Missing Feminist Revolution in Sociology" (1985), an essay we had coauthored more than a decade earlier. Burawoy offered "no apologies for romanticizing feminism since my intention is to counter the jaded disquisition of Stacey and Thorne" (1996, 5). Compounding the paradox, in the same symposium, feminist theorist Dorothy Smith gently took us to task for erring in the opposite direction: she believed that we had mistakenly indulged in feminist self-congratulation despite the appalling conditions of political backlash, co-optation, and free market intellectual triumphalism that now

[1] All quoted definitions in this essay are from the *American Heritage Dictionary of the English Language,* 3d ed. (Boston: Houghton Mifflin, 1992).

[2] Burawoy 1996; Catapano and Wasserman 1998; Kaye/Kantrowitz 1999.

[*Signs: Journal of Women in Culture and Society* 2000, vol. 25, no. 4]

confront feminist scholars. As the century and millennium turn, is the academic feminist glass half full or half empty? Half and half? All or none of the above? Opinions differ widely and fluctuate wildly, not only among diverse feminist scholars but within most of us internally as well.

The question that my title poses is intentionally provocative, of course, and somewhat jesuitical. By literal dictionary standards, academic feminism is *by definition* oxymoronic. If an academic is someone "scholarly to the point of being unaware of the outside world" who pursues knowledge that is "theoretical or speculative without a practical purpose or intention" and produces work "having no practical purpose or use," such an intellectual should find herself categorically at odds with the fundamentally political character of the "F" word. Readers of this journal don't need to be reminded of the profoundly worldly origins and ambitions of academic feminism — this very wanted, nurtured child of the grassroots activism of the "second wave." Original subscribers to *Signs,* like me, probably stockpile memories of sit-ins, demonstrations, petition drives, and vigorous direct-action efforts through which we struggled to introduce women's studies courses, programs, faculty, and ideals into our universities. And yet I doubt that many readers will be shocked by the discouraged sentiments expressed in the first of the multiple-choice statements above or surprised to learn that they represent the views of Joan Catapano and Marlie Wasserman, two feminist editors at major university presses who have been publishing our books for more than two decades.

However oxymoronic the concept may be in theory, in practice academic feminism has become a social fact. Few of us "women of a certain age" who have reaped a disproportionate share of the professional privileges and burdens of its remarkable growth can be strangers to recurrent angst-ridden exchanges in corridors, seminars, or kitchen table conferences over this uncomfortable theme. For what was once the subversive, intellectual arm of a thriving grassroots movement has been institutionalized and professionalized, while the movement that launched our enterprise is far less activist, confident, or popular. Today more than six hundred women's studies programs in the United States alone, some with departmental status, grant degrees at the bachelor's, master's, and even doctoral levels, and women's studies programs, courses, and projects continue to spread globally. Feminist professional associations, conferences, journals, presses, book series, prizes, fellowships, conferences, archives, institutes, list servs, foundations, and the like abound. Feminists occupy senior faculty and administrative positions, including endowed chairs for feminist scholarship, throughout most disciplines and professional schools, even at the nation's most elite universities. Indeed, numerous feminists actively participate in the global jet set of an academic commodity market whose excesses compete with those parodied in the novels of David Lodge (1975, 1985). Boasting our own celebrity system replete with agents, speaking tours, publicists, photo shoots, and even fanzines, many feminist scholars too often do produce works that are quite literally "academic"—that is, "theoretical or speculative without a practical purpose or intention"—as Catapano and Wasserman lament, composed in ungainly prose infused with gratuitous displays of arcane jargon. How sobering to note that academic feminist "sisterhood" has proven powerful enough to replicate many of the less endearing status hierarchies, anxieties, affectations, and schisms of "normal science."

Signs is not a dictionary, however, and neither this symposium nor my title invites such a literalist response to the question my title poses. Otherwise, I could end my essay on this depressingly "affirmative," but unconstructive, note. Instead, I want to identify a few of the paradoxical challenges, both external and internal, to the future of feminism in the academy that our professional success has produced. The external threats are the most obvious and perhaps the most serious. Dorothy Smith is unequivocally correct that in "a surrounding climate becoming more deeply conservative and more deeply committed to sustaining the power of the wealthy over the people, it is difficult for the academy to sustain the independence on which feminist sociology [and feminist scholarship generally] has relied" (1996, 4). Like Smith, I too worry that "present technological and managerial transformations of the academy may subdue altogether the values of enlightenment and freedom in the academy which enabled feminism to struggle to the level of success" we have achieved (4). This clear and present danger threatens the ultimate survival of academic feminism and other progressive knowledge projects, as well as most of the worldly dreams of the social movements that spawned them.

I lack space or spirit to rehearse here the ubiquitous consequences of these unfavorable winds—the chilling effects of university retrenchment and of the backlash against affirmative action and "political correctness," which include not only broad assaults on the humanities and on the tenure system itself, but also increasingly direct attacks on feminist scholarship and teaching. Particularly dispiriting to those of us old and confessional enough to admit that we once naively endorsed the slogan "sisterhood is powerful" is the fact that these days an almost unimaginable oxymoron spearheads many of these attacks—a highly vocal, articulate cadre of *antifeminist* academic "feminists," such as Christina Hoff-Sommers, Jean Bethke Elshtain, Elizabeth Fox-Genovese, and Camille Paglia, to name but a few. It should not surprise us therefore, that state and local legislators have begun to take direct aim at women's studies programs. The week I began to compose these reflections in February 1999, for example, I received an e-mail alert that some Arizona legislators were attempting to eliminate funding for women's studies programs at their state's public universities. Likewise, following the successful repeal of affirmative action admissions policies at the University of California, some conservative legislators began to challenge the educational legitimacy of women's studies and ethnic studies programs in my home state. While feminists can read such threats as testimonies to our success, they should also remind us that, however ambivalent we may feel about the oxymoronic character of academic feminism, by no means can we take for granted its institutional survival.

Moreover, two major intellectual developments internal to academic feminism also threaten its future as an autonomous enterprise. Paradoxically, the staggering transdisciplinary growth of feminist scholarship has propelled an increasing level of disciplinary specialization. It was not immodest for those of us who began to study and teach women's studies in the early 1970s to aspire to comprehensive, cross-disciplinary expertise in feminist theory and scholarship. The literature was so limited that reading across the disciplines was not daring; it was both feasible and necessary. We debated the pros and cons of building an autonomous new "discipline" that would draw from and transcend traditional boundaries of knowledge. However, one of the ironic by-products of the staggering proliferation of feminist scholarship has been a sharp decline in interdisciplinarity. In academia today, *feminist* typically functions as an adjectival modifier to the established disciplines. Few scholars can achieve comprehensive knowledge of the feminist literature even in their own disciplinary subfields, let alone indulge in the "dream of a common language" in which feminist scholars might write and speak fluently in an intellectual world without disciplinary borders.

Of course, potent political and intellectual developments have compelled most white, Western, heterosexual feminists to renounce universalistic longings for sisterhood, identity, and transparency, and in my view these pose the most challenging questions about the institutional future of academic feminism. Indeed, they threaten to pull the intellectual rug out from under the autonomous status of women's studies or gender studies programs. I now title my (doggedly interdisciplinary) graduate seminar in contemporary feminist theory "The Decentering of Gender in Feminist Theory: Different Differences and Significant Others." The seminar focuses on twin deconstructive challenges to universalistic theories of gender posed by critiques derived from identity politics and from the post-Enlightenment "theory revolution." Since the early 1980s, lesbians, feminists of color, postcolonial critics, and queer theorists, as well as postfeminists and antifeminist women, have exposed the ethnocentric conceits and consequences of the foundational categories of Western feminist thought—women, gender, and sex. Meanwhile, post-Marxist critical theories have been relentlessly deconstructing the illusory grounding of all foundational categories. Consequently, feminist theory now proceeds from the premise that gender never operates uniformly or in isolation from race, nationality, sexuality, class, or any other powerful axis of identity and power. But this admirable principle presents a dilemma: if feminists can no longer profess the primacy of gender as a category of analysis, does this leave us any disciplinary or discursive domain that we can claim to be distinctively feminist? As my course description asks, "What constitutes feminist theory after gender has been radically decentered? Can there be a feminism without woman? Without women? Without illusions?"

These are not merely "academic" questions. Nettlesome, decidedly practical matters governing curriculum, departmental structure, and staffing hinge on our answers. How can we prevent feminist studies from condensing de facto into straight white feminist studies? Must (or rather, can) feminist scholarship always devote "equal time" to gender, race, class, sexuality, and other major categories of cultural difference and social domination? Consider just the question of selection criteria for required course readings: Does *The Alchemy of Race and Rights* (1991) by critical legal theorist Patricia Williams qualify as a specifically feminist work? What about *The Epistemology of the Closet* (1990), Eve Sedgwick's canonical contribution to queer theory, or *Ghostly Matters* (1997), a stunningly original contribution to cultural studies by Avery Gordon? Or Anne McClintock's postcolonial theory opus, *Imperial Leather* (1995)? None of these works makes gender the central category of analysis; all four have appeared on my recent feminist theory syllabi.

Analogously, how can or should we identify, recruit, and hire feminist faculty whose work does not center on women or gender? What institutional relationships should we promote between gender studies and academic programs in ethnic studies, gay and lesbian and queer studies, cultural studies, and their progressive kin? Is the feminist author of the second multiple-choice statement above correct that "we should be yoking together Women's Studies, Ethnic Studies, Jewish Studies and Queer Studies under the rubric of Liberation Studies"? If so, can we evade the snares of being identified as "grievance studies" by friends and foes alike, thereby intensifying the likelihood of debilitating ideological battles within and political assaults from without? And how could we protect our intellectual progeny from a traditional "unhappy marriage" that once again consigned feminist theory to a subordinate helpmeet status? These are but a few of the very real conundrums that academic feminists now confront in our institutions, classrooms, and scholarship.

If I go back to my dictionary, I must conclude that academic feminism is indeed an oxymoron, "a rhetorical figure in which incongruous or contradictory terms are combined, as in *a deafening silence* or *a mournful optimist.*" Conceding this enables us to take justifiable pride in our collective accomplishments, even as we feel threatened by enemies without and fissures and ambivalence within. Mournful optimism seems a fitting sensibility to adopt as we observe the rituals of Y2K reflections. In that spirit, let us raise our half-full, half-empty glasses in a toast to the irrepressible ghosts of academic feminism — past, present, and future.

Sociology Department
University of Southern California

References

Burawoy, Michael. 1996. "The Power of Feminism." *Perspectives: The ASA Theory Section Newsletter* 18(3):4–6.

Catapano, Joan, and Marlie P. Wasserman. 1998. "Is Publishing Perishing?" *Women's Review of Books* 15(5):22.

Gordon, Avery. 1997. *Ghostly Matters Haunting and the Sociological Imagination.* Minneapolis: University of Minnesota Press.

Kaye/Kantrowitz, Melanie. 1999. "Liberation Studies Now." *Women's Review of Books* 16(5):15.

Lodge, David. 1975. *Changing Places: A Tale of Two Campuses.* London: Secker & Warburg.

———. 1985. *Small World: An Academic Romance.* London: Secker & Warburg.

McClintock, Anne. 1995. *Imperial Leather: Race, Gender, and Sexuality in the Colonial Contest.* New York: Routledge.

Sedgwick, Eve Kosofsky. 1990. *Epistemology of the Closet.* Berkeley: University of California Press.

Smith, Dorothy E. 1996. "Response to Judith Stacey's and Barrie Thorne's Essay." *Perspectives: The ASA Theory Section Newsletter* 18(3):3–4.

Stacey, Judith, and Barrie Thorne. 1985. "The Missing Feminist Revolution in Sociology." *Social Problems* 32(4):301–16.

———. 1996. "Is Sociology Still Missing Its Feminist Revolution?" *Perspectives: The ASA Theory Section Newsletter* 18(3):1–3.

Williams, Patricia J. 1991. *The Alchemy of Race and Rights.* Cambridge, Mass.: Harvard University Press.

Irene Dölling

Sabine Hark

She Who Speaks Shadow Speaks Truth:
Transdisciplinarity in Women's and Gender Studies

As arbitrary as such demarcations may be, the end of the century raises the question of the future of women's and gender studies. Caught between a visible trend toward normalization and a renewed struggle over the legitimacy of women's and gender studies, feminism is undergoing a critical reexamination, as women's studies' own disciplinary location brings renewed attention to the necessary role of transdisciplinarity in women's and gender studies.

A trend toward repositioning women's and gender studies within the "field of science" (Bourdieu 1998) has been visible for some time now. Although women's studies is often still not fully accepted, with increasing institutionalization (as evinced by the creation of professorships and courses of study), it has moved from margin to center. Even given the variations among individual disciplines, women's and gender studies has long since ceased to be a matter pursued by a few scholars from an outsider or marginal position in the academic field, and its construction of new research perspectives and subjects is also no longer connected per se with a critique of the system of knowledge production called "scholarly research." For women's and gender studies, as for other disciplines, increasing institutionalization carries with it the threat of a loss of critical potential, especially the capacity to reflect upon its own modes of knowledge production. Moving into the center, however, necessitates a higher level of self-reflexivity. Transdisciplinarity, understood as a critical evaluation of terms, concepts, and methods that transgresses disciplinary boundaries can be a means to this higher level of reflexivity.

Moreover, the social transformations that are now taking place or becoming visible serve notice of the end of industrial capitalism, and with it the transformation of all of the subsystems of "modern" society. This process confronts women's and gender studies with the task of testing whether, and to what degree, the disciplinary or interdisciplinary perspectives applied thus far are adequate to analyzing and representing these

[*Signs: Journal of Women in Culture and Society* 2000, vol. 25, no. 4]

changes. New types of inequality and social divisions are becoming visible, as are new phenomena in the "feminization" of social groups, activities, and life-styles, which no longer necessarily obey gender lines and cannot be grasped simply in terms of (social and cultural) differentiations within a genus group. With modification, however, the hierarchical construct of a two-gender system can definitely continue to be useful in naming and signifying these new boundaries.

The progress in genetic and reproductive technologies also makes transdisciplinary approaches crucial if we are to address the development of a modern "bio-power" with the intention of creating life (Foucault 1993). At the end of the twentieth century, it is impossible to overlook the discursive entrance of a "new species" that leaves behind the limitations and ecologically threatened human, bound by a "naturally given" body. Whether gender differentiation is meaningful in the cultural construction of this new species and in what way this cultural construction can be influenced from a feminist perspective constitute challenges to women's and gender studies that not only call into question terms and patterns of thought thus far held to be valid but also demand the abandonment of disciplinary boundaries in the formulation of research subjects.

If women's studies has moved further toward the center, then it can no longer easily claim a critical marginality from which to challenge the established canon of knowledge. Under what conditions, then, can feminist theory as a critique of the dominant order be maintained? What capabilities do feminist scholars require in order to act as dissidents in the face of increasingly commodified and identity-oriented production of scholarly knowledge? These questions are being debated in feminist contexts—and other places—under the rubric of transdisciplinarity. As an epistemological and methodological strategy, transdisciplinarity proceeds from the insight that disciplines are conventionally thought of territorially, as independent domains with clear boundaries. In fact, however, disciplines are characterized by multiple interconnections and shot through with cross-disciplinary pathways. Consequently, the boundaries between them must be understood—much like physical territorial borders—as arbitrary products, effects of social activity: as sociological facts that formulate themselves in space, as Georg Simmel (1992) puts it.

Transdisciplinarity as a structural principle for scholarly work attempts to take seriously the idea that disciplines are less constituted around a core than organized like knots in a netlike structure. The task lies, then, in tracing these interlacings to untangle the separate strands, "to recognize from the beginning the actual transdisciplinary constitution of disciplinary content" (Welsch 1996, 947). Transdisciplinarity is thus not a new demand on the production of scholarly knowledge; it is its structuring principle. In a certain sense, it denotes that scholarly practice is becoming more self-reflective, questioning identity as the privileged mode of knowledge formation. That is, true transdisciplinarity is characterized by a continual examination of artificially drawn and contingent boundaries and that which they exclude.

This last point, especially, could be decisive as a future foundation for the production of feminist scholarly knowledge as a critique of the dominant order. The past two decades have been characterized by vehement worldwide struggles over the epistemological and political "we" of feminism. This has led to a decentering and questioning of the representativeness of any one version of feminism. In the course of these struggles it has become clear that while reference to an epistemological "we" is basic to the production of feminist scholarly knowledge, it must also be simultaneously relativized, displaced, and reformulated by the thematization and treatment of differences and inequalities between women. This is in no way to be understood as a misfortune or childhood illness of a still-young scholarly practice; it can be regarded rather as a significant indicator of the direction feminist theory should take. A women's/gender studies that understands itself to be critical of the dominant order must constantly reassign itself the task of questioning its own epistemological foundations in the spirit of antifoundationalism (as defined by Judith Butler [1994], among others). Feminist theory must reflect upon the contingency of its own premises and constructions to maintain its awareness of the difference between the thought and the thinkable. It is less a matter of working out a subject core (e.g., gender) than one of developing a range of tools for analyzing the logic of power relations and power struggles. A scholarly practice that aims to critique power and hegemony must be forthright about its own complicity in given relationships of power. The unsaid must also appear in the said. Transdisciplinarity, while hardly feminist scholarship's last word in response to this challenge, accepts the task of making itself transparent by thematizating the conditions of its own speech. "In the ideal case, this transparency of conditions," the philosopher Wolfgang Welsch commented, leads to "an explicit delineation of the boundaries and exclusions of the respective conditional framework" (1996, 938).

Feminist theory has repeatedly resisted the procedures of exclusion inherent in the disciplinary organization of knowledge. In doing so, it has provoked a reconsideration not only of disciplinary structure itself but also of what qualifies as knowledge in any discipline. Feminism's openness to self-reflection and subsequent changes have been largely the result of its attention to women's contradictory social experiences. On its intricate path from margin to center, women's studies now is in danger of giving up its dialogue with the other in favor of a dialogue with the canonized powers. It behooves us to bear in mind Paul Celan's remark that "[s]he who speaks shadow speaks truth" (1983, 135) — that full speech is realized only when the unspoken appears in the spoken, that, as Bourdieu put it, "acts of recognition are unavoidably acts of misrecognition" (1997, 96).

Understood thus, transdisciplinarity can be an opportunity to retain the dissident potential of women's/gender studies while also transforming it into a well-honed, central tool for scholarly analysis of the problems of the next century.

Women's Studies Department
University of Potsdam

References

Bourdieu, Pierre. 1997. "Maennliche Herrschaft Revisited." *Feministische Studien* 15(2):88–99.

———. 1998. *Vom Gebrauch der Wissenschaft: Fuer eine klinische Soziologie des wissenschaftlichen Feldes.* Konstanz: Universitaetsverlag.

Butler, Judith. 1994. "Against Proper Objects." *differences: A Journal of Feminist Cultural Studies* 6(2):1–26.

Celan, Paul. 1983: "Sprich auch du." In his *Von Schwelle zu Schwelle.* In *Gesammelte Werke*, Bd. 1, 135. Frankfurt am Main: Suhrkamp.

Foucault, Michel. 1993. "Leben machen und sterben lassen: Die Geburt des Rassismus." In *Bio-Macht*, 27–50. DISS-Texte, Nr. 25. Duisburg: Duisburger Institute für Sprach- und Sozialforschung.

Simmel, Georg. 1992. "Der Raum und die raeumlichen Ordnungen der Gesellschaft." In his *Soziologie: Untersuchungen ueber die Formen der Vergesellschaftung.* Gesamtausgabe 11. Frankfurt am Main: Suhrkamp.

Welsch, Wolfgang. 1996. *Vernunft: Die zeitgenoessische Vernunftkritik und das Konzept der transversalen Vernunft.* Frankfurt am Main: Suhrkamp.

Signs: The Stanford Years, 1980–1985

In April 1998, **Myra Strober** and I were asked to participate in the Jing Lyman lecture series, sponsored by the Institute for Research on Women and Gender at Stanford University, by recalling our experiences during the years that *Signs* was housed at Stanford. Myra, when director of the institute (then called the Center for Research on Women), had initiated the bid to have *Signs* come to the center, its first editorial move after its brilliant success under Catharine Stimpson's editorship at Barnard. Myra was also one of the group of associate editors while the journal was at Stanford, and I was its editor.[1]

These distinctions — editor, associate editor — had an administrative necessity, designating lines of responsibility that the University of Chicago Press needed as part of the journal's structure, but in our internal organization we worked as a collective. The managing editors and I had primary responsibility for editing accepted essays, but the whole group — associate editors, the managing editors, and I — was involved in brainstorming and in handling different aspects of editorial review. Not surprisingly, then, the event that Myra and I most emphasized in recalling our experience was the conference "Communities of Women" that *Signs* had sponsored. Planning for it began almost as soon as we caught our breath after the steep learning curve that followed *Signs's* arrival. The conference was held at Stanford on February 18–20, 1983, almost precisely the midpoint of the journal's presence there. The special issue of *Signs* based on the conference appeared in Summer 1985, as we were packing up the boxes to send to *Signs's* next home under Jean O'Barr's editorship at Duke–University of North Carolina.

The context and circumstances in which Myra and I made our 1998

---

[1] Because the mastheads of *Signs* serve as the only record of participants in the Stanford group, let me list them here. The first associates were Estelle Freedman, Carol Nagy Jacklin, Nannerl O. Keohane, Michelle Zimbalist Rosaldo, Myra H. Strober, and Margery Wolf. In 1983, Jane Fishburne Collier and Sylvia Yanagisako joined the group. Margaret Weeks was the first managing editor and Clare C. Novak the assistant editor. After a year, Clare became managing editor, and Susan L. Johnson joined the staff, first as assistant, then as co-managing editor.

[*Signs: Journal of Women in Culture and Society* 2000, vol. 25, no. 4]

presentation permitted — even demanded — a nostalgia not appropriate in the look forward into the new millennium that I'm attempting here. We noted — as I see we did in our editorial in the "Communities of Women" issue — our initial delight in the editorial collective as an indicator that the "sisterhood" that was so much a catchword of the day could indeed be actualized. We recalled the importance of Nan Keohane's contribution to the journal before, to our prideful dismay, she became president of Wellesley College; we celebrated the life of Shelly Rosaldo and mourned her loss. In describing the conference, Myra and I remembered it as an extraordinary outpouring of community feeling, recalled the dynamism with which Sister Joan Chittister, in the conference's closing, called on us to reaffirm a spirit of collaboration that resists the violence inherent in competition. And, as I look to corroborative documents, I see that we remembered rightly, but in that presentation at the institute we did not tell the whole story.

The years during which *Signs* was at Stanford marked the point of "turn" in feminist experience of sisterhood. Under analysis, our experience itself gave rise to harsh and searching questions: Is a group of predominantly white women at a private university to take itself as model for women's interactions? Is the concept of powerful sisterhood at all liberatory for women of color, when their struggle must of necessity be a racial one in solidarity with men? Is the celebration of sisterhood itself not shot through with an ideological blindness to racism, classism, and homophobia within as well as outside the women's movement? Sober and thoughtful in its tone, the editorial for the "Communities" issue raises these strong caveats about the very concept we had originally planned to celebrate.

That soberness has taken a turn almost to the somber (or such is my impression) in the fifteen years since *Signs* left Stanford. The essentialism, separatism, classism, and racism present in the early years of the twentieth-century women's movement have rightly come under judgment, but what rallying cry do we have to replace "sisterhood" as a call to common action? Is common action possible or even appropriate at this historical moment? Questions like these darkened my mood as, through the winter quarter of the 1998–99 academic year, I did the preliminary work of articulating my feelings that this short essay demands. What are my hopes for the future? Do I actually have any? Or do I have primarily fears? Would I just as soon, therefore, not think of this subject at all?

As it happens, I consider these questions in the very room in which, fifteen years ago, I edited *Signs*. I have agreed to serve for part of this year as acting director of the feminist studies program while its director, my friend and *Signs* associate Estelle Freedman, is on sabbatical. The program is housed at the Institute for Research on Women and Gender in the rooms once used by *Signs*. I sit, therefore, at my old desk. The tasks are administrative, active: outreach to other programs and departments on campus, participation in meetings of the program's Committee-in-Charge, attendance at functions—all with the program's administrator, Cathy Jensen, along with her assistants, Heather McCallum and Masum Momaya, as my aides and mentors. The performance of these duties returns me to the world of interdisciplinary feminist study and a consciousness of feminist activism that I have not experienced since the *Signs* days. And therefore—pondering, struggling for discernment—I find myself looking to routine events as themselves potential signs. My feelings while engaged in these tasks help me to assess the present and thereby project a possible future.

Monday, February 1, 4:30–6:00, Reception for the New Women Faculty. Each year the provost's office, the institute, and the feminist studies program sponsor this event. New women faculty members are asked to introduce themselves and to speak briefly about their areas of interest, while women already on the faculty are encouraged to attend and to welcome the newcomers. It is a celebration, then, of Stanford's "community of women." This year the number of women added to the faculty—thirty-two—brought exclamations of pleased surprise from the old guard. At least as hopeful a sign of change was the range of disciplines represented: four in engineering, ten in the medical school, four in the sciences, two in the law school, one in the business school. And, with a busy quarter already under way, twenty-three of these new faculty members came to the reception.

Standing beside Cathy Jensen, I was among the pleased exclaimers. Cathy joined me but murmured, "There are very few of the regular women faculty here." True—and I knew in part the reason. February is the height of the hiring season. The English department was hosting a candidate in its ongoing senior search, and there were job talks being given in other departments as well. With crowded schedules and competing demands, women necessarily find themselves choosing to work within their separate departments. Therefore, the increased number of women on the faculty does not in itself bring increased interdisciplinary communication.

A far more serious problem shadows my pleasure in these added numbers of women faculty. The pressures on all untenured faculty members involve not simply schedule but also the steady rise in the height of the bar for tenure. How many of the untenured among the thirty-two arrivals actually will be granted tenure? The last tenure appointment made through the ranks from the English department (bracketing my own half-time appointment) dates back more than ten years. Such signs do not augur well for the future.

Tuesday, March 2, 12:00–2:00, lunch with a friend. The friend, not a member of the English department, is one among many people — including what appears to be a disproportionate number of women — who have recently been denied tenure at Stanford. Our lunch was nonetheless in great part a celebration: she had just accepted a chaired professorship from another institution. It was also a chance for me to learn something more of the class-action suit being brought against Stanford by the Labor Department. The question posed is whether Stanford is an academic workplace inimical to women and minorities.

In this connection a report to the Faculty Senate on the situation of women at Stanford, drawn up last year by a committee of the Women's Caucus chaired by Estelle Freedman (history) and Cecelia Ridgeway (sociology) highlighted an extremely important point that might otherwise have gone unnoticed. In the 1980s, when women's presence on the Stanford faculty made a noticeable advance, the administration then in place subscribed to a policy of affirmative action at both the hiring and tenure levels. This policy did not allow a lower standard for minorities and women, but it did take the position that, when there might be two opposed judgments about the quality of a tenure candidate's work, those ruling in the matter should favor the more positive view. That policy was subsequently changed under a provost who is an African-American woman; now affirmative action is operative at the entry level to Stanford but not at the tenure level. The Stanford Faculty Senate was never consulted about this policy change; it was a unilateral administrative decision, and in 1999 there appear to be no procedures in place whereby it can be overruled. Not a happy sign.

Thursday, March 4, 4:00–5:30, feminist studies alumnae panel. As we move toward spring quarter, graduating seniors often experience separation anxiety. For those majoring in feminist studies this can be the moment when actual voices or voices in their heads say, "I told you you'd be better off majoring in English if you planned to go to law school." As a practical response to this difficulty, Masum, the undergraduate coordinator, has for the past two years organized a session in which graduates from the program meet with the seniors. The alumnae describe their experiences on the job market and in their present work, thereby transforming the unknown into something imaginable and so less threatening. My presence at the gathering was simply ex officio — a courtesy to Masum and the alumnae and an indication to the seniors of the program's interest in their decision-making process. I did not expect myself to be one of those receiving wisdom or help.

As part of the plan to show as many options as possible within limited time, each panelist represented a different area of choice. But as I listened, I noticed a common theme. Each one, without for a moment "preaching," simply took two points as given: first, that majoring in feminist studies had been her way of analyzing the sources of injury and injustice to be found at the intersections of race, class, gender, and sexual preference; and second, that the work she chose after college must in some way resist and negate those sources. Backlash against feminism and the "me first" mentality taken as characteristic of the 1990s have not gone away, but I was hearing testimony to another attitude at work in the world as well. The dream of a community of women may have had deep flaws, but here were women building community and doing so, at least in part, because of that earlier dream, despite its flaws and mistakes. Perhaps, after all, we had learned something from the mistakes.

My life rooted here at Stanford, I did not come to the meeting with the alumnae burdened with the seniors' anxieties. Yet, as the narrative above suggests, I did come with fears about the imagined future, the twenty-first century, as a world of escalating competition filled with attendant violence, injustice, and self-concern. Those realities cannot be blinked away, but they are also not the whole truth by any means, as I could tell from the narratives of these former feminist studies majors. The very last words spoken at the "Communities of Women" conference were Sister Joan Chittister's: "This conference was designed to call all of us to begin again, begin anew." They still seem appropriate several months into the year 2000.

English Department
Stanford University

Jean F. O'Barr

My Master List for the Millennium

Like many who will read this essay, I am a list maker. What do I plan to do and when do I need to do it? And every once in a while, I enter the major leagues and make a list of my lists. What have I committed myself to do and how will I prioritize those commitments? And, like some who will read this essay, I do not quarrel with using events such as the millennium to encourage reflection. I find such events an ideal time to make lists, for they focus me both backward and forward simultaneously.

My colleague Mary Armstrong, who read this essay in draft form, suggested that list making is indeed a feminist practice. Feminism, she observed, is constantly in the process of thinking of, and consistently and repeatedly fighting for the recognition of, its own history and the history of women. Feminism envisions the future with an ongoing consciousness. In short, the work of feminism is the work of always having the master lists in mind. The millennium may help us acknowledge the very special consciousness we try to cultivate and maintain as feminists.

In rethinking my personal habit in light of her comments about our collective tendencies, I plunged ahead to compile a list of the commitments I believe feminism needs to pursue, with some notes on how to get going. And like all lists, some items will be scratched off over time and others will reappear under various headings for decades.

Challenges that confound me

1. *Negotiating the many languages of feminism.* Figure out how to talk to feminist colleagues in our own specialized and theoretical language at one moment and in the next moment discuss feminist issues with my campus and community colleagues in terms that are meaningful for them.

2. *Pursue the tough research questions interdisciplinarily* in a climate that pretends there are few if any left to pursue. Seek outlets to publish interdisciplinary analyses and then build a *curriculum vitae* of works that meets the measure of senior colleagues who bring disciplinary judgments to bear in campus decision making.

3. *Keep political commitments at the core of all these endeavors.* When

[*Signs: Journal of Women in Culture and Society* 2000, vol. 25, no. 4]

colleagues say that feminist scholarship is political, remember that theirs was too — at some point every discipline arose in response to a social problem. When colleagues resist a feminist proposal on political grounds (but never saying so), remember that according women and gender center stage always causes discomfort since it means a rearrangement of power. And when colleagues worry that feminists disagree, agree with them — healthy disagreement is a key marker of vigorous intellectual inquiry, so celebrate it.

4. *Work with the folks who have more power and different politics.* To achieve institutional compromise, to choose the battle that might be won at the moment (and, hopefully, will not backfire later), is to maintain the long view while surviving in the short run. Be around, and active, for the long haul.

5. *Learn to talk to the next generations, whose experiences are different from my own.* Repeat to myself that their issues show a difference on the surface but that underneath there is a substantial similarity. And remember not to tell them to be grateful for all that we have done.

6. *Find the balance between arrogance and apathy* (a Charlotte Bunch phrase) when it comes to women from backgrounds and cultures other than my own. Acknowledge that (*a*) they have many of the keys to understanding their own needs, (*b*) some of the strategies people like me have developed might aid their success, and (*c*) they have much to teach and we have much to learn in the exchange.

7. *Turn jokes about women and feminism around,* driving a point home but leaving out the egregious insults.

Ideas about what to do

1. *Develop a complex agenda.* Get out of the either-or mentality when thinking about what to do and go for the both-and strategy (although maybe not in the same day). Remember that, along with most women who have assumed multiple tasks and roles in family, work, and community, I am accomplished at doing several things at once.

2. *Get space.* Space of all kinds, so that we can come together across the lines that demarcate us now: campus space in offices, classrooms, hallways, parking lots, mailrooms, and toilets; community space where women from many locations find common ground; public space at national and regional conferences on disciplinary and topical issues; intellectual space at research conferences of our own that are genuinely interdisciplinary; organizational space in an association that speaks for feminists, with us, about us as a field of inquiry; space in print and on electronic media that spreads the ideas and options we are developing about women, gender, and feminism.

3. *Foster coalitions.* Individuals and groups always have agendas. Their agendas will not be identical to ours, but our agendas will overlap. Think about ways to come together at those intersections. This applies to community-campus interfaces, to the relationships between various theories in the academy, and to the myriad policy decisions in institutions of higher education. Note that coalition building will be helped by a multitask agenda and some spaces to pursue it.

4. *Do not get stuck.* Think of the feminist toolbox as having everything — master's tools, new tools, and old tools that can be deployed for new purposes. Use the toolbox: spend energy on deciding which tools to use, not only on how to equip the toolbox. I will know what I need when I try using the tools that I have — then I can search out others.

5. *Write, speak, think, argue, reinforce.* Be conscious of our history and develop a sense of responsibility to communicate it. Do whatever it takes to leave a richer legacy than the one inherited. That includes leaving private papers to a library and telling children and younger friends what all this fuss about women has meant.

6. *Change structures.* (This is the hardest one.) Begin by changing women and the circumstances in which they sometimes find themselves and the ways many present themselves and are represented. Do not stop with changing people: get people to change structures. Remember: only when there is a shift in institutional patterns of power can people sustain the changes they have initiated.

7. *Persist, persist, persist and then take a few days off.* (No, this is the hardest one.) There is no way to battle sexism constantly and stay balanced. Feed the spirit and tend the body so that the mind can soar. Be passionate in commitment and use the power of that passion, knowing that the glass is better imagined as half full than as half empty.

Women's Studies Program
Duke University

Noliwe M. Rooks

Like Canaries in the Mines: Black Women's Studies at the Millennium

The United States should have closed down and examined its every intention, institution, and law on the very first day a black woman observed that the collard greens tasted like water.
— Walker 1988, 35

Recently, one of her colleagues mentioned that Lani Guinier is working on a theory about the similarities between black communities and the canaries once used by coal miners to detect poisonous gas in the mines. She believes that, in much the same way as the death of the tiny birds would signal the presence of poison gas and give the larger, stronger miners a chance to make a quick retreat before they were harmed, the collective gaspings, reelings, and collapses of urban black communities signals the approach of evils that threaten us all. Her point, much like that of the above quote of Alice Walker, is that we need to pay attention to what happens "over there to those people," because "there" can become "here" and "them" can become "us" rather quickly.

While it is my contention that the health of black women's studies parallels that of larger fields (women's studies, history, English) within the academy, in the few short pages that follow, I want to look specifically at one aspect of the academic life and health of black women's studies — the circulation of ideas, scholarship, and theoretical paradigms. Black women's scholarly space is shrinking (if cited at all, the work of black women scholars is often buried in a footnote), bodies are disappearing (the work of the actual black women in black women's studies is often forgotten entirely), and those without an elevator to carry them up out of the mines are staring at each other in wide-eyed wonder (many whose work falls within the confines of the field find themselves engaged in scholarly conversation only with each other). If I had a lot more space and a little more courage, I would now turn to a number of recent and historical examples that illustrate my point. However, given the limitations of both, anecdotal evidence will have to suffice.

At a recent conference on African-American studies hosted at an East

[*Signs: Journal of Women in Culture and Society* 2000, vol. 25, no. 4]

Coast institution, a black woman colleague and I marveled at the fact that, with the exception of the panel on gender, few black women scholars had been invited to participate. While the gender panel was composed entirely of black women academics, the six remaining panels included only two invited black women scholars. Additionally, we noticed that we did not hear anyone who was not black and female utter the name or mention the work of an African-American woman academic. It was not that such work was not relevant, but the conference was not specifically about black women and so neither their brains nor their bodies were seen as crucial. This state of affairs is either a form of academic apartheid or death. I'm not sure which, but I am sure that the greens are tasting mighty watery. I also know that this was not a turn of events I had anticipated when I graduated from college and entered graduate school in 1987.

By the late 1980s, black women's studies seemed poised to take over the universe. Toni Morrison and Alice Walker were popular publishing phenomena; Paula Giddings had recently initiated a popular interest in African-American women's history and club movements; Barbara Christian had already traced a history of black feminist criticism; bell hooks was writing a staggering amount in various forms and forums about black women's relationship to feminism, representation, power, and ideology; Hortense Spillers and Mae Henderson had introduced the world to black women's relationship to deconstruction and various critical theories; a whole host of graduate students were writing dissertations, theses, research papers, and conference presentations on subjects that situated black women at the center of numerous discourses and disciplines; and there was serious interdisciplinary exploration of black women's past and present lives, literatures, and histories. That period was undeniably a high-water mark for work and interest in African-American women's studies. Even so, those canaries have been chirping away, trying to tell the rest of us something.

Indeed, in a 1994 article published in this journal, Ann duCille wrote passionately about what she termed "The Occult of True Black Womanhood" (1994). She asked who owned the field and why the overwhelming interest in the subject was functioning to exclude the scholarship of black women academics. She wanted to know how it was that fellowships, jobs, and tenure for people working in black women's studies seemed to pass black women by. In short, she raised an alarm while at the same time making clear that she was in no way interested in policing the boundaries of the field or acting as a gatekeeper to determine what kind of people engaged in this work. All were welcome to either visit or move into the neighborhood; duCille just wanted to remind them that there were already people living there. Although that article was authored in the early 1990s, there are still some striking similarities to the state of the field as we put a period on the decade and begin a new century. At first blush, it does not appear that duCille's warnings resulted in quick action. While there are some slight differences between then and now, they generally are not for the better.

If one of the primary problems for black women's studies in the mid-1990s was a sort of historical amnesia with regard to the contributions of pioneers in the field of black women's studies, as well a distressing lack of academic support for black women who wanted to work in the field, at the end of the century it no longer is deemed necessary to become familiar with the work of contemporary black women academics or, once one becomes familiar with the work, to give credit for the ideas used. There are, for example, any number of black women academics who have had the experience of leafing through a book or article that directly relates to some work we have published and finding our work unmentioned or of listening to a talk and hearing the substance of our work come back at us out of the mouths of the speakers. It's just our *names* that are missing, although, we are always assured, "You are in the footnotes—somewhere."

Black women's studies has gained some and lost some in the the past ten-odd years since I entered graduate school and began to work in the field. However, I'm not sure the fundamental dynamics of space and power have been reconfigured in any significant way during that period. This in and of itself should serve as a warning to the rest of us. In the meantime, we are left to wonder about the place of African-American women's scholarship in the academy and to ask whether we intend to pay attention to the health of the canaries in the mines: leave them to their insistent chirping without a backward glance or free them to fly into the bright sunlight of a new century. We should decide while the decision is still ours to make.

History Department
Princeton University

References

duCille, Ann. 1994. "The Occult of True Black Womanhood: Critical Demeanor and Black Feminist Studies." *Signs: Journal of Women in Culture and Society* 19(3):591–629.

Walker, Alice. 1988. "Longing to Die of Old Age." In her *Living by the Word: Selected Writings, 1973–1987*. New York: Harcourt Brace Jovanovich.

Regrets

This little essay bothers me greatly, because I want to write it and I want to write it right: to think about what has changed, what research remains to be done, what advice I'd give to younger scholars. But try as I may, I'm not sure I can even show up. Every time I sit down to write, especially when I think about the academy in the next five years, exasperation overflows my computer.

For twenty-five years I've been hearing too much of the same frustrations from my colleagues of color. Too little has changed for me to cherish the "progress" I know to lie at the core of a mandatory narrative from scholars of color. We can complain, but only after praising how far we have come and how much things have changed for the better, thank you. But I can't write the "progress" narrative. Managing mainstream feminists just saps too much energy for me to perform it at the end of the academic year.

How can I reflect on how far we have come when American historians still divide not only the American past but also American historiography into "real" history, which counts, and African-American history, which does not count and need not be read or cited, unless produced by whites?

How can I speak of progress when I know that young African-American historians' fear that they will not be judged fairly by their professors is founded?

How can I assure my younger colleagues that things have changed when only white historians receive prestigious prizes for writing African-American history?

When black women professors are vulnerable to harassment from male students of all races?

When white colleagues routinely forget they have black colleagues?

When we in the minority are still expected to smile gently when we're the only one, time after time after time?

When isolation, exhaustion, and frustration sit at the end of every working day, little energy remains for the contemplation of issues beyond how to make it to the next day and the end of each semester.

[*Signs: Journal of Women in Culture and Society* 2000, vol. 25, no. 4]

After such a long time and still so many of the same old frustrations, I'm just plain worn out.

African-American Studies Program and History Department
Princeton University

Barbara Ransby

Black Feminism at Twenty-One: Reflections on the Evolution of a National Community

After mourning the loss of several stillborn black feminist organizations over the course of the 1990s, the midwives were beginning to feel cursed. Why did the baby keep dying before she could be nursed to life? Why did we seem unable to sustain a national organization beyond the moment of crisis or celebration that inspired its conception? There were political and personality differences at play, to be sure, and there was also the sheer enormity of the task and the lack of resources, time, and stamina, given all the other battles we were fighting simultaneously. But there had to be something else. After all, we knew there was a constituency for black feminist ideas and issues. There was the African-American Women in Defense of Ourselves (AAWIDOO) mobilization of sixteen hundred women in response to the Anita Hill-Clarence Thomas hearings in 1991. A few years later, in response to the Million Man March (MMM), there was another series of gatherings, a public statement critical of the march, and several follow-up gatherings under the banner of African-American Agenda 2000. And in Chicago in 1998, a historic gathering of the Black Radical Congress (BRC) inspired the formation of a Black Feminist Caucus. But by 1999, it appeared that all of these attempts at creating a national black feminist entity centered on the politics of grassroots organizing had failed.

After all of our meetings, conferences, mobilizations, listservs, draft documents, retreats, and rallies, what did we have to show for our efforts? There was no name, no structure, no office, no budget, not even a voice-mail or post-office box. There was no organization for black feminists/womanists on par with the National Organization for Women or the National Association for the Advancement of Colored People—no national marker that we actually existed. But we do exist—a loose network of black

This article, constrained by time and space, does not profess to be a comprehensive survey of black feminist political work or scholarship; rather, it highlights those struggles and campaigns in which I have been directly involved and the scholarly literature that intersects with my own research and writing.

[*Signs: Journal of Women in Culture and Society* 2000, vol. 25, no. 4]

women activists and a few male fellow travelers and nonblack supporters who have established a tangible political history together and, more important, have established the parameters of a shared political consensus. It is that consensus, as well as the awkward but protracted process by which it was achieved, that offers hope for a more democratic and inclusive progressive movement in the twenty-first century.

When Deborah King, Elsa Barkley Brown, and I launched the AAWI-DOO campaign to protest Clarence Thomas's nomination to the Supreme Court and to highlight the issue of sexual harassment and the media's silencing of black women, we did not talk about our long-term goals. As it turned out, our ideas about where the mobilization was headed and at what pace were quite different, and, after several local branches in Chicago, New York, and Philadelphia failed to sustain themselves without the support of a national body or solidly planted roots, the entire AAWIDOO initiative slowly and quietly faded out of existence. Nevertheless, a collective silence had been broken. Not since the National Black Feminist Organization and its more well-known offshoot, the Combahee River Collective, made their marks in the mid-1970s had black women in the United States organized around a feminist/womanist agenda and made a national public intervention. We raised more than $50,000 in a short time to place ads in the *New York Times* and African-American newspapers around the country, and we compiled a mailing list of over two thousand names, which itself became a vital resource for subsequent local and national mobilizations. The campaign represented a growing consensus among an often invisible network of activists and intellectuals who at least partly shared a political vision, even if we were not all card-carrying members of any one club.[1]

In 1993, black feminist writer Jill Nelson, activist Gail Garfield, and others organized a series of rallies to protest plans by the predominantly male political establishment of Harlem to give Mike Tyson, a convicted rapist, a hero's welcome after his release from prison. Black feminist activists in Harlem took the principled but unpopular position that rape was both a feminist issue and a black community issue and that, racism within the criminal justice system notwithstanding, rapists could not be celebrated as heroes in our community. The Harlem activists requested the AAWI-

---

[1] During the MMM mobilization, the *New York Times Magazine* featured a story on black feminism by a novice writer who distorted and obscured more about black feminism than she revealed (Zooks 1995). This type of skewed media coverage reinforces invisibility as much as outright silence does. For more carefully researched studies of black feminism and black women's political activism, see Smith 1983; Giddings 1984; Guy-Sheftall 1995; Collins 1998.

DOO mailing list to publicize and garner support for their campaign, and AAWIDOO's strategy of buying newspaper ads served as an inspiration and model for St. Louis activists who organized a similar campaign against the exaltation of Tyson in their community.[2]

The growing network of black feminists across the country again became visible in 1995 when the aspiring patriarch of black politics, Nation of Islam minister Louis Farrakhan, convened a gathering of men in the nation's capital to reclaim their rightful places as heads of their families and leaders of the entire black community. Feminist activist and law professor Kimberle Crenshaw organized a national meeting in New York in the spring of 1995 to explore how black feminists should respond to the MMM. We formed an ad hoc committee, issued a public statement, and participated in several community forums. Our response to the MMM and the increasing male-centeredness of black politics and community priorities represented a deepening national consensus among black feminists. The black community as a whole was sharply divided over the march, with the majority in support. The issue, for many, was not clear cut: for some, opposing Clarence Thomas's sexism had been easy because there were so many other reasons (having to do with his conservative antiblack politics) to oppose him, but to challenge a charismatic religious icon like Farrakhan or a superstar athlete like Tyson was a different matter altogether. Nevertheless, black feminists once again mobilized on fairly short notice to do precisely that.

The black feminist statement issued on the eve of the MMM, like AAWIDOO's four years earlier, was not a narrow, single-issue document. It outlined both the sexism and unprecedented gender exclusivity of the MMM and also the conservative class message of the march's principal spokesman. A core of activists held several follow-up meetings and a three-day-long retreat to try to map out a way forward after the march. Again, old phone chains from previous mobilizations were activated and relationships reestablished. There was a clear sense of a tangible national constituency. While most of those who participated were college educated and, to a large extent, middle class, we were engaged in many different areas of political work: international human rights; antiviolence; opposition to the prison industrial complex; welfare rights and antipoverty work; civil rights and sexual harassment litigation; alternative media; lesbian, bisexual, gay, and transsexual work; and student organizing. Some of the members of this group, which called itself African-American Agenda 2000, later became key organizers of either the African American Policy Forum or the

---

[2] White 1999 provides an excellent detailed analysis of the St. Louis campaign.

Feminist Caucus of the Black Radical Congress (two groups that reconnected to work on the Tabitha Walrond case in the summer of 1999).[3] Even though questions of strategy and tactics have divided us at times, our politics keep bringing us back together.

So, what are the politics that unite a disparate cross section of organizers under the rubric of black feminism? Let me first address the method and style of organizing and then, briefly, the ideological content. Over the past decade, the style of black feminist work has represented a democratic impulse within the larger progressive movement, with decentralized mobilization efforts, informal leadership, and flexible structures. This has not always been the most efficient way to organize, but the political benefits have outweighed the inconvenience. Moreover, we have benefited from such organizational structures, which have consisted of less hierarchical steering committees and coordinating groups rather than chairpersons, presidents, and officers in the more common linear fashion. Over the years, black women have evolved organization styles consistent with the specific cultural, economic, and historical realities that have defined our lives. I cannot, within the confines of this article, outline all of the nuanced variations, but one predominant strain is a decentralized, group-centered, grassroots democratic model, best exemplified by the lifelong work of Ella Jo Baker and Septima Poinsette Clark.[4] Given this history, it is not surprising that no single charismatic figure has emerged to personify and symbolize the movement. For example, there is no dark-skinned version of Gloria Steinem or Betty Friedan in black feminist circles; there are no female counterparts to Louis Farrakhan or Jesse Jackson, Sr. in terms of political visibility. Angela Davis, Barbara Smith, and bell hooks are perhaps the most renowned living black feminist personae, but, for different reasons, each has admirably resisted and declined icon status.

But what are the ideological tenets around which black feminists have organized? Perhaps strongest is the notion that race, class, gender, and sexuality are codependent variables that cannot readily be separated and ranked in scholarship, in political practice, or in lived experience. The main tension within diverse political coalitions has been the tendency to rank

---

[3] Walrond was a young black woman on welfare who, in May 1999, was convicted of negligent homicide for her baby's death. She had attempted unsuccessfully to breast-feed the baby, was not given adequate medical support, and was denied medical treatment for the child a short time before he died because his Medicaid card had not yet arrived in the mail. A coalition of groups supported Walrond's case, citing it as an example of sexism, racism, economic injustice, and the growing emphasis on prisons over social services.

[4] On the democratic character of many of black women's organizing efforts, see Brodkin 1988; Payne 1995; Robnett 1997.

different systems of oppression and thus prioritize the liberation agendas of certain groups within the coalition. Because any political agenda that addresses the realities of most African-American women's lives must deal with the four major systems of oppression and exploitation—race, class, gender, and sexuality—black feminist politics radically breaks down the notion of mutually exclusive, competing identities and interests and instead understands identities and political process as organic, fluid, interdependent, dynamic, and historical. The openness of our political processes and the permeability of our multiple identities help create the potential for collaborations that transcend social boundaries and reject elitist criteria for leadership. Instead of policing boundaries, racial or otherwise, black feminists have more often than not penetrated these barriers, expanding the meaning of "we" and "community" in the process.

Contrary to those who argue that black struggles, women's struggles, queer struggles narrow our range of vision and divide us into factions, the radical organizers and theorists within these so-called identity-based movements actually offer the terms for a higher level of unity, integration, and interaction. Radicals within the feminist, lesbigay-trans, and people of color communities generally see fighting against economic exploitation as intimately related to, and inseparable from, the fight against racism, sexism, and heterosexism and as a critical component of their political agenda. Thus, these forces are potentially the connective tissue between various social change movements and constituencies, rather than the wedge that divides them. Nothing embodies this spirit better than the founding statement of the Combahee River Collective, conceived nearly a quarter-century ago by black lesbian feminist activists in Boston, many of whom continue to play central roles in progressive struggles today. It reads: "The most general statement of our politics at the present time would be that we are actively committed to struggling against racial, sexual, heterosexual, and class oppression and see as our particular task the development of integrated analysis and practice based upon the fact that the major systems of oppression are interlocking. The synthesis of these oppressions creates the conditions of our lives" (Combahee River Collective [1977] 1995, 232).

It is no coincidence, then, that black feminist organizers around the country have deeply immersed themselves in struggles that incorporate but are not isolated to gender issues.[5] In the decades since the formation of the

---

[5] For example, Beth Richie's (1995) work on domestic violence has connections with larger antiviolence, antipoverty, and prisoners' rights movements, as does Angela Davis's work on the prison industrial complex. Atlanta-based black feminist Loretta Ross and Washington D.C.-based organizer and law professor Lisa Crooms have worked on international and domestic human rights projects that incorporate many issues in addition to gender.

short-lived Combahee River Collective, black feminist practice has evolved, not so much reinventing itself as building on the foundational vision, outlined in 1977, of an inclusive, multi-issue political agenda built on a fluid democratic practice. And while we often bemoan the absence of a tangible physical place of our own, black feminists are not invisible, nor have we been effectively silenced. A wealth of scholarship has helped to forge a heterogeneous body of work that explores and debates the applications and interpretations of black feminist political ideology. More important, because of our persistent efforts—the lessons learned, strategies explored, trust established, storms weathered—perhaps now we have the kind of history that can give us greater optimism for the future, optimism that might enable the forging of an independent black feminist organization with links and ties to multiple other oppositional and visionary movements of the twenty-first century.

African-American Studies Department
University of Illinois at Chicago

References
Brodkin, Karen. 1988. *Caring by the Hour: Women, Work, and Organizing at Duke Medical Center.* Urbana: University of Illinois Press.
Collins, Patricia Hill. 1998. *Fighting Words: Black Women and the Search for Justice.* Minneapolis: University of Minnesota Press.
Combahee River Collective (Barbara Smith, Beverly Smith, and Demita Frazier). (1977) 1995. "A Black Feminist Statement." In Guy-Sheftall 1995, 232–40.
Giddings, Paula. 1984. *When and Where I Enter: The Impact of Black Women on Race and Sex in America.* New York: Morrow.
Guy-Sheftall, Beverly, ed. 1995. *Words of Fire: An Anthology of African-American Feminist Thought.* New York: New Press.
hooks, bell. 1984. *Feminist Theory from Margin to Center.* Boston: South End.
Payne, Charles M. 1995. *I've Got the Light of Freedom: The Organizing Tradition and the Mississippi Freedom Struggle.* Berkeley: University of California Press.
Richie, Beth. 1995. *Compelled to Crime: The Gender Entrapment of Battered Black Women.* New York: Routledge.
Robnett, Belinda. 1997. *How Long? How Long? African-American Women in the Struggle for Civil Rights.* New York: Oxford University Press.

Barbara Smith's long and diverse career of outspoken activism (as chronicled in Smith 1998) on issues from police brutality to the case of political prisoner Mumia Abu-Jamal belies the stereotype that the political agenda of a black lesbian is narrow or parochial. And the late black lesbian feminist poet-activist Audre Lorde was the embodiment of such broad-based politics: all issues having to do with injustice were her issues (and, since her death, the New York-based Audre Lorde Project has carried on her tradition) (see also hooks 1984).

Smith, Barbara. 1998. *The Truth That Never Hurts: Writings on Race, Gender, and Freedom.* New Brunswick, N.J.: Rutgers University Press.

Smith, Barbara, ed. 1983. *Home Girls: A Black Feminist Anthology.* New York: Kitchen Table/Women of Color.

White, Aaronette M. 1999. "Talking Feminist, Talking Black: Micromobilization Processes in a Collective Protest against Rape." *Gender & Society* 13(1):77–100.

Zooks, Krystal Brent. 1995. "A Manifesto of Sorts for a New Black Feminist Movement." *New York Times Magazine,* November 12.

Once More into the Streets

Millennium, schmillennium. I'll be happy to survive the next few years of "friendly" fire—the continued transfer of the public purse from the needy to the greedy and of young men of color from schools to prisons, the castigation of white women for daring to have abortions and of women of color for daring to raise children. With "friends" like these, as a dead white European man once said, "what is to be done?" To answer that question, I turn to history, looking backward to find the way forward. Yes, I know about subjectivity, that my history is not necessarily yours, that there are many histories and no one truth. But some histories and subjectivities can suggest ways forward, while others leave us in despair. (Guess which get more play in mass and scholarly media?) My history is of the former kind.

I am an affirmative-action baby. Thanks to the civil rights and black freedom movements, I'm a very comfortable middle-aged, middle-class white woman, thank you. Second-wave feminism, my own included, was just a bud when all those funds that put me through graduate school magically appeared. And I wasn't even one of the targeted beneficiaries. But a beneficiary I certainly was. And so were lots of other white women—and men—of my generation. I know who put us where we are—lots and lots of mainly working-class black and brown women and men. And now it's payback time. Make no mistake, my history tells me that payback is good for white folks too, and it's especially good for white feminists.

Like many middle-class white feminists who finished their undergraduate years in the early to mid-sixties, I got a virtually free ride through graduate school, mostly from fellowships large enough to support me. The sixties and early seventies were years when public funding to train more college teachers grew sharply. Most of us wannabe academics were white and middle class because, before the civil rights movement, that's who college was mainly for. There was precious little about gender equity in any of this (I was told by a senior colleague at my first teaching job that he

This essay and the following one, by France Winddance Twine, come from conversations between the two authors across race and generation.

[*Signs: Journal of Women in Culture and Society* 2000, vol. 25, no. 4]

liked to hire women because they worked much harder and you didn't have to pay them much).

The reason that money went into expanding graduate education and training college teachers was that undergraduate education had expanded. And most of that expansion was a result of pressure by the black freedom and allied social justice movements to desegregate higher education so that more than token numbers of people of color and working-class whites could attend college. That pressure also produced Medicare, Medicaid, Head Start, and the reform and expansion of Aid for Families with Dependent Children (AFDC). Health, education, and welfare for all Americans. Hardly small change.

The combination of social movements and urban uprisings gave birth to a wave of public community-college building in general and in neighborhoods of color in particular. For example, years of pressure from African Americans for a community college in Detroit, a predominantly black city surrounded by largely white counties with such colleges, produced nothing—until the 1967 Detroit uprising. Two weeks after the fires died out, politicians found funds for Wayne County Community College. In New York, City University expanded exponentially, instituted open admissions, hired many of my graduate-school peers and professors, and, as a tuition-free institution, became a model for public higher education nationally. New York's state university system and California's three-tier system also expanded greatly in a more democratic direction than they had before and than they have since. These developments greatly increased multiracial access to higher education for undergraduates, graduates, and faculty. The result, despite a couple of decades of backsliding, is that U.S. universities today are considerably more colorful than they were when the sixties began.

This was the history that gave birth to the feminist movement. The white—and black and Chicana—feminists who animated the second wave came out of the civil rights, Chicano, and other movements that were part of a broad tapestry of movements working to broaden democracy in America. The idea that all the early feminists were white or that feminism was only about white women obliterates the contributions of African-American and Chicana feminist activists who were working and writing in 1970 (e.g., Toni Cade Bambara, Frances Beal, Eleanor Holmes Norton, the Black Women's Liberation Group, Elizabeth Sutherland, and Enriqueta Longauex y Vasquez).

Twenty-five years ago, the lines between feminism in the academy and activism in the streets were much more blurred than they are today. As a result of contributing to Robin Morgan's anthology *Sisterhood Is Powerful*

(1970), I received more mail than I could answer. As a new faculty member at Oakland University near Pontiac, Michigan, I invited my activist and feminist undergrads to form a group to answer the mail and to join in helping women from across southern Michigan set up their own consciousness-raising groups. In those years when abortion was illegal, we were also involved, with local clergy, in helping pregnant women get abortions, first in Canada, then in New York. Three older, returning women students in my anthropology class and three young ones in Carol Andreas's sociology class organized a campus movement for a child-care center. It became a mass movement that included campus workers and their demands of pay equity and culminated in a sit-in child-care center in the university president's office. My university was not a high profile place; it was not famous for activism; we didn't make headlines. But our activism was probably not that unusual either.

Women's studies was but one of many institutions—like battered women's shelters, women's clinics, rape crisis centers, political organizations and women's buildings—that we hoped would help save women's lives. Broad movement activism made curricular space for the then-bizarre notion of women's studies programs, which we envisioned as one among many institutions whose mission was to support equality for women as part of a wider push for democracy for all.

That was then; this is now. All of those social justice programs, like the affirmative-action programs under such heavy attack today, benefited everyone. They were not zero-sum games; rather, they expanded greatly the institutions that served health, education, housing, and welfare needs. National priorities were democratized because there was a social movement, a coalition of movements, strong enough to do it. These truths of my history are hard to find in today's mass-produced historical record.[1]

Mass-produced histories explain the wholesale shift away from public responsibility for social service toward a military/prison/police-centered state as necessary and good. Racist gender stereotypes are at the heart of these histories: demonizing women on welfare as African-American welfare queens and caricaturing African-American and Latino men as gangbangers and criminals are part of a history designed to show that social welfare programs created monsters of color. The message was unspoken

---

[1] Not surprisingly, some of the self-appointed stewards of U.S. higher education were less than pleased by these trends: in 1968, the Carnegie Commission worried that, by the nineties, the majority of the nation's tenured faculty would be those whose ideas were formed in the antiracist and democratic political environment of the sixties, and the Committee for Economic Development recommended greatly increasing the size and strength of university administration as an antidote to faculty power (see Sacks 1978).

but loud and clear: whiteness is heterosexuality, is subordination of women, is "respectable," is rightness, and rightness doesn't make waves.

So now it's payback time. Perhaps more than other social movements, campus programs, and organizations created to further social justice, women's studies has grown in size and strength. True, it has also lost much of its fire and has remained too white, but, still, at some level, we believe that our mission is to further social justice for all women — in the curriculum, in the university, in society. Payback means translating our multiracial feminist analyses into words of one syllable and taking them back to the streets, repoliticizing ourselves, and helping to rebuild the alliances that can redemocratize politics today. Feminist and critical race scholars developed the theory; women's studies programs need to put it more consistently into practice. In that spirit, I have three concrete recommendations for the immediate future:

1. Women's studies curricula should be reorganized around a critical analysis of the counterpoint between the gendered racism of public policy and dominant discourses (domestic and global) on the one hand, and the variety of challenges and alternatives to these on the other.
2. Women's studies programs should become much more vocally and visibly involved in fights to preserve and expand affirmative action.
3. As the largest organized voice of feminism (with more than 1,500 programs in the United States alone), women's studies should take the lead in amplifying feminist voices on these issues.

Women's Studies, as the largest of the programs created by earlier racial and social justice movements, has the responsibility to initiate the kinds of coalition-building needed to reanimate these campus and community movements. The time to start is now.

Anthropology Department
University of California, Los Angeles

References

Sacks, Karen Brodkin. 1978. "Survival of the Fattest." *Radical Teacher* (March): 33–37.

Feminist Fairy Tales for Black and American Indian Girls: A Working-Class Vision

In 1998 I was invited to participate in a workshop, "Feminism's Race Question," organized by feminist historians Ellen DuBois and Brenda Stevenson at UCLA. I left this conference revitalized and affirmed after listening to sessions that included Rosalyn Terborg-Penn, Evelynn Hammonds, Tessie Liu, Michael Awkward, and Eric Avila, among others. It was the first time that I had participated in panels that included black and Chicano male feminists from working-class origins along with established middle-class feminists. This workshop was the first I had attended that approached what I imagined a utopic feminist space/project to be: one that included women and men of color, working-class scholars, gay, lesbian, and queer scholars, as well as scholars trained in different disciplines and of different generations all engaged in dialogue.

What I envision two decades from now is working-class American Indian and U.S. black children claiming feminisms to empower themselves. I desire for the next generation what I was exposed to as a working-class girl living under American apartheid—a feminism that empowered me. I would like my experience of inclusion in feminist antiracist projects extended to future generations of working-class U.S. black and American Indian children who do not possess the cultural or financial capital to access a university education without a social justice movement. I want them to learn that feminism(s) can work for them. Is this "fairy tale" possible today in communities that differ from the segregated, working-class, and Catholic world in which I learned to claim feminism in Chicago two decades ago?

My journey to a feminist antiracist identity may be interpreted by some as a black feminist fairy tale, but it was a real product of the civil rights and women's movements. As a black girl (with an American Indian father) attending Catholic schools, I was taught by a series of feminists—mainly Irish Catholic nuns struggling to chart their own paths to antiracism. I

This essay and the previous one, by Karen Brodkin, come from conversations between the two authors across race and generation.

[*Signs: Journal of Women in Culture and Society* 2000, vol. 25, no. 4]

learned in contradictory spaces that feminism belonged to me. I have no personal memories of a monolithic middle-class feminism not attached to an antiracist agenda, and it was not until the early 1980s, as a member of a feminist writers group (consisting mainly of Jewish feminist poets), that I read about the history of U.S. feminism and learned of various forms of exclusion and racism as practiced by white feminists. But I read this as past history because I had grown up with feminist antiracists of all ethnic backgrounds in my life. My earliest memories are of the civil rights and women's movements, and although I was too young to participate actively, I was taught that these social justice movements gave me access to a university education.

I had neither U.S. black feminist nor American Indian feminist mentors in the two departments (anthropology and sociology) in which I trained as a doctoral student. I entered the graduate program in anthropology at the University of California, Berkeley, in 1989 and was surprised to find no students of working-class origin, no U.S. blacks, and no American Indians in my cohort. Moreover, I was one of the few students who lacked a pedigree of academic parents or grandparents. This was a radical departure from my experience as an undergraduate at Northwestern University, a private institution that had a U.S. black student population of 12 percent and a significant number of working-class students at that time. While I encountered no working-class feminists among my peers in anthropology at Berkeley, I was mentored by several white feminist scholars, including Kristin Luker and Margaret Conkey, whose support (along with that of several black male scholars) prevented me from dropping out in response to the ongoing racism and elitism that prevailed.

In 1994, when I considered applying for academic positions as a U.S. black feminist trained in anthropology, I decided that the ideal place to synthesize my feminist and antiracist commitments was in a women studies department. I was thrilled when I was offered a women studies position, and I began my first lecture to two hundred students with these words: "I am here today because of the civil rights movement and the women's movement, and many of you are here because of these same movements." I then asked them to close their eyes and imagine a prefeminist world that lacked women faculty, feminist journals, feminist books, feminist publishers, and women graduate students.

While I have had several white feminist colleagues of working-class origins in the departments in which I have taught, there has been a continued absence of working-class U.S. black and American Indian faculty. The "diversity" criteria employed by some of my academic colleagues often assumes monolithic "white" and "women of color" categories that are not

inflected by class. The absence of sustained reflection on the complex intersections of racism and class inequality—and their particular impact on U.S.
blacks and brown-skinned American Indians who possess neither white
skin privilege nor class privilege—has consequences for the future of
women studies and gender studies departments. I am concerned about the
lack of a sustained discussion of the exclusion from the tenured ranks in
many women studies programs of U.S. working-class women (of all racial
and ethnic backgrounds), particularly those who lack prestigious creden-
tials from Ivy League or Ivy League–equivalent schools. I have witnessed
patterns of recruitment and hiring that fail to consider how the valorization
of scholars who possess class and cultural privilege (as measured by the
"quality" of their degrees and letters) undermines the egalitarian ideals that
women studies claims as a value. Consider the essays in *Working-Class
Women in the Academy,* edited by Michelle M. Tokarczyk and Elizabeth Fay
(1993). This volume includes essays by white working-class women struggling with pressures to devalue their cultural training, cultural style, and
nonacademic lineage, which raises the question, Is it enough to simply
consider hiring women of working-class origins and culture? The answer
is No.

Feminist scholars must challenge the aristocratic leanings of institutional reward structures external to their departments that exclude non-
elites. For example, scholars who possess certain "lineages," which include
prestigious degrees, postdoctoral fellowships, and letters from "brand-
name" mentors, are typically assumed to be superior to scholars who are
resource-deprived, their actual scholarly production notwithstanding. I
have been privy to conversations in which feminist scholars who had produced work that I consider equal if not "superior" in terms of both quantity and quality were judged less qualified. Scholars with less prestigious
degrees often have to overproduce to compensate for their poor lineage,
but this situation is rarely acknowledged openly. In his analysis of the "hab-
itus" of the academy, Paul Rabinow (1991) provides an example of how
senior faculty assess the "character" of job candidates through their table
manners. He argues, "The extent to which this art of symbolic navigation
is a product of class and status socialization is revealed and highlighted by
the entry of newer minorities into the arena, who, while mastering in diverse ways the codes of the academic world, reveal . . . how habitual the
'docility' in its strict sense is. . . . It is dangerous for the candidate or her
supporters to point out these class- and status-based prejudgements to the
old boys, who, proclaiming their perfect neutrality, will almost never engage on this ground" (69). Rabinow's analysis of the criteria used to exclude candidates whose bodily practices fail to conform to middle-class

ways of comportment can also be applied to women of working-class origin attempting to secure positions in women studies departments.

In the 1980s the Reagan administration initiated a legislative assault on working-class students seeking higher education. Grants and low-interest loans of the sort that I received were eliminated. Today, working-class students have much less access to government-sponsored financial support for a university education than I did two decades ago. As affirmative action and poverty continue to be criminalized, academic feminists struggle to sustain a viable feminist antiracist project that is accountable to and includes non-elite women. Implementing diversification in ways that benefit primarily the most privileged women threatens to replicate structural inequalities while also reproducing impoverished university communities. Excluding scholars who lack prestigious pedigrees contributes to the political isolation of women studies programs in working-class communities. If women studies programs and departments are perceived to function as exclusive clubs that fail to actively recruit and support working-class women, they risk lacking political and moral credibility in working-class communities. Feminists have been central in creating more egalitarian spaces in the past, and we must continue the struggle to build antiracist and anti-elitist spaces of belonging.

Department of Sociology
University of California, Santa Barbara

Henry M. Jackson School of International Studies
University of Washington

References

Rabinow, Paul. 1991. "For Hire: Resolutely Late Modern." In *Recapturing Anthropology: Working in the Present*, ed. Richard Gabriel Fox, 59–72. Santa Fe, N.M.: School of American Research Press.

Tokarczyk, Michelle M., and Elizabeth Fay. 1993. *Working-Class Women in the Academy: Laborers in the Knowledge Factory*. Amherst: University of Massachusetts Press.

Barbara Laslett

Johanna Brenner

Twenty-First-Century Academic Feminism in the United States: Utopian Visions and Practical Actions

The twentieth century began as the century of modernism with the hope that science, rationality, and technological progress would overcome the social and political ills so evident in nineteenth-century capitalism and colonialism. Decades of objection to the modernist worldview have exposed its exclusions and repressions as well as the limitations of the utopian countermovements that constituted the radical politics of the modernist century, with their premature political certainties and grandiose claims to universalism. Unfortunately, postmodernist deconstruction has remained primarily a critique, and critique without alternatives leads to cynicism. The next century will require a postmodernism that is politically activist and envisions rather than rejects the possibility of broad social change. In place of cynicism, academic feminists ought to be considering ways to recapture at least some of the spirit of our earlier political action. Admittedly, the conditions under which feminists work in this new century are different from those of the second wave. Still, we believe that it is possible and necessary for academic feminists to think and talk about alternatives, to create new feminist visions, new feminist utopias for the future.

Academics, scholars, teachers, and administrators in the United States are fortunate to have the space to engage in imagining a different, more just world. As feminists we can draw on our understandings of human beings and social life, of human agency and socially necessary organization, of how people create and change, and of how to use technology to foster creativity and make work a place of growth and satisfaction, not stagnation and alienation. These visionary questions are important not only for ourselves but also for our students, who should be encouraged to think beyond the limits of what is immediately possible. In this sense, our commitment to knowledge and scholarship is founded on the modernist belief that knowledge is a basis for action. In this spirit, this essay revisits the choices academic feminists have made, not as an exercise in critique or guilt production but rather as a way of understanding the choices of the past

[*Signs: Journal of Women in Culture and Society* 2000, vol. 25, no. 4]

and therefore how choices may be made in the present and the future. To truly know our history is to understand how the contexts within which we act shape what we consider possible.

In the second-wave movements, many academic feminists saw their political practices to be the encouragement and institutionalization of feminism and gender awareness and the production of feminist scholarship. Victory was celebrated every time another feminist was hired, every time a woman stepped into a position of authority, every time women's studies gained another faculty line. And, to that end, there have been many successes and some (but fewer) failures. The historical context within which academic feminists decided to pursue these goals made them seem simultaneously necessary, possible, and even radical. There was a sense of connection to women's struggles in their families, workplaces, and communities. In addition, many of the innovations in academia, as in so many other parts of American life, were inspired by the liberation movements of the 1960s. Establishing academic feminism was hard work, often done in hostile environments, but there was the élan, the spirit, of a social movement that sustained these efforts in the face of opposition. While attacks on academic feminism have not been completely silenced, today it has defenders even among nonfeminists. So it is perhaps now time to rethink the original goals, not to renounce them but to reframe the possibilities for academic feminism and academic feminists today. We need to consider the political-action implications of being committed to utopian visions of human and environmental well-being. But how can this process of reframing be truly dialogic—not an autocritique, but a real conversation among feminists of different generations?

It has been thirty years since the birth of the second wave. Today's new Ph.D.s are the first generation of women who grew up with feminism, who never experienced a prefeminist world. There is a palpable sense of generational difference, framing how both second-wave and current feminists understand the experience of being women, of developing a gendered subjectivity, of taking on a feminist political identity. The differences, however, are shaped by much more than each generation's relationship to feminism as a political, cultural, and intellectual phenomenon. Women of the second-wave generation had to battle to enter the male-dominated institutions that governed the world of work and politics. Today's feminists enter an economy with greater opportunity for women but even greater insecurity and intensified competition. The academy has not been insulated from these changes. If anything, they are felt even more profoundly in academia than elsewhere, since, until recently, academic institutions have been at least somewhat protected from market forces. Today, the shape of academic institutions both internally and in relation to one another looks more like the U.S. economy as a whole: an elite of extremely privileged "winners" and a growing body of disempowered "losers" in a highly competitive game.

The continuing overproduction of Ph.D.s relative to the supply of jobs is unlikely to wane, given the various interests driving it. On the one hand, there are enough successes to encourage people to enter graduate programs, and, on the other hand, academic departments need a supply of graduate students to maintain their programs, so they have no reason to cut back on admissions. And, given the alternatives available to intellectually oriented young people today, academia remains an attractive option. Insofar as the older generation fails to acknowledge the historical particularity of their present position, they conceal the class nature of the academy — the inequalities of control over one's intellectual choices, working conditions, and income between scholars at nonelite institutions and those at elite ones. Defining academic success in terms that emphasize striving toward the goal of reaching the most privileged locations in academia, and acting as if this were a realistic possibility for the majority of their graduate students, senior women academics, like their senior male colleagues, often obscure class realities and divert attention from a far more important possibility: the development of strategies that confront rather than accommodate the distributions of power within and between academic institutions. The collective "networking" that passes as feminist organization in academia today simply helps the lucky few to negotiate the hurdles and ascend the career ladder. It does little for those whose career ladders have a horizontal rather than vertical form.

The same changes that are reshaping the professoriate are challenging the heart of feminism on campus: women's studies programs. Here, too, failing to recognize significant changes in the way higher education institutions work will turn out to be profoundly disempowering. Although many feminist scholars recognize the crucial importance of "intersectionality" and the need to incorporate this insight into the women's studies curriculum, the consequences for feminist political strategy have been only dimly realized. In the first place, the recognition of "difference" has become, in too many instances, an intellectual exercise removed from the practical problems of creating political oppositional groups or forces based in common interests and goals. Even when difference is analyzed politically, the goal tends to be narrowly focused on overcoming divisions among women in order to create a stronger feminist/women's movement.

It remains crucial for gender to be acknowledged as a pervasive dimension of inequality, of social organization, social meaning, and cultural symbolism. Nevertheless, in this historical period, it is impossible to build a women's movement separate from an oppositional politics that recognizes all kinds of social inequalities. The creation of a multi-issue coalitional politics linking feminism, antiracism, queer liberation, radical environmentalism, labor movements, and broader working-class political agendas, is no longer only a utopian dream. It is a pragmatic necessity.

There are, however, real barriers. Not least of these is that within the academy the acquisition of resources for building up women's studies programs has rested on assertions of a unique and, in some respects, unitary identity. (For example, the claim that women's studies is a specialized field of study legitimates demands for a core curriculum and a core faculty.) In expansionary periods, there has been more room for new programs and thus for women's studies, ethnic studies, black studies, and so forth, all to lay claim to resources. In today's academic world, the drive to stabilize and expand women's studies may intensify competitive relations with other programs that otherwise ought to be our allies. The point here is *not* that women's studies ought to "defer" our ambitions. Rather, we need to reconceptualize how we are going to further the cause. Thirty years ago, feminists on campus were "outsiders within" who relied, at least in part, on our connections to a radical women's liberation movement outside the academy. Feminist academics need to rekindle that admittedly tension-filled relationship, allying ourselves wherever we can with organizations and groups that oppose corporate dominance.

A coalition politics means taking risks and making alliances with the least powerful groups within academia — with unionizing graduate students and part-time faculty, for instance, rather than with sympathetic administrators. It means taking part in struggles to expand funding for higher education not through the business-as-usual mode of shifting state dollars from another function (e.g., social services) but through coalitions with labor and community groups (in the United States, organizations such as Jobs with Justice and ACORN) organizing for reforms that redistribute income and economic resources in general.

In times when we feel especially pressured and politically weak, being called on to challenge economically and politically powerful forces may seem unfair. And, given that so many others are scrambling simply to stay afloat, to stake our future on a coalitional politics may seem utopian. Surely, the wiser course is to continue a strategy that has allowed feminism to make really unprecedented gains. But gains for whom? For which women? If we are to have a twenty-first-century feminism capable of making the same kinds of truly radical changes that the first and second waves made for their times, we will need new strategies that correspond to the new opportunities as well as the new difficulties of these times. It is truly practical to hold on to our utopian visions for social justice, for they encourage us to reach for the best that we might accomplish.

Sociology Department
University of Minnesota (Laslett)

Women's Studies Department
Portland State University (Brenner)

Gender Aporias

Does gender operate as an individual choice or a social mandate, or as something in between? How do we conceive of gender roles over time and across cultures? If gender is not to be conceived as a simple mechanism that dictates behavior, and if we are to avoid the trap of merely replacing biological determinism with cultural determinism, how exactly does gender work? Can we construe gender in a way that addresses changing stereotypes and that can be challenged, transformed, and refigured? What kind of flexibility does it have as a category, and to what does it owe its authority? If women are not assigned to subservience and passivity by some inflexible, innate nature but are accustomed to cultural roles, then rescripting those cultural roles should make transformation possible. But who writes the scripts, and how do they avoid privileging their own experiences and subject positions in a way that mimics precisely the alleged neutrality that patriarchal values uphold?

A useful way of considering how feminism has developed during this century, and where it might be going in the next, is to focus on how it has been served by the language of sex and gender. My intention is not to identify any feminist thinker or group of thinkers with a single approach but rather to isolate general tendencies, in order to clarify how best to carry forward our thinking about sex and gender, and to reflect upon whether these terms remain useful. To that end I distinguish three typical models of the relation between sex and gender and show how each is inadequate. I indicate the direction in which we need to go in order to ensure the usefulness of the categories of sex and gender, which might serve as a starting point for reflecting on the next millennium.

The logic of sex and gender

The relation between the terms *sex* and *gender* can be characterized as necessary, as arbitrary, or as contingent. At the beginning of the twentieth century, U.S. suffragists were trying to combat traditional conceptions of the relation between what later came to be called "sex" and "gender." The female sex was defined by certain physical, biological, and psychological

[*Signs: Journal of Women in Culture and Society* 2000, vol. 25, no. 4]

characteristics that were taken to be innate, unchanging, and causally related to activities, behaviors, and customs that were defined socially, culturally, and historically. To be defined as a member of the female sex, on this model, necessarily entailed a specific and limited range of activities such as nurturing and child rearing, based on claims such as "women are naturally good mothers" or "the feminine constitution is unfit for the rigors and demands of the masculine world." Once such language gained currency, the causal relation that was traditionally posited between nature and culture could be cashed out as producing a relation of necessity between the terms *sex* and *gender*.

Feminism challenged the idea that women were naturally destined for certain prescribed roles and unsuited for others by construing the relation of sex and gender not as one of necessity but rather as one that allowed some free play. But what kind of free play? Are women (and, by implication, men as well) completely free in relation to their sex? That is, should the relation between sex and gender be understood as one of full autonomy? Is gender free of any determining force deriving from sex, or is it still constrained in some ways? If it is constrained, what sort of constraint is involved, and how is it to be thought?

Is the connection between sex and gender arbitrary?

During the 1960s, *gender* became the preferred category of analysis because it offered a flexibility that *sex* did not appear to. But how exactly can gender free itself from its apparently necessary connection to sex? Are these categories to be seen as entirely independent of one another? Is the relationship simply one of habitual association, such that to point to the logical independence of gender from sex is also effectively to dismantle their apparent symbiosis — or at least to create the conditions for such dismantling? If gender is only arbitrarily attached to sex, if sex places no restriction on gender, then any number of cultural behaviors and gender identifications become available for adoption and reevaluation, and being a woman no longer entails being restricted by the traditional sphere of feminine activities. By positing the relation between sex and gender as arbitrary, feminist theory seemed to be rendering the body unimportant, collapsing sex into gender and claiming that gender could become the sole explanatory category.

For all the possibilities it may seem to open up, construing the relation between sex and gender as arbitrary poses a number of problems and leaves important questions unanswered. It implies not only that there is no reason for the habitual association of gender with sex but also that sex has nothing to do with gender. It is important to bear in mind, however, that severing the relation of necessity between sex and gender does not mean there is no connection whatsoever. In fact, experience suggests that gender has everything to do with sex: if a girl is treated like a girl, it is precisely because she has a female body. Furthermore, there must be some explanation for the consistent linking of sex and gender, other than mere historical accident. Even if the explanation turns out to be grounded on faulty beliefs, those beliefs have held sway in ways that have systematically shaped social and cultural formations and institutions, so that some avenues of expression seem possible and legitimate while others are closed off as impossible and illegitimate.

What, then, does it mean to assert an arbitrary connection between sex and gender? It cannot mean that simply redescribing the relation can reinvent it or that choosing not to conform to old stereotypes will free one of old restrictive ways of thinking. It cannot mean that gender identity can be re-created merely by a voluntary act of individual will that bears no relation to the social forces that create cultural stereotypes. Whatever it means, the assertion that the connection between sex and gender is arbitrary, in order to have any effect, must involve a constitutive or performative element; it must involve a transformation of the systemic aspects of established and traditional roles. Gender is not simply a matter of choice, or even a series of choices, at the individual level.

Is the connection between sex and gender contingent?

To conceive of the relation between sex and gender as contingent, rather than arbitrary, allows feminists to acknowledge the significance of bodies: it is because a girl's body identifies her with the female sex that she is taught to be, and expects herself to be, feminine. To see the relation as contingent acknowledges the force of social pressure but leaves room for a certain amount of discrepancy between cultural norms and an individual's ability or desire to reject them. An individual may well feel the weight of tradition that demands behavior considered normal for the gender assigned to her sex by society, but she will not necessarily conform to those gender expectations. If individuals challenge gender norms, then gender norms themselves will reflect such challenges and over time become less restrictive, as a wider spectrum of gendered behavior comes to be tolerated, accepted, and, finally, normalized. Construing the relation between sex and gender as contingent allows for some, but not total, free play. It concedes that bodies are relevant to gender identity but not determinative of them. The connection between sex and gender is not conceived as entirely static or fixed but as capable of absorbing challenges and as changing over time. In this view, the relation between sex and gender is construed more loosely than on the model of necessity, but some kind of causality is maintained, rather than simply denied, as it is when the relation is considered arbitrary. The contingent model characterizes the relation of sex and gender as one of probability rather than necessity: having a female body makes it likely, although not necessary, that one will be influenced by cultural imperatives to act in traditionally feminine ways.

The problem with the arbitrary model of sex and gender is that, by collapsing sex into gender and treating the entire arena of sexuality as a normative, constructed dimension, it seems to disregard the relevance of the body. The contingent model responds to this potential eclipse of the body by ushering it back into play, but to do so it must posit the body as given. It seems to ignore the fact that the body is not the unchanging and natural ground it was once thought to be, that bodies themselves are sites capable of change. Work on transgender studies in the 1990s has brought this new understanding to the fore. Bodies do not necessarily naturally fall into the categories of male and female; they are made to fit these categories. Through a variety of techniques, including fashion, technology, surgery, and bodybuilding, we are able to reshape and resculpt our bodies. Does this ability suggest that perhaps the arbitrary model has more credibility than it first appeared? Should we embrace the idea that sex is really gender, or that sex is merely a normative projection of a binary heterosexual matrix? Such a model absorbs bodies into cultural norms, without leaving any space to consider the effects of materiality on these norms.

Each of the three models I have outlined makes one of two mistakes. Either it assumes that sex and gender are logically autonomous categories that have a relation of necessity or probability or it assumes that one category can be subsumed by the other. One must therefore be the founding and original category and the other merely a symptom or effect. We need a more porous model, in which neither category is evacuated of meaning but both are constituted, in relation to one another, as permeable and unstable. The challenge, it seems to me, is to resist both the tendency to collapse one term entirely into the other and the tendency to assume the initial integrity and independence of both and then ask how they can be brought into relation with one another. We must find ways of conceptualizing the sex-gender relation that avoid both. Otherwise, not only will we be forced to leave aside a proper investigation of bodies and materiality, we will also fail to think through the complexities of race, class, ethnicity, and other axes of oppression.

Some theorists have embraced the language of sexual difference in an effort to formulate experience as both gendered and embodied, while at the same time recognizing that such formulations themselves are never immune from ideological inflection. If the terms *sex* and *gender* are to retain their purchase, their meanings must be able to shift as the relation between them is rethought, rather than always being strictly oppositional or mutually exclusive. We cannot be content to construe gender as belonging to society or culture and sex as dictated by physical nature; we must understand that the domains we designate as gendered can have material effects, as when medical technology reorganizes bodies to cohere with normalized gender definitions. We must be prepared to think sex and gender as always in dynamic relation and the distinctions between the two realms as not fixed or rigid but malleable and flexible.

Philosophy Department
University of Memphis

Millennial Bodies

By the time this essay is published, the year will have turned and many of us will find ourselves in the twenty-first century. I say "many of us" because there are plenty of folks for whom next year is neither the end nor the beginning of an era, millennium, or age. January 1, 2000, will be 5760 according to the Jewish calendar, 2543 according to the Theravadan Buddhist calendar, and Heisei 12 according to the traditional Japanese calendar. Yet, despite these and other examples, one hears daily of the great event that will take place as clocks worldwide sweep us into a global celebration of the New Millennium.

I begin an essay on feminism at the millennium thus not just to make the obvious point that assuming a global phenomenon bespeaks a kind of calendarial centrism but also to suggest that if the arbitrary demarcations of hundred- or thousand-year periods are one way to mark historical shifts and significant changes, the positioning of Asian Americans and other communities of color in the United States may very well undermine any celebratory gestures prompted by the changing of the calendar year.

I say this based on a comparative glance over the past hundred years or so. At the turn of the past century, as in the present, populations of color were predicted to increase their numbers through immigration and birth rate. Alarmist pamphlets and "studies" decried the influx of the "rising tide of color." Asians were the targets of several U.S. anti-immigration acts between 1882 and 1924, and Asian women in particular were seen as a threat to the white American nation-state because of their capacity for reproduction. Such anxieties are mirrored in present-day rhetoric of Asian overrepresentation and fear of Latino population growth. In response, the last five years of the twentieth century have been characterized by neoconservative attacks on the gains made by people of color in the past twenty-five years. California's infamous Proposition 187 disproportionately affects Asian Americans and Latinos, and anti–affirmative action legislation around the country is attempting to cut into the already small numbers of people of color represented in the educational and public sectors. In this climate, Asian American women function doubly as acceptable "twofers"

[*Signs: Journal of Women in Culture and Society* 2000, vol. 25, no. 4]

(providing a race-and-gender alibi) and as members of the bogeywomen-of-color cadre who are supposedly saturating the job market in venues ranging from newscasting to medicine.

Meanwhile, we are inundated with a "postracist" rhetoric of tolerance, inclusion, and color blindness, and with a persistent valorization of ideals of diversity in which we "celebrate the differences," a phrase that suggests a hodgepodge of happy inclusive plurality but obscures the extent to which such claims rely on images of equality that do little or nothing to guarantee actual structures of equality. Liberal multiculturalist rhetoric has, with little exception, failed to do much more than bring some color to prime-time television and insert food-and-culture learning units into kindergarten classrooms. It's one thing to eat sushi and pancit and talk about how the Chinese invented firecrackers. It is entirely another to talk about the history of exclusion and racism that defines much of the Asian American experience, and still another to talk about current positionings of Asian Americans in the racialized landscape of the United States.

In other words, we are presented with images wherein difference functions as healthy variety promoted by well-meaning folks for whom it is a singular sign of bad manners and bad taste to mention the realities of race. From telephone commercials to fast-food ads to magazines, a steady stream of images assures us that we (a white, black, brown, red, and yellow "we") are no longer in the bad old days of racist segregation. Interracial couples are increasingly represented on prime-time television, and the faces of multiracial children are read as visual proof that we really can all get along, and better than anyone would have guessed.

But while such fantasies flicker before us, there is the fact that monies for poor and immigrant children are shrinking at an alarming rate; that hate crimes against people of color and gays and lesbians are on the rise; that affirmative action programs on both local and national levels are being eliminated; and that political and social control over female bodies is being steadily reestablished. There is the fact that the only structures in which you will find a majority of color are state and federal prisons.

In such a contradictory and contestatory climate, it is more crucial than ever to articulate the terms of what meaningful intervention might be, and it seems reasonable to expect that progressive and radical feminisms ought to play some role in that articulation. Yet, in the latter half of 1998, it was still possible for Susan Gubar, in a by-now-infamous essay, to rail against women of color for taking the fun out of feminism and breaking up the supposed unity of "women."[1] Gubar is not the only, nor will she be the

---

[1] See also the incisive reply to Gubar by Robyn Wiegman (1999).

last, feminist theorist to lob such complaints. I won't spend time refuting her claims here; rather, I want to point out that much feminist theory, like the reactionary Right and the liberal Left, has yet to come to terms with racialized embodiment. That is, feminism has failed to deal adequately with difference and particularity as both are registered by the body and as the body is registered by the social and material economies of the U.S. nation-state. To accuse women of color of theorizing out of a righteous and reductionist identity politics is, to my mind, to participate in a violent erasure of a body whose markedness gives rise to a very different articulation of what politics, feminism, and feminist politics might be.

Cheryl Harris (1998), a professor of law, has pointed out that the language in which any of us might speak about race is never inherently tied to a particular and assumed politics. In the past ten years, feminist and other theories have evoked race as a social construction. Yet such a recognition does not of itself signify an antiracist discourse, nor does it perforce lead to structural change. This is evidenced not only by conflicts within feminist theories — even putatively antiracist ones — that continue to construct women of color as the problematic reminders that gender never was and never will be a discrete axis of identity and subjectivity; it is also indicated by theories that focus on the constructedness of race to suggest that the disavowal of racist biologism is the key to the problem of racism. But where does that really get us? As Ian Haney López (1996) has demonstrated, discourses of race have vacillated between biologism and constructivism over the course of the twentieth century, and there is nothing to suggest that racist repression was less intense in those periods during which race was spoken of as a social construction. Feminist theory, too, has long "understood" race to be a social construction that does not "really" exist, but this understanding often has only obscured a problem with difference that masquerades under the guise of concern about feminism generally.

When I ask what difference the work we do makes, I ask not out of an expectation that all theorizing must translate directly and immediately into street politics but rather out of a worry that sharpens with each invocation to "celebrate the differences" in a "global village" that seems increasingly to be home and host for casually, and sometimes radically, racist individuals and groups, many in positions of structural power. I am increasingly concerned with feminist theories that seem unable to think through the apparent conundrum of race as figure and race as literalization, or that invoke global subjects as a code for "third-world women," a phrase that often both assumes and elides U.S. women of color. If we are to deal with the rampant contradictions that have marked the past century and threaten to follow us into the next, we need to think seriously about what it means to identify and be identified with the bodies we do or do not inhabit. We need to stop confusing anti-essentialist politics with anti-body politics. Words are powerful; discourse indeed shapes thought. But let us not fool ourselves into forgetting that structures are not discursive only and do not conveniently remain in the realm of the abstract: they lay the landscape for the social and material world in which we live, a world in which bodies that do not matter are increasingly at risk because of something — race — that supposedly "doesn't exist."

English Department
University of California, Riverside

References

Gubar, Susan. 1998. "What Ails Feminist Criticism?" *Critical Inquiry* 24(4):878–902.

Harris, Cheryl. 1998. Paper presented at "What, Then, Is 'White'?" University of California, Riverside, February.

López, Ian F. Haney. 1996. *White by Law: The Legal Construction of Race.* New York: New York University Press.

Wiegman, Robyn. 1999. "What Ails Feminist Criticism? A Second Opinion." *Critical Inquiry* 25(2):362–79.

Devon A. Mihesuah

A Few Cautions at the Millennium on the Merging of Feminist Studies with American Indian Women's Studies

At the millennium, more scholars than ever are writing about feminist theory. To borrow from Kramarae and Spender, the field has exploded with theory, diverging opinions, and unanswered questions about women's marginalization. At the same time, American Indian Studies has also grown to the point that Standing Rock Sioux writer Vine Deloria, Jr., has written, "I can see no useful purpose for any additional research or writing on Indians, other than as a form of entertainment" (1991, 461).

Though the integration of American Indian women's studies and feminist studies would seem a logical project for the new millennium, the progress on such an initiative should be both cautious and deliberate. The introduction of the multifaceted lives and values of American Indians into feminist discourse will necessarily and appropriately confuse the understanding of "women's" experiences. Indeed, while clarity about gender may be compelling, it is often at the expense of the visibility, agency, and identity of those represented. I therefore add my cautions here to the arguments put forth by other women of color, seeing both the need for appreciating women's heterogeneity and the need for more sensitivity in studying and writing about individuals outside one's racial and cultural group. I believe all feminists can learn from American Indians, but care must be used in researching, interpreting, and formulating ideas about "others."

At the year 2000, and 502 years after what Natives commonly refer to as the beginning of the "invasion," thousands of books and articles have been written about Natives. With the exception of works of fiction, the vast majority of these are written by whites who analyze their subjects using Eurocentric standards of interpretation not Natives' own versions of their cultures and histories. Because whites are usually the ones speaking about women outside their group, as well as gathering information, creating theories, and benefiting from all of this writing, Natives' images are

Many thanks to Joseph Boles, director of women's studies at Northern Arizona University, for his gentle critique of this essay.

[*Signs: Journal of Women in Culture and Society* 2000, vol. 25, no. 4]

often at the mercy of author bias, power positions, and the personal agendas of scholars and of authors of popular literature.

Scholars often rationalize that because they are armed with written documentation and theories (often formulated by thinkers who have never met an Indian), they can write from a Native perspective. It is dangerous and unethical to presume to know what motivates Native women without talking to them, but scholars do it all the time. Some refuse to speak with Natives, believing that informants who are not formally educated have no information worth garnering. Occasionally, shyness or respect keeps researchers away, as in the example of a former non-Native graduate student of mine who never completed her nicely conceptualized dissertation on the activist women at Wounded Knee in 1973 because of my requirement that she conduct interviews with Native women present at the encounter. My personal standards — gut feelings, actually — are that I should not produce a manuscript about my tribe or another tribe unless it is useful to them and that I will not write about historic Native women unless the project benefits their descendants.

Feminist scholars who wish to write about American Indian women must be aware of the various voices among them. For example, some writers suggest that traditionalist Native women are the authoritative voices on Indian issues rather than those more assimilated. In the four pages that M. Annette Jaimes and Theresa Halsey devote to feminism in their 1992 essay "American Indian Women at the Center of Indigenous Resistance in Contemporary North America," they criticize prominent Native writers such as Shirley Hill Witt and Suzan Shown Harjo because, in their opinion, these women are too assimilated and are more concerned with fighting for "civil rights" than with fighting for tribal sovereignty. Crow Creek Sioux novelist and editor Elizabeth Cook-Lynn offers a similar thesis in her 1998 essay "American Indian Intellectualism and the New Indian Story," in which she argues that the writings produced by mixed-blood authors are rooted in "a deconstruction of a tribal nation-past, hardly an intellectual movement that can claim a continuation of the tribal communal story or an ongoing tribal literary tradition" (128). She also contends that successful writers such as Louise Erdrich, Paula Gunn Allen, and Wendy Rose (and males Sherman Alexie and Gerald Vizenor) exude "excesses of individualism" when she believes they should be advocating tribal unity.

These stances include two of the important political issues within American Indian Studies among Natives. The first is identity politics: the women whom Jaimes and Halsey take to task actually are strong advocates for tribal rights, and Cook-Lynn tends to ignore the reality that the majority of Indians today are of mixed blood, often disassociated with their tribe's culture perhaps, but still possessing strong Native identities. Within and outside the academy, these voices debate, validate, and negate each other. Second, these sentiments contribute to my answer to the question of authoritative voice: there isn't a single one among Native women, and no one feminist theory totalizes Native women's thought. Rather, there is a spectrum of multiheritage women, in between "traditional" and "progressive," who possess a multitude of opinions on what it means to be a Native female. The label "third world women" is only a large umbrella under which another umbrella, "Natives," may fit, but underneath that umbrella are all of the three hundred or so modern U.S. tribes and, further still, all female members of those tribes. Thousands more umbrellas are needed to account for the tribal and individual sociocultural changes that occur over time. The complexity of Native women and the elements that make up their values and personalities are addressed in my essay "Commonalty of Difference: American Indian Women and History" (1998), in which I also warn that identifying and categorizing these overlapping variations among Native women are formidable tasks. Knowledge of these complexities, however, is crucial to understanding the rationales behind the Native voice the scholar hears, in addition to knowing that it is not representative of all Natives.

Non-Natives must take care that the voice they hear actually *is* Native. Within the academy, numerous "wannabe" and "marginal" Natives with few connections to their tribes publish with the claim of writing from an Indian perspective. The voices of Native women have also been undermined by the cultural and literary appropriations of New Age fraudulent "medicine women" who have convinced the public that theirs are the truthful works about Native religion and culture. For instance, the well-published charlatan Lynn Andrews distorts the reality of traditional Native male-female relationships and advises her followers that their quests to find their true "feminine" selves are hindered by male oppression.[1] Native writers such as Wendy Rose and Andrea Smith discuss the potential damage done to constructive cross-cultural relationships between authentic American Indians and non-Indians when these "plastic" medicine women and men (whose works have found their way onto university required reading lists) assert that they are the authoritative voices on Native spirituality.[2]

Assuming that a given researcher has real American Indian informants in mind, she must be aware that many tribes have strict research guidelines

---

[1] Andrews is the author of, most notably, *Medicine Woman* (1981), *Jaguar Woman* (1985), *Star Woman* (1986), and *Crystal Woman* (1987).

[2] See Andrea Smith 1991; Rose 1992; Andy Smith 1994.

that outsiders must follow when interviewing tribal members, as do universities with institutional review boards (see Mihesuah 1993). And, good intentions do not always garner results. While some Natives are willing to share information with researchers, others are tentative and will discuss only bits and pieces of their lives and tribal goings-on. Traditional Native women—who might more accurately be called "tribalists" because they believe they are disadvantaged by the colonialist ideologies that disempower their race and contribute to dysfunctional tribal gender roles—have no interest in white feminist theory because they know from experience that white women have enjoyed the power privileges that come with being white at the expense of women of color. They are aware that white scholars usually just want information that they use to build their academic careers, while the knowledgeable "objects of study" receive nothing in return.

If feminist scholars want to learn about themselves and others and to contribute to their discipline, they should approach American Indian women only because of genuine, but respectful, curiosity about another way of life. If allowed to enter the lives of Natives, researchers should be forewarned that interviewing American Indians is very time consuming, that interviewers must be sensitive to the privacy and self-respect of those women, and that they must have a project that is important to the women whose voices they utilize. They must abandon any posturing about being an expert on what counts as important knowledge about Native women. If feminist scholars can engage in reciprocal, practical dialogue with their informants, then Native voices, too, will become a part of feminist discourse.

Applied Indigenous Studies
Northern Arizona University

References

Andrews, Lynn V. 1981. *Medicine Woman.* San Francisco: Harper & Row.
———. 1985. *Jaguar Woman and the Wisdom of the Butterfly Tree.* San Francisco: Harper & Row.
———. 1986. *Star Woman.* New York: Warner.
———. 1987. *Crystal Woman.* New York: Warner.
Cook-Lynn, Elizabeth. 1998. "American Indian Intellectualism and the New Indian Story." In *Natives and Academics: Researching and Writing about American Indians,* ed. Devon A. Mihesuah, 111–38. Lincoln: University of Nebraska Press.
Deloria, Vine, Jr. 1991. "Commentary: Research, Redskins, and Reality." *American Indian Quarterly* 15(1):457–68.

Jaimes, M. Annette, and Theresa Halsey. 1992. "American Indian Women: At the Center of Indigenous Resistance in Contemporary North America." In *The State of Native America: Genocide, Colonization, and Resistance,* ed. M. Annette Jaimes, 311–44. Boston: South End.

Mihesuah, Devon A. 1993. "Suggested Research Guidelines for Institutions with Scholars Who Study American Indians." *American Indian Culture and Research Journal* 17 (Fall): 131–39.

———. 1998. "Commonalty of Difference: American Indian Women and History." In *Natives and Academics: Researching and Writing about American Indians,* ed. Devon A. Mihesuah, 37–54. Lincoln: University of Nebraska Press.

Rose, Wendy. 1992. "The Great Pretenders: Further Reflections on White-shamanism." In *The State of Native America: Genocide, Colonization, and Resistance,* ed. M. Annette Jaimes, 403–22. Boston: South End.

Smith, Andrea. 1991. "The New Age Movement and Native Spirituality." *Indigenous Woman* 1 (Spring): 18–19.

Smith, Andy. 1994. "For All Those Who Were Indian in a Former Life." *Ms.* 2(3):44–45.

On Teaching through the Millennium

What do students want? The more time I've logged in as a professor at a university that prides itself on good teaching, the less certain I am of the answer to that question. I know *I* want to tell students about what I find important, interesting, and useful in the world. I know I would like to see them all become activist citizens, young feminists, committed to equal opportunity for all races and ethnicities, willing to climb tall first-growth trees to save the environment, and much, much more. But can we transmit to the next generation the values devised from our own struggles, the lessons learned from our own mistakes, the knowledge gained by our own post-Enlightenment approaches to understanding the world? This is always the challenge teachers face, one made symbolically more poignant because we are at the foot of that heavily trafficked bridge into the twenty-first century.

I am poised beyond the halfway mark in my life and academic career, with many of my parents' generation now dead and with those remaining numbering among the senior seniors. Being of "that certain age" has pushed me to reflect on how the previous generation shaped my own life. Perhaps those reflections can, in turn, help me better understand my own role as a teacher of following generations. I am a "red diaper daughter"— and on one side of the family a red diaper granddaughter too.[1] I grew up with stories of struggle—how my grandfather was exiled to Siberia for taking part in a May Day parade in Tsarist Vilna, how Russian Communists taught my grandmother to read in secret woodland meetings, how my father hid an axe handle under his coat when he went to the second Peekskill Concert featuring Paul Robeson. (The first had been attacked and disrupted by police and an anticommunist mob.) Our parents, despite— or perhaps because of— the 1950s, made every effort to educate us as good communists. During some summers I attended the interracial Pioneer Youth Camp, where counselors took us to meet Eleanor Roosevelt and we enjoyed regular visits from Pete Seeger and other progressive folk musicians. During the winters I frequented a discussion group developed

---

[1] See Kaplan and Shapiro 1998; Mishler 1999.

[*Signs: Journal of Women in Culture and Society* 2000, vol. 25, no. 4]

especially for the red kids of Westchester County (not actually an oxymoron!). We read Marx, Engels, Lenin, and others and found friends and refuge from an often hostile and alien world.

Recently, I had a conversation with another red diaper daughter in which we talked about the inevitable deaths in our parents' generation. These "grown-ups" were remarkable, she said, but although we've done them proud, we are not them. We are not them because our world is not theirs. To begin with, there is no longer a single, believable international movement in which to place our faith. Instead there are dozens of movements — reproductive rights, gay rights, civil rights, environmentalism, the shelter movement, and many more. The Enlightenment concept of universal brotherhood has given way to the postmodern notion of multiple and fragmented identities. Many of us have chosen to do political work (including both academic and teaching endeavors), but there is no longer a single political leadership to follow nor an indisputable chosen group — as the working class was to my parents and grandparents. The truth, both exciting and difficult, is that, politically and culturally speaking, my generation has flown by the seat of its pants. There were none before us to develop the field of gender and science (for example). But we used tools given to us by the best of the previous generation — combining a dash of daring with vision, a passion for social change, and a critical mindset.

What is true when we compare ourselves with our parents' generation is equally true when we compare ourselves with our students. We cannot hope that they will be us. Nor can we expect them to understand more than a few fragments of our lives. I look out at the young people in my classes and know that they have not a clue as to who I am now, how I got here, and what I feel about the world. And I, also, have little insight into what they really think, what their eyes see, what makes them tick. With so little overlapping ground, how can I create the mutual empathy that I think is essential for teaching and learning? What can I teach them? I can't possibly fill in all the information they are missing about the past or even about the present. But I can offer them what my parents' generation gave me — a vision of the future. I can't tell them how to get there, but I can give them research skills and urge them to learn how to organize. I can offer them undying intellectual curiosity. Some will accept the offer. That others will not is one of those difficult facts of life for a teacher.

Although I work well with individual students in one-on-one situations, I feel fairly certain that my days as an effective classroom teacher of students in late adolescence are about over. Oedipus and Electra haunt my classroom, and I am not interested in being the resident Mother target. My position as a feminist scientist often alienates me from science students who can't figure out what to make of me. (For example, I recently had a student drop a course in the history of genetics and embryology because there was too much history in it. Note the title and go figure!) But because I really love science and teach it (even in the history course), women's studies students also avoid me. Like most women's studies programs around the country, Brown's does not require its majors to study science—something I have written about elsewhere.[2]

Intellectually and pedagogically, I have found myself most at home in a new academic field—science studies.[3] Those who gravitate to this new field have had to accept the existence of a feminist analysis of science (as one of several critical approaches to studying science as culture). Furthermore, these colleagues are generally not allergic to the idea that science studies students need straight science courses and technological literacy. So, once again, I find myself advocating at my university for a new course of study—one that elicits a certain degree of puzzlement or hostility from departments unfamiliar with this new body of research and one that is as interdisciplinary as gender studies and as exciting to its subset of students as early women's studies courses were to the young feminists of the 1970s and 1980s.

Although, with age, I have grown less happy in the classroom, my intellectual work now brings me more pleasure than ever. Finally, thirty years into the game, I feel like I understand a little something about how the world works. That it has taken me so long is, perhaps, in the nature of truly interdisciplinary work. One has to become mistress of several fields and also learn how to work profitably at the borders connecting particular disciplines. Part of my alienation from the classroom certainly lies in the fact that I want nothing more, at the moment, than to work—alone or with others—at the level of sophistication it has taken me so long to develop. Teaching at this level is not possible with undergraduates who must first learn the basics. But here too, I have made a choice about teaching. I decided, for example, to write my new book *Sexing the Body: Gender Politics and the Construction of Human Sexuality* (2000) for a general readership, banishing the more arcane academic and technical discussions to the endnotes. This form of writing utilizes my teaching skills outside of the classroom, where, in the end, I reach a larger and more diverse audience than I can ever hope for through in-person contacts.

[2] Fausto-Sterling 1992. See also the Web site of the American Association of Colleges and Universities for various projects aimed at overcoming the kinds of difficulties I discuss (http://www.aacu-edu.org/Initiatives/scilit.html).
[3] See Hess 1997.

Our professional strengths and weaknesses change as we age. I sometimes wonder whether teaching is a profession better suited to younger colleagues who by virtue of their youth share more experiences and points of view with their students. And I think it is possible that we really do get wiser with age. If I am right about this double surmise, then it would make sense for the university of the twenty-first century to allow scholars gradually to transform their focus as they age. Such a transformation could take advantage of the certain knowledge that the skills and needs of beginning teachers, scholars, and feminists differ from those who have been at it for thirty years. I often used to joke that my generation of feminists would not take menopause lightly, that there would be an explosion of books on aging, public protests about estrogen, and more. Sure enough, the list of menopause books grows apace. In the same way, I hope that our generation of feminists will struggle out loud with what it means to age within the academy. Perhaps this brief essay will start the discussion.

Professor of Biology and Women's Studies
Brown University

References

Fausto-Sterling, Anne. 1992 "Building Two-Way Streets: The Case of Feminism and Science." *National Women's Studies Association Journal* 4(3):336–49.

———. 2000. *Sexing the Body: Gender Politics and the Construction of Human Sexuality*. New York: Basic.

Hess, David J. 1997. "If You're Thinking of Living in STS: A Guide for the Perplexed." In *Cyborgs and Citadels: Anthropological Interventions in Emerging Sciences and Technologies,* ed. Gary Lee Downey and Joseph Dumit, 143–64. Santa Fe, N.M.: School of American Research Press.

Kaplan, Judy, and Linn Shapiro. 1998. *Red Diapers: Growing Up in the Communist Left*. Urbana: University of Illinois Press.

Mishler, Paul C. 1999. *Raising Reds: The Young Pioneers, Radical Summer Camps, and Communist Political Culture in the United States*. New York: Columbia University Press.

Masculinity, the Teening of America, and Empathic Targeting

Millennial changes are conducive to paranoid fantasies. This is mine: I imagine that the world is ruled by a few rich white men.[1] They control multinational corporations and the media, yet they want even more wealth and power. Their success produces problems they need to manage. Some want their daughters as well as their sons to inherit their power.

Here in the United States, women have made significant gains over the past thirty years, and so have rich people. These trends are partly contradictory. Fewer U.S. men and women believe women are inferior to men or even very different from them, yet women still have less money, less power, and less freedom than men, while social classes have become more polarized.[2] Thus, widespread acceptance of some feminist ideas has not improved the lot of all women as much as we second-wave feminists hoped. My fantasy imagines ways that current trends adapt gender to economic change yet continue to uphold a male dominant status quo.

Despite increasing numbers of male gender rebels, dominant masculinity seems to serve many men well. Few want to exchange it for androgyny or genderlessness. However, retaining male privilege without male supremacist ideology requires new strategies. Midcentury breadwinner roles, which opposed rational masculine producers to emotional feminine nurturers and consumers, today seem dull and out of date.[3] Now multinational corporate culture needs fewer high-wage producers and managers

---

[1] The following brief essay is a satire or caricature, a schematic simplification that permits itself broad generalizations in order to sketch some current directions in the constructions of gender. For more complete documentation on these topics, see my essay " 'South Park,' Blue Men, Anality, and Market Masculinity" (2000). That essay and this one relate to my book-in-progress on masculinity in feminist theory, which proposes the advantages of developmental rather that oppositional masculinities. One influential book on contemporary masculinities is Connell 1995.

[2] For women's economic status in the current economy, see, e.g., Sidel 1996.

[3] On the decline of 1950s patriarchy, see Ehrenreich 1983, 1995.

[*Signs: Journal of Women in Culture and Society* 2000, vol. 25, no. 4]

but even more consumers. I imagine that new kinds of masculinity help to compensate for men's reduced roles as breadwinners and to reassert gender difference in response to feminist gains and economic changes.

I see the new masculinities as products that are niche marketed and the processes they involve as operating like handball: men increase their solidarity with one another through competition more than direct contact, their relationships bouncing off walls of media images. For example, the Superstar line of masculinity bonds men to athletes who act as living action figures, while the Slacker line glamorizes lightly employed young middle-class white men, free from family obligations, not as sixties rebels against the consumer culture but as its hip, cynical connoisseurs. Thugs' wrappings, however, package the same behavior as practiced by young men of color, while the Cyberinforcer line persuades young men passively seated in front of computer screens that they are tough and manly.

Altered masculinities also appear in the reconfiguration and regendering of age categories, which I call the "teening of America."[4] This trend extends the imagery and lifestyle of adolescence throughout the age span, simultaneously promoting consumption for both genders and reinforcing gender differences. Since adolescence is the age of maximum gender differentiation, such teening strengthens gender polarization when other social forces, such as feminism, work to erode it. Teening promotes images of youthful sexuality keyed to lifetime feminine attractiveness for women and athletic fun and fitness for men. It cuts across races and classes, although it is differently inflected in each. Moreover, it helps smooth the transition from liberal individuality, with its focus on personal rights and responsibilities, to consumer individualism, which isolates people from commitment to the welfare of others and refracts their identities through brand loyalties.

Traditional social divisions can be maintained more easily when most people are kept isolated and insensitive to the needs of others, and it is harder to bomb people elsewhere if people at home notice that real people like themselves are being hurt. However, my paranoia believes that aggression against others is required to maintain a stably inegalitarian world. Around the globe, young men serve as soldiers enforcing the status quo, and they are often incited to anger and aggression, the feelings considered most appropriate to men. However, gender maintenance and power stabilization here in the United States seem to rely more on emotional socialization than on force. In an economy where many men are receiving a lower patriarchal dividend in terms of power and pay than they used to, emo-

---

[4] Bly 1996 puts forward a conservative and sexist version of this idea.

tional reconfigurations help keep gender divisions firm: I fantasize that there are invisible Emotional Maintenance Organizations, which manage people's emotions the way HMOs manage health care.

Empathy is paradigmatic of current reshapings of emotional responsiveness. Empathy potentially serves equality, letting all people understand the sufferings of the oppressed and exploited and so motivating calls for social justice.[5] Women have traditionally been judged more empathic than men, and women are also more inclined than men to sympathize with efforts for redistributive justice. Only a generation ago, women were largely relegated to unpaid nurturing and men to paid labor. Keeping women empathic, my vision hints, is still necessary to providing underpaid caregivers for infants, the disabled, and the elderly. Now, however, more women can be detached from providing personal services in order to increase the market for receiving them. Sex, love, food preparation, personal safety, and psychological insight are all available in the open market.

Boys are not fixed in patriarchal masculinity by either biology or female caregiving but must be rigorously trained throughout youth, often through humiliation by older peers.[6] Boys tease and shame other boys in schools and playgrounds, and men's work sites also foster edgy defensiveness against a culture of mutual attack. Men in our culture typically prove their manhood by resisting impulses to empathize with victims and by showing themselves impervious to the insults of others. Thus antiempathy training still seems an important part of masculine gendering.

Some popular culture of the 1990s teaches young men to identify with the vulnerability of boys, then to rebuff sentiment and empathy in favor of cool, tough, and selfish responses, including, for example, glee at a cartoon child's recurrent murder.[7] Humor targeted to college men is both antiempathic and masculinity-reinforcing. For example, a list of comic maxims argues, "If men really ruled the world," "nodding and looking at your watch would be deemed an acceptable response to 'I love you,' " and "it'd be considered harmless fun to gather thirty friends, put on horned helmets, and go pillage a nearby town."[8] Such anti-empathic elements in popular

---

[5] For references on empathy and gender, see, e.g., Gardiner 1994, 1998.

[6] See Chodorow 1998, which alters the views earlier expressed in Chodorow 1978. For children's gendering of empathy, see Eder et al. 1995.

[7] The character Kenny in the television series *South Park* is killed in nearly every program in purportedly humorous circumstances.

[8] I received these maxims as part of an anonymous e-mail posting circulated among college students, titled "If Men Really Ruled the World," credited to *Maxim Magazine* (November 1998).

culture apparently keep male bonding instrumental rather than erotic or political and also strengthen class and race hierarchies.

Furthermore, I picture male loyalty to masculinity as reinforced through identification with power and prestige, whether that of superathletes, movie heroes, billionaires, or political leaders. Conversely, dominant U.S. masculinity invites men to attack weakness in others and ridicule those already shamed. This habit created a painful contradiction for many men when a popular president, instead of being a site for identification with idealized power, was sexually exposed and humiliated for adolescent sexual behavior that seemed neither powerful nor traditionally masculine.

At the same time, powerful men may now want to enjoy more emotional goods themselves, including love, passion, empathic capacities, and children's attachment and admiration. They want to feel emotionally alive and in touch with their inner, even childhood, selves. One solution I envision is the narrowly targeted empathic moment, an interlude of child care or family affection that is kept apart from business or political life. Such empathic moments are available vicariously through the media as well as at home. For example, famous athletes cry on television about impending illness or deceased parents. The athletes, who already serve as masculinity prostheses for other men, thus also become their emotional surrogates. Politicians, too, claim to "share the pain" of the suffering and exploited without seeking to end it.

One practice that inhibits empathy is the eighty-hour workweek, whether the workaholic executive's one job or the needy moonlighting worker's two, which reduces labor costs. In my fantasy, such overtime by the rich serves chiefly to isolate high-paid professionals from their families and their communities and from fellow feeling with the poor, whom they believe work less hard and therefore deserve less. This system also permits a few privileged women to join ruling-class occupations if they conform to its time regimen and individualist disdain for family and community attachments.

Thus, empathy is incited and targeted only to those most like oneself— or, if more broadly, then only briefly—at the same time that anti-empathic forces are also being strengthened. These complex possibilities modernize older, simpler connections between femininity and empathy and between masculinity and aggression, while increasing the contradictions and humiliations that keep men's social feelings in check.

Hegemonic masculinity bolsters male dominance. Feminists therefore have an interest in encouraging more democratic masculinities. Developmental rather than oppositional gender schema are promising in this regard. They define being a man not in opposition to being a woman or a male homosexual but as the result of growing beyond being a boy. Even less polarized masculinities, however, will be truly egalitarian only when they are built on empathy rather than humiliation and shame.

Millennial realities are far more difficult, complex, and multivalent than my schematic fantasies. There are no central emotional managers or masculinity marketers masterminding the construction of consumer individualist gender. Nevertheless, my fantasies at least articulate a hope that U.S.-based feminist theorists engage with masculinity and age studies, as well as other global knowledges, in order to work more effectively toward a gender-just future for all.

Department of English
University of Illinois at Chicago

References

Bly, Robert. 1996. *The Sibling Society.* Reading, Mass.: Addison-Wesley.

Chodorow, Nancy. 1978. *The Reproduction of Mothering.* Berkeley: University of California Press.

———. 1998. "The Enemy Outside: Thoughts on the Psychodynamics of Extreme Violence with Special Attention to Men and Masculinity." *JPCS: Journal for the Psychoanalysis of Culture and Society* 3(1):25–38.

Connell, R. W. 1995. *Masculinities.* Berkeley: University of California Press.

Eder, Donna, with Catherine Colleen Evans and Stephen Parker. 1995. *School Talk: Gender and Adolescent Culture.* New Brunswick, N.J.: Rutgers University Press.

Ehrenreich, Barbara. 1983. *The Hearts of Men: American Dreams and the Flight from Commitment.* New York: Anchor.

———. 1995. "The Decline of Patriarchy." In *Constructing Masculinity,* ed. M. Berger, B. Wallis, and S. Watson, 284–90. New York: Routledge.

Gardiner, Judith Kegan. 1994. "Empathic Ways of Reading: Narcissism, Identity Politics, and Russ's *Female Man.*" *Feminist Studies* 20(1):87–111.

———. 1998. "Feminism and the Future of Fathering." In *Men Doing Feminism,* ed. Tom Digby, 255–73. New York: Routledge.

———. 2000. " 'South Park,' Blue Men, Anality, and Market Masculinity." *Men and Masculinities* 2(3):251–71.

Sidel, Ruth. 1996. *Keeping Women and Children Last: America's War on the Poor.* New York: Penguin.

Thomas J. Gerschick

Toward a Theory of Disability and Gender

As **feminist theory** has developed, scholars increasingly have attended to how gender intersects with other social characteristics, including sexual orientation, class, and race and ethnicity, to shape the perceptions, experiences, and life chances of women and men. More recently, activists and scholars have applied feminist insights, theory, and methods to the intersection of disability and gender.[1] However, comprehensive theories about the relationship between disability and gender remain elusive. This essay contributes to the development of such theory by addressing the following questions: How does disability affect the gendering process? How does it affect the experience of gender? How does having a disability affect women's and men's abilities to enact gender? In what ways are the experiences of women and men with disabilities similar and different?[2]

Developing a theory of disability and gender provides insight into the lives of a large number of people. The U.S. Census Bureau estimates that in 1994 more than 20.6 percent of the U.S. population, or about fifty-four million people, had some level of physical or mental disability; for 9.9 percent of the population, or twenty-six million people, this disability was severe (McNeil 1997, 1).[3] After women, then, people with disabilities represent the largest minority population in the United States. Given that the likelihood of developing a disability increases with age, and given that the baby-boom generation is aging, the proportion of the U.S. population with disabilities will likely continue to increase. Moreover, accounting for the experiences of women and men with disabilities makes feminist theories of gender more inclusive, complex, and nuanced. Finally, a

This essay is dedicated to the memory of Adam S. Miller (1971–99), friend and frequent coauthor. I would like to thank Bob Broad and Georganne Rundblad for their comments on previous drafts of this essay and Ryan Hieronymous for research assistance.

[1] See Fine and Asch 1988; Hillyer 1993; Morris 1993a, 1993b; Gerschick and Miller 1995; Wendell 1996, 1997; Gerschick 1998.

[2] Space limitations necessitate that I focus on disabilities primarily in the United States in this essay. See Lynn and Wilkinson 1993 for a number of international perspectives on women and disability.

[3] McNeil 1997 provides Census Bureau definitions and measures of disability.

[*Signs: Journal of Women in Culture and Society* 2000, vol. 25, no. 4]

theory of the relation between gender and disability provides another tool that people with disabilities can use to understand and challenge their oppression.

In order to contextualize the experiences of women and men with physical disabilities, we need to attend to three sets of social dynamics: the stigma assigned to disability, gender as an interactional process, and the importance of the body to enacting gender.

To have a disability is not only a physical or mental condition; it is also a social and stigmatized one (Goffman 1963). As anthropologist Robert Murphy observes, "Stigmatization is less a by-product of disability than its substance. The greatest impediment to a person's taking full part in this society are not his physical flaws, but rather the tissue of myths, fears, and misunderstandings that society attaches to them" (1990, 113). Thus, stigmatization is embedded in the daily interactions between people with disabilities and the temporarily able-bodied.[4] In order to enact gender, people with disabilities must be recognized by others as "appropriately" masculine or feminine (West and Zimmerman 1987). Much is at stake in this process, as one's sense of self rests precariously on others' validation or rejection of one's gender performance. Successful enactment bestows status and acceptance; failure invites embarrassment and humiliation (West and Zimmerman 1987). Thus, people with disabilities are engaged in an asymmetrical power relationship with their temporarily able-bodied counterparts.

Bodies are central to achieving recognition as appropriately gendered beings. Bodies operate socially as canvases on which gender is displayed and kinesthetically as the mechanisms by which it is physically enacted. Thus, the bodies of people with disabilities make them vulnerable to being denied recognition as women and men. The type of disability, its visibility, its severity, and whether it is physical or mental in origin mediate the degree to which the body of a person with a disability is socially compromised. For instance, a severe case of the Epstein-Barr virus can lead to disability; however, typically the condition is not readily apparent and, as a consequence, does not trigger stigmatization and devaluation. Conversely, having quadriplegia and using a wheelchair for mobility is highly visual, is perceived to be severe, and frequently elicits invalidation.[5] Moreover, the

---

[4] I intentionally use the term *temporarily able-bodied* to highlight the facts that aging is often disabling and that many of us will develop a disability during our lifetime. In 1994, e.g., the disability rate among the U.S. population ages 65–79 years was 47.3 percent; for those ages 80 years and older, it rose to 71.5 percent (McNeil 1997).

[5] Of course, the degree to which one's body is compromised is also affected by other social characteristics, including race and ethnicity, social class, age, and sexual orientation. Unfortunately, exploring these other characteristics is beyond the scope of this essay.

degree to which a person with a disability is legitimized or delegitimized is context-specific and has both material and nonmaterial consequences.

Disability affects the gendering process in many ways. My current research suggests that the age of onset combines with the type, severity, and visibility of a person's disability to influence the degree to which she or he is taught and subjected to gendered expectations. As C. West and D. H. Zimmerman (1987) note, no one escapes being gendered, including people with disabilities. However, all people do not experience the same degree and type of gender socialization and expectations. For instance, if an infant has a congenital disability and if that disability is severe, as in the case of spina bifida, parents and others in the infant's social world will assign her or him to sex and gender categories but will likely hold fewer gender expectations than for an infant who has a milder disability, such as a visual impairment. Conversely, when the onset of a disability occurs later in a child's life, she or he already will have experienced a significant amount of gender socialization and internalized many gendered expectations. Thus, her or his struggles for social validation as a woman or man will begin with a different level of awareness and commitment to gender. For people with disabilities, then, gendering is conditional.

Furthermore, theories of gender presume that everyone has the same ability to learn, understand, respond to, and be held accountable for gendered expectations. However, for people with a mental disability, these abilities are compromised to different degrees. For example, a person with profound mental retardation may not be able to comprehend many aspects of gender and consequently would largely be beyond the reach of sanctions, while the same does not hold true for a person with a learning disability. Additionally, mental illness can vary individuals' gender enactment. Kay Redfield Jamison (1995), for instance, eloquently describes how her gender performance varied depending on whether she was manic or depressed.

Although women and men with disabilities share similar experiences of devaluation, isolation, marginalization, and discrimination, their fortunes diverge in important ways. Two stigmatized statuses converge in the lives of women with disabilities, further diminishing their already devalued gender status. As M. Fine and A. Asch note, they experience "sexism without the pedestal" (1988, 1). Conversely, for men with physical disabilities, masculine gender privilege collides with the stigmatized status of having a disability, thereby causing status inconsistency, as having a disability erodes much, but not all, masculine privilege.

Although there is much that we do not know regarding the extent of violence that people with disabilities experience, research suggests that children with disabilities are 70 percent more likely to be physically or sexually abused than their able-bodied counterparts (Crosse, Kaye, and Ratnofsky 1993). This abuse is likely to be chronic rather than episodic and to be perpetuated by someone the victim knows, such as a family member or personal attendant (Sobsey and Doe 1991). Furthermore, this abuse is gendered; females with disabilities are more likely to be sexually assaulted, whereas males with disabilities are more likely to experience other forms of physical abuse (Sobsey, Randall, and Parrila 1997). Thus, having a disability exacerbates one of the worst, most direct elements of oppression.

In the contemporary United States, to be perceived as physically attractive is to be socially and sexually desirable. As a result of their invalidated condition, women and men with disabilities are constrained in their opportunities to nurture and to be nurtured, to be loved and to love, and to become parents if they so desire (Fine and Asch 1988, 13). Writer Susan Hannaford explains, "I discovered on becoming officially defined as 'disabled' that I lost my previous identity as a sexually attractive being" (1985, 17). This dynamic, in addition to being mediated by degree, type, and severity of disability, may also be gendered. For example, Hannaford maintains that women are four times as likely as men to divorce after developing a disability (18) and only one-third to one-fourth as likely to marry (76). Fine and Asch (1988, 12–23) provide a range of supporting evidence. Ironically, this may also mean that women with disabilities are less likely than their able-bodied counterparts to be limited by many of the gendered expectations and roles that feminists have challenged.

Women and men with physical disabilities are also economically more vulnerable than nondisabled people. Among people of working age, women with disabilities are less likely to participate in the labor force than both nondisabled women and men with disabilities. This gap varies by gender and the severity of the disability. For instance, according to the U.S. Census Bureau, nondisabled women's labor force participation rate in 1994 was 74.5 percent. For women with a mild disability, the percentage dropped to 68.4 percent, and it plunged to 24.7 percent for women with severe disabilities. For men, the respective numbers were 89.9 percent, 85.1 percent, and 27.8 percent (McNeil 1997). Women with disabilities are also more susceptible to being tracked into low-wage service-sector jobs.

Similarly, gender and the severity of one's disability affect median monthly earnings. Among women 21–64 years of age in 1994, median monthly earnings were $1,470 among those with no disability, $1,200 among those with a nonsevere disability, and $1,000 among those with a severe disability. Comparable figures for men were $2,190, $1,857, and

$1,262 (McNeil 1997). As a consequence, women and men with disabilities are poorer than their able-bodied counterparts, and women with disabilities fare worst of all (LaPlante et al. 1999).

In brief summary, disability has a profound effect on the material and nonmaterial experience of gender. Yet, there is still much we do not know about this dynamic: How and under what conditions do social characteristics such as race, class, age, and sexual orientation further mediate the relationship between gender and disability? How does gender affect the experience of disability? How do the dynamics identified in this essay vary by culture in a global context? How might the stigmatization and marginalization that women and men with disabilities face contribute to the creation of alternative gender identities? As we enter a new millennium, I encourage the readers of *Signs* to take up these questions and to add further inquiries of their own so that we can soon develop more comprehensive theories about the relationship between disability and gender.

Department of Sociology
Illinois State University

References

Crosse, S. B., E. Kaye, and A. C. Ratnofsky. 1993. *Report on the Maltreatment of Children with Disabilities.* Washington, D.C.: National Center on Child Abuse and Neglect.

Fine, M., and A. Asch. 1988. "Introduction: Beyond Pedestals." In *Women with Disabilities: Essays in Psychology, Culture, and Politics,* ed. M. Fine and A. Asch, 1–37. Philadelphia: Temple University Press.

Gerschick, T. J. 1998. "Sisyphus in a Wheelchair: Men with Physical Disabilities Confront Gender Domination." In *Everyday Inequalities: Critical Inquiries,* ed. J. O'Brien and J. A. Howard, 189–211. Oxford: Blackwell.

Gerschick, T. J., and A. S. Miller. 1995. "Coming to Terms: Masculinity and Physical Disability." In *Men's Health and Illness: Gender, Power, and the Body,* 183–204. Thousand Oaks, Calif.: Sage.

Goffman, E. 1963. *Stigma: Notes on the Management of Spoiled Identity.* New York: Touchstone.

Hannaford, S. 1985. *Living Outside Inside: A Disabled Woman's Experience.* Berkeley, Calif.: Canterbury.

Hillyer, B. 1993. *Feminism and Disability.* Norman: University of Oklahoma Press.

Jamison, K. R. 1995. *An Unquiet Mind.* New York: Knopf.

LaPlante, M. P., J. Kennedy, H. S. Kaye, and B. L. Wenger. 1999. *Disability and Employment.* Available on-line at http://dsc.ucsf.edu/default.html.

Lynn, M., and S. Wilkinson, eds. 1993. "Women and Disability," special issue of *Canadian Woman Studies,* vol. 13, no. 4.

McNeil, J. M. 1997. *Americans with Disabilities, 1994–95*. Current Population Report No. P70-61. Washington, D.C.: Bureau of the Census.

Morris, J. 1993a. "Feminism and Disability." *Feminist Review,* no. 43 (Spring): 57–70.

———. 1993b. "Gender and Disability." In *Disabling Barriers—Enabling Environments,* ed. J. Swain, V. Finkelstein, S. French, and M. Oliver, 85–92. Thousand Oaks, Calif.: Sage.

Murphy, R. F. 1990. *The Body Silent.* New York: Norton.

Sobsey, D., and T. Doe. 1991. "Patterns of Sexual Abuse and Assault." *Sexuality and Disability* 9(3):243–59.

Sobsey, D., W. Randall, and R. K. Parrila. 1997. "Gender Differences in Abused Children with and without Disabilities." *Child Abuse and Neglect* 21(8):707–20.

Wendell, S. 1996. *The Rejected Body: Feminist Philosophical Reflections on Disability.* New York: Routledge.

———. 1997. "Toward a Feminist Theory of Disability." In *The Disability Studies Reader,* ed. L. Davis, 260–78. New York: Routledge.

West, C., and D. H. Zimmerman. 1987. "Doing Gender." *Gender & Society* 1(2):125–51.

The U.S. Women's Health Research Agenda
for the Twenty-First Century

In **1999,** the National Institutes of Health (NIH) published a research agenda for the beginning of the next century, based on activities during the past two decades. In this essay, I examine the NIH women's health research agenda as a guide for women's health research, and consider the sociopolitical context in which it was developed, and also evaluate the adequacy of this agenda for advancing women's health science from the perspectives of feminist critics of science.

The 1999 NIH women's health research agenda originated with the work of the U.S. Public Health Service Task Force on Women's Health Issues and its publication of a two-volume report (1985). The task force recommended that "biomedical and behavioral research should be expanded to insure emphasis on those conditions and diseases unique to, or more prevalent in, women in all age groups" as well as those conditions for which the interventions were different, or the health risks greater, for women than for men (6). In 1986 the NIH Advisory Committee on Women's Health recommended that investigators include women in studies, especially in clinical trials; explain exclusion of women from their proposals when that was seen as appropriate; and evaluate gender differences in their findings. In 1990, a Government Accounting Office study found that the policy was not being implemented and that only $778 million (or 13.5 percent) of the NIH budget was spent on women's health issues. In 1990 the Congressional Caucus on Women's Issues drafted the Women's Health Equity Act. In September 1990, the House and Senate conducted hearings on women's health research being funded by the NIH, and the Office of Research on Women's Health (ORWH) was created within the Office of the Director, NIH, with three objectives: (1) to ensure that issues pertaining to women are adequately addressed, including "diseases, disorders, and conditions that are unique to, more prevalent among, or far more serious in women, or for which there are different risk factors or interventions for women than for men"; (2) to ensure appropriate participation in clinical research, especially clinical trials; and (3) to foster increased

[*Signs: Journal of Women in Culture and Society* 2000, vol. 25, no. 4]

involvement of women in biomedical research, especially in decision-making roles in clinical medicine and research environments (U.S. Public Health Service 1992). Beginning in February 1991, no Public Health Service grant applications were accepted unless women were adequately represented in clinical research, except in cases where their exclusion was justified.

In 1991 the ORWH convened the NIH Task Force on Opportunities for Research on Women's Health and charged it with assessing the current status of women's health research, identifying research opportunities and gaps in knowledge, and formulating a cross-NIH plan for future directions for women's health research. The task force heard public testimony in June 1991 from scientists, health professionals, and women's health advocates. The ORWH summary of the public testimony indicated that high priority should be given to prevention of cancer (especially breast cancer), cardiovascular disease, osteoporosis, autoimmune diseases, sexually transmitted diseases, domestic violence, and AIDS, and to postnatal care and consequences of women's hormonal cycles for pharmacotherapy. In addition, it strongly emphasized the need for behavioral research and for attention to the diversity of women's health needs, particularly with regard to populations such as African-American, Hispanic, and poor women.

The Workshop on Opportunities for Research on Women's Health held in Hunt Valley, Maryland, in September 1991 included experts in basic and clinical sciences, women's health clinicians, and representatives of women's organizations. The goal was to develop recommendations for research activities on behalf of all U.S. women. The framework for development of a research agenda included the formation of working groups to address major divisions of the lifespan and scientific areas that cut across women's health throughout life (U.S. Public Health Service 1992). Groups also addressed cross-cutting areas of science: reproductive biology, early developmental biology, aging processes, cardiovascular function and disease, malignancy, and immune function and infectious diseases.

Critics of the 1991 agenda asserted that greater consideration should be given to diverse groups of women, for example, to the special health issues of women of particular age and racial groups (Grisso and Watkins 1992). In addition, some suggested that the agenda should be broader, including consideration of community factors such as employment opportunities, hygiene, and transportation; family factors such as household income; and personal factors such as genetics (Leslie 1992). Others advocated including mental health, which was absent from the NIH agenda (McBride 1987; Russo 1990).

In addition to criticizing the content of the agenda, some offered critiques of the methods used to generate knowledge about women's health. In particular, some expressed concern that unless research questions were grounded in an understanding of the nature of women's lives they were not likely to generate knowledge for women.[1] Others wondered whether the research agenda would address questions that women themselves wanted answered — for example, questions about prevention of heart disease, cancer, AIDS/HIV, and violence against women (Lather 1991; Narrigan et al. 1997). Still others pointed out that the perspectives of the predominantly white, middle-class male investigators funded by NIH would not be likely to reflect the perspectives of women whose identities spanned a range of race, class, and culture (Woods 1994; Olesen et al. 1997; Ruzek, Olesen, and Clarke 1997).

In setting the 1999 agenda, the ORWH engaged a task force of governmental and nongovernmental experts in planning a one-year process that included three regional meetings, in Philadelphia in 1996, New Orleans in 1997, and Santa Fe in 1997. At each meeting, women's health advocates and scientists engaged in discussions and presentations and heard public testimony. A final meeting was convened in Bethesda in 1997 to revise and update the agenda for research on women's health for the twenty-first century on the basis of the testimony and presentations at the regional meetings.

Informed by the 1994 *NIH Guidelines on the Inclusion of Women and Minorities as Subjects in Clinical Research,* some discussions focused explicitly on health problems of specific ethnic groups of women, such as African Americans, Hispanics, and Asian Pacific Islanders (U.S. Public Health Service 1994). In addition, some sessions focused on women living with disabling conditions. An explicit distinction was made between sex and gender in the report, pointing out the need to consider which health effects were mediated by biology (e.g., the X chromosome) and which by social roles. Emphasis on emerging research issues related to genetic testing and its role in prevention, diagnosis, and treatment was evident throughout the conferences, demonstrating progress related to the Human Genome Project.

The final report reflects the deliberations and recommendations from the hearings; assesses the current status of research on women's health and identifies continuing gaps in knowledge; identifies sex and gender differences that may influence women's health and factors that influence

---

[1] Klein 1983; Duffy and Hedin 1988; Harding 1991; Parker and McFarlane 1991; Woods 1994.

differences among populations of women; addresses emerging research resulting from basic clinical and applied research that can facilitate better prevention, diagnosis, and treatment; develops strategies for improving the health status of all women, regardless of race, ethnicity, age, or other population characteristics; discusses career issues for women scientists; and recommends a research agenda for women's health for the twenty-first century (U.S. Public Health Service 1999).

The scientific chapters in the report address disorders and consequences of the use of alcohol, tobacco, and other drugs; behavioral and social sciences; bone and musculoskeletal disorders; cancer; cardiovascular disease; digestive diseases; immunity and autoimmune diseases; infectious diseases and emerging infections; mental disorders; neuroscience; oral health; pharmacologic issues; reproductive health; and urologic and kidney conditions. Of particular note are chapters focusing on the use of sex and gender to define and characterize meaningful differences between men and women (Fishman, Wick, and Koenig) and a series of chapters addressing issues in research design. Among these are chapters titled "Health of Special Populations of Women" (Sarto), "Sex and Gender Differences" (Counts, Brawley, Sagraves, and Hutter), "Racial, Ethnic, and Cultural Diversity" (Cain, Rodriguez-Trias, and Avila), and "Multidisciplinary Perspectives" (Grady, Strom, and Farer). Taken together, these chapters create a new framework for studying women's health that could transform the landscape of women's health research; however, whether the material in this section of the report can be integrated into the work recommended in the scientific chapters will depend on the willingness of scientists to expand their frames of reference beyond the biomedical view. What remains to be seen is the degree to which the recommendations in this report are embraced by the senior scientists who judge the scientific merit of research proposals and the advisory council members who shape science policy for NIH.

What is missing from the agenda? There is relatively little emphasis on the health consequences of poverty, of power differences between men and women, and of the gendered allocation of work in the society. The agenda also needs to develop further a global perspective on women's health, including examination of the women's health consequences of economic development and social policy.

In the final analysis, the adequacy of the women's health research agenda will be demonstrated by future research that includes women in studies that generate information about health issues that matter to women; informs practice for diverse groups of women, addressing differences in ethnicity, race, socioeconomic status, and sexual orientation; and has significant consequences for advancing the health of all women in the world.

School of Nursing
University of Washington

References

Duffy, M., and B. Hedin. 1988. "New Directions for Nursing Research." In *Nursing Research: Theory and Practice,* ed. N. Woods and M. Catanzaro, 530–39. St. Louis: Moody.

Grisso, J., and K. Watkins. 1992. "A Framework for a Women's Health Research Agenda." *Journal of Women's Health* 1(3):177–87.

Harding, S. 1991. *Whose Science? Whose Knowledge? Thinking from Women's Lives.* Ithaca, N.Y.: Cornell University Press.

Klein, R. 1983. "How to Do What We Want to Do: Thoughts about Feminist Methodology." In *Theories of Women's Studies,* ed. G. Bowles and R. Klein, 88–104. London: Routledge & Kegan Paul.

Lather, P. 1991. *Getting Smart: Feminist Research and Pedagogy with/in the Postmodern.* New York: Routledge.

Leslie, J. 1992. "Women's Lives and Women's Health: Using Social Science Research to Promote Better Health for Women." *Journal of Women's Health* 1(4):307–18.

McBride, A. B. 1987. "Developing a Women's Mental Health Research Agenda." *Image* 19(1):4–8.

Narrigan, D., J. Zones, N. Worcester, and M. Grad. 1997. "Research to Improve Women's Health: An Agenda for Equity." In *Women's Health: Complexities and Differences,* ed. S. Ruzek, V. Olesen, and A. Clarke, 551–79. Columbus: Ohio State University Press.

Olesen, V., D. Taylor, S. Ruzek, and A. Clarke. 1997. "Strengths and Strongholds in Women's Health Research. In *Women's Health: Complexities and Differences,* ed. S. Ruzek, V. Olesen, and A. Clarke, 580–606. Columbus: Ohio State University Press.

Parker, B., and J. McFarlane. 1991. "Feminist Theory and Nursing: An Empowerment Model for Research." *Advances in Nursing Science* 13(2):59–67.

Russo, N. 1990. "Forging Research Priorities for Women's Mental Health." *American Psychologist* 45(3):368–73.

Ruzek, S., V. Olesen, and A. Clarke. 1997. "Conversing with Diversity: Implications for Social Research." In *Women's Health: Complexities and Differences,* ed. S. Ruzek, V. Olesen, and A. Clarke, 607–35. Columbus: Ohio State University Press.

U.S. Public Health Service. 1992. *Opportunities for Research on Women's Health.* Bethesda, Md.: National Institutes of Health.

———. 1994. *NIH Guidelines on the Inclusion of Women and Minorities as Subjects in Clinical Research.* Washington, D.C.: Department of Health and Human Services.

———. 1999. *A Report of the Task Force on the NIH Women's Health Research Agenda for the Twenty-First Century.* NIH publication no. 99-4386. Bethesda, Md.: National Institutes of Health.

U.S. Public Health Service Task Force on Women's Health Issues. 1985. *Women's Health: Report of the Public Health Services.* 2 vols. U.S. Department of Health and Human Services publication no. PHS-85-50206. Washington, D.C.: Public Health Service.

Woods, N. 1994. "The United States Women's Health Research Agenda: Analysis and Critique." *Western Journal of Nursing Research* 16(5):467–79.

Melancholia in the Late Twentieth Century

Like hysteria at the turn of the last century, melancholia at the turn of this one has come largely to define how we think about our subjectivities. Freud's initial research with J. M. Charcot challenged hysteria's historical connection with the traumatized female body by linking it as well to the traumatized (Jewish) male body.[1] However, Freud's subsequent and most famous case histories on hysteria—such as Dora—reconfigured the disease once again as largely descriptive of a (deracinated) female condition. This genealogy of hysteria as pathological female subjectivity—as the uncontrollable "wandering womb"—continues to endure.

Freud also connected melancholia to the female condition. In "Mourning and Melancholia" ([1917] 1963), he suggests that while melancholia might be pathological for men, it describes normative female subjectivity—a suggestion that feminist thinkers such as Julia Kristeva (e.g., 1989) have developed in their work on women and depression. Unlike hysteria, however, at the turn of the twentieth century melancholia has come to encompass a wide spectrum of subjectivities exceeding any gendered distinctions. Indeed, melancholia and its generalized connection with depression in the popular imagination have come to describe numerous subjectivities inhabiting multiple areas of the globe. How might we account for this proliferation of melancholia? And what does it mean for feminisms at the millennium?

I I I

In *States of Injury*, Wendy Brown notes that the "late modern liberal subject quite literally seethes with *ressentiment*" (1995, 69). She argues that the genealogy of identity politics in the late twentieth century must be thought in large part as both a product of and a reaction to this condition of *ressentiment*. For Brown, discourses of injury and grief not only give form to marginalized identities; they are identity politics' very condition

---

[1] For histories of male hysteria and Jewish identity, see Gilman 1991; Geller 1992; Boyarin 1995; Pellegrini 1997. For analyses of male hysteria in relation to the traumas of modernity and industrialization, see Hertz 1983; Kirby 1988; Smith 1993.

[*Signs: Journal of Women in Culture and Society* 2000, vol. 25, no. 4]

of possibility. What, then, would it mean if minoritarian group identities were defined not through a particular set of physiological distinctions or cultural bonds but through a collective group memory of historical loss and continued suffering?

As Freud's premier theory of unspeakable loss and inexorable suffering, melancholia serves as a powerful tool for analyzing the psychic production, condition, and limits of marginalized subjectivities predicated on states of injury. In this regard, melancholia as a theory of unresolved grief is useful for investigating the formation of not only gendered subjects but also a host of other minoritarian group identities mobilized through identity-politics movements of the last quarter-century. In the remainder of this short essay, I propose a genealogy of melancholia in relation to gendered, queer, racialized, and postcolonial subjects. I argue that, even if melancholia has proliferated beyond Freud's gendered framework, gender nevertheless remains a crucial analytic lens through which to investigate these multiple social hierarchies. Ultimately, a critical reevaluation of melancholia in terms of these intersecting subject positions allows us to strategize ways of challenging liberal society's refusal, as Brown points out, to recognize the very possibility of multiple states of injury even as it expressly blames those who experience them for their own conditions of suffering (1995, 70).

I   I   I

Freud argues in "Mourning and Melancholia" that melancholia is a pathological form of mourning: unable "properly" to grieve the loss of an object, a place, or an ideal, the melancholic, according to Freud, repudiates the finite process of mourning, languishing instead in the refusal to grieve ([1917] 1963). The melancholic is so militant in his or her denials that the lost object is finally incorporated into the self, turned into the shelter of the ego, and preserved as a form of ghostly identification. In this refusal to sever any attachments to the lost object, the melancholic becomes instead haunted by it. Loss denied is incorporated into the ego, and the ego thus becomes a remainder of unresolved grief.

The turning of the lost object into the ego not only marks a turning away from the external world of the social to the internal world of the psyche, it also simultaneously transforms all possible reproaches against the loved object into reproaches against the self: "Thus the shadow of the object fell upon the ego, so that the latter could henceforth be criticized by a special mental faculty like an object, like the forsaken object" (170). Marking this turning from the external world of lost desires to the internal world of pathological identifications, Freud summarizes: "In grief the world becomes poor and empty; in melancholia it is the ego itself" (167).

While Freud attempts to characterize melancholia as a mode of pathological mourning, he cannot sustain this distinction. In *The Ego and the Id* ([1923] 1960), he revises his theory of melancholia, contending that the ego, in fact, is composed of abandoned object-cathexes preserved as identifications. Freud admits that he had failed earlier to "appreciate the full significance of the [melancholic] process and did not know how common and typical it is," and he concludes that identification with lost objects has "a great share in determining the form taken by the ego and that it makes an essential contribution towards building up what is called its 'character' " (23). The ego is created through an originary loss predicated on a melancholic incorporation and identification. As such, there can be no ego without, or prior to, melancholia. Melancholia is the privileged psychic mechanism by which "abandoned" and "forsaken" objects are simultaneously preserved by and as the ego. In *The Ego and the Id,* Freud comes, then, to recognize this psychic entity as one of melancholy's effects. The melancholic turning inward establishes the ego, which only then can claim the "proper" work of mourning. In this respect, melancholia cannot be regarded as pathological. To the contrary, it must be thought of as entirely normative — as a constitutive psychic mechanism engendering subjectivity itself.

In *The Psychic Life of Power* (1997), Judith Butler delineates the formation of gendered identity as a product of this melancholic framework. She notes that for Freud's little boy the primary lost object is the father. In other words, the little boy must give up his forbidden attachments to the father as an object of (homo)sexual desire in favor of a constitutive identification with him. This melancholic loss and turning inward of the father, Butler suggests, establishes the little boy's ego by simultaneously segregating and orienting his identifications (with the father) and desires (for the mother). The boy's subjectivity is thus created as a gendered identity governed by a system of compulsory heterosexuality. The masculine is formed from the refusal to grieve the father as a possibility of love, and this melancholic system reifies a "cultural logic whereby gender is achieved and stabilized through a heterosexual positioning, and where threats to heterosexuality become threats to gender itself" (135). In this scenario, the masculine is formed through an identification consolidated by the disavowal of loss. However, if a system of gender regulation and compulsory heterosexuality emerge through the logics of melancholia, not all gendered subjects, I must emphasize, are finally melancholic ones, as the normative heterosexual male on whom Freud's gendered productions focus remains largely untroubled by this condition. If the ego itself is established through loss, why is it that the normative heterosexual male is not enjoined to face this lack—to see himself either as a subject or as an object of loss? Why is it that women, homosexuals, people of color, and postcolonials seem to be at greatest risk for melancholia and depression in contemporary society? How do we account for the fact that it is these minoritarian groups and not normative heterosexual male subjects who bear the greatest burden of unresolved grief?

Freud states that melancholia comes about through the loss of—and the inability to relinquish—an object, a place, or an ideal. While he makes no social distinctions between the various lost objects engendering melancholia, we must. A political reading of this aspect of melancholia is crucial, for the social status of the lost object seems largely to determine whether the subject is fated to an existence of depression and despair. In a society organized by compulsory heterosexuality, the little boy has tremendous support—indeed psychic pressure as well as material incentive—to cede the father as an object of desire for a socially sanctioned identification with him. Here, melancholia functions to regulate, to normalize, and to designate a sphere of prevailing gender norms and acceptable attachments. At the same time, it also delimits a sphere of unacceptable objects and abjected identifications.

Unlike Freud's little boy, women, homosexuals, people of color, and postcolonials are all coerced to relinquish and yet to identify with socially disparaged objects on their psychic paths to subjectivity. This ambivalent attachment to devalued objects, like *ressentiment,* comes to define—indeed, to produce—minoritarian subjectivities. Can the melancholic's psychic ambivalence toward the lost object—an ambivalence turned against the ego as self-reproaches that undermine and destabilize the ego's coherence—be thought of as a direct effect of social conflict between the melancholic's desire to preserve a lost object that dominant society refuses to support or to recognize? If, for instance, there is no public language by which a loss can be recognized, then melancholia assumes a social dimension of contemporary consequence that must be acknowledged and analyzed as a problem of the political. This attention to the social dimensions of melancholia insists on a thinking of the dis-ease less as individual pathology than as a model of group formation. As Stanley Cavell notes, "massive depression has, whatever else, a political basis" (1999, 246).

Thinking this dynamic of coerced loss and ambivalent preservation in terms of gender and feminism, Kaja Silverman has written extensively on the production of normative female subjectivity as a melancholic forfeiture. In *The Acoustic Mirror,* she argues that the development of Freud's little girl into a mature woman requires her sacrifice of the mother of plenitude for a forced identification with the mother of lack (1988, 141–86). This trajec-

tory traces a movement from interdicted activity to culturally enforced passivity—a movement that enacts the difficult transfer of erotic investments
from the phallic (clitoral) to the genital (vaginal).

Reading melancholia from the vantage of queer politics, Douglas Crimp
(1989) challenges us to imagine a discourse of identification in the age of
AIDS that could mean anything other than silence, retribution, and death.
He notes that the innumerable losses of socially excoriated, dead young
men remains unspeakable within the public realm. And insofar as this grief
remains unspeakable, Butler adds, "the rage over the loss can redouble by
virtue of remaining unavowed. And if that rage is publicly proscribed, the
melancholic effects of such a proposition can achieve suicidal proportions"
(1997, 148). Unsure whether we will share this fate as sad young survivors, we become the vehicles of self-inflicted violence. These dead young
men — these lost objects of desire — unspeakable and unspoken, are melan-
cholically withdrawn into the world of the psyche. There they remain ambivalent identifications of violence, guilt, and death, vexed psychic efforts
to annul the tragic losses that a homophobic world repeatedly demands.

Little has been written on the question of racial difference and melancholia until quite recently (see Cheng 1997; Muñoz 1997; Eng and Han,
in press), though it is not difficult to imagine the ways melancholia comes
to animate racial identity. In a Western social order configured by unattain-
able ideals of whiteness—a world Frantz Fanon summarizes through the
social imperative "*turn white or disappear*" (1967, 100)—assimilation into
dominant society for people of color means the acquiescence to racial self-
erasure. In *Black Skin, White Masks,* Fanon writes about the classroom as a
site of colonialist regulation and assimilation that compels a melancholic
"devaluation of self" (75) through forced identification with socially disparaged ideals of blackness and, I would add, brownness and yellowness.
"Forever in combat with his own image" (194), the racialized subject lives
the social fate of Ralph Ellison's invisible man as a normative structure of
daily life.

Fanon's examples, taken from experiences in French Martinique and Algeria, also bring us to the question of melancholia and postcolonial identity. Postcolonial Hong Kong identity, for instance, is constituted through
the loss of a socially disparaged place. Largely seen, that is, by the world as
decadent—neither properly "Chinese" nor properly "British"—with little
political history or cultural distinction, Hong Kong comes into existence
only at its moment of disappearance. Writing about the 1997 turnover of
this colonial port from Great Britain to China, Ackbar Abbas observes,
"The cause of this interest in Hong Kong culture—1997—may also cause
its demise. The change in status of culture in Hong Kong can be described

as follows: from reverse hallucination, which only sees desert, to a culture of disappearance, whose appearance is posited on the imminence of its disappearance" (1997, 7). In turn, postcolonial Hong Kong subjectivity emerges precisely at this moment of forfeiture and loss — through an inexorable logic of melancholic incorporation and identification that the vocabulary of diaspora, exile, and dispersion continually traces in its language of lost origins (see Eng 1999).

The proliferation of melancholia beyond its gendered distinctions insists, along with the scholarship of third-world feminists, that feminisms at the millennium can no longer think about gender in isolation — that the subjects of feminism must always consider gender through the multiple and intersecting registers of sexuality, race, and postcoloniality. At the same time, the cleaving between gendered labor and capital demand a rethinking of the ways gender organizes the global subject in our contemporary age. Indeed, in a recent lecture titled "Feminism without Frontiers" (1999), Gayatri Chakravorty Spivak suggests that while we might consider the colonial subject as classed and the postcolonial subject as raced, we must regard the global subject as gendered.

As a psychic paradigm in which the lost object holds pride of place, melancholia's tenacious attachment to objects of loss convinces us, finally, of something we might otherwise doubt: our enduring attachment to (disparaged) others (see Phillips 1997). In this formulation lies a nascent political protest. Is not the internal violence of melancholia, Butler asks, "a refracted indictment of the social forms that have made certain kinds of loss ungrievable" (185)? If the proliferation of melancholia in the late twentieth century insists that gender is not the only or the primary guarantor of loss that organizes our psychic and social lives, an expansion of melancholia as nascent political protest allows us to resituate gender and feminisms at the millennium as crucial sites of progressive politics in their renewed configurations on the global stage.

Department of English and Comparative Literature
Columbia University

References

Abbas, Ackbar. 1997. *Hong Kong: Culture and the Politics of Disappearance.* Minneapolis: University of Minnesota Press.

Boyarin, Daniel. 1995. "Freud's Baby, Fleiss's Maybe: Homophobia, Anti-Semitism, and the Invention of Oedipus." *GLQ: A Journal of Lesbian and Gay Studies* 2(1–2):115–47.

Brown, Wendy. 1995. *States of Injury: Power and Freedom in Late Modernity.* Princeton, N.J.: Princeton University Press.

Butler, Judith. 1997. *The Psychic Life of Power: Theories in Subjection.* Stanford, Calif.: Stanford University Press.

Cavell, Stanley. 1999. "Benjamin and Wittgenstein: Signals and Affinities." *Critical Inquiry* 25(2):235–46.

Cheng, Anne Anlin. 1997. "The Melancholy of Race." *Kenyon Review* 19(1):49–61.

Crimp, Douglas. 1989. "Mourning and Militancy." *October* 51 (Winter): 3–18.

Eng, David L. 1999. "Melancholia/Postcoloniality: Loss in *The Floating Life*." *Qui Parle* 11(2):137–50, 161–64.

Eng, David L., and Shinhee Han. In press. "A Dialogue on Racial Melancholia." *Psychoanalytic Dialogues* 10(4).

Fanon, Frantz. 1967. *Black Skin, White Masks.* Trans. Charles Lam Markmann. New York: Grove Weidenfeld.

Freud, Sigmund. (1917) 1963. "Mourning and Melancholia." In *General Psychological Theory,* ed. Philip Rieff, 164–79. New York: Collier.

———. (1923) 1960. *The Ego and the Id.* Trans. Joan Riviere. New York: Norton.

Geller, Jonathan. 1992. " 'A Glance on the Nose': Freud's Inscription of Jewish Difference." *American Imago* 49:427–44.

Gilman, Sander. 1991. *The Jew's Body.* New York: Routledge.

Hertz, Neil. 1983. "Medusa's Head: Male Hysteria under Political Pressure." *Representations* 4 (Fall): 26–54.

Kirby, Lynne. 1988. "Male Hysteria and Early Cinema." *Camera Obscura: A Journal of Feminism and Film Theory* 17:113–31.

Kristeva, Julia, 1989. *Black Sun: Depression and Melancholia.* Trans. Leon S. Roudiez. New York: Columbia University Press.

Muñoz, José Esteban. 1997. "Photographies of Mourning: Melancholia and Ambivalence in Van Der Zee, Mapplethorpe, and *Looking for Langston*." In *Race and the Subject of Masculinities,* ed. Harry Stecopoulous and Michael Uebel, 337–57. Durham, N.C.: Duke University Press.

Pellegrini, Ann. 1997. *Performance Anxieties: Staging Psychoanalysis, Staging Race.* New York: Routledge.

Phillips, Adam. 1997. "Keep It Moving: Commentary on Judith Butler's 'Melancholy Gender/Refused Identification.' " In Butler 1997, 151–59.

Silverman, Kaja. 1988. *The Acoustic Mirror: The Female Voice in Psychoanalysis and Cinema.* Bloomington: Indiana University Press.

Smith, Paul. 1993. *Clint Eastwood: A Cultural Production.* Minneapolis: University of Minnesota Press.

Spivak, Gayatri Chakravorty. 1999. "Feminism without Frontiers." Paper presented in the Feminist Interventions series, Institute for Research on Women and Gender, Columbia University, February 1.

Women and Music on the Verge of the New Millennium

n February 1999 Lauryn Hill set a record by winning five Grammy Awards for her album *The Miseducation of Lauryn Hill* (Ruffhouse/Columbia, 1998). She was, moreover, the fifth woman (along with Bonnie Raitt, Natalie Cole, Alanis Morissette, and Celine Dion) to receive the accolade "Album of the Year" in the 1990s: in other words, more women than men have earned the highest prize offered by the music industry in the past ten years. In the field of classical composition, two women — Ellen Taafe Zwilich and Shulamit Ran — have been honored with recent Pulitzer Prizes for their music (in 1983 and 1991, respectively), while Meredith Monk became a MacArthur Fellow in 1995. And over the course of the 1990s, feminist scholars (including Catherine Clément, Susan Cook, Suzanne Cusick, Ellen Koskoff, Ruth Solie, Judith Tick, Elizabeth Wood, myself, and others) have transformed radically the goals, methods, and subject matter of the academic discipline of musicology — a field hitherto devoted to upholding the all-male canon of European art music.

If we were to judge only on the basis of the last decade of the second millennium, we might conclude that North American men and women share equally in the production and study of music, that the biases that have plagued the rest of the culture do not obtain in this domain. Indeed, women in the field of music today feel unusually optimistic — more so than at any previous time in Western history. Many even deny the need for what they regard as the special pleading of feminism.

But the long view would advise us to temper our optimism with caution. Until the 1990s, few music-history textbooks so much as mentioned a single woman. Although feminist scholars have now brought to light earlier moments of female creativity in European art music, these artists had faded from memory over the centuries, and our new biographies of these female composers reveal over and over again the exceptional tenacity demanded of women who attempted to participate in public arenas of music making. Moreover, despite the increasing prominence of women in contemporary popular music, periodicals such as *Rolling Stone* still tend to write about them in "gee whiz!" articles that marvel at the sheer existence of such creatures, rather like the proverbial dancing dog. Ten years of

[*Signs: Journal of Women in Culture and Society* 2000, vol. 25, no. 4]

equity (and mostly in North America) out of two thousand — a mere blip on the screen of time.

No one can predict the future. Certainly very few arbiters of taste in 1899 would have guessed on the basis of the ragtime craze that the dominant innovations of the next century would be those of African-American musicians, with their successive contributions of jazz, blues, rock, rhythm and blues, soul, disco, funk, rap, and so on. Thus, although the success of female artists in the 1990s might quickly sink without a trace into the well of history, awaiting rediscovery by yet-unborn generations of feminist scholars, it *could* happen that the rise of women in music during the 1990s constitutes but the beginning of a long-term trajectory.

We who identify ourselves as feminists sometimes worry about the tendency of these successful female artists to reject the label themselves. In interview after interview they recite what sounds to our ears like the very core of feminist thought, only to punctuate their statements with the phrase, "But I'm *not* a feminist!" Like many of our students, who likewise bristle at the F-word, they happily benefit from the struggles of the 1970s women's movement while disavowing any affiliation. Any feminist critic who has approached an idolized female artist — say, Queen Latifah, Polly Jean Harvey, or Thea Musgrave — and been rebuffed knows the keen disappointment of the gap between apparent affinities and verbal confirmation.

Yet if we accept the notion that feminism is as feminism does, we might see that we are surrounded by far more powerful strains of pro-woman art than those available even at the zenith of the women's movement. Why the repudiation of feminist identification? Part of the answer lies with the successful media backlash that has painted such a ludicrous picture of the movement that only the most intrepid younger women admit to feeling hailed by it; most imagine that signing on as a feminist would mean declaring war on men and refusing to wear anything besides sackcloth and ashes.

In music, however, an additional cause of this distancing is the feel-good, folk-based repertory that circulated at 1970s women's music festivals. To be fair, that musical style derived its effectiveness from its aggressive simplicity, which both facilitated communal participation and also served as an unobtrusive vehicle for conveying lyrics. The efficacy of the women's movement depended at the outset on its ability to produce a cohesive social world, and so-called womyn's music played a role similar to that of Luther's chorales or national anthems: the practice of congregational singing makes palpable in the here-and-now the reality of a unified community, a kind of experience at which verbal theories can only gesture provisionally.

But feminist theory itself called into question the one-size-fits-all model of political organization. We may interpret the move from the sisterhood of twenty-five years ago to the radically individualized performativity of the 1990s as yet another splintering of the Left. Or we may choose to read it as evidence that feminism (or whatever we want to call the emergence of inventive, self-possessed women) has acquired sufficient strength to sustain an indefinite number of very different voices.

According to received wisdom, music lags behind the other arts; it picks up ideas from other media just when they have become outmoded. But Jacques Attali, in his influential little book *Noise* (1985), argues the opposite: that music — because of the flexibility it acquires through its relative indeterminacy — often foreshadows structures of feeling only later discernible in other, more concrete cultural media. Thus, while some critics of the early 1980s saw Madonna's videos as evidence of reactionary sexual politics, others recognized in her work the masquerade of femininity, the ever-changing performed identities later verbalized by cutting-edge feminist theorists; the much-loathed Yoko Ono is now coming into her own as an avant-garde artist rather than just the dragon lady who broke up the Beatles; and that weird opera project by Gertrude Stein and Virgil Thomson, *Four Saints in Three Acts,* can finally be grasped as the fundamentally queer text it always was, long before we had words to label its deconstructive mischief.

One of the most heartening aspects of recent music by women is its courage to defy stereotypes of sanctioned female behavior. In the arena of popular culture, we have, for instance, Tori Amos's candid accounts of rape and recovery from abuse, the wry jazz-based ruminations of Erykah Badu, PJ Harvey's searing visions of ecstasy, and the Afro-Peruvian protest songs of Susana Baca; in the classical realm, we have the haunting string quartets of Sofia Gubaidulina, the dynamic orchestral allegories of Joan Tower, the woman-centered operas of Thea Musgrave and Meredith Monk, and the transgressive performance art of Diamanda Galas and Shelly Hirsch; and in musicology, we have an increasing number of biographies and reference works dealing with female musicians. But even more important, feminist criticism has opened the field to the study of genders, sexualities, bodies, emotions, and subjectivities as articulated in a vast range of musics — popular and classical, Western and non-Western, ancient and contemporary; it has, in other words, brought musicology into the conversations that have dominated the humanities in the past twenty years. If this spectrum lacks the focused uniformity of the 1970s, it represents far more faithfully the diverse negotiations faced by women now at the fin de siècle.

Although we live in a commercially dominated culture, the music industry, despite its many faults, more closely approaches a meritocracy and offers opportunities to a wider spectrum of artists than any other form of support—certainly more than the patronage systems of old. Music by women can continue to flourish in the public sphere, but only so long as it manages to sell tickets and recordings: the unexpected success of the Lilith Fair concerts, featuring exclusively female artists, confirmed not only the artistry of the participating musicians but also the willingness of a mass audience to support their efforts.

Needless to say, we have witnessed in the past decade an unusually talented cluster of women in music, although we must keep in mind that such bursts of female creativity have occurred and vanished in the past. I would like to believe, however, that something new happened in the 1990s: namely, that audiences began to rise to the occasion, producing the critical mass and public attention that must precede professional acclaim and (eventually) entry into the history books. If the trajectory of prominent female musicians is to continue well into the new millennium, it will require our collective efforts at active reception.

In short, do your part: Attend concerts. Buy CDs. Listen up.

Department of Musicology
University of California, Los Angeles

References

Attali, Jacques. 1985. *Noise: The Political Economy of Music.* Minneapolis: University of Minnesota Press.

Ellie M. Hisama

Feminist Music Theory into the Millennium:
A Personal History

A **composer friend** in her fifties recently commented that some days she wishes she had been born fifteen years later so that her formal training could have included studying music by women and exploring some of the feminist scholarship about music that is now abundantly available. Her wistful remark got me to thinking about my own training in music during the 1990s and the opportunities that I enjoyed as a graduate student, ones that far too few women experienced in the 1970s: diverse course offerings that attended to the ways women, gender, and sexuality have informed music making, the chance to study with tenured women professors and to work with an adviser sympathetic to feminist methodologies, and encouragement and financial support to write a feminist dissertation. In this essay, I retrace my professional footsteps over the past decade in order to share my experience of how a woman with feminist sensibilities interested in pursuing a Ph.D. in music theory successfully navigated a course through graduate school and into the profession.

As an undergraduate, I never met—let alone studied with—a female music theory professor. Yet I assumed that there must be women theorists somewhere; they just didn't teach at my college. Only later would I become aware of the degree to which men dominated the discipline, which is characterized by formalist approaches and by attention to musical structure. After completing two years of graduate school, I encountered a female music theorist for the first time, at the conference "Feminist Theory and Music," which was held in Minneapolis in June 1991. Meeting Marianne Kielian-Gilbert, who chaired a panel on which I presented an analysis of a string quartet movement by Ruth Crawford within a feminist theoretical framework, demonstrated to me that a woman could succeed in the profession—a woman who did feminist work, no less (Kielian-Gilbert 1994).

The conference proved to be a watershed for me in other ways as well.

I am grateful to Anton Vishio for several helpful discussions about this essay.

[*Signs: Journal of Women in Culture and Society* 2000, vol. 25, no. 4]

Not only was I able to present my work in a public forum without facing skepticism about the validity of analyzing instrumental music from a feminist perspective, but I also found a small, committed community of theorists who were interested in exploring feminist questions about music. What I believed could exist, but of which I had never previously seen any evidence — that women and music theory, and feminism and music theory, could be conjoined — was made tangible in Minneapolis that summer.

Since 1991, I have witnessed feminist work in music take root. "Feminist Theory and Music" conferences have taken place biennially, providing a regular forum for the presentation of feminist research; music by women has engaged the attention of several theorists; and considerations of gender, sex, and sexuality have shaped work in theory, analysis, and the history of theory.[1] The paper I gave in Minneapolis became a book chapter (Hisama 1995) and then the foundation of my dissertation, which will be published in revised form as a book (Hisama, in press).

My interest in developing a branch of music theory that is markedly feminist has led me to consider elements not typically incorporated into music analysis. Situating compositions within their historical and social contexts, I perform close readings that recognize the impact of the composer's gender, politics, and social views on the "music itself"; relate each piece to specific incidents in the composer's life that occurred at roughly the time of composition; and link narratives in the pieces to the composer's identity as projected in her writings and in reflections by contemporaries. My analyses, moreover, do not speak with a disembodied authority; they are marked by my own identity. By virtue of feminism's increased visibility and its current tentative acceptance in music scholarship, I enjoy the freedom to work on music outside the analytical canon and to develop feminist ways of hearing and analyzing music without feeling obligated to write on more traditional topics.

A few years ago, I taught at a school of music in which there were four women on the theory faculty: two tenured, one untenured, and one visiting. This unusually large concentration of women faculty made it possible for many of our majors to take courses in harmony, post-tonal theory, ear training, theory pedagogy, and form and analysis entirely with female instructors. I am certain that at least a few students emerged from these classes firmly convinced that the field of music theory is dominated by

---

[1] For theoretical work on music by women, see Lochhead 1992; Straus 1995; Burns 2000. On music theory and gender, sex, and sexuality, see Lewin 1992; Citron 1993; Maus 1993; Cusick 1994; Guck 1994; McClary 1994.

women. Attending an annual meeting of our professional society, the Society for Music Theory (SMT), however, would quickly deflate that notion. According to a 1999 study, women constitute only 18 percent of SMT's membership (Society for Music Theory 1999). Although progress has been made on a local level here and there, much work still needs to be done with regard to the inclusion of women nationally.

Teaching at a large university, I have often pondered the question of how I might present music theory to my students in ways informed by feminist insights. Since the need to forge a feminist discourse about music has motivated my own work as a scholar, I am interested in introducing the element of gender into my courses as a possible way to kindle students' enthusiasm for music theory. However, because the academic study of music traditionally has been inhospitable to approaches that concern any kind of socially constructed layer of identity, the task of introducing gender into one's teaching in the supposedly objective discipline of music theory can prove daunting. In a recent seminar I taught on popular music, one topic proved particularly useful in raising students' consciousness about the relevance of my subjectivity as a woman — specifically as an Asian American woman — to the works under discussion: the ways in which Asian women have been represented in the work of the saxophonist and composer John Zorn.

The liner of Zorn's 1991 compact disc *Torture Garden* includes eight stills from a pornographic film that depict Japanese women engaged in various sadomasochistic acts; a ninth still is imprinted on the CD itself. The front cover shows a Japanese woman, wearing only a garter belt, about to whip a second Japanese woman, who is restrained with a thick leash. The inner photos show women tied up with ropes and chains, bound and gagged, and hung upside down, their mouths wide open in pain; on the back cover, an elderly couple gapes at a roped and chained nude woman through a window.

Torture Garden comprises forty-two provocatively titled pieces, including "Osaka Bondage," "Victims of Torture," "The Noose," and "S&M Sniper." Heavily indebted to a thrash music aesthetic, the pieces on *Torture Garden* are marked by Zorn's characteristic writing in sound blocks and juxtaposition of disparate styles, punctuated by screams of a male vocalist that establish the one-sided nature of pleasure and control in this scenario. Zorn's music has been frequently upheld as an exemplar of postmodernist composition for its reliance on elements of popular and mass culture, juxtaposition of elements from different musical genres, and use of pastiche.

But listening to *Torture Garden* from the position of the object Zorn represents, that of a Japanese woman, I would characterize the CD not simply as a clever mix of styles and quotations but rather as a disturbing collage of racist and misogynist narratives contained in a sleek postmodernist package. When discussing works such as "Osaka Bondage" in the seminar, I made it clear that I find Zorn's visual and textual representations of Asian women's bodies extremely disturbing and argued that these images are inextricably linked to the compositions they encase. In other words, I encouraged my students to understand the structure of these compositions and their politics as interwoven.

By presenting specific pieces of music as studies in the variety of ways gender, race, sexuality, and nation are part and parcel of music, I try to convey an understanding of the relationship between a piece's structure and how it accomplishes its cultural work. My status as the only Asian American full-time member of my department and one of only a few on the university faculty at large presents a valuable opportunity to reach students whose first extended academic encounter with an Asian person might very well be their undergraduate music theory class with me. I have found that not only are my students interested in learning about harmony and voice leading, they are also curious about who I am and how I hear music; analyzing works such as "Osaka Bondage" helps them to understand the subject position of an Asian American woman through the perspective of someone they respect rather than through the distorting stereotypes perpetuated in popular culture.

I am committed in my teaching to developing these and other approaches that acknowledge the role of gender in analyzing music because I am convinced that feminist scholarship, feminist pedagogy, and equity are intertwined. As my own experience has shown, alternative approaches and repertories can attract a woman to the discipline of music theory and can convince her to build a life there, making women music theorists, previously unseen, visible, and feminist music theory, previously unimaginable, a reality.

Conservatory of Music and Ph.D. Program in Music
Brooklyn College and Graduate Center, CUNY

References

Burns, Lori. 2000. "Analytic Methodologies for Rock Music: Harmonic and Voice-Leading Strategies in Tori Amos's 'Crucify.' " In *Expression in Pop-Rock Music: A Collection of Critical and Analytical Essays,* ed. Walter Everett, 213–46. New York: Garland.

Citron, Marcia J. 1993. "Music as Gendered Discourse." In her *Gender and the Musical Canon,* 120–64. Cambridge: Cambridge University Press.

Cusick, Suzanne G. 1994. "Feminist Theory, Music Theory, and the Mind/Body Problem." *Perspectives of New Music* 32(1):8–27.

Guck, Marion A. 1994. "A Woman's (Theoretical) Work." *Perspectives of New Music* 32(1):28–43.

Hisama, Ellie M. 1995. "The Question of Climax in Ruth Crawford's String Quartet, Mvt. 3." In *Concert Music, Rock, and Jazz since 1945: Essays and Analytical Studies,* ed. Elizabeth West Marvin and Richard Hermann, 285–312. Rochester, N.Y.: University of Rochester Press.

———. In press. "Gendering Musical Modernism: The Music of Ruth Crawford, Marion Bauer, and Miriam Gideon." Cambridge: Cambridge University Press.

Kielian-Gilbert, Marianne. 1994. "Of Poetics and Poesis, Pleasure and Politics — Music Theory and Modes of the Feminine." *Perspectives of New Music* 32(1):44–67.

Lewin, David. 1992. "Women's Voices and the Fundamental Bass." *Journal of Musicology* 10(4):464–82.

Lochhead, Judy. 1992. "Joan Tower's 'Wings' and 'Breakfast Rhythms I and II': Some Thoughts on Form and Repetition." *Perspectives of New Music* 30(1):132–57.

Maus, Fred Everett. 1993. "Masculine Discourse in Music Theory." *Perspectives of New Music* 31(2):264–93.

McClary, Susan. 1994. "Paradigm Dissonances: Music Theory, Cultural Studies, Feminist Criticism." *Perspectives of New Music* 32(1):68–85.

Society for Music Theory. 1999. Report from the Committee on the Status of Women. *SMT Newsletter: A Publication of the Society For Music Theory* 22(2):6–7.

Straus, Joseph N. 1995. *The Music of Ruth Crawford Seeger.* Cambridge: Cambridge University Press.

Beyond Recognition, Beholden:
Toward a Pedagogy of Privilege

The cusp of the third (Christian) millennium coincides with the start of my career on the tenure track at the University of Minnesota, where I teach dramatic literature and theater of the Americas. Although I am new enough to experience this transition as vibrant with possibility, my perspective is also informed by my prior careers: for a chunk of the Reagan/ Bush decade, I worked in an international mutual fund investment firm; I spent most of the following decade in graduate school and a series of part-time teaching jobs that helped fund my research on indigenous theater and women's theater collectives in Mexico. Together, these experiences have conspired to turn me into a materialist feminist with a commitment to postcolonial theorizing about theater and other forms of cultural production.

Thus, when I taught my first "Theatre of the Americas" class at Minnesota, I emphasized how porous the border is between what many in the United States solipsistically call "America" and what lies south of it. I showed a film that brilliantly illustrates this point through the lexicon of popular music, congratulating myself on finding something my students could relate to.[1] Nevertheless, at the film's end one of them, a bright and talented actress of northern European descent, sighed and said, "I wish I had a culture. You know, with feathers."

Such "feather longing" is understandable, given the variety of marketplace discourses that help to determine it — everything from tourism commercials to direct-mail catalogs and music videos purveying artifacts and

This essay is dedicated to Danielle. My gratitude goes to my students; to Maria Brewer, Sarah Bryant-Bertail, Ananya Chatterjea, Christopher Danowski, Fortaleza de la Mujer Maya, Izetta Irwin, Katie Johnson, Jennifer Jones, Amy Kaminsky, Michal Kobialka, Sonja Kuftinec, Jo Lee, Megan Lewis, Joanna O'Connell, Tina Redd, Cynthia Steele, Paul and Donna Lee Buccelli Underiner, Matthew Wagner, and E. J. Westlake; and to Federated Investors, Inc., for waking me up.

[1] The film is *Fronterilandia/Borderland* (Lerner and Ortiz-Torres 1995), a postmodern pastiche of music and architecture showing culture to be a simulacrum produced in a two-way expression of border-crossing desire.

images of "tribal" custom and spirituality. In "American" consumerism, the ideological imperative to buy produces the experience of a lack of the desired object, even when that object is culture (and it *is* objectified in such discourse). It is but a small step, then, to imagine that culture is something that only "other" people have.

The discourses that produce culture as exotic also work hard to produce whiteness as normative, creating a kind of white-blindness in the process, or what Peggy McIntosh (1997) calls the "invisible knapsack" of white privilege.[2] This perceived normalcy makes it difficult for my students to connect with the experiences of women in the developing world who use theater to resist and transgress both ethnic and gender essentialism—in effect, to redefine and produce their own culture. Their responses to these women's experiences tend to fluctuate between two unfelicitous extremes: fetishization and indifference. As white "Americans," their economic privilege, relative to these women, is not hard for them to realize. However, that they are not only privileged but, as consumers in a global economy of (cultural) desire and goods, are also producers of the privilege gap is something that eludes their grasp. And that their relative privilege is intimately imbricated with their skin color is an understanding that their upbringing in "can-do America," with its interlocking but largely invisible systems of privilege, works hard to prevent. It is hard for them to see their whiteness and even more difficult to recognize all of the symbolic capital that goes with it.[3]

Because I teach theater majors, finding a classroom praxis to work through this obstacle has become my priority, since many of my students will go on to become arbiters of taste and controllers of representations, in professions that produce images that, if left unexamined, will perpetuate the invisible systems that allow "a white person [to] recede into privilege and not worry about racism whenever she or he chooses, [while] people of color cannot" (Wildman 1996, 163). Fortunately, theater history is rich with examples, from before Corneille to beyond Brecht, of work that revels in its ability to unmask the conditions of its own representation, and contemporary theater and performance art have done much to render visible the sociocultural operations that produce normative categories like gender

[2] For background on the growing interdisciplinary field of whiteness studies, see, e.g., Frederickson 1981; Frye 1983; Roediger 1991, 1994, 1998; hooks 1992; Frankenberg 1993; Allen 1994; Wildman 1996; Hill 1997.

[3] McIntosh's essay, "White Privilege: Unpacking the Invisible Knapsack," enumerates the components of this symbolic capital and distinguishes "earned strength which is earned and unearned power which is conferred systemically" and works for dominance over the systemically underadvantaged (1997).

and sexuality.[4] It seems logical to me that theater similarly can become an important site for rendering visible the invisible where white privilege is concerned — if those who hold it, and for whom it confers more opportunities to actually work in "American" theater, can come to see it first for themselves.

How, then, can I help my students move beyond a recognition of and confrontation with their privilege that doesn't reify the difference between "white and other" that, as Susan Stanford Friedman (1995) points out, produces mostly impasse (the rock of fetishization, the hard place of indifference)? Her solution, drawing on both poststructural and postcolonial insights, is to reconfigure identity as far too fluid, situational, and relational a phenomenon to be successfully approached only through fixed categories of ethnicity, gender, class, and so forth. Such a reconfiguration would allow for the possibility of multiple, shifting positionings and for transformative alliances across mythical categories. Still, as Friedman acknowledges and as is true for my often all-white classes, it is difficult to get *beyond* whiteness and otherness until one has spent time working *through* these categories.

One way out of the dilemma is to deploy the dramatic canon with a vengeance. I not only use it as an example of institutionalized and invisible whiteness produced through the rhetoric of liberal humanism, I also put it in direct confrontation with newer voices whose work directly and indirectly interrogates its authority. These are not new strategies by any means, but their reception in my classes tells me that they are still altogether necessary. An example: in a recent class several students criticized Suzan-Lori Parks' *The America Play* (1995) for its painstaking phonetic recreation of a kind of black dialect. They believed this would have the effect of perpetuating stereotypes of such dialect among, say, the largely white audiences for University shows — and they may be right, given the power of normative white privilege. Therefore, they argued, the play merited its highly acclaimed reputation as a radical de/reconstruction of "American" history only in intention, not in effect. Still, they had a difficult time seeing this as a systemic flaw rather than a dramaturgical one, and many felt that to produce it might do more harm than good. Their unconscious assumption

---

[4] See, e.g., Corneille's play *The Theatrical Illusion* (recently adapted and made popular anew by Tony Kushner) and Brecht's materialist theater, which worked on every level to expose the means of its own production. Brecht's techniques, if not his politics, have found their way into much contemporary theater that calls attention to its own theatricality. Contemporary performers whose work similarly exposes the machinery behind sociocultural categories include Caryl Churchill, Karen Finley, Split Britches, Bloolips, and Annie Sprinkle, to name just a few.

was that white audiences are the "normal" audience for such works (a disputable claim at best), and they had difficulty seeing their own good intentions as yet another silencing of an alternative voice. I suggested that, as an option for their final projects, they attend a canonical or contemporary "American" play whose "universal values" were embodied in the drama of unmarked white men and remark to their companions, "Hey, did you notice how stereotypically white those characters sounded?" They could then report on or perform the conversations that resulted. Although my students eventually got the point, none is doing such a project; this teaches me much about how hard it is to move from awareness to action.

If this kind of work is designed to help render the invisible visible, it still doesn't go far enough. I chafe at a pervasive reluctance in my classes, even when privilege comes to be recognizable, to see it as both contingent and relational: manifest through an accident of birth and maintained by the blood, sweat, and creativity of others the world over, who are the true labor of the "American" way. Beyond a general pigmentocratic privilege, there are also privileges hard won by work of earlier generations (feminists and civil-rights workers, e.g.), whose results have similarly come to be naturalized in a "post-" conscious "America."[5] I see this as a dangerously unhealthy ingratitude.

To counter it, I have begun to consider the possibilities for reenvisioning gratitude itself as a critical site for the excavation and responsible uses of unexamined privilege, as a way of seeing the world and its relationship to the perceiving self. Although gratitude is a tenet of many of the world's spiritual traditions—and psychologists such as Melanie Klein (1987) and Abraham Maslow (1996) and moral philosophers from Immanuel Kant ([1791] 1964) to Terrance McConnell (1993) agree on its importance to the healthy development of the individual and/in society (admittedly in a rather unreconstructed universal humanist kind of way)—the (too little) scholarly work on theories of gratitude is often caught up in the vocabulary of exchange—to whom is it owed, and under what circumstances?[6] And although such a vocabulary can be productive in unmasking the relational nature of privilege that I am trying to foreground, I am aiming at something more: an unblinking, aggressively unsentimental gratitude, a gratitude with attitude, a rigorous mental discipline that will help the contemporary mind overcome its addiction to binaries. For, to the extent that gratitude itself embeds a relationship between giver and

[5] My thanks to an unknown colleague who left the word *pigmentocracy* on the blackboard in the class before mine. I am not otherwise aware of its coinage.

[6] For a critique of this view's limitations from a Buddhist perspective, see Fitzgerald 1998.

receiver, benefactor and beneficiary, it can help answer Friedman's call to move beyond fixed categories of white and other toward a relational pedagogy of privilege.

Like any critical tool, this one has at least two edges, one of which can produce a dangerously conservative complacency (Amato 1982), and as an ethical practice it compels specification both historically and culturally. But, like the dramatic canon, it is also a notion that can be used strategically to highlight how privilege is constructed in relationships before it goes into systemic hiding. Whatever else theater is and does, it is always also an act of beholding. Taking this an etymological step further, a pedagogy of privilege in the theater classroom can become a site for the realization that, in very important ways, we are all beholden to one another.

Theatre Arts and Dance Department
University of Minnesota

References

Allen, Theodore W. 1994. *The Invention of the White Race*. London: Verso.

Amato, Joseph Anthony II. 1982. *Guilt and Gratitude: A Study of the Origins of Contemporary Conscience*. Westport, Conn.: Greenwood.

Fitzgerald, Patrick. 1998. "Gratitude and Justice." *Ethics* 109 (October): 119–53.

Frankenberg, Ruth. 1993. *White Women, Race Matters: The Social Construction of Whiteness*. Minneapolis: University of Minnesota Press.

Frederickson, George. 1981. *White Supremacy: A Comparative Study of American and South African History*. Oxford: Oxford University Press.

Friedman, Susan Stanford. 1995. "Beyond White and Other: Relationality and Narratives of Race in Feminist Discourse." *Signs: Journal of Women in Culture and Society* 21(1):1–49.

Frye, Marilyn. 1983. "On Being White: Thinking toward a Feminist Understanding of Race and Race Supremacy." In her *The Politics of Reality: Essays in Feminist Theory*, 110–27. Trumansburg, N.Y.: Crossing.

Hill, Mike, ed. 1997. *Whiteness: A Critical Reader*. New York: New York University Press.

hooks, bell. 1992. "Representations of Whiteness." In her *Black Looks: Race and Representation*, 165–78. Boston: South End.

Kant, Immanuel. (1791) 1964. *The Doctrine of Virtue*. Pt. 2 of *The Metaphysics of Morals*. Trans. Mary J. Gregor. Philadelphia: University of Pennsylvania Press.

Klein, Melanie. 1987. *Envy and Gratitude, and Other Works*. London: Hogarth.

Lerner, Jesse, and Rubén Ortiz-Torres. 1995. *Fronterilandia/Borderland*. Mexico City: IDERA Films.

Maslow, Abraham H. 1996. "Regaining Our Sense of Gratitude." In *Future Visions: The Unpublished Papers of Abraham Maslow*, ed. Edward Hoffman, 78–79. Thousand Oaks, Calif.: Sage.

McConnell, Terrance. 1993. *Gratitude.* Philadelphia: Temple University Press.

McIntosh, Peggy. 1997. "White Privilege: Unpacking the Invisible Knapsack." In *Race: An Anthology in the First Person,* ed. Bart Schneider, 120–26. New York: Three Rivers.

Parks, Suzan-Lori. 1995. *The America Play and Other Works.* New York: Theatre Communications Group.

Roediger, David. 1991. *The Wages of Whiteness: Race and the Making of the American Working Class.* London: Verso.

———. 1994. *Towards the Abolition of Whiteness: Essays on Race, Politics, and Working-Class History.* London: Verso.

———, ed. 1998. *Black on White: Black Writers on What It Means to Be White.* New York: Schocken.

Wildman, Stephanie M. 1996. *Privilege Revealed: How Invisible Preference Undermines America.* New York: New York University Press.

Dale M. Bauer

Priscilla Wald

Complaining, Conversing, and Coalescing

Almost as soon as we decided to write this essay together we encountered our first obstacle: Priscilla wanted to revisit Bernice Johnson Reagon's claim that "the principles of coalition are directly related" to the opportunity for feminists "to have something to do with what makes it into the next century" (Reagon 1983, 356), while Dale looked instead to "the mass experience of intimate female identification" central to feminist politics that Lauren Berlant also puts at the center of feminist theorizing (1988, 238). At first glance, these differences seemed difficult (at best) to reconcile in five to six pages. But we decided to begin a conversation and see what emerged. During the process we realized that the emergent essay witnessed our collaboration even as it chronicled our differences, that we were engaged in exactly the kind of conversation that has characterized our more than decade-long friendship, and that our conversation corresponds to key debates within feminism.

Dale began the exchange with an e-mail to Priscilla: "You asked me to write this essay with you for the *Signs* millennium issue in the spirit of coalition and collaboration. I am happy to comply. You want for us to write about possibilities for a united front for feminisms in the 21st century, since you claim that with the proliferation of feminisms, we are in need of ever more creative venues and strategies for our collective work. I agree." The collaboration began with a mutual misunderstanding, for Dale wanted to focus on imagining the possibilities for "a united front," and she assumed that was what Priscilla had meant by "coalition." Dale was interested in seeking new models for coalition, attracted especially to the urgency that Berlant marshals in her investigation of genre. Priscilla, however, was more concerned with investigating the challenges of working as a coalition and found in Reagon's ideas about the "principles of coalition" an especially useful way to think about some of the difficulties inherent in feminist work, as well as some of the intrinsic contradictions of feminist institutions.

"You're not really doing no coalescing" unless "most of the time you feel

[*Signs: Journal of Women in Culture and Society* 2000, vol. 25, no. 4]

threatened to the core," Reagon told the audience assembled at Yosemite National Forest for the 1981 West Coast Women's Music Festival (Reagon 1983, 356). For her, the threat marked the challenge to and of feminism, and our work as feminists depended on our ability — and willingness — to endure it; the nearly two decades since her remarks have given feminists ample opportunity to experience it.

Like Reagon's, Berlant's essay begins with a woman standing in front of a diverse group of women, but this woman, Erica Jong, refuses the opportunity for introspection that coalition offers, responding defensively to her audience's evident displeasure when she "was virtually booed off the stage by a feminist audience of the lesbian-separatist variety for reading a series of poems that celebrated pregnancy and birth while affirming a woman's strength and power" (Berlant 1988, 237). No one said coalescing would be easy. Coalition politics does not offer a united front of feminism. Reagon keeps the uncertainty very much in view. *Coalition politics*, for her, refers to the choice people make to struggle for a common cause, despite the multitude of differences among them. It is very uncomfortable, she says: it is not "done in your home. Coalition work has to be done in the streets. And it is some of the most dangerous work you can do" (Reagon 1983, 359). The differences are always in view and always potentially disruptive. The danger in coalition work seems to inhere in the vulnerability of the human ego. Maybe we grow up thinking that we know who we are and that what concerns us most deeply should concern everyone else, but in coalitions, we can count on not having who we think we are mirrored back to us and on finding out that our deepest concerns are not shared by the other members of the coalition. So when we coalesce — come together — we have to give up any secure sense of self. We merge, and we change. And we cannot count on a supportive environment. A coalition comes together to get some work done, not to nurture. We have to confront our biases and bigotries; insincere pieties disrupt the work of coalition, and we will be asked to own — and get over — them.

Feminism has been at the forefront of exploring the principles of coalition. Feminists are more than ever in the public view, and as a group we are more self-conscious than ever about our differences. "It is not surprising," writes Berlant, "that in the moment of public display, feminists deploying their gender as if alone in a private, protected, intimate space, became shocked and horrified by their mutual alienation." At precisely the moment of ostensible possibility for female speech, we confront the failures and contradictions of feminism. Berlant calls it a "rupture of identification" that "must open the question of *whether feminism does, in fact, have 'a' potential constituency in 'all women'* " (Berlant 1988, 238). Issues of race, class, sexuality, religion, and globalization have revised and reshaped feminism, prompting us to confront our complicity in a patriarchy in which we may be invested. Our discussions have pushed us (and we say this hopefully) to explore our privileges — to understand, for example, that race or class privilege means not having to see (and therefore often not seeing) racism or elitism when we are not immediately or apparently affected by its expression. That self-awareness is a necessary prerequisite to coalescing. Feminist work at its best enjoins us at once to articulate our viewpoints and concerns fully and to decenter our perspectives. That, as we understand her, is what Reagon means by "the principles of coalition."

Our own disagreement really centers on what to do with the principles of coalition. Feminists in the nineties have taken up this question in an activist context, but Dale wants to consider its ramifications for literary critics as well. She finds a model for this approach in Berlant, who casts the problem in generic terms: the difficulties of group consciousness that emerge from women's competing affiliations and identifications find voice, for her, in "the complaint," which she offers "as a paradigm of public female discourse" (1988, 238). Observing that old complaints do not provide adequate models for contemporary coalitions, some feminists have wondered whether it might be time to dissolve the coalitions. Dale disagrees but believes it is time to invent a new genre, to replace the complaint with something other than the manifesto (a seventies genre), the confession (an early nineties mode, which is already dividing feminists from one another and alienating others), or letters. She thinks we need a genre less conscripted, less oppositional — one with no melodrama, sentimentality, or domestic irony, one that will allow us to disidentify with the homogenizing constructions of "woman" that produce our multiple complaints.

Priscilla disagrees with the premise of this response; she has difficulty imagining how the principles of coalition could be expressed through genre. Coalition is by nature protean; it changes shape with each new issue and concern. Work in women's studies — or in the study of women and gender — has increasingly registered a suspicion of homogenizing claims and desires, demonstrating, in the process, the impact of the principles of coalition on the very shape (or shapelessness) of the field. Thus, Priscilla agrees with Dale's quest for a "genre-shattering" response (Berlant 1988, 241) but resists her impulse to replace the complaint with another genre.

We agree that it is still important to have some space set aside for women and women's issues in the academy and in society. And we agree with the need to preserve rough edges and to make room for the difficulties of difference — even for incompatibility. In fact, that is what holds this essay together, what allows it to be written. The rough edges are evident not only in our professed disagreements but also in our prose: in, for example, our somewhat alienating references to ourselves in the third person, an alienation that may well be endemic to coalition, marking the feeling of discomfort—the uncanny sense of not being at home—that Reagon describes. Not only have we put our voices together somewhat discordantly, but we have also brought together scholars who were not speaking directly to each other and presented them as though they were engaged in conversation, perhaps misreading both in the process. These are some of the risks of collaboration, which may be the closest thing to a written counterpart to coalition.

It has been especially hard for us, in writing this essay, to agree to preserve our own rough edges, which leads us to wonder how we might learn to be comfortable with them, even celebrate them, not so much as postmodernism does (as a decentering aesthetic) but as an acceptable form of scholarly production. Our own discomfort has led us to consider again the difficulties of preserving the principles of coalition within the academy—or in any context of institutional feminism. While seeking a united front, how might we allow our differences to surface, and to remain unresolved, even as we continue to negotiate externally imposed criteria for evaluation (for tenure, promotion, curricular, and other program decisions) in the context of pressure exerted by an (often unsympathetic) institution? How, in particular, can we keep in mind the possibility of the coalition's dissolution—and the certainties of its endless transformation—without undermining its transformative power within the institution? How, in other words, do we respond to our own feminist demands in an institutional context?

Our own collaboration began with generative disagreements and misunderstandings. We have not attempted to gloss them over; we work from within them. We work from mutual respect and a commitment to dialogue, the basis for collaboration that is also at the heart of coalition. We have not come to an agreement, and we do not have a neat conclusion for the essay. Instead what we offer is a form of conversation that we believe is central to feminism and that partly explains the centrality of feminism to the future. And with coalition, collaboration, and conversation, we offer terms that we think are key to our futures as feminists.

English and Women's Studies Departments
University of Kentucky (Bauer)

English Department
Duke University (Wald)

References

Berlant, Lauren. 1988. "The Female Complaint." *Social Text,* no. 19–20 (Fall), 237–59.

Reagon, Bernice Johnson. 1983. "Coalition Politics: Turning the Century." In *Home Girls: A Black Feminist Anthology,* ed. Barbara Smith, 356–68. New York: Kitchen Table—Women of Color Press.

About the Contributors

Edna Acosta-Belén is Distinguished Service Professor of Latin American and Caribbean studies and women's studies and director of the Center for Latino, Latin American, and Caribbean Studies (CELAC) at the University at Albany, SUNY. She is also editor of *The Latino(a) Research Review*. She is author of *The Puerto Rican Diaspora: Its History and Contributions* (Albany, N.Y.: CELAC, 2000); editor of *The Puerto Rican Woman: Perspectives on Culture, History, and Society* (New York: Praeger, 1986, 2d ed.); and coeditor, with Barbara R. Sjostrom, of *Hispanic Experience in the United States: Contemporary Issues and Perspectives* (New York: Praeger, 1988) and, with Christine E. Bose, of *Researching Women in Latin America and the Caribbean* (Boulder, Colo.: Westview, 1993).

Carolyn Allen is professor of English and adjunct professor of women studies at the University of Washington. She is author of *Following Djuna: Women Lovers and the Erotics of Loss* (Indianapolis: Indiana University Press, 1996) and articles on a variety of topics in twentieth-century studies and in feminist theory. Her most recent project is on cultural power and theories of emotion. She is coeditor of *Signs: Journal of Women in Culture and Society*.

Tani E. Barlow is a historian of modern China teaching in the women studies department at the University of Washington. She is coeditor, with Jing Wang, of *Cinema and Desire: The Cultural Politics of Feminist Marxist Dai Jinhua* (London: Verso, in press). Her most recent article, "'green blade in act of being grazed': Late Capital, Flexible Bodies, Critical Intelligibility," appears in *differences: A Journal of Feminist Cultural Studies* 10, no. 3 (1998): 119–58. She has recently completed a book manuscript titled "The Question of Women in Chinese Feminism."

Dale M. Bauer is professor of English at the University of Kentucky. She is author of *Feminist Dialogics: A Theory of Failed Community* (Albany: State University of New York Press, 1988), *Edith Wharton's Brave New Politics* (Madison: University of Wisconsin Press, 1994), and essays on feminist theory and pedagogy. She has edited *The Yellow Wallpaper* (Boston: Bedford, 1998) and, with Phil Gould, is completing "The Cambridge Companion to Nineteenth-Century American Women's Writing." She is also at work on a study of sex expression and American women writers from 1860 to 1950.

Catherine Belsey is chair of the Centre for Critical and Cultural Theory at Cardiff University. Her most recent books are *Desire: Love Stories in Western Culture*

(Oxford: Blackwell, 1994) and *Shakespeare and the Loss of Eden: The Construction of Family Values in Early Modern Culture* (New Brunswick, N.J.: Rutgers University Press, 1999). She is coeditor, with Jane Moore, of *The Feminist Reader: Essays in Gender and the Politics of Literary Theory* (Malden, Mass.: Blackwell, 1997, 2d ed.).

Paola Bono teaches English drama at the University of Roma Tre. She is author of *Esercizi di differenza: Letture partigiane del mondo e dei suoi testi* (Ancona: Costa & Nolan, 1999); coauthor, with M. Vittoria Tessitore, of *Il mito di Didone: Avventure di una regina tra secoli e culture* (Milan: Bruno Mondadori, 1998); editor of *Questioni di teoria femminista* (Milan: La Tartaruga, 1993); and coeditor, with Sandra Kemp, of both *Italian Feminist Thought: A Reader* (Oxford: Blackwell, 1991) and *The Lonely Mirror: Italian Perspectives on Feminist Theory* (London: Routledge, 1993). She is on the editorial boards of *DonnaWomanFemme* and *European Journal of Women's Studies*.

Liana Borghi (liborg@unifi.it), a member of WISE/WILD and the Società Italiana delle Letterate, teaches Anglo-American literature at the University of Firenze. She has written on Mary Wollstonecraft, nineteenth-century ethics and literature, women travelers, and women's fiction and has translated into Italian works by Kate Chopin, Adrienne Rich, and Donna Haraway. Her interest in contemporary women's writing ranges from poetry to lesbian fiction to science fiction to Jewish-American women's literature. She is coeditor of *S/oggetti Immaginari: Letterature comparate al femminile* (Urbino: QuattroVenti, 1996), a volume of essays on women's comparative literature, and editor of a companion volume, *Passaggi: Letterature comparate al femminile* (Urbino: Quattro Venti, 2000).

Christine E. Bose is associate professor of sociology, with joint appointments in the Latino, Latin American, and Caribbean studies and women's studies departments at the University at Albany, SUNY. She publishes in the areas of stratification and work, development, and gender studies. She is coeditor, with Edna Acosta-Belén, of *Women in the Latin American Development Process* (Philadelphia: Temple University Press, 1995) and has just completed a book titled "Gateway to the Twentieth Century: Women and the U.S. Political Economy in 1900" for Temple University Press. She is also editor of *Gender and Society*.

Laura Brace (lb21@leicester.ac.uk) is lecturer in political theory at the University of Leicester, where she teaches courses in political ideas and feminist political theory. She is author of *The Idea of Property in Seventeenth-Century England: Tithes and the Individual* (Manchester: Manchester University Press, 1998); coeditor, with John Hoffman, of *Reclaiming Sovereignty* (London: Pinter, 1997); and coauthor, with Julia O'Connell Davidson, of "Desperate Debtors and Counterfeit Love: The Hobbesian World of the Sex Tourist," *Contemporary Politics*, vol. 2, no. 3 (1996).

Rosi Braidotti is professor of women's studies on the arts faculty at Utrecht University and scientific director of the Netherlands Research School of Women's Studies.

She coordinates ATHENA, the European Thematic Network of women's studies for the SOCRATES program of the commission for the European Union. She has published extensively in feminist philosophy, epistemology, poststructuralism, and psychoanalysis. Her most recent books are *Nomadic Subjects: Embodiment and Sexual Difference* (New York: Columbia University Press, 1994) and "Metamorphoses," forthcoming from Polity.

Johanna Brenner (brennerj@pdx.edu) is chair of the women's studies department at Portland State University, a welfare rights activist, and founder of Portland's nonprofit feminist bookstore for women, In Other Words: Women's Books and Resources. A book of her essays titled "Women and the Politics of Class" is forthcoming from Monthly Review Press.

Karen Brodkin teaches anthropology and women's studies at the University of California, Los Angeles. Her research centers on women and grassroots activism and the dynamics of race, class, and gender in the United States. She is author of *Sisters and Wives: The Past and Future of Sexual Equality* (Urbana: University of Illinois Press, 1982, 2d ed.), *Caring by the Hour: Women, Work, and Organizing at Duke Medical Center* (Urbana: University of Illinois Press, 1988), and *How Jews Became White Folks and What That Says about Race in America* (New Brunswick, N.J.: Rutgers University Press, 1998) and coeditor, with Dorothy Remy, of *My Troubles Are Going to Have Trouble with Me: Everyday Trials and Triumphs of Women Workers* (New Brunswick, N.J.: Rutgers University Press, 1984).

Sue-Ellen Case is professor and chair of theatre and dance at the University of California, Davis. Her numerous works on feminism, performance, and lesbian cultural theory include *The Domain-Matrix: Performing Lesbian at the End of Print Culture* (Bloomington: Indiana University Press, 1996) and *Decomposition: Post-Disciplinary Performance* (Bloomington: Indiana University Press, 2000).

Tina Chanter is author of *Ethics of Eros: Irigaray's Rewriting of the Philosophers* (New York: Routledge, 1995) and *In the Time of Death: Levinas, Heidegger and the Feminine* (Stanford, Calif.: Stanford University Press, in press) and editor of *Feminist Interpretations of Emmanuel Levinas* (Philadelphia: Pennsylvania University Press, in press). She has published articles in the journals *differences, Research in Phenomenology, Graduate Faculty Philosophy Journal,* and *Philosophy and Social Criticism*.

Drucilla Cornell is professor of law, women's studies, and political science at Rutgers University and has authored numerous articles on critical theory, feminism, and "postmodern" theories of ethics. Her latest book is *At the Heart of Freedom: Feminism, Sex, and Equality* (Princeton, N.J.: Princeton University Press, 1998). Her plays *The Dream Cure* and *Background Interference* have been performed in New York and Los Angeles.

Irene Dölling is professor of women's studies at Potsdam University. She is author of *Der Mensch und sein Weib: Frauen- und Männerbilder, Geschichtliche Ursprünge und Perspektiven* (Berlin: Dietz, 1991) and coeditor, with Beate Krais, of *Ein Alltägliches Spiel: Geschlechterkonstruktion in der sozialen Praxis* (Frankfurt am Main: Suhrkamp, 1997). Articles by Dölling have appeared in *Signs, Feminist Review,* and the *European Journal of Women's Studies.*

David L. Eng is assistant professor of English and comparative literature and affiliate faculty of Asian American studies at Columbia University. He is author of "Racial Castration: Managing Masculinity in Asian America" (Durham, N.C.: Duke University Press, forthcoming) and coeditor, with Alice Y. Hom, of *Q & A: Queer in Asian America* (Philadelphia: Temple University Press, 1998), which received a 1998 Lambda Literary Award. The essay included here will appear in the forthcoming anthology "Loss: Mourning and Melancholia in the Late Twentieth Century," edited by Eng and David Kazanjian.

Cynthia Enloe is professor of government and director of women's studies at Clark University. She is author of *Ethnic Soldiers: State Security in Divided Societies* (London: Penguin, 1980), *Bananas, Beaches, and Bases: Making Feminist Sense of International Politics* (Berkeley: University of California Press, 1990), *The Morning After: Sexual Politics at the End of the Cold War* (Berkeley: University of California Press, 1993), and *Maneuvers: The International Politics of Militarizing Women's Lives* (Berkeley: University of California Press, 2000).

Anne Fausto-Sterling is professor of biology and women's studies at Brown University. In addition to scholarly articles in the fields of developmental biology, history of biology, and gender and science, she is author of *Myths of Gender: Biological Theories about Women and Men* (New York: Basic, 1992, 2d ed.) and *Sexing the Body: Gender Politics and the Construction of Sexuality* (New York: Basic, 2000).

Patricia Fernández-Kelly holds a joint position in the Office of Population Research and the sociology department at Princeton University. Her field is international development, with special attention to gender, migration, and race and ethnicity, and she has conducted extensive research on economic internationalization and women's employment in export-processing zones. She is coproducer, with filmmaker Lorraine Gray, of the Emmy award–winning documentary *The Global Assembly Line* (New York: New Days Films, 1986); author of *For We Are Sold, I and My People: Women and Industry in Mexico's Frontier* (Albany, N.Y.: SUNY Press, 1983); and coeditor, with June Nash, of *Women, Men, and the International Division of Labor* (Albany, N.Y.: SUNY Press, 1983). She is also founder of Parent Plus, an endeavor to facilitate partnerships between families of unequal means to improve educational and social opportunities for inner-city children.

Michelle Fine is professor of social psychology and women's studies at the Graduate Center, CUNY. She is coauthor, with Jane Balin and Lani Guinier, of *Becoming*

Gentlemen: Women, Law School, and Institutional Change (Boston: Beacon, 1997) and, with Lois Weis, of *The Unknown City: Lives of Poor and Working-Class Young Adults* (Boston: Beacon, 1998) and coeditor, with Linda Powell, Lois Weis, and Mun Wong, of *Off White: Readings on Race, Power, and Society* (New York: Routledge, 1997).

Małgorzata Fuszara is professor at Warsaw University and, with Bozenna Chołuj, codirector of the Institute of Applied Social Sciences and Gender Studies. She is author of *Codzienne konflikty i odświętna sprawiedliwość* (Everyday conflicts and festive justice) (1988) and *Rodzina w sądzie* (The family at court) (Warsaw: Zakład Socjologii Obyczajów i Prawa, Instytut Stosowanych Nauk Spolecznych, Uniwersytet Warszawski, 1994), as well as more than 50 articles and chapters, many dealing with the situation of women and gender equality. She is also coauthor, with Eleonora Zielińska, of a draft bill on the equal status of men and women.

Judith Kegan Gardiner (gardiner@uic.edu) is professor of English and women's studies at the University of Illinois at Chicago. Her scholarship addresses Renaissance English literature, twentieth-century writing by women, and psychoanalytic and feminist theories. She is author of *Rhys, Stead, Lessing, and the Politics of Empathy* (Bloomington: Indiana University Press, 1989) and editor of *Provoking Agents: Gender and Agency in Theory and Practice* (Urbana: University of Illinois Press, 1995). She is currently writing a book about masculinity in feminist theories and editing a volume titled "Masculinity Studies and Feminist Theories: New Directions." She is one of the editors of *Feminist Studies*.

Barbara Charlesworth Gelpi (bgelpi@leland.stanford.edu) is professor emerita of English at Stanford University. She is author of *Dark Passages: The Decadent Consciousness in Victorian Literature* (Madison: University of Wisconsin Press, 1965) and *Shelley's Goddess: Maternity, Language, Subjectivity* (New York: Oxford University Press, 1992) and coeditor, with Albert Gelpi, of *Adrienne Rich's Poetry*, later revised and retitled *Adrienne Rich's Poetry and Prose: Poems, Prose, Reviews and Criticism* (New York: Norton, 1975, 1993). She is currently at work on two projects: "Working in Common," a study of Victorian medievalism as it centered in Oxford, and "Before I Forget," a family memoir.

Tom Gerschick (tjgersch@ilstu.edu) is associate professor of sociology at Illinois State University. His interests include gender, disability, undergraduate education, and pedagogy. His publications have focused on how men with physical disabilities create and maintain self-satisfactory gender identities, the gender domination that men with disabilities experience, and the politics of teaching about social inequality. He is currently finishing a reader on gender for Pine Forge Press, due out in 2000, and studying how gender is being taught in sociology departments in North America. His future research will compare the gender identity formation and maintenance strategies of people with disabilities. He is temporarily able bodied.

Federica Giardini is working on a Ph.D. in philosophy at the University of Roma Tre; her dissertation gives a feminist reading of Husserl. She is author of essays on the imaginary as corporeal relation and is on the editorial boards of the women's philosophical journal *Sofia: Materiali di filosofia e cultura di donne* and the feminist journal *DonnaWomanFemme*.

Elizabeth Grosz holds the Julian Park Chair in Humanities at the State University of New York at Buffalo, where she teaches comparative literature. She is author of *Space, Time, and Perversion: Essays on the Politics of Bodies* (New York: Routledge, 1995) and editor or coeditor of a number of feminist theory anthologies. She is currently working on a book on virtual architectures.

Sandra Harding is a philosopher in the graduate school of education and information studies and director of the Center for the Study of Women at the University of California, Los Angeles. Her most recent books are *Is Science Multicultural? Postcolonialisms, Feminisms, and Epistemologies* (Bloomington: Indiana University Press, 1998) and, with Uma Narayan, an edited collection titled *Decentering the Center: Philosophy for a Multicultural, Postcolonial, and Feminist World* (Bloomington: Indiana University Press, 2000). Beginning in July 2000, she will be coeditor, with Kathryn Norberg, of *Signs*.

Sabine Hark is assistant professor of women's studies at Potsdam University. She is author of *Deviante Subjekte: Die paradoxe Politik der Identität* (Opladen: Leske & Budrich, 1999, 2d ed.) and numerous feminist articles on lesbian identity politics, queer theory, and theories of subject formation.

Ellie M. Hisama is associate professor of music at Brooklyn College and the Graduate Center, CUNY, and director of the Institute for Studies in American Music at Brooklyn College. She is author of "Postcolonialism on the Make: The Music of John Mellencamp, David Bowie, and John Zorn," *Popular Music* 12, no. 2 (1993): 91–104; "Voice, Race, and Sexuality in the Music of Joan Armatrading," in *Audible Traces: Gender, Identity, and Music,* ed. Elaine Barkin and Lydia Hamessley (Zurich and Los Angeles: Carciofoli, 1999); and "From *L'Étranger* to 'Killing an Arab': Representing the Other in a Cure Song," in *Expression in Pop-Rock Music: A Collection of Critical and Analytical Essays,* ed. Walter Everett (New York: Garland, 2000). Her book "Gendering Musical Modernism: The Music of Ruth Crawford, Marion Bauer, and Miriam Gideon" is forthcoming from Cambridge University Press.

Judith A. Howard is professor of sociology and adjunct professor of women studies at the University of Washington. She studies gender dynamics and their intersections with race, class, and sexuality, emphasizing micro-level cognitions and interpersonal interactions. She is coauthor, with Jocelyn A. Hollander, of *Gendered Situations, Gendered Selves: A Gender Lens on Social Psychology* (Thousand Oaks, Calif.: Sage, 1997) and coeditor, with Jodi O'Brien, of *Everyday Inequalities: Critical In-*

quiries (Malden, Mass.: Blackwell, 1998). She is coeditor of *Signs: Journal of Women in Culture and Society* and of Sage Publications' Gender Lens book series, which promotes scholarship and pedagogies that contribute to analyses of social inequalities based on race, class, gender, and sexuality.

Ruth-Ellen Boetcher Joeres (joere001@tc.umn.edu) is professor of German and women's studies at the University of Minnesota. She was coeditor, with Barbara Laslett, of *Signs* from 1990 to 1995. Her most recent book is *Respectability and Deviance: Nineteenth-Century German Women and the Ambiguity of Representation* (Chicago: University of Chicago Press, 1998). Her scholarly interests include the social and literary history of German women from the eighteenth to the twentieth centuries, comparative feminist theories, and women's personal narratives. She is at work on a volume of theoretical and autobiographical essays centering on her reflections as a teacher and scholar in the fields of German studies and feminist inquiry.

Sydney Janet Kaplan (sydneyk@u.washington.edu) is professor of English and adjunct professor of women studies at the University of Washington. She is author of *Feminine Consciousness in the Modern British Novel* (Urbana: University of Illinois Press, 1975) and *Katherine Mansfield and the Origins of Modernist Fiction* (Ithaca, N.Y.: Cornell University Press, 1991). She recently received a National Endowment for the Humanities Fellowship to work on a book manuscript titled "Circulating Genius: Virginia Woolf, Katherine Mansfield, T. S. Eliot, and John Middleton Murry."

Artis Lane, a painter and sculptor, first turned to classical figurative sculpture in the 1980s. Working primarily in bronze, she draws on her spiritual beliefs and on ancient Egyptian, African, and Roman cultures, seeking to explore qualities beyond the physical, at times removing the figure, still electric and alive, from its context — a fossil unearthed after a millennium spent underground, a shell delivering up secret contents.

Barbara Laslett is professor of sociology at the University of Minnesota. She was coeditor, with Ruth-Ellen Boetcher Joeres, of *Signs* from 1990 to 1995. Her research and writing have focused primarily on the historical sociology of the family, the history of American sociology, and feminist social theory. She is currently working, with Mary Jo Maynes and Jennifer Pierce, on a book on the uses of personal narratives in the social sciences.

Elaine Marks is Germaine Brée Professor of French and women's studies at the University of Wisconsin — Madison and former president of the Modern Language Association of America. Her teaching and research interests are in nineteenth- and twentieth-century French literature, women writers, and French and Italian Jewish writers of the twentieth century. Her most recent book is *Marrano as Metaphor:*

The Jewish Presence in French Writing (New York: Columbia University Press, 1996). She is currently writing a book manuscript called "The Death of God from Fin-de-siècle to Fin-de-siècle" and delivering talks and writing essays on the status of imaginative literature.

Susan McClary is professor of musicology at the University of California, Los Angeles, specializing in the cultural criticism of both classical and popular music. Best known for her book *Feminine Endings: Music, Gender, and Sexuality* (Minneapolis: University of Minnesota, 1991), she is also author of *Georges Bizet: Carmen* (Cambridge: Cambridge University Press, 1992) and *Conventional Wisdom: The Content of Musical Form* (Berkeley: University of California Press, 2000) and coeditor, with Richard D. Leppert, of *Music and Society: The Politics of Composition, Performance, and Reception* (Cambridge: Cambridge University Press, 1987). She was awarded a MacArthur Foundation Fellowship in 1995.

Devon A. Mihesuah (devon.mihesuah@nau.edu) is professor of history at Northern Arizona University and member of the Choctaw Nation of Oklahoma. She is author of *Cultivating the Rose Buds: The Education of Women at the Cherokee Female Seminary, 1851–1909* (Urbana: University of Illinois Press, 1993); *American Indians: Stereotypes and Realities* (Atlanta: Clarity, 1996); *Natives and Academics: Researching and Writing about American Indians* (Lincoln: University of Nebraska Press, 1998); *Repatriation Reader: Who Owns American Indian Remains?* (Lincoln: University of Nebraska Press, 2000); and *The Roads of My Relations: Stories* (Tucson: University of Arizona Press, 2000). She is currently working on a manuscript titled "Essays on American Indian Women's Racial and Ethnic Identities" and is editor of *American Indian Quarterly*.

Henrietta L. Moore is professor of anthropology at the London School of Economics and was director of the Gender Institute there from 1994 to 1999. She is editor of *Anthropological Theory Today* (Cambridge: Polity, 1999) and coeditor, with Bwire Kaare and Todd Sanders, of *Those Who Play with Fire: Gender, Fertility, and Transformation in East and Southern Africa* (London: Athlone, 1999). Her interests include changing family relations, gender and social structure, social and feminist theory, the anthropology of East and Central Africa, and multiculturalism and ethics.

Uma Narayan is associate professor of philosophy at Vassar College. She is author of *Dislocating Cultures: Identities, Traditions, and Third-World Feminism* (New York: Routledge, 1997) and numerous scholarly articles on issues such as affirmative action, homelessness, and human rights. She is coeditor, with Mary Lyndon Shanley, of *Reconstructing Political Theory: Feminist Perspectives* (University Park: Pennsylvania State University Press, 1997) and, with Julia J. Bartkowiak, of *Having and Raising Children: Unconventional Families, Hard Choices, and the Social Good* (University Park: Pennsylvania State University Press, 1999).

Julie A. Nelson (julie.nelson@rcn.com) is visiting professor of economics at the University of Massachusetts, Boston. Her previous affiliations include the U.S. Bureau of Labor Statistics, the economics departments at the University of California, Davis, and Brandeis University, and the women's studies program at Harvard. She is author of *Feminism, Objectivity, and Economics* (London: Routledge, 1996) and coeditor, with Marianne A. Ferber, of *Beyond Economic Man: Feminist Theory and Economics* (Chicago: University of Chicago Press, 1993). Her most recent article is "Of Markets and Martyrs: Is It OK to Pay Well for Care?" in *Feminist Economics* 5, no. 3 (1999): 43–59.

Jean F. O'Barr is Margaret Taylor Smith Director of Women's Studies at Duke University, the first endowed women's studies directorship in the United States. A political scientist by background, she has led the Duke program since 1983. Her most recent publications are *Feminism in Action: Building Community and Institutions through Women's Studies* (Chapel Hill: University of North Carolina Press, 1994) and the collection *Women Imagine Change: A Global Anthology of Women's Resistance from 600 B.C.E. to Present* (New York: Routledge, 1997), coedited with Eugenia DeLamotte and Natania Meeker. She was editor of *Signs* from 1985 to 1990.

Julia O'Connell Davidson (jod@leicester.ac.uk) is reader in sociology at the University of Leicester. Her research focuses on prostitution and sex tourism, and she has recently completed a study of tourist-related prostitution in the Caribbean funded by the Economic and Social Research Council. She is author of *Prostitution, Power, and Freedom* (Cambridge: Polity, 1998) and numerous articles and chapters on prostitution, sex tourism, and the commercial exploitation of children.

Oyeronke Oyewumi (oyewumi@alishaw.ucsb.edu) is assistant professor of black studies at the University of California, Santa Barbara. She has been a Rockefeller Humanist-in-Residence at the Center for Advanced Feminist Studies at the University of Minnesota and has held a Rockefeller fellowship at the Institute for the Study of Gender in Africa at the University of California, Los Angeles. Her research interests include critical social theory, Western culture, and African societies and cultures in their local and global dimensions. She is author of *The Invention of Women: Making an African Sense of Western Gender Discourses* (Minneapolis: University of Minnesota Press, 1997) and editor of *African Women and Feminism: Reflecting on the Politics of Sisterhood* (Trenton, N.J.: Africa World Press, 2000).

Nell Irvin Painter is Edwards Professor of American History and director of African-American studies at Princeton University. She is author, most recently, of *Sojourner Truth: A Life, a Symbol* (New York: Norton, 1996) and editor of the Penguin Classics editions of the *Narrative of Sojourner Truth* and *Incidents in the Life of a Slave Girl*. She has advised nearly a score of dissertation writers and serves on several feminist editorial boards, including that of *Signs*.

Barbara Ransby (bransby@uic.edu) is assistant professor of African American studies and history at the University of Illinois at Chicago. She is completing a biography of civil rights activist and intellectual Ella Jo Baker (1903–86), which will be published by the University of North Carolina Press in 2001. In addition to her scholarly publications, she is also a freelance writer who has published columns and editorials in more than three dozen newspapers nationwide. She is on the editorial boards of the London-based journal *Race and Class* and the Chicago-based Crossroads Foundation and has been active in progressive politics for the past twenty years. She was a founder of a national Black feminist network, African American Women in Defense of Ourselves, and an initiator of the Black Radical Congress in 1998 and is currently active in the Ida B. Wells CommUniversity Project.

Beth E. Richie (brichie@uic.edu) is a sociologist and activist on the faculty of the criminal justice and women's studies departments at the University of Illinois at Chicago and is senior research consultant with the Institute in Violence, Inc., a model program funded by the National Institute for Justice. Her work emphasizes the ways race/ethnicity and social position affect women's experiences of violence, with particular attention to African American battered women and sexual assault survivors. She is author of numerous articles and books, including *Compelled to Crime: The Gender Entrapment of Battered Black Women* (New York: Routledge, 1996). Her current work is on the gender dimensions of youth violence and focuses on African American girls and young women in low-income communities and on the conditions of confinement in women's prisons.

Mary Romero (mary.romero@asu.edu) is professor of justice studies in the College of Public Programs at Arizona State University. Her research and teaching interests are feminist and racial justice, law, and narrative. She is author of *Maid in the U.S.A.* (New York: Routledge, 1992) and coeditor, with Abigail J. Stewart, of *Women's Untold Stories: Breaking Silence, Talking Back, Voicing Complexity* (New York: Routledge, 1999); with Pierette Hondagneu-Sotelo and Vilma Ortiz, of *Challenging Fronteras: Structuring Latina and Latino Lives in the U.S.: An Anthology of Readings* (New York: Routledge, 1997); and, with Elizabeth Higginbotham, of *Women and Work: Exploring Race, Ethnicity, and Class* (Thousand Oaks, Calif.: Sage, 1997). Her most recent articles have appeared in the *American University Journal of Gender, Social Policy and the Law; University of Miami Law Review; NWSA Journal;* and *Race and Society.*

Noliwe Rooks is visiting assistant professor in history and African-American studies at Princeton University. She is author of *Hair Raising: Beauty, Culture, and African American Women* (New Brunswick, N.J.: Rutgers University Press, 1996), which received the Choice Award for Outstanding Academic Book, and coeditor, with Asake Bomani, of *Paris Connections: African American Artists in Paris, 1920–1975* (Fort Bragg, Calif.: Q.E.D, 1992), which won an American Book Award. She is currently at work on a social history of African-American women's magazines between 1891 and 1975.

Hilary Rose is professor emerita of social policy at Bradford University, visiting professor of sociology at City University, and joint professor of physic at Gresham College, London. She has published extensively in the sociology of science, from *Science and Society* (London: Allen Lane, 1969) to *Love, Power, and Knowledge: Towards a Feminist Transformation of the Sciences* (Cambridge: Polity, 1994). "The Commodification of Virtual Reality: The Iceland Health Sector Database," a report from her work in progress on genomics, is forthcoming from the Wellcome Trust (London).

Kathy Rudy is assistant professor of ethics and women's studies at Duke University. She is author of *Beyond Pro-Life and Pro-Choice: Moral Diversity in the Abortion Debate* (Boston: Beacon, 1996), *Sex and the Church: Gender, Homosexuality, and Contemporary Christian Politics* (Boston: Beacon, 1997), and "Moral Support: An Argument about Illness, Narrative, and Human Meaning" (in press). She also has published articles on abortion and reproduction, sexual and feminist ethics, bioethics, and feminist theory and is currently working on a project charting the history of feminist theory in the United States.

Therese Saliba is faculty of third world feminist studies at Evergreen State College and an associate editor of *Signs*. Her recent publications include "Resisting Invisibility: Arab Americans in Academia and Activism," in *Arabs in America: Building a New Future*, ed. Michael Suleiman (Philadelphia: Temple University Press) and, with Jeanne Kattan, "Palestinian Women and the Politics of Reception," in *Going Global: Third World Women in a Transnational Frame*, ed. Amal Amireh and Lisa Suhair Majaj (New York: Routledge, in press). She is also coeditor of the forthcoming collection "Intersections: Gender, Nation, and Community in Arab Women's Novels."

Ilaria B. Sborgi is a Ph.D. student in Anglo-American literature at the University of Firenze. She helped found the feminist student group Cassandra in 1993 and is also affiliated with Next GENDERation and 30 Something, European and Italian networks of women in gender studies. She has published essays in the journals *Leggere Donna, Feminist Europa, Tutte Storie, Inchiesta,* and *DonnaWomanFemme*.

Londa Schiebinger (LLS10@psu.edu) is professor of history of science and women's studies at Pennsylvania State University. She is author of *The Mind Has No Sex? Women in the Origins of Modern Science* (Cambridge, Mass.: Harvard University Press, 1989), the prize-winning *Nature's Body: Gender in the Making of Modern Science* (Boston: Beacon, 1993), and *Has Feminism Changed Science?* (Cambridge, Mass.: Harvard University Press, 1999). She is the first woman historian to win the senior international Alexander von Humboldt Research Prize and is a research fellow at the Berlin Max Planck Institute for History of Science for the 1999–2000 year. Her current research explores gender in the European voyages of scientific discovery.

Mrinalini Sinha teaches history at Southern Illinois University at Carbondale. She is author of *Colonial Masculinity: The "Manly Englishman" and the "Effeminate Bengali" in the Late Nineteenth Century* (Manchester: Manchester University Press, 1995), editor of *Selections from Mother India* by Katherine Mayo (New Delhi: Kali, 1998), and coeditor, with Donna Guy and Angela Woollacott, of *Feminism and Internationalism* (Oxford: Blackwell, 1999). She currently serves as the North American coeditor for *Gender and History*.

Dorothy E. Smith is in the sociology and equity studies department at the University of Toronto. For the past twenty years she has been concerned with the implications of feminism for sociology. She is author of *The Everyday World as Problematic: A Feminist Sociology* (Boston: Northeastern University Press, 1987), *The Conceptual Practices of Power: A Feminist Sociology of Knowledge* (Boston: Northeastern University Press, 1990), *Texts, Facts, and Femininity: Exploring the Relations of Ruling* (London: Routledge, 1990), and *Writing the Social: Critique, Theory, and Investigations* (Toronto: University of Toronto Press, 1998).

Judith Stacey is professor of sociology and gender studies at the University of Southern California. Her publications include *In the Name of the Family: Rethinking Family Values in the Postmodern Age* (Boston: Beacon, 1996) and *Brave New Families: Stories of Domestic Upheaval in Late Twentieth-Century America* (reprint, University of California Press, 1998). She is a founding member of the Council of Contemporary Families, a group committed to public education about research on family diversity.

Catharine R. Stimpson, founding editor of *Signs,* is professor and dean of the Graduate School at New York University.

Dorothy Q. Thomas advises the program on human rights in the United States at the Shaler Adams Foundation. She was founding director of the women's rights division of Human Rights Watch from 1989 to 1998, where she investigated a wide range of rights abuses, including wartime rape, custodial sexual abuse, domestic violence, and trafficking in women. In 1998 she received the Eleanor Roosevelt Human Rights Award and a MacArthur Foundation Fellowship for her work on women's human rights. She is author of numerous reports and articles on human rights, including *All Too Familiar: Sexual Abuse of Women in U.S. Prisons* (New York: Human Rights Watch, 1996).

Barrie Thorne is professor of women's studies and sociology at the University of California, Berkeley. She is author of *Gender Play: Girls and Boys in School* (New

Brunswick, N.J.: Rutgers University Press, 1993) and coeditor, with Marilyn Ya-lom, of *Rethinking the Family: Some Feminist Questions* (Boston: Northeastern University Press, 1992, 2d ed.) and, with Barbara Laslett, of *Feminist Sociology: Life Histories of a Movement* (New Brunswick, N.J.: Rutgers University Press, 1997). Thorne is currently at work on an ethnography of childhoods in contemporary California.

France Winddance Twine, an enrolled member of the Creek (Muskogee) Nation of Oklahoma, teaches feminist studies at the University of California, Santa Barbara, and international studies at the University of Washington. She is author of *Racism in a Racial Democracy: The Maintenance of White Supremacy in Brazil* (New Brunswick, N.J.: Rutgers University Press, 1998) and coeditor of four volumes, including, with Jonathan W. Warren, *Racing Research, Researching Race: Methodological Dilemmas in Critical Race Studies* (New York: New York University Press, 2000) and, with Helena Ragoné, *Ideologies and Technologies of Motherhood: Race, Class, Sexuality, and Religion* (New York: Routledge, 2000).

Tamara Underiner (under009@tc.umn.edu) is assistant professor in Theatre of the Americas at the University of Minnesota. Her research interests include gender and performance, especially as they relate to Latin American and U.S. Latino/a theater. Her recent publications include "Incidents of Theatre in Chiapas, Tabasco, and Yucatán: Cultural Enactments in Mayan Mexico," *Theatre Journal* 50, no. 3 (1998): 349–69, and "International Negotiations: Contemporary Mayan Theatre," in the *Oxford Comparative History of Latin American Literary Cultures* (Oxford: Oxford University Press, in press). Since submitting this essay for *Signs,* she is most grateful for the birth of her daughter, Eliana.

Priscilla Wald is associate professor of English at Duke University. She is author of *Constituting Americans: Cultural Anxiety and Narrative Form* (Durham, N.C.: Duke University Press, 1995) and coeditor, with Christine Di Stefano and Judith Wei-senfeld, of a special issue of *Signs* titled "Institutions, Regulation, and Social Control" vol. 24, no. 4 (1999). She is currently at work on a project on contagion and Americanism.

Lois Weis is professor of sociology of education at the State University of New York, Buffalo. She is author of *Working Class without Work: High School Students in a De-Industrializing Economy* (New York: Routledge, 1990); coauthor, with Michelle Fine, of *The Unknown City: Lives of Poor and Working-Class Young Adults* (Boston: Beacon, 1998); and coeditor, with Michelle Fine, of *Beyond Silenced Voices: Class, Race, and Gender in United States Schools* (Albany: SUNY Press, 1993), with Maxine Seller, of *Beyond Black and White: New Faces and Voices in United States Schools* (Albany: SUNY Press, 1997), and, with Michelle Fine, Linda Powell, and Mun Wong, of *Off White: Readings on Race, Power, and Society* (New York: Routledge, 1997).

She has received two Spencer Foundation grants and a Carnegie Foundation grant and is an editor of *Educational Policy.*

Nancy Fugate Woods is dean of the School of Nursing, professor of family and child nursing, and cofounder (in 1989) of the Center for Women's Health Research at the University of Washington. She has an extensive list of publications on premenstrual symptoms, the menstrual cycle, and menopausal transition and has authored or edited several books on health care for women. Her current research focuses on midlife women and health and health-seeking behavior patterns, including women's decisions about using hormone replacement therapy and the relationship of endocrine and social factors to symptoms during the menopausal transition.

Traise Yamamoto is associate professor of English at the University of California, Riverside. She is author of *Masking Selves, Making Subjects: Japanese American Women, Identity, and the Body* (Berkeley: University of California Press, 1999) and is currently at work on a book of essays on Asian American feminism.

Index